Lecture Notes in Computer Science 1060

Edited by G. Goos, J. Hartmanis and J. van Leeuwen

Advisory Board: W. Brauer   D. Gries   J. Stoer

Springer
Berlin
Heidelberg
New York
Barcelona
Budapest
Hong Kong
London
Milan
Paris
Santa Clara
Singapore
Tokyo

Tibor Gyimóthy (Ed.)

Compiler Construction

6th International Conference, CC'96
Linköping, Sweden, April 24-26, 1996
Proceedings

 Springer

Series Editors

Gerhard Goos, Karlsruhe University, Germany

Juris Hartmanis, Cornell University, NY, USA

Jan van Leeuwen, Utrecht University, The Netherlands

Volume Editor

Tibor Gyimóthy
Hungarian Academy of Sciences, Research Group on Theory of Automata
Aradi vértanúk tere 1, H-6720 Szeged, Hungary

Cataloging-in-Publication data applied for

Die Deutsche Bibliothek - CIP-Einheitsaufnahme

Compiler construction : 6th international conference ;
proceedings / CC '96, Linköping, Sweden, April 24 - 26, 1996.
Tibor Gyimóthy (ed.). - Berlin ; Heidelberg ; New York ;
Barcelona ; Budapest ; Hong Kong ; London ; Milan ; Paris ;
Santa Clara ; Singapore ; Tokyo : Springer, 1996
  (Lecture notes in computer science ; Vol. 1060)
  ISBN 3-540-61053-7
NE: Gyimóthy, Tibor [Hrsg.]; CC <6, 1996, Linköping>; GT

CR Subject Classification (1991): D.3.4, D.3.1,F.4.2, D.2.6, I.2.2

ISBN 3-540-61053-7 Springer-Verlag Berlin Heidelberg New York

© Springer-Verlag Berlin Heidelberg 1996
Printed in Germany

Typesetting: Camera-ready by author
SPIN 10512669   06/3142 – 5 4 3 2 1 0   Printed on acid-free paper

Preface

This volume contains the papers accepted for presentation at the 6th Conference on Compiler Construction (CC'96), held in Linköping, Sweden, 24/26 April 1996.

This conference is held every two years and provides a forum for the presentation and discussion of recent developments in the area of compiler construction, language implementation, and language design. Its scope ranges from compilation methods and tools to pragmatic issues in the design, development, and implementation of programming languages, with an emphasis on experimental results and practical experience.

In 1994 the CC'94 was co-located with the conferences Colloquium on Trees in Algebra and Programming (CAAP'94) and European Symposium on Programming (ESOP'94) in Edinburgh, Scotland. The aim of the synchronization of these conferences was to provide a European conference week covering a range of subjects, both practical and theoretical, related to programming languages and their implementation. The good result of this joint event shows the need for such forums, therefore CAAP'96, CC'96, and ESOP'96 have also been organized in this way.

The program committee of CC'96 selected 23 of the 57 papers received in response to the call for papers. Further papers were selected for a poster session. These were printed in a technical report at the Department of Computer and Information Science, Linköping University.

Each submitted paper was read by at least three assigned members of the program committee. The committee then held a one-day session in which they considered each paper carefully before coming to a consensus on the 23 papers selected for presentation at the conference. The conference program was completed with a keynote speech by Professor William M. Waite on the subject "Compiler construction: craftsmanship or engineering?"

Thanks very much to the authors who submitted their papers to CC'96, irrespective of acceptance. I would like to express my thanks for the work of the program committee and others who helped review the papers.
Special thanks to the invited keynote speaker, Professor William M. Waite from the University of Colorado, U.S.A. I also gratefully acknowledge the work of all those who contributed to organizing the conference, especially the local organizers at Linköping University and also Chris Hankin, who organized the joint program committee meeting in London.

Szeged, January 1996   Tibor Gyimóthy

Program Chairman:

Tibor Gyimóthy (Academy of Sciences, Szeged, Hungary)

Program Committee:

Miklós Bartha	(Memorial University of Newfoundland, Canada)
Paul Franchi—Zanettacci	(ESSI, France)
Peter Fritzson	(Linköping University, Sweden)
Rajiv Gupta	(University of Pittsburgh, USA)
R. Nigel Horspool	(University of Victoria, Canada)
Stefan Jähnichen	(Technical University of Berlin, Germany)
Martin Jourdan	(INRIA—Rocquencourt, Paris, France)
Uwe Kastens	(University of Paderborn, Germany)
Kai Koskimies	(University of Tampere, Finland)
Boris Magnusson	(University of Lund, Sweden)
Thomas Reps	(University of Wisconsin—Madison, USA)
Günter Riedewald	(University of Rostock, Germany)
Barbara Ryder	(Rutgers University, USA)
Jürgen Uhl	(IBM, Germany)
David A. Watt	(University of Glasgow, UK)

List of Referees

We gratefully acknowledge the following individuals who assisted the program committee in the reviewing process:

Zoltán Alexin
Niclas Andersson
Isabelle Attali
Rastislav Bodik
Jan Borowiec
Manuel Chakravarty
Jason Corless
Evelyn Duesterwald
Javier Elices
Thilo Ernst
Carlos Escalante
Jacques Farre
Carine Fedele
Adrien Fiech
István Forgács
Robert Gabriel
Marc Gaetano
Erick Gallesio
Éva Gombás
Jim Grundy
Rolf Haenisch
Görel Hedin
Stephan Herrmann

Clara Jaramillo
Mariam Kamkar
Emmanuel Kounalis
Igor Litovsky
Ferenc Magyar
Thomas Marlowe
Merik Meriste
Tony Middleton
Jean-Chrisophe Mignot
Henrik Nilsson
Soner Onderr
Mikael Pettersson
Jean-Paul Rigault
Johan Ringstrom
Friedrich Schoen
Andreas Schramm
Philip Stocks
István Tóth
Lars Viklund
Jyh-shiarn Yur
Michael Zastre
Wlodek Zuberek

Table of Contents

Pipelining-Dovetailing: A Transformation to Enhance Software Pipelining for Nested Loops*

Jian Wang and Guang R. Gao

School of Computer Science
McGill University
3480 University Street
Montréal, QC
Canada, H3A 2A7
email: {*jwang, gao*}@*acaps.cs.mcgill.ca*

Abstract. The objective of software pipelining is to generate code which can maximally exploit *instruction-level parallelism* (ILP) in modern multi-issue processor architectures, such as VLIW and superscalar processors. Since the amount of ILP is usually fixed to a small number, four - eight, using state-of-the-art software pipelining scheduling techniques, modern compilers have been able to schedule instructions in a small window of successive iterations and keep the machine resources usefully busy. To maximally take advantage of software pipelining, it is beneficial if the number of iterations of the loops to be software pipelined is large (called *trip counts* in this paper). Therefore, software pipelining of nested loops becomes important, especially when the innermost loops have smaller trip counts.

This paper presents a loop transformation which extends software pipelining from the innermost loops to the enclosing loop nests. Unlike some popular loop transformation techniques (e.g. *unimodular transformation*) targeted to multi-processor machines (where the goal has been to maximally expose loop-level parallelism i.e. the transformed loop nests have maximum number of doall loops), the goal of our transformation, *pipelining-dovetailing*, is to extend the software pipelining of the innermost loop to the surrounding loop nests. Thus all iterations of the loop nests can be smoothly software pipelined through, and the number of effective trip counts is maximized. We also define the condition under which pipelining-dovetailing is valid. As a result, a software pipelining framework is derived for loop nests which integrates software pipelining and pipelining-dovetailing together.

Keywords: Instruction-Level Parallelism, Fine-Grain Parallelism, Software Pipelining, Loop Scheduling, Nested Loop, Very Long Instruction Word(VLIW), Superscalar

---

* This work was supported by research grants from NSERC, Micronet – Network Centers of Excellence, Canada.

1 Introduction

Exploiting Instruction-Level Parallelism [1] for loop programs has become a major challenge in the design of optimizing compilers for high-performance computer architectures. To this end, software pipelining has been proposed to schedule instructions from several consecutive iterations of an innermost loop for overlapped execution. Over the past decade, software pipelining has been widely studied and it is now successfully used in modern compilers to effectively exploit instruction-level parallelism under the resource and register constraints [2, 3, 4, 5, 6, 7, 8, 9].

Up to now, most proposed software pipelining approaches have only focused on the innermost loops and little work has been done to apply software pipelining across a whole loop nest[2]. For a uniprocessor architecture, which has been the primary target of software pipelining, the available hardware parallelism is quite limited and software pipelining of the innermost loops is quite effective. Note that in order to take advantage of software pipelining, it is desirable that a loop to be software pipelined should have a large number of iterations (called *trip counts* in this paper). In many applications the innermost loops do have reasonably large trip counts, making software pipelining beneficial.

There are three reasons that software pipelining of outer loops is becoming increasingly important. First, since the speeds of innermost loops with long trip counts have already been improved significantly by software pipelining, handling of those with smaller trip counts may become important – an incentive to extend software pipelining to outer loops. Secondly, modern compilers may introduce loop transformations such as *tiling* to improve data locality, as a result the transformed loop tiles may have a much smaller trip count at the innermost level. Finally, for multiprocessor machines, a loop nest may be partitioned to different processors, consequently the loops to be executed on one processor may also have smaller trip counts at the innermost level.

In this paper, we study a software pipelining method applicable to nested loops. A main feature of our methodology is to retain the existing (and quite mature) framework of software pipelining techniques for innermost loops, and investigate how such a framework can be naturally *extended* from the innermost loops to the enclosing loops. The key question to be answered is how can such an extension be done in a smooth and efficient fashion ?

At the center of our approach there is the following observation: for a majority of innermost loops to which software pipelining has been successfully applied, there is enough instruction-level parallelism across a few iterations of the loop body to fully utilize the hardware parallelism within the resource and register constraints in modern uniprocessor architectures. Therefore, our objective here is not to further "widen" the parallelism of the software pipeline (already being exploited very well for the innermost loop) by globally scheduling instructions from several outer-loop iterations together. Instead, taking a 2 dimensional loop nest as an example, we will apply software pipelining to the innermost loop as

---

[2] In this paper, we use "loop nest" and "nested loop" interchangeably.

before, but try to "dovetail" the end of one outer loop iteration – an already software pipelined loop body – to the beginning to the next (also software pipelined). In other word, we would like to effectively stretch the whole loop nest as a long software pipeline with a fixed width (the same as the innermost one), such that the total trip count is now increased to the number of iterations of the entire loop nest.

This paper will present a new transformation – called *pipelining-dovetailing* to make the above "dovetail" possible. However, this transformation is quite different from some popular loop transformation techniques (e.g. *unimodular transformations*) targeted to multiprocessor machines where the goal has been to *maximally* expose loop-level parallelism i.e. the transformed loop nests should have maximum numbers of **doall** loops [10, 11, 12, 13]. The goal of our transformation is to effectively extend the software pipelining of the innermost loop to the surrounding loop nests so that all iterations of the loop nests can be smoothly software pipelined through, and the number of effective trip counts is maximized. Our loop transformation does not need to make the innermost loop or any of the enclosing loops into **doall** loops! In other word, our loop transformation does not perform any global scheduling and that explains the simplicity of the resulting algorithm.

It is important to note that we should view our techniques and previous loop transformation techniques (e.g. unimodular transformation, tiling, etc.) as complementary to each other — each can be applied for their own purpose at a different phase in a compiler. For example, one can imagine that some unimodular transformation or tiling may be performed at an earlier phase of compilation for parallelization or storage optimization, then our technique can be applied at the later code generation phase.

This paper is organized as follows: The next section gives a brief introduction to software pipelining and the data dependence representation of loop nests, making this paper self-contained. Section 3 consists of the motivating examples which highlight the principle of pipelining-dovetailing and discusses the relation with unimodular loop transformation. In Section 4, we present a sufficient condition under which pipelining-dovetailing is valid. The performance analysis is given in Section 5. Section 6 compares our approach with the related work. People assume the last section is a conclusion.

2 Background

2.1 Software Pipelining

Software pipelining is an efficient instruction-level loop scheduling technique. It tries to overlap the execution of operations from several consecutive iterations of a loop under the constraints of data dependences and resources. Figure 2.1 gives an example of software pipelining. A software pipelined loop consists of three parts: the prelude and the postlude which are executed exactly one time, and the software pipelined loop body[3] which may be executed many times. The length of the software pipelined loop body is called *initiation interval(II)*. $II = 1$ for this example.

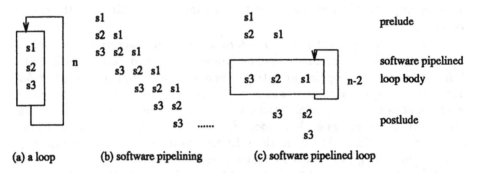

Figure 2.1 An example of software pipelining

Software pipelining can be combined with a loop unrolling transformation to improve its performance. We often consider a software pipelining technique with loop unrolling in such a way that we first unroll the loop and then software pipeline the unrolled loop without any unrolling.

The data dependences of a single-level loop can be represented by a Data Dependence Graph (DDG), (O, E, λ, δ), where O is the operation set, E is the dependence edge set, λ is the *dependence distance* and δ is the *delay*. λ and δ are two non-negative integers associated with each edge. For example, $e = (op, op')$ and $(\lambda(e), \delta(e))$ denote that op' can be only issued $\delta(e)$ cycles after the start of the operation op of the $\lambda(e)$th previous iteration [14]. Not more formally, we can define software pipelining without loop unrolling as follows:

Construct a loop schedule σ, a mapping function from $O \times N$ to N (N is the positive integer set), $\sigma(op, i)$ denotes the execution cycle where the instance of operation op of ith iteration is issued. If the following constraints are satisfied:

1. Resource constraints: In each cycle, the same resource can not be used more than once.

2. Dependence constraint: $\forall e = (op_i, op_j) \in E$, $\forall k \in N$, $\sigma(op_i, k) + \delta(e) \leq \sigma(op_j, k + \lambda(e))$.

3. Cyclicity constraint: σ must be expressible in the form of a loop, that is, $\exists II \in N$, $\forall op \in O$, $\forall i \in N$ and $i > 0$, $\sigma(op, i) = \sigma(op, 1) + II * (i - 1)$.

then we say that σ is a valid loop schedule for the given loop. II is called the initiation interval of σ. The goal of software pipelining is to find a valid loop schedule with the minimum initiation interval.

---

[3] There are some other names, e.g. the steady state, the repeating pattern, the new loop body.

2.2 The Data Dependence Representation of Loop Nests

The data dependence representation of a single-level loop should be extended for loop nests. For simplicity of formulation, we only consider normalized perfect nested loops[4] [15] as shown in Figure 2.2, but the ideas presented in this paper can be extended to any nested loop.

```
for i1 = 1 to N1 do
    for i2 = 1 to N2 do
    ......
        for im = 1 to Nm do
        begin
        s1;
        s2;
        ......
        sn;
        end
```

Figure 2.2 The perfect nested loop

Each iteration in a nested loop of depth m is identified by its index vector $(i_1, i_2, ..., i_m)$, where i_k is the value of the kth loop index in the nested loop, numbered successively from the outermost loop to the innermost loop. In a sequential loop, the iterations are thus executed in *lexicographic order* of their index vectors [15].

Therefore, an instance of an operation *op* in a nested loop is represented as $(op, (i_1, i_2, ..., i_m))$. For any two instances, $(op, (i_1, i_2, ..., i_m))$ and $(op', (i'_1, i'_2, ..., i'_m))$, if there is a data dependence between them, then we say there is a data dependence between *op* and *op'* with a *distance vector* [15] of $(d_1, d_2, ..., d_m)$, where $d_k = i'_k - i_k$, $\forall k = 1, 2, ..., m$. Like the data dependences in a single-level loop, there is also a delay δ associated with each dependence in a nested loop.

However, for some nested loops, their data dependences may not be representable with a finite set of distance vectors. In this case, extensions to include *direction vector* [15] are necessary.

The direction vector $(\theta_1, \theta_2, ..., \theta_m)$ of two iterations $(i_1, i_2, ..., i_m)$ and $(i'_1, i'_2, ..., i'_m)$ is defined by, for all j $(1 \le j \le m)$

$$\theta_j = \begin{cases} '<' \text{ if } i'_j - i_j > 0 \\ '=' \text{ if } i'_j - i_j = 0 \\ '>' \text{ if } i'_j - i_j < 0 \end{cases}$$

---

[4] In this paper, "nested loop" or "loop nest" refers to the normalized perfect nested loop unless it is specified.

A direction vector may contain the symbol '*' which stands for an arbitrary relationship between corresponding components of two iterations. $(=, <, *)$, for example, stands for the set $\{(=, <, <), (=, <, >), (=, <, =)\}$.

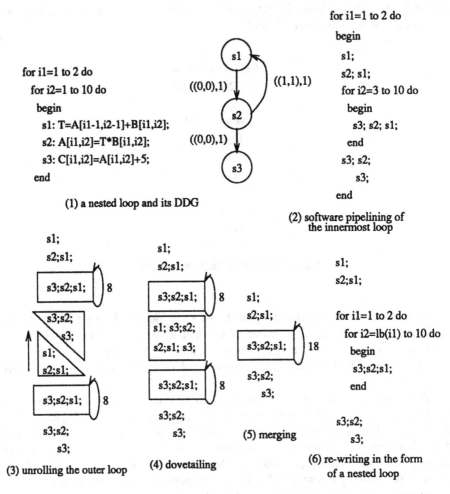

(1) a nested loop and its DDG

(2) software pipelining of the innermost loop

(3) unrolling the outer loop

(4) dovetailing

(5) merging

(6) re-writing in the form of a nested loop

Figure 3.1 The Principle of Pipelining-Dovetailing

3 Pipelining-Dovetailing: Motivating Examples

3.1 The Principle of Pipelining-Dovetailing

Let us first describe the principle of pipelining-dovetailing with a simple nested loop shown in Figure 3.1(1), where the value on each dependence edge denotes the distance vector and the delay. The distance vector $(0,0)$ represents a loop-independent dependence. Assume we software pipeline the innermost loop as shown in Figure 3.1(2). Imaging that we fully unroll the outer loop as shown in Figure 3.1(3). Now, we present a transformation, called *dovetailing*, to transform Figure 3.1(3) to (4). In Figure 3.1(3), the prelude of the second software pipelined loop can be moved upward to fit together with the postlude of the first software pipelined loop, thus generating Figure 3.1(4). It is easy to check that all data dependences are satisfied in Figure 3.1(4) so the dovetailing is valid for this example. Guaranteeing a valid dovetailing will be theoretically detailed in the next section. After dovetailing, the loop in Figure 3.1(4) can be *merged* as shown in Figure 3.1(5), which is always valid since we do not change the execution order of the loop iterations. We re-write the merged loop in the form of a nested loop as shown in Figure 3.1(6), where $lb(i1)$ means that $i2$ should count from 3 if $i1 = 1$, otherwise from 1. We call *"pipelining-dovetailing"* the transformation from Figure 3.1(2) to Figure 3.1(6).

3.2   Two Full Examples of Pipelining-Dovetailing

Next we discuss two examples to illustrate the applications of pipelining-dovetailing. The first example illustrates how pipelining-dovetailing improves the efficiency of software pipelining of the innermost loop. We can also see the simplicity, the low computation complexity and the low implementation cost of pipelining-dovetailing in the first example. The second example can not be pipelining-dovetailed due to data dependence constraint.

The first example is shown in Figure 3.2(a). After the innermost loop is software pipelined, we get the nested loop shown in Figure 3.2(b). Although the instruction-level parallelism within the innermost loop is fully exploited, its prelude and postlude are executed $N1 * N2$ times, thus the whole nested loop can not be efficiently executed on a VLIW/superscalar processor. If we apply pipelining-dovetailing to it, however, then the final nested loop is shown in Figure 3.2(c) where the prelude and the postlude are only executed once. The lower bound of $i3$ should be rewritten so that it counts from 5 instead of 1 when $i1 = 1$ and $i2 = 1$. We can see that the whole nested loop is in the form of software pipelining in Figure 3.2(c). It is not difficult to check that all dependences are satisfied in the loop of Figure 3.2(c) so pipelining-dovetailing is valid for this example.

Now we do a simple quantitative analysis to see how pipelining-dovetailing improves the efficiency of software pipelining. Let $N1 = N2 = N3 = 10$, and the execution time of each operation is one cycle, then the original nested loop in Figure 3.2(a) needs $T_{ori} = (1 + 1 + 1 + 1 + 1) * 10 * 10 * 10 = 5000$ cycles; the loop in Figure 3.2(b) needs $T_{inn} = (4 + 4) * 10 * 10 + 1 * 10 * 10 * 6 = 1400$ cycles; the loop in Figure 3.2(c) needs $T_{pd} = 4 + 4 + 1 * (10 * 10 * 10 - 4) = 1004$ cycles. Therefore, software pipelining of the innermost loop gets the speedup of $T_{ori}/T_{inn} = 3.57$ over the original loop; but software pipelining plus pipelining-dovetailing can get the speedup of $T_{ori}/T_{pd} = 4.98$ over the original loop, and an improvement of 28.29% over software pipelining the innermost loop only.

We give the second example in Figure 3.3. The nested loop in Figure 3.3(a) can not be pipelining-dovetailed due to the dependence edge from s_2 to s_1.

Readers can easily check that this edge will be violated if we software pipeline the innermost loop and then do pipelining-dovetailing directly.

The next section will develop a condition under which pipelining-dovetailing is guaranteed to be valid.

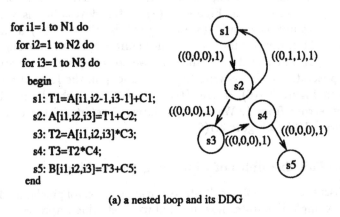

```
for i1=1 to N1 do
  for i2=1 to N2 do
    for i3=1 to N3 do
      begin
        s1: T1=A[i1,i2-1,i3-1]+C1;
        s2: A[i1,i2,i3]=T1+C2;
        s3: T2=A[i1,i2,i3]*C3;
        s4: T3=T2*C4;
        s5: B[i1,i2,i3]=T3+C5;
      end
```

(a) a nested loop and its DDG

```
for i1=1 to N1 do
  for i2=1 to N2 do
    begin
      s1;

      s2; s1;
      s3; s2; s1

      s4; s3; s2; s1;
      for i3=5 to N3 do
        begin

          s5; s4; s3; s2; s1;
        end
      s5; s4; s3; s2;
        s5; s4; s3;
          s5; s4;
            s5;

    end
```

```
s1;

s2; s1;
s3; s2; s1;

s4; s3; s2; s1;
for i1=1 to N1 do
  for i2=1 to N2 do
    for i3= L(i1,i2) to N3 do
      begin
        s5; s4; s3; s2; s1;
      end

s5; s4; s3; s2;
  s5; s4; s3;
    s5; s4;
      s5;
```

(b) software pipelining   (c) valid pipelining-dovetailing
of the innermost loop

Figure 3.2 Example 1

3.3 Relation with Unimodular Loop Transformation

It is important to highlight relation between the pipelining-dovetailing transformation we develop in this paper and the unimodular loop transformation [16, 10]

```
for i1=1 to 10 do
  for i2=1 to 10 do
    for i3=1 to 10 do
      begin
        s1: T=A[i1-1,i2+9,i3+8]+C1;
        s2: A[i1,i2,i3]=T*C2;
        s3: B[i1,i2,i3]=A[i1,i2,i3]+C3;
      end
```

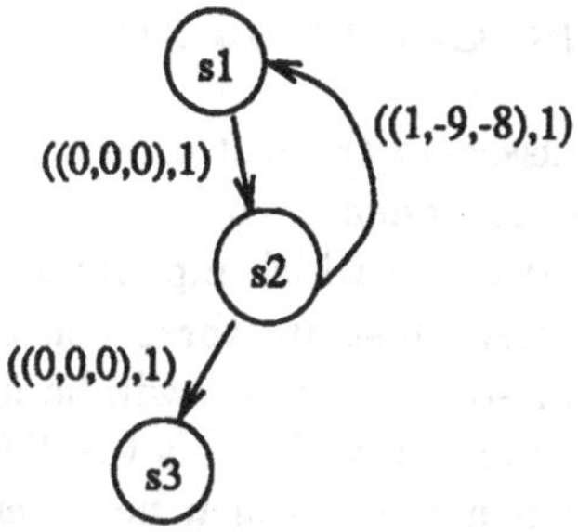

(a) a nested loop and its DDG

```
for i1=1 to 10 do
  for i2=1 to 10 do
    begin
      s1;
      s2; s1;
      for i3=3 to 10 do
        begin
          s3; s2; s1;
        end
      s3; s2;
      s3;
    end
```

(b) software pipelining
of the innermost loop

```
s1;
s2; s1;
for i1=1 to 10 do
  for i1=1 to 10 do
    for i3= L(i2,i1) to 10 do
      begin
        s3; s2; s1;
      end
    s3; s2;
    s3;
```

(c) invalid pipelining-dovetailing

Figure 3.3 Example 2

which is well known in the field of optimizing and parallelizing compilers. Unimodular loop transformation provides a novel matrix representation to combine loop transformations such as loop interchange, loop reversal and loop skewing. Its goal has been to maximally expose loop-level parallelism, i.e. the transformed loop nests have maximum number of doall loops. Consider the example as shown in Figure 3.1(1), since the innermost loop is already a **doall** loop in effect, unimodular loop transformation may not do anything to further transform it for exposing instruction-level parallelism in the innermost loop. However, our method would perform dovetailing to extend the software pipelining to the outer-loop.

In fact, we can view pipelining-dovetailing and unimodular loop transformation to be complement with each other — each can be applied for their own purpose at a different phase in a compiler. For example, one can imagine that some unimodular transformation or tiling may be performed at an earlier phase of compilation for parallelization or storage optimization, then pipelining-dovetailing can be applied at the later code generation phase.

4 The Condition for Valid Pipelining-Dovetailing

As discussed in the last section, pipelining-dovetailing is not always valid due to data dependence constraint. In this section, a sufficient condition will be presented under which pipelining-dovetailing is valid.

We first illustrate three concepts – innermost DDG, linearized DDG and pipelining-depth – which will be used as a basis in the following discussion.

The *innermost DDG* is the DDG of the innermost loop, which retains only those dependences which have zeros on all outer dimensions. Figure 4.1(a) is an example of the innermost DDG of the nested loop shown in Figure 3.2(a). Innermost DDG is traditionally used when software pipelining is applied to the innermost level only.

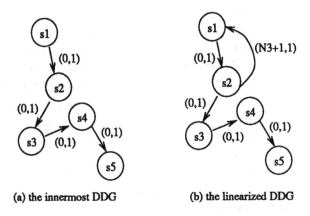

(a) the innermost DDG   (b) the linearized DDG

Figure 4.1 The innermost DDG and the linearized DDG
of the nested loop in Figure 3.2(a)

The *linearized DDG* is a new concept we present in this paper, which has the same node set and the same edge set as the DDG of a nested loop, but each dependence edge's distance vector is *linearized* into a scalar. For example, the dependence distance $(0,1,1)$ of the edge from s2 to s1 in Figure 3.2(a) is linearized into $0 * N2 * N3 + 1 * N3 + 1 = N3 + 1$, which is the dependence distance of the edge from s2 to s1 in Figure 4.1(b). The linearized DDG can be exactly defined as:

Given a nested loop and its DDG, $G = (O, E, (d_1, d_2, ..., d_m), \delta)$ where O is the node set, E is the edge set, $(d_1, d_2, ..., d_m)$ is the distance vector and δ the delay on each edge, the linearized DDG of G, $G' = (O', E', \lambda', \delta')$, is defined by:

(1) $O' = O, E' = E$;

(2) For each edge e,

$\lambda'(e) = N_2 * N_3 * ... * N_m * d_1(e) + N_3 * N_4 * ... * N_m * d_2(e) + ... + N_m * d_{m-1}(e) + d_m(e)$;

(3) For each edge e, $\delta'(e) = \delta(e)$.

In general, given a nested loop, its linearized DDG and its innermost DDG have the same node set. Moreover, the edge set of the innermost DDG is a subset of the edge set of the linearized DDG. While the innermost DDG is the data dependence constraint when software pipelining is only applied to the innermost loop, the linearized DDG is the data dependence constraint when software pipelining is applied to the *linearized* loop of the nested loop. By "linearizing a loop nest", we mean that the loop nest is first completely unrolled and then re-rolled into a single level loop. Figure 4.2(1) is an example of a "linearized loop". As we can see, the two dimensional iteration space (i1,i2) in Figure 3.1(1) is linearized into a one-dimensional iteration space $((i1,i2) \rightarrow (i1*10+i2))$ in Figure 4.2(1).

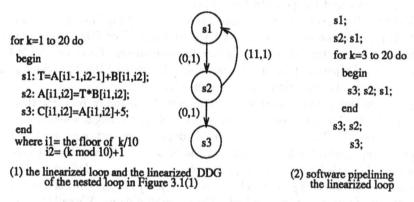

for k=1 to 20 do
  begin
    s1: T=A[i1-1,i2-1]+B[i1,i2];
    s2: A[i1,i2]=T*B[i1,i2];
    s3: C[i1,i2]=A[i1,i2]+5;
  end
  where i1= the floor of k/10
        i2= (k mod 10)+1

(0,1)   (11,1)
(0,1)

s1;
s2; s1;
for k=3 to 20 do
  begin
    s3; s2; s1;
  end
  s3; s2;
  s3;

(1) the linearized loop and the linearized DDG
    of the nested loop in Figure 3.1(1)

(2) software pipelining
    the linearized loop

Figure 4.2 Linearizing a loop nest and software pipelining

The *pipelining-depth* is defined as the number of different iterations which are overlapped in the software pipelined loop body. For example, in Figure 3.2(b), the pipelining-depth is 5 since there are 5 different iterations being overlapped in the software pipelined loop body; while in Figure 3.3(b), the pipelining-depth is 3. Pipelining-depth is of an important property: If the dependence distance of a loop-carried dependence is greater than or equal to the pipelining-depth, then this loop-carried dependence can be omitted during software pipelining. This property is very useful when we software pipeline a loop nest: After the loop nest is linearized, some dependence edges may have long dependence distances and removal of these edges may simplify the data dependence graph. For example, in Figure 4.2, the dependence distance of the edge from s2 to s1 is 11, which is much greater than the pipelining-depth, 3.

Now we derive a sufficient condition on the basis of the above three concepts under which pipelining-dovetailing is valid. Let us recall the principle of pipelining-dovetailing illustrated in Figure 3.1. That is, we first software pipeline the innermost loop and then do pipelining-dovetailing. This can be regarded as to first linearize the loop nest into a single level loop and then software pipeline the linearized loop, as shown in Figure 4.2.

We now see that if the linearized DDG and the innermost DDG are the same, pipelining-dovetailing is definitely valid. If the linearized DDG has more dependence edges than the innermost DDG and those edges have large dependence distances (greater than or equal to the pipelining-depth), according to the property of pipelining-depth, pipelining-dovetailing is still valid. Let us take the example of Figure 4.2. Although the linearized DDG has an edge from s2 to s1 which is not in the innermost DDG, the dependence distance of this edge is 11, greater than the pipelining-depth, 3, thus pipelining-dovetailing is valid for this loop nest. Therefore, we have the following theorem.

Theorem 4.1 Given a nested loop, let its innermost DDG be (O, E, λ, δ), the linearized DDG be $(O, E', \lambda', \delta')$, assume pd is the pipelining-depth. If $E = E' - \{e|e \in E' \text{ and } \lambda'(e) \geq pd\}$, Then the nested loop can be validly pipelining-dovetailed.

Readers can find the proof in the Appendix.

Although Theorem 4.1 can be used to determine if pipelining-dovetailing is valid, it needs to construct innermost DDG and linearized DDG. Our question is: can we directly check each dependence distance vector of a given nested loop to determine if pipelining-dovetailing is valid? Theorem 4.1 itself provides a hint that we can give the question a positive answer.

The sufficient condition stated in Theorem 4.1 actually requires that the (linearized) DDG of the nested loop does not include the edges which are not in the innermost DDG and whose (linearized) dependence distances are less than the pipelining-depth. We have found that the distance vectors of those edges can be expressed in the form of $(0, ..., 0, 1, 1 - N_{i+1}, ..., 1 - N_{m-1}, d_m)$ where $1 \leq i < m$[5], d_m is a negative integer of less than $(pd - N_m)$, N_j $(1 \leq j \leq m)$ is the number of iterations of the level-j loop and pd is the pipelining-depth. We call those edges *dovetailing-preventing edges* since they prevent the valid pipelining-dovetailing. Figure 3.3 gives an example of dovetailing-preventing edges, where the edge from s2 to s1 has the distance vector $(1, -9, -8)$, in the form of $(1, 1 - 10, -8)$ where $d_m = -8$ is less than $pd - N_m = 3 - 10 = -7$. As discussed in section 3.2, This edge prevents the valid pipelining-dovetailing. Thus, we have Theorem 4.2 (readers can find the proof in the Appendix).

Theorem 4.2 Given a nested loop, if there is not any dovetailing-preventing edge in its DDG, then the nested loop can be validly pipelining-dovetailed.

Theorem 4.2 gives a very feasible method for applying pipelining-dovetailing.

Finally, we want to point out that, the above results can be easily extended to the nested loops whose data dependences may include direction vectors. Here we only use a simple example to illustrate the extension.

Given the nested loop, for simplicity, let the number of levels, $m = 2$. A direction vector, say $(=, <)$, is a set of distance vectors, $\{(0, 1), (0, 2), ..., (0, N_2 - 1)\}$. When we construct the DDG of the innermost loop and the linearized DDG, we only take the worst case, that is $(0, 1)$. When we consider the data dependences in Theorem 4.2, we still only take the worst case, $(0, 1)$.

The direction vector, $(=, >)$, is also a set of distance vectors, $\{(0, -1), (0, -2), ..., (0, -N_2 + 1)\}$. When we construct the DDG of the innermost loop and the

---

[5] If $i = m$, the edge is in the innermost DDG.

linearized DDG, we only take the worst case, that is $(0, -N_2 + 1)$. When we consider the data dependences in Theorem 4.2, we still only take the worst case, $(0, -N_2 + 1)$.

5   Applicability and Performance Improvement

The applicability of pipelining-dovetailing depends on how many loop nests in practical programs satisfy the condition of Theorem 4.2. According to the form of the distance vector of a dovetailing-preventing edge, the condition is quite relaxed and we expect that most loop nests may not include any dovetailing-preventing edge and satisfy the condition.

In order to verify the applicability of our method we studied three well known benchmarks from SPECfp92 – fppp.f, tomcatv.f and ora.f. We have identified all loop nests which are suitable for software pipelining. For each such loop nest we examined the dependence relation of the loop body and checked it against the condition for dovetailing outlined in the last section. We found that all such loop nests in these three programs satisfy the condition so that the dovetailing can be successfully applied [6].

It is beyond the scope of this paper to fully assess the performance impact of pipelining-dovetailing. However, we found it useful to provide some preliminary analysis based on a straight-forward back-to-the-envelop calculation as detailed below.

Given an m-level nested loop, let the execution time of the original loop body be T, $N^0 = N_1 * N_2 * ... * N_{m-1}$ where N_j is the number of iterations of level-j loop, then the execution time of the original nested loop is $t_0 = N^0 * N_m * T$.

Assume we only software pipeline the innermost loop, let II be the initiation interval, then the execution time of the software pipelined loop is

$$t_{sp} = N^0 * 2II * (\lceil \frac{T}{II} \rceil - 1) + N^0 * (N_m - \lceil \frac{T}{II} \rceil + 1) * II = N^0 * (N_m + \lceil \frac{T}{II} \rceil - 1) * II.$$

We pipelining-dovetail the software pipelined loop. It is not difficult to compute the execution time of the loop which is software pipelined and pipelining-dovetailed

$$t_{sp-pd} = 2II * (\lceil \frac{T}{II} \rceil - 1) + N^0 * N_m - \lceil \frac{T}{II} \rceil + 1) * II$$

Provided $N^0 * N_m$ is large enough compared to $\lceil \frac{T}{II} \rceil$, we get the following result approximately $t_{sp-pd} = N^0 * N_m * II$.

We can compute the performance improvement below

$$\Delta = \frac{t_0}{t_{sp-pd}} - \frac{t_0}{t_{sp}} = \frac{T}{II} * \frac{1}{\eta + 1} \qquad \ldots\ldots\ldots \quad (6.1)$$

---

[6] We also develop a loop transformation to transform those loop nests which include dovetailing-preventing edges such that they satisfy the condition. However, due to the limitation of the paper's length, we can not present this work in this paper.

Where $\eta = \frac{N_m}{\lceil \frac{T}{II} \rceil - 1}$.

From equation (6.1), we directly have the following conclusions:

1. The efficiency of pipelining-dovetailing only depends on $\frac{T}{II}$ and N_m;

2. When $\frac{T}{II}$ is large and N_m is small, the efficiency of pipelining-dovetailing is significant;

3. When $\frac{T}{II}$ is small and N_m is large, it is not necessary to do pipelining-dovetailing;

4. After software pipelining the innermost loop, we can get $\frac{T}{II}$, thus make a decision whether or not it is worth to do pipelining-dovetailing;

5. Note that, in order to transform the innermost loop into a doall loop, the leading loop transformation techniques [10] tend to cause a large $\frac{T}{II}$ and a small N_m of the innermost loop, which indicating that pipelining-dovetailing is very promising.

6 Related Work

Most of existing software pipelining methods have been focused on the innermost loops. In [17] and [4], an approach has been presented to deal with nested loops (in [4], it is called hierarchical reduction); that is, first software pipeline the innermost loop, then reduce the software pipelined loop as a single node in the body of outer loop so that the outer loop can be software pipelined further.

Another software pipelining method for nested loops has been presented in [18], where the loop schedule σ was defined as

$$\sigma(s_j, (i_1, i_2, ..., i_m)) = \lfloor \frac{T_1 * i_1 + T_2 * i_2 + ... + T_m * i_m + A(s_j)}{r} \rfloor$$

$T_1, T_2, ..., T_m, A(s_j), \forall j = 1, 2, ..., n$, are non-negative integers, r is a positive integer, called periodicity. For software pipelining without unrolling, $r = 1$ and the above formula can be simplified below

$$\sigma(s_j, (i_1, i_2, ..., i_m)) = T_1 * i_1 + T_2 * i_2 + ... + T_m * i_m + A(s_j)$$

In [18], a method has been presented to determine the optimal $T_1, T_2, ..., T_m$ and $A(s_j)$ while, in [19], a method has been presented to generate the new loop based on $T_1, T_2, ..., T_m$ and $A(s_j)$. The computational complexity of this method appears to be quite high. In addition, it remains to be a challenge to handle the resource constraint under this method.

Many loop transformation techniques have been proposed to exploit coarse-grain parallelism for multi-processor architectures and vector machines [15, 12, 20, 21, 11]. Unimodular loop transformation provides a framework to combine the loop transformations such as loop interchange, loop reversal and loop skewing to exploit the maximum degree of parallelism [16, 10]. In [13], the affine transformation technique has been presented to extend the work of [10]. We have already highlighted the differences of these work from ours in section 1 and 3.3.

7 Conclusion

In this paper, we have proposed pipelining-dovetailing as a simple method to extend software pipelining from the innermost loop to the enclosing loops in a loop nest. We have also formulated the condition under which pipelining-dovetailing is legal.

We anticipate that software pipelining will become increasingly important for future generation processor architectures with ample instruction-level parallelism. The method developed in this paper has the advantage that it can be built upon on the existing software pipelining method, and appears to be simple to implement. Nevertheless, much work remains to be done to assess its feasibility in practical compilers.

Acknowledgments

We would like to thank Dr. Christine Eisenbeis, Dr. Andreas Krall and Prof. Bogong Su for their comments, and thank Mr. Hisham Petry for proof-reading. We would also like to appreciate the helpful suggestions from Prof. Uwe Kastens and our anonymous referees for improving the presentation of this paper.

References

1. B. R. Rau and J.A. Fisher. Instruction-level parallel processing: History, overview and perspective. *The Journal of Supercomputing*, 7(1), January 1993.
2. B.R. Rau and C.D. Glaeser. Some scheduling techniques and an easily schedulable horizontal architecture for high performance scientific computing. In *proceedings of the 14th International Symposium on Microprogramming and Microarchitectures (MICRO-14)*, pages 183–198, October 1981.
3. K. Ebcioglu and T. Nakatani. A new compilation technique for paralelizing loops with unpredictable branches on a vliw architecture. In A. Nicolau D. Gelernter and D. Padua, editors, *Languages and Compilers for Parallel Computing*, pages 213–229. Pitman/The MIT Press, London, 1989.
4. M.S. Lam. *A Systolic Array Optimizing Compiler*. PhD thesis, CMU, 1987. CMU-CS-87-187.
5. C. Eisenbeis, W. Jalby, and A. Lichnewsky. Compile-time optimization of memory and register usage on the cray-2. In *proceedings of the second Workshop on Languages and Compilers*, 1989.
6. A. Aiken and A. Nicolau. A realistic resource-constrainted software pipelining algorithm. In T.Gross A. Nicolau, D. Gelernter and D. Padua, editors, *Languages and Compilers for Parallel Computing*, pages 274–290. Pitman/The MIT Press, London, 1991.
7. R. Huff. Lifetime-sensitive modulo scheduling. In *proceedings of ACM SIGPLAN PLDI*, pages 258–267, June 1993.
8. Q. Ning and G.R. Gao. A novel framework of register allocation for software pipelining. In *proceedings of POPL*, January 1993.

9. Jian Wang, Christine Eisenbeis, Martin Jourdan, and Bogong Su. Decomposed Software Pipelining: A new perspective and a new approach. *International Journal of Parallel Programming*, 22(3):357–379, 1994.

10. Michael E. Wolf and M. S. Lam. A loop transformation theory and an algorithm to maximize parallelism. *IEEE Transactions on Parallel and Distributed Systems*, 2(4), 1991.

11. U. Banerjee. *Loop Transformations for Restructuring Compilers*. Kluwer Academic, 1993.

12. A. Darte, L. Risset, and Y. Robert. Loop nest scheduling and transformations. In *proceedings of Environments and Tools for Parallel Scientific Computing*, 1992.

13. Amy W. Lim and M. S. Lam. Communication-free parallelization via affine transformations. In *proceedings of LCPC'94*, 1994.

14. F. Gasperoni. Compilation techniques for vliw architectures. Technical Report TR435, New York University, March 1989.

15. Hans Zima and Barbara Chapman. *Supercompilers for Parallel and Vector Computers*. ACM Press, New York, 1990.

16. U. Banerjee. Unimodular transformations of double loops. In *proceedings of the 3rd Workshop on Languages and Compilers for Parallel Computing*, 1990.

17. Bogong Su, Shiyuan Ding, Jian Wang, and Jinshi Xia. GURPR–a method for global software pipelining. In *proceedings of the 20th Annual International Workshop on Microprogramming (MICRO-20)*, pages 88–96. ACM and IEEE, November 1987.

18. Guang R. Gao, Qi Ning, and Vincent Van Dongen. Extending software pipelining techniques for scheduling nested loops. In *proceedings of the 6th Workshop on Languages and Compilers for Parallel Computing*, 1993.

19. Ki chang Kim and Alexandru Nicolau. Parallelizing tightly nested loops. In *proceedings of International Conference on Parallel Processing*, 1991.

20. P. Feautrier. A collection of papers on the systematic construction of parallel and distributed programs. Technical Report Hors-serie, Lab. MASI, Universite P. et M. Curie, 1992.

21. M. J. Wolfe. *Optimizing Supercompilers for Supercomputers*. MIT Press, Cambridge, MA, 1989.

Appendix: The Proofs of Theorem 4.1 and 4.2

Theorem 4.1 Given a nested loop, let its innermost DDG be (O, E, λ, δ), the linearized DDG be $(O, E', \lambda', \delta')$, assume pd is the pipelining-depth. If $E = E' - \{e|e \in E'$ and $\lambda'(e) \geq pd\}$, Then the nested loop can be validly pipelining-dovetailed.

Proof: We first software pipeline the innermost loop and then do pipelining-dovetailing for the whole nested loop, which is equivalent to that we software pipeline the whole nested loop in its lexicographic order under the data dependence constraints given in the linearized DDG. Therefore, we only need to show that, given the condition of the theorem, the linearized DDG is satisfied if the DDG of the innermost loop is satisfied. From the property of pipelining-depth, we can remove those loop-carried dependences whose dependence distances are greater than or equal to pd since they will be automatically satisfied. Furthermore, from the condition of the theorem, after those loop-carried dependences are removed, the remaining linearized DDG and the DDG of the innermost loop have the same data dependence edges, which has proven our theorem. □

Theorem 4.2 Given a nested loop, if there is not any dovetailing-preventing edge in its DDG, then the nested loop can be validly pipelining-dovetailed.

Proof: First, each data dependence with distance vector $(d_1, ..., d_m)$ of a nested loop maps to , one by one, an edge in the linearized DDG whose dependence distance is below

$$\lambda = N_2 * N_3 * ... * N_m * d_1 + N_3 * N_4 * ... * N_m * d_2 + ... + N_m * d_{m-1} + d_m.$$

We need to prove that, if a dependence edge of the linearized DDG whose corresponding distance vector is not $(0, ..., 0, 1, 1 - N_{i+1}, ..., 1 - N_{m-1}, d_m)$ and d_m is a negative integer of less than $(pd - N_m)$, then it is in the innermost DDG or its dependence distance is greater than or equal to pd.

For any edge whose corresponding distance vector is $(0, ..., 0, d_i, ..., d_m)$ and $d_i > 0$, if $i = m$, then the edge is in the innermost DDG; now let us consider $1 \leq i < m$. We define $(0, ..., 0, d_i', ..., d_m')$ where $d_i' = 1, d_{i+1}' = 1 - N_{i+1}, ..., d_{m-1}' = 1 - N_{m-1}$ and d_m' is any integer. We have

$$\lambda = N_{i+1} * N_{i+2} * ... * N_m * d_i + N_{i+2} * ... * N_m * d_{i+1} + ... + N_m * d_{m-1} + d_m.$$

$$\lambda' = N_{i+1} * N_{i+2} * ... * N_m * d_i' + N_{i+2} * ... * N_m * d_{i+1}' + ... + N_m * d_{m-1}' + d_m' = N_m + d_m'.$$

and

$$\lambda - \lambda' = N_{i+1} * N_{i+2} * ... * N_m * (d_i - d_i') + N_{i+2} * ... * N_m * (d_{i+1} - d_{i+1}') + ... + N_m * (d_{m-1} - d_{m-1}') + d_m - d_m'.$$

There are only two cases:

(1) $d_i = d_i', ..., d_{m-1} = d_{m-1}'$, but $d_m \geq pd - N_m$: we have $\lambda - \lambda' = d_m - d_m' \geq pd - N_m - d_m'$, that is, $\lambda \geq pd$;

(2) There at least exists $d_j > d_j'$ $i \leq j \leq m - 1$: we have $\lambda - \lambda' \geq N_{j+1} * ... * N_{m-1} * N_m + d_m - d_m'$, that is, $\lambda \geq N_{j+1} * ... * N_{m-1} * N_m + d_m + N_m$. Since $N_{j+1} * ... * N_{m-1} \geq 1$ and $d_m > -N_m$, $\lambda > N_m$. Note that, we software pipeline the innermost loop thus the pipelining-depth is always less than or equal to the number of iterations of the innermost loop, so we have $\lambda > pd$.

Therefore, from Theorem 4.1, the nested loop can be validly pipelining-dovetailed.□

A Comparison of Modulo Scheduling Techniques for Software Pipelining

Peter Pfahler, Georg Piepenbrock[1]
Universität-GH Paderborn, Fachbereich 17, D-33095 Paderborn/Germany
Email: peter@uni-paderborn.de

Abstract

Software pipelining is a well-known and effective technique for generating compact loop schedules for instruction level parallel computers. This paper presents the results of an experimental evaluation and comparison of different scheduling algorithms that generate software pipelines. We implemented these algorithms in an uniform retargetable compiler environment that can be instantiated by providing target machine descriptions. This environment and a carefully designed benchmark suite enable us to perform a fair comparison of the implemented techniques. We evaluate well-known non-hierarchical and hierarchical schedulers and a hybrid technique developed in our group. Our analysis indicates that scheduling algorithms based on variations of the "classical" non-hierarchical modulo scheduling technique will probably yield the most effective software pipelines.

Keywords

Software Pipelining, Instruction Level Parallelism, Superscalar Processors, VLIW

1 Introduction

The compilation for high performance computer architectures such as VLIW, superscalar and pipelined processors heavily depends on techniques that make use of the offered instruction level parallelism. Besides local and global scheduling techniques parallelizing code arrangement for loops is one of the major challenges in the design of an optimizing code generation for such processors. Software pipelining is a well-known and effective technique for generating compact loop schedules for instruction level parallel computers. Software pipelining aims at reducing the run time of program loops by overlapping the execution of adjacent iterations. The overlap is achieved by generating a schedule for the loop body in which instructions from different iterations are executed in parallel.

Various heuristic techniques for generating software pipelines have been published in the past decade (see [RaF93] for an overview). All these techniques generate pipelined loop code which shows impressive speed-ups compared to code produced by simple local instruction schedulers. One important and well-known family of techniques for generating software pipelines is *Modulo Schedul-*

---

[1]supported by the "Deutsche Forschungsgemeinschaft", DFG project "Übersetzungs-methoden für VLIW-Parallelrechner-Architekturen"

ing introduced by Rau and Glaeser [RaG81] (see Sect. 3).

This paper presents the evaluation of two "classical" modulo scheduling algorithms [RaG81] [Lam88] and compares them with the *RSPS* algorithm developed in our group [Pie95]. We used an uniform evaluation environment where these three schedulers have been implemented. This evaluation environment is machine independent and can be instantiated by providing a target processor specification. It allows us to analyze and compare the pipeline scheduler's performance for different target processors with more or less constrained resources. Even more interesting results are achieved by investigating how the pipeline algorithms cope with different source loop characteristics. Besides using realistic input programs (Livermore loops, loops from numerical applications) we designed a small suite of synthetic benchmarks. These benchmarks consist of loops of different size and varying dependence characteristics (see Sect. 2.3 for details).

The rest of this paper is organized as follows: In Sect. 2 we describe the evaluation environment. Sect. 3 gives a concise overview over software pipelining in general and presents the techniques that we investigated, including RSPS. Sect. 4 presents the comparative evaluation and discusses its results.

2 The Evaluation Environment

The quality of pipeline scheduling techniques can only be compared if these techniques generate code for the same target processor. Furthermore, the effectiveness of pipeline schedules clearly depends on specific target processor and source code characteristics (e.g. the number of parallel functional units, the number and size of recurrence cycles). Consequently, one of the main goals of our work was to make the different software pipelining approaches comparable by evaluating them in an uniform and machine independent environment.

2.1 The Compiler Environment

Our code generators start from an intermediate language representation produced by an ANSI C frontend. This intermediate representation is transformed into the *Operation Dependence Graph (ODG)* by the code selection phase. The ODG is the central data structure for the following code generation tasks (functional unit assignment, register assignment, and scheduling). It consists of nodes representing machine operations and edges that model the data and control flow between machine operations. It is the task of a dependence analysis phase to compute the data dependence relations in a way that leaves the greatest possible freedom for the following scheduling phase. The Omega dependence test [Pug92] is used in our environment.

The functional unit assignment phase maps the operations in the ODG to the target processor's functional units (FUs). If the functional units are different in instruction set, speed, resource consumption, or connection to storage units (e.g.

register banks), the chosen assignment can have a great influence on the quality of the resulting schedules. If, for instance, the target processor is organized in clusters having individual register banks [CNO87], the FU assignment phase has to compute a mapping which both distributes the operations over the FUs for parallel execution and keeps data-dependent operations locally on the same cluster to avoid inter-cluster copy operations. The functional unit assignment technique from [Ell86] works in this way and yields very good results for acyclic dependence graphs. Our compilers use this technique in an enhanced form which makes it suitable for pipeline scheduling by taking modulo resource constraints (see Sect. 3) into account [Pie95].

The register assignment phase maps symbolic registers to physical register banks and registers of the target processor. Like the assignment of functional units, register assignment in pipeline schedules can have a great influence on the quality of the generated code [Pin93] [HGA92] [GoH88][DGS92]. In our environment we use postpass register assignment, i.e. the registers are assigned after instruction scheduling. This phase ordering does not unnecessarily restrict scheduling freedom by introducing additional dependencies due to register reuse. On the other hand, postpass register assignment can lead to problems caused by overlapping register lifetimes in software pipelines. These problems are addressed in Sect. 4.

2.2 Machine Modeling

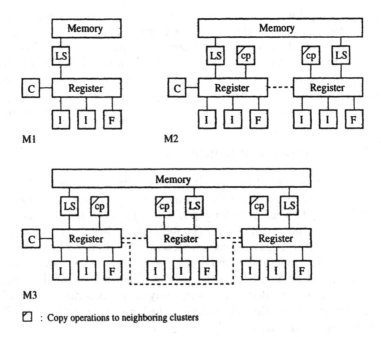

□ : Copy operations to neighboring clusters

Figure 1: The Machine Models

To be able to easily retarget our compiler environment we isolated all machine specific information in a module called *MachSpec*. All other compiler modules access machine-dependent information only via MachSpec. MachSpec (which is generated from a machine description language) provides the processor specific information required in the code generation phase, i.e. the resource requirement of machine operations, the instruction set of the functional units and structural information such as the reachability of register banks from the different functional units.

We used three different processor models for our evaluation. All models are built of integer units (I), floating point units (F), a control unit (C) for branching, load/store units (LS) for memory access, and copy units (cp) implementing the data transfer between register banks in cluster-structured machines. Fig. 1 shows the machine models. Processor M1 imitates the structure of the PowerPC 604 superscalar processor. Processors M2 and M3 are two and three cluster architectures. They use the M1 structure inside their clusters with an additional copy unit for data transfer between clusters. The design of these processor models was guided by the instruction frequency distribution in typical realistic input programs. Consequently, an evenly balanced load can be expected on the functional units of these processors.

2.3 Benchmarks

We used three classes of benchmarks for evaluating the pipeline schedulers:

The Livermore Loops as a classical benchmark set turned out to be very well suited for demonstrating impressive speedups due to software pipelining in general. Some of the loops, however, are only of limited significance for comparing the effectiveness of different pipelining algorithms (see Sect. 4).

The synthetic benchmarks set SCC contains 5 source programs. It evaluates the performance of the pipeline schedulers when the number of strongly connected components (SCC) grows[2]. The SCCs are cyclic subgraphs of the ODG caused by loop carried data dependencies in the source programs. This benchmark set stresses the SCC characteristics because handling cyclically dependent nodes turns out to be the major challenge for software pipeline schedulers (see Sect. 3).

The third class of benchmarks contains four numerical source programs ("sor": sequential overrelaxation, "horner": polynomial evaluation, "convol": convolution, "matrix": matrix multiplication). These programs have been transformed on the source level by SRP (*skewing, reversal, permutation*) transformations to increase parallelism in the innermost loop [WoL91]. Applying such transformations prior to software pipelining can lead to speed-up factors of 2 to 4 compared to pipelining the original loops [SPP94]. On the other hand these transformations lead to more complex loop exit conditions and index expressions, which makes them a challenging benchmark suite for comparing pipeline schedulers.

Since the evaluation described in this paper considers the software pipelining

---

[2]The SCC number ranges from 3 (SCC1) to 7 (SCC5).

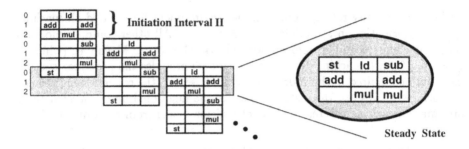

Figure 2: Overlapping loop iterations (a) and steady state of a software pipelined loop (b)

algorithms in their basic versions, our benchmark programs do not contain loops with internal control flow.

3 Pipeline Scheduling Techniques

Software Pipelining exploits instruction level parallelism by overlapping the execution of consecutive loop iterations. This is achieved by starting the execution of a loop iteration before its predecessor iteration is finished. The constant number of cycles between the start of consecutive iterations is called *initiation interval II*. Fig. 2(a) shows this pipelined execution of a loop.

The task of a software pipelining scheduler is to construct a static loop schedule, which, when executed, leads to this pipelined execution. For this purpose, the scheduler makes use of the fact that after a few cycles the software pipeline executes a repeating pattern of instructions. This repeating pattern is called *steady state* (see Fig. 2(b)) and becomes the body of the generated loop code. The number of instructions in the steady state is equal to the initiation interval II. The instructions that are executed before the steady state is reached are coded in the so-called *prologue*. After leaving the steady state, the remaining iterations are ended in the *epilogue* code. Thus, software pipelining can also be seen as a loop transformation technique transforming the original loop schedule into the prologue, steady state (the new body) and epilogue parts.

Software pipelining is constrained by both machine and source code characteristics. Resource constraints of the target machine clearly limit the possible amount of iteration overlapping II, since the steady state code of length II must be a conflict-free arrangement of all operations contained in the original loop schedule. This fact is used to compute a lower bound for the initiation interval called the *minimum resource II* (ResMII) from the resource requirement of the original loop.

Data dependencies in the source code are the second source for pipelining constraints. Loop carried dependencies, like e.g. "operation a from iteration $i+k$

must not be executed before operation b from iteration i" clearly limit the possible amount of iteration overlapping. Such dependencies lead to a second lower bound on II, the *minimum precedence II* (RecMII): The II can not be smaller than the sum of delay times on dependence cycles $d(c)$ in the ODG divided by the sum of the iteration distances $p(c)$ on these cycles. The lower bound on the initiation interval MII is defined to be the maximum of RecMII and ResMII.

All modulo scheduling algorithms try to construct loop schedules for a single iteration that can be software pipelined with an initiation interval of II cycles. They start their search for a pipeline schedule with an II value of MII. Compared to schedulers for straight-line code (*local schedulers*) they have to deal with two additional problems: An operation scheduled for cycle c of the loop code will be executed in parallel with all operations from cycles k where $c \bmod II = k \bmod II$. This fact is easily modeled by replacing the local scheduler's resource reservation table with a table of length II which is indexed modulo II[3]. As opposed to local schedulers, the modulo scheduler can fail because of these so-called *modulo resource constraints*.

Dependence cycles lead to the introduction of scheduling ranges for operations. Like local schedulers the modulo schedulers have to obey earliest possible scheduling positions of operations depending on the positions of their predecessors. Additionally, the initiation interval and the scheduling decisions for successors in subsequent iterations determine a latest possible scheduling position (*recurrence constraint*). As opposed to local scheduling, scheduling can now fail if an operation cannot be placed within its legal scheduling range.

In both cases of failure the partial pipeline schedule can not be extended to a valid pipeline schedule for the whole loop. The initiation interval has to increased and the scheduling process restarts. The schedule length of an unpipelined loop iteration serves as a natural upper bound for effective initiation intervals. Asymptotically, the length of the initiation interval, being equal to the number of cycles in the steady state, determines the execution time of the software pipelined loop. Therefore, the II values are generally used to judge and compare different pipeline scheduling techniques.

Flat Modulo Scheduling (FMS)

Flat modulo scheduling [RaG81] has initially been proposed for so-called *Generalized Vector Computations (GVC)*, i.e. loops without recurrences that have a known trip count. The resulting acyclic dependence graph is processed by a list scheduling algorithm which uses typical critical path aspects for priorizing operations. [RaG81] also describe a straight-forward extension to loops with recurrences. By ignoring backward edges in the dependence graph the list scheduler for GVCs can be reused. Operation priority is again determined by the critical paths in the acyclic graphs. Additionally the scheduler has to obey the recurrence constraint that assures correctly timed inter-iteration dataflow.

---

[3]This is where the name "Modulo Scheduling" comes from.

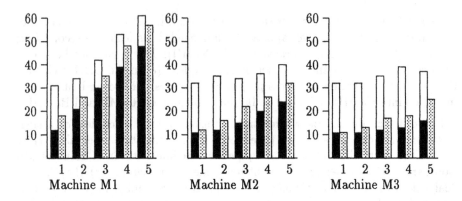

Figure 3: FMS results for the SCC(1..5) benchmarks: II (grey bar) compared to MII (black bar) and length of the unpipelined loop (white bar)

In this basic version FMS does not give priority to time-critical operations on dependence cycles. This clearly leads to sub-optimal initiation intervals if the resources for such operations are occupied by previously scheduled non-critical operations. Fig. 3 demonstrates this effect by comparing the size of initiation interval produced by FMS to the minimum possible initiation interval MII and the maximal useful II (size of the unpipelined loop schedule). FMS is only able to construct optimal or near-optimal results if both the number of cyclicly dependent operations is small and the resource pressure is low, i.e. on machines which offer a sufficient number of parallel functional units.

The results of the original FMS can clearly be improved by extending the list scheduler to take time-critical dependence cycles into account when determining scheduling priorities. This has been proposed by a number of authors [DeT93], [WHS92], [LVA95].

Hierarchical Software Pipelining (HMS)

We consider hierarchical modulo scheduling as proposed by Lam [Lam88]. This algorithm first processes the dependence graph's strongly connected components (SCC) induced by source loop recurrences separately and independently. If this succeeds for one II value for all SCCs this first scheduling phase terminates.

In the second phase an acyclic dependence graph is constructed by reducing the SCCs to hypernodes which are connected to all predecessors and successors of the component (*acyclic condensation*). The hypernodes have complex resource patterns, which correspond to the resource usage in the precomputed SCC schedules. The reduced dependence graph has to be scheduled with the initiation interval used in scheduling the SCCs. Since the reduced graph is acyclic, a simple local scheduler for modulo-constrained resources can be used. The scheduling is successful, if all operations, including the meta operations representing the SCCs, can be integrated in the schedule. If scheduling fails because

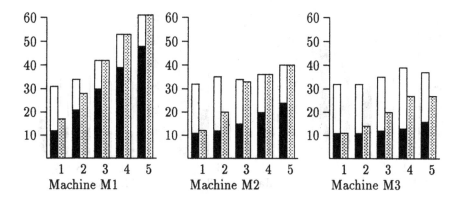

Figure 4: HMS results for the SCC(1..5) benchmarks: II (grey bar) compared to MII (black bar) and length of the unpipelined loop (white bar)

of the modulo resource constraint, all scheduling decisions are discarded and the whole process repeats with an increased II.

HMS clearly gives priority to the operations in recurrence cycles by scheduling them independently in its first phase. Furthermore its hypernode reduction strategy can easily be extended to handle loops with internal control flow . The severe drawback of HMS lies in the fact that although compact pipeline schedules for the SCCs can be generated, these schedules lead to complex resource usage patterns for the hypernodes in the second scheduling phase. Thus, HMS frequently fails in its second phase due to resource conflicts leading to sub-optimal II results. Fig. 4 illustrates this.

Resource Sensitive Software Pipelining (RSPS)

Resource Sensitive Pipeline Scheduling has been developed to improve the results of the hierarchical algorithm HMS [Pie95]. RSPS is similar to HMS, the main difference being, that SCCs are scheduled with knowledge of the resource usage in the previously scheduled components. During the first scheduling phase the resource requirement of the components is kept stored in the modulo resource reservation table. The so computed SCC schedules always fit together in the second phase because they cannot cause resource conflicts with each other. The order in which the SCCs are processed is determined by their cycle length to prioritize time critical subgraphs. One essential difference between RSPS and HMS lies in the fact that the resource sensitive approach fixes the modulo positions of the SCC members in its first scheduling phase whereas HMS does so when finally arranging the hypernodes in the second phase.

The reservation table resulting from scheduling the SCCs is reused for arranging the acyclic condensation. Simple (non-SCC) operations are placed in positions where they do not conflict with the previously scheduled components. Arranging the meta operations always succeeds because their resource requirement is

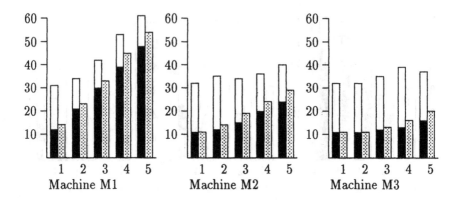

Figure 5: RSPS results for the SCC(1..5) benchmarks: II (grey bar) compared to MII (black bar) and length of the unpipelined loop (white bar)

already reserved in the resource reservation table. The only thing to be done is finding a schedule cycle satisfying the precedence constraints and the modulo positions of the components members. Scheduling a simple operation can of course fail because of the modulo resource constraint.

RSPS can be considered as a hybrid approach between flat and hierarchical modulo scheduling. It is no flat algorithm since it uses precomputed schedules for the SCCs. It is not really an hierarchical technique, since it doesn't process the SCCs independently. The scheduling results in Fig. 5 show that the goal of generating near-optimal pipeline schedules has been reached by the RSPS algorithm.

4 Evaluation

The results for the SCC benchmarks shown in Sect. 3 give a first impression of the performance of the investigated scheduling algorithms. This section provides more benchmarking results and a detailed performance analysis. In addition to the comparison on the base of the II length we will investigate the register requirement of the pipelined loop code generated by the three schedulers.

4.1 Execution time

MATH Benchmark

The SRP transformed numerical programs (c.f. Sect. 2.3) are characterized by large loop bodies with many strongly connected components where some of the SCCs are quite large. Nevertheless the loop's resource usage dominates the lower bound on II (MII = ResMII). The results in Fig. 6 show that only the RSPS algorithm computes pipeline schedules with an initiation interval close to or at the lower bound.

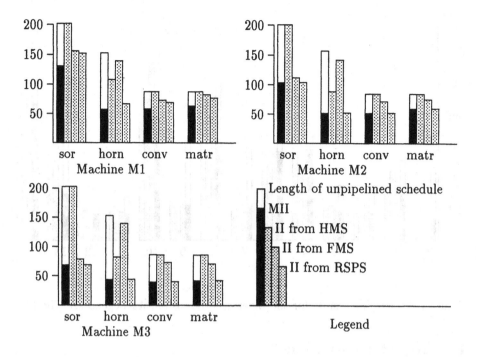

Figure 6: Pipelining results for the MATH benchmark.

Livermore Benchmark

We use the first 14 Livermore loops to generate software pipelined loop code for processor M2[4]. The speed-up for the software pipelined loops on M2 ranges between 3.8 (loop 7) and 1.3 (loop 5) compared to the parallel schedule of one loop iteration.

In loops 8, 9, 10 and 13 the lower bound for II is determined by resource usage (MII = ResMII). Therefore the results of the scheduling algorithms for these programs are similar to the results obtained for the synthetic benchmarks. In loops 5, 6 and 14 the resource pressure is very small because of long dependence cycles (MII = RecMII). With the exception of FMS in loop 14 all scheduling algorithms generate pipeline schedules with an optimal initiation interval. The remaining loops are small with a low resource pressure. Here the FMS algorithm generates the poorest results which once again is clearly due to the fact that cyclicly dependent operations are not given scheduling preference. HMS and RSPS almost always achieve optimal initiation intervals for these loops.

---

[4]The scheduling results for M1 and M3 are similar and are omitted in this paper.

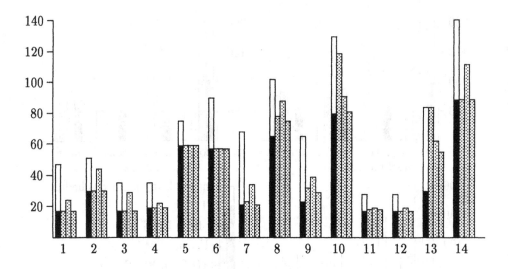

Figure 7: Pipelining results for the Livermore Loops on M2(Legend see Fig. 6)

4.2 Register requirement

In addition to the length of the initiation interval the register requirement of the generated loop code deserves attention. The register requirement grows with growing concurrency caused by modern processors with more instruction level parallelism and/or effective parallelization techniques, like software pipelining. If the generated schedule requires more registers than available spill code has to be inserted. This can lead to a serious performance degradation due to additional machine cycles and the necessary memory accesses.

Apart from the growing register requirement, one particular problem shows up in software pipelined code: Register lifetime may exceed the length of the initiation interval. Fig 8 illustrates this fact. Register r1 with a lifetime of 5 cycles exceeds the length of the II (3 cycles). This leads to overwriting the r1 value before reading it in the steady state. Fig. 8 also shows two ways to solve this problem. One can make use of *register queues* to store living register values. If such queues are not supported by the target hardware they can be implemented by register-to-register copies (Fig. 8b). The second approach is called *Modulo variable expansion* [Lam88]. The steady state code is duplicated an appropriate number of times. Each copy uses a different register to propagate the value in question (Fig. 8c). The best way, however, to avoid this problem is to have a scheduler that tries to minimize register lifetimes.

None of the investigated scheduling algorithms considers the minimization of register pressure. Being based on the level-oriented as-soon-as-possible list scheduling algorithm, they all tend to generate longer register lifetimes than e.g. the subtree-oriented strategies used in classical compiler code generation. Nevertheless, there are striking differences.

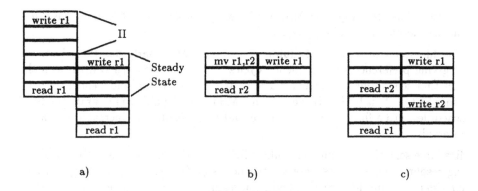

Figure 8: Register Lifetime exceeds the II (a), register queue (b) and Modulo variable expansion (c)

FMS generated software pipelines have the least register lifetimes that exceed the initiation interval (0.6 register values on the average for the Livermore benchmarks on all three machines). HMS produced 3.5 and RSPS 5.6 exceeding register values. The other benchmark sets led to similar results. The reason for this effect is obvious: HMS must move whole SCC schedules to find a conflict-free scheduling position for the hypernodes. This lengthens the lifetime of all values flowing into the SCC nodes from outside. With RSPS the situation is still worse: Since the modulo-positions of the prescheduled SCC nodes are fixed, the second scheduling phase can only place them at these modulo positions, i.e. every IIth cycle. As our tests show this can cause extremely long register lifetimes.

To summarize our discussion we would like to classify the investigated scheduling techniques by four criteria:

a) preferential treatment of recurrence cycles

b) independent scheduling or recurrence cycles

c) time of decision binding for the relative positions of nodes on dependence cycles (i.e. the construction time of the SCC schedules).

d) time of decision binding for modulo positions of nodes on dependence cycles (i.e. the time when a SCC member's modulo position is fixed).

The following table summarizes this classification:

	SCC		Binding	
	preference	independence	relative pos.	modulo pos.
HMS	yes	yes	early	late
RSPS	yes	resource dependence	early	early
FMS	no	no	late	late

For two-phase techniques (HMS, RSSP) *early* simply means the first phase, *late* means the final scheduling phase.

The hierarchical modulo scheduling technique HMS clearly has the advantage of giving preference to dependence cycles. The problem with HMS lies in the fact that scheduling decisions for a SCC are fixed early and independently from other SCCs. This frequently results in HMS not being able to integrate the SCC schedules into a final schedule in its second phase leading to increased initiation intervals.

Resource sensitive pipeline scheduling RSPS avoids these problems by considering resource dependences between the nodes of different SCCs. This approach considerably simplifies SCC integration leading to optimal or near-optimal initiation intervals. This advantage, however, must be paid for in terms of register requirement because the early binding of modulo positions for cyclicly dependent nodes may cause very long register lifetimes. This early binding, on the other hand, is necessary to model the resource interdependence of different SCCs.

Flat modulo scheduling FMS results in reasonable register pressure although register minimization is not regarded in this algorithm. Late binding of all scheduling decisions and the individual arrangement of operations clearly influences register lifetimes positively. The clear disadvantage of FMS in its original form lies in the suboptimal initiation intervals of the generated software pipelines. This is certainly due to not giving preference to nodes on recurrence cycles in the FMS version we used for this evaluation.

Summarizing, non-hierarchical modulo scheduling in an enhanced form that preferences recurrence cycles seems to be the most promising technique. As mentioned in Sect. 3 such enhancements have been proposed by some authors. A recent publication [LVA95] additionally integrates register minimization aspects. Unfortunately, this technique has not yet been integrated into our evaluation environment.

5   Summary and Conclusion

We compared different software pipelining techniques by implementing them in an uniform compiler environment and having them generate code for different instruction parallel machines. In this paper we investigated the non-hierarchical technique FMS [RaG81], the hierarchical technique HMS [Lam88], and the hybrid variant RSSP [Pie95].

The evaluation of our experiments shows that the hierarchical approach has problems scheduling the hypernodes in the acyclic condensation of the data dependence graphs because the schedules for the hypernodes have been produced independently. This problem is especially severe if resource pressure is high, i.e. we have large dependence graphs or small machines. Current instruction level parallel processors provide a quite limited amount of parallel resources. Therefore, pipeline schedulers face both resource and register pressure. Furthermore, specialized optimization techniques applied before pipeline scheduling tend to further decrease cycle length or remove cycles by moving dependencies out of inner loops. Thus, resource consumption dominates the minimal initiation interval and pipeline schedulers must be able to cope with hard resource constraints. This excludes HMS from the list of promising pipeline scheduling approaches.

The RSSP variant avoids hypernode arrangement problems by taking the resource consumption of previously scheduled components into account while scheduling SCCs. In most cases the RSSP algorithm yields smaller initiation intervals. This advantage, however, must be paid for in terms of register requirement because the early binding of modulo positions for cyclically dependent nodes may cause prohibitively long register lifetimes.

The basic non-hierarchical pipeline scheduling algorithm suffers from not giving cyclicly dependent operations (SCCs) preference over acyclic operations. Especially if the minimal initiation interval is dominated by the length of cyclic dependence paths, non-critical operations tend to occupy resources required by critical operations on cyclic paths. This prevents FSP from achieving optimal or near-optimal initiation intervals. Register pressure is low in FMS generated software pipelines. This is clearly due to its ability to schedule all operations individually. Furthermore, FMS turns out the most flexible approach which is open for integrating additional optimization criteria. Recent publications, e.g., propose enhanced versions of FMS integrating both preferential treatment of recurrence cycles and register minimization heuristics [LVA95].

Together with the fact that the FMS implementation is considerably simpler than the implementation of the hierarchical technique, non-hierarchical pipeline schedulers turn out to be the most promising candidate for future production quality instruction schedulers.

References

[CNO87]   Colwell, R. P., Nix, R. P., O'Donnel, J. J., Pappworth, D. B. and Rodman, P. K., *A VLIW Architecture for a Trace Scheduling Compiler*, in Proc. 2nd Int'l Conf. on Arch. Support for Progr. Languages and Operating Systems, Oct 87, 180 – 192.

[DeT93]   Dehnert, J. C. and Towle, R. A., *Compiling for the Cydra-5*, Journal of Supercomputing (7) (May 1993), 181–227.

[DGS92]   Düsterwald, E., Gupta, R. and Soffa, M. L., *Register Pipelining: An Integrated Approach to Register Allocation for Scalar and Subscripted Variables*, in Proc. 4th International Conference on Compiler Construction, CC'92, vol. 641, Springer-Verlag, 1992, 192–206.

[Ell86]   Ellis, J. R., *Bulldog: A Compiler for VLIW Architectures*, MIT Press, Cambridge, MA, 1986.

[GoH88]   Goodman, J. R. and Hsu, W. C., *Code Scheduling and Register Allocation in Large Basic Blocks*, in Proc. International Conference on Supercomputing, ACM, 1988, 442–452.

[HGA92]   Hendren, L. J., Gao, G. R., Altman, E. R. and Mukerji, C., *A Register Allocation Framework Based on Hierachical Cyclic Interval Graphs*, in Proc. 4th International Conference on Compiler Construction, CC'92, vol. 641, Lecture Notes in Computer Science, Springer-Verlag, 1992, 176–191.

[Lam88]   Lam, M., *Software Pipelining: An Effective Scheduling Technique for VLIW Machines*, in Proc. SIGPLAN 88 Conf. on Programming Language Design and Implementation, June 1988, 318 – 328.

[LVA95]   Llosa, J., Valero, M. and Ayguade, E., *Bidirectional Scheduling to Minimize Register Requirements*, in 5th Workshop on Compilers for Parallel Computers, Malaga Spain, 1995.

[Pie95]   Piepenbrock, G., *Methoden des Software-Pipelining für Prozessoren mit Instruktionsparallelität*, PhD Thesis Universität-GH Paderborn (1995).

[Pin93]   Pinter, S. S., *Register Allocation with Instruction Scheduling: a New Approach*, in Proc SIGPLAN 93 Conference on Programming Language Design and Implementation, 1993, 248–257.

[Pug92]   Pugh, W., *A Practical Algorithm for Exact Array Dependence Analysis*, Communications of the ACM 35-8 (1992), 102–114.

[RaG81]   Rau, B. R. and Glaeser, C. D., *Some Scheduling Techniques and an Easily Schedulable Horizontal Architecture for High Performance Scientific Computing*, in Proc. 14th Annual Microprogramming Workshop, 1981, 183–198.

[RaF93]   Rau, B. R. and Fisher, J. A., *Instruction-Level Parallel Processing: History, Overview and Perspective*, Journal of Supercomputing 7 (May 1993), 9–50.

[SPP94]   Slowik, A., Pfahler, P. and Piepenbrock, G., *Compiling Nested Loops for Limited Connectivity VLIWs*, in Proc. 5th International Conference on Compiler Construction, CC'94, vol. 786, Lecture Notes in Computer Science, Springer-Verlag, 1994, 143–157.

[WHS92]   Warter, N. J., Haab, G. E., Subramanian, K. and Bockhaus, J. W., *Enhanced Modulo Scheduling for Loops with Conditional Branches*, Proc. 25th Intern. Symposium on Microarchitecture, Portland (1992).

[WoL91]   Wolf, M. E. and Lam, M. S., *A Loop Transformation Theory and an Algorithm to Maximize Parallelism*, Transactions on Parallel and Distributetd Systems 2/4 (Oct. 1991), 452–471.

Removing Anti Dependences by Repairing

M. Anton Ertl   Andreas Krall
{anton,andi}@mips.complang.tuwien.ac.at

Institut für Computersprachen
Technische Universität Wien
Argentinierstraße 8, A-1040 Wien, Austria
anton,andi@mips.complang.tuwien.ac.at
http://www.complang.tuwien.ac.at/home.html
Tel.: (+43-1) 58801 4474
Fax.: (+43-1) 505 78 38

Abstract. Anti dependences (write-after-read dependences) constrain
the reordering of instructions and limit the effectiveness of instruction
scheduling and software pipelining techniques for superscalar and VLIW
processors. Repairing solves this problem: If the definition of a variable
is moved before a previous use of that variable, compiler-generated repair code reconstructs the value that the definition destroyed. Repairing features several potential advantages over register renaming, another
technique for removing anti dependences: less register pressure, less loop
unrolling and fewer move instructions.
Key Words: anti dependence, repairing, register renaming, instruction-
level parallelism, speculative execution

1 Introduction

Computer designers and computer architects have been striving to improve
uniprocessor performance since the invention of computers. The next step in
this quest for higher performance is the exploitation of significant amounts of
instruction-level parallelism. Therefore, superscalar and VLIW (very large instruction word) machines have been designed, which can execute several instructions in parallel. In order to use these resources the instructions are reordered by
the hardware [Tho64, Tom67, PHS85, Soh90] or by compiler techniques like basic
block instruction scheduling [LDSM80, HG83, GM86, EK92], trace scheduling
[Fis81, Ell85] and software pipelining [RG81, Lam88, Rau94]. To ensure correctness, the order between dependent instructions must be maintained, which
restricts reordering and parallelism.

Dependences exist between writes and reads (data flow dependences), reads
and writes (anti dependences) and between writes (output dependences) to the
same register or memory location. In this paper, we will discuss only dependences
through registers. We will also concentrate on anti dependences. Although the
techniques discussed here can be used to eliminate output dependences, (partial)
dead code elimination [KRS94, BC94] is more appropriate for this purpose.

Another problem for exploiting significant amounts of instruction-level parallelism is the limited amount of registers (e.g., ≤ 32 integer registers on all

popular architectures). By contrast, functional units tend to become abundant; compilers will have a hard time utilizing all of them all the time.

We discuss anti dependences and existing techniques for dealing with them in Section 2. In Section 3 we introduce a new technique, that often reduces register pressure, but usually pays for this with more instructions: repairing. In Section 4 we demonstrate the advantages of repairing with a small example. Finally, we show the potential of repairing with empirical data derived from instruction traces of real-life applications (Section 5).

2 Anti Dependences

Anti dependences (and output dependences) are, in some sense, false dependences. They are not caused by the data flow between instructions, but by reusing registers. Several methods for dealing with anti dependences have been proposed:

2.1 Register Renaming

Anti dependences can be removed (or at least moved) by register renaming [PW86]. This technique can be implemented in hardware [Tom67, PHS85, Soh90] and as compiler optimization [PW86, Lam88]. Note that only compiler-based renaming techniques can increase the reordering freedom for the compiler.

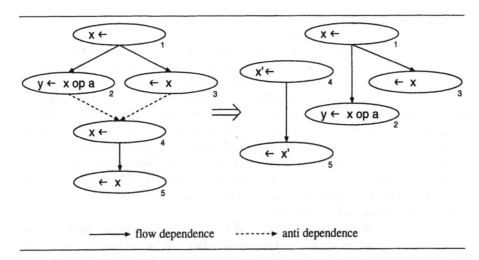

Fig. 1. Register renaming

Figure 1 shows how register renaming works: Originally, register x is used in two live ranges, resulting in two anti dependences, one from each use (read) of the first live range to the definition (write) of the second live range. Register renaming transforms the second live range such that it uses the register x'.

Renaming has two restrictions:

- Renaming the whole second live range may be impossible, because one of the uses requires a specific register (e.g., to satisfy the calling convention).
- Renaming does not work, if the two dynamic live ranges involved are statically the same live range (e.g., a live range in a loop).

Both problems can be solved by moving x' to x as soon as the first live range no longer needs x (at the cost of an additional move instruction). The second problem can also be solved by separating the live ranges statically by code replication (e.g., loop unrolling).[1]

2.2 Rematerialization

Instead of renaming one of the live ranges such that the definition of the second does not destroy the value used in the first live range, the compiler can reconstruct the value of the first live range just before the value is used. Rematerialization reconstructs the value by simply recomputing it. Rematerialization of constants has been proposed [CAC+81] and successfully used [BCT92] as an alternative to spilling in register allocation.

Figure 2 shows, how the scheduler can rematerialize a constant (in instruction $\bar{1}$). In this example, rematerialization moved instruction 3 down across 4 and 5, which originally (anti-) depend on 3. The resulting code still contains antidependences, but they are different and may hinder scheduling less (if this arrangement were not profitable, the compiler would use rematerialization differently or not at all).

Rematerialization reduces the lifetime of the result of a computation, but it may increase the lifetime of the source operands. This may cause higher register pressure and more loop unrolling. A simple way to avoid this problem is to rematerialize only constants, because they have no input operands. This approach is used by [BCT92].

3 Repairing

Like rematerialization, repairing reconstructs the value that was in the register before it was overwritten by the definition of the second live range. In contrast to rematerialization, repairing reconstructs the value from downstream values using the inverse operation.

In Figure 3, the value of the first live range is used to compute y in instruction 2. Later, y is used to reconstruct that value in register x' using the inverse operation $\overline{op}$ (instruction $\bar{2}$).

To apply this transformation, the following conditions must be satisfied:

---

[1] The combination of register renaming and loop unrolling is known as modulo variable expansion [Lam88].

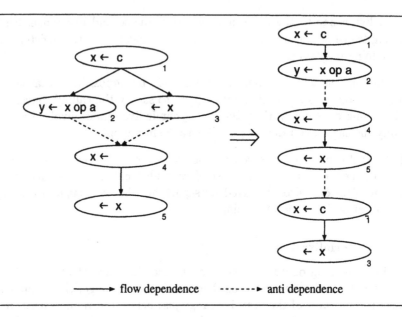

Fig. 2. Rematerialization of a constant

- Another value has been computed from the value destroyed by the second definition.
- This computation is invertible. This includes arithmetic and logic operations like add (with modulo arithmetic), subtract, rotate, exclusive or, negation and bitwise complement, but not multiply or floating point operations, which can lose information.

At first sight, repair code seems to make the program worse, especially when compared to register renaming, which (apparently) costs nothing but a few loop unrollings. But in many cases the repair code can use an otherwise unused execution unit, can be combined [NE89] with other operations or optimized in some other way.

Repairing also introduces new data flow dependences ($2 \to \overline{2} \to 3$ in Figure 3). These dependences pose no problem to the scheduler. It can chose between repairing and other methods depending on the way in which it wants to arrange the instructions 2, 3 and 4. The data dependences introduced by repairing just mean that repairing cannot be used for certain arrangements. Fortunately, for those arrangements where repairing offers the greatest benefits (i.e., the scheduler wants to move instruction 3 far down), it can be applied.

The potential advantages of repairing over register renaming are:

less register pressure Repairing often uses one register less between the time when the value is destroyed and the time when it is repaired.
less loop unrolling If the lifetime of a variable is l cycles, and a loop iteration is initiated every s cycles, then at least $\lceil l/s \rceil$ values for the variable must

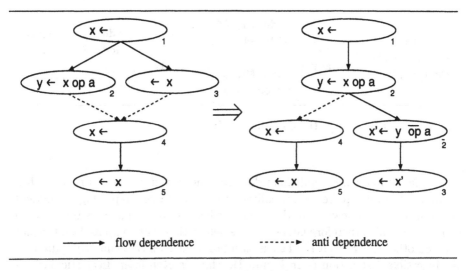

Fig. 3. Repairing using the inverse operation ($\overline{op}$)

be kept alive concurrently. The loop must be unrolled that many times in order to to address the values in different registers. Repairing shortens the lifetime of registers, which in turn lowers $\lceil l/s \rceil$ and the unrolling factor.

fewer move instructions Unless the compiler performs an unhealthy amount of code replication, register renaming introduces move instructions at control flow joins. These moves can often be avoided with repairing.

However, repairing also has a potential for making a program worse. Apart from adding an operation, it can also lengthen the lifetime of the values that are needed for the reconstruction. The result of the operation to be inverted (y in Figure 3) is used elsewhere anyway, and keeping it alive for repairing is certainly better (with respect to register pressure) than keeping the original value alive; but lengthening the lifetime of the other operand (a in Figure 3) can cause higher register pressure than register renaming. Of course, if the operation needs only one operand in a register (i.e., the operation is unary or it has an inline (small constant) operand), repairing is guaranteed to be profitable with respect to register pressure.

In some cases, the repairing operation and the operation using this repaired value can be combined [NE89], providing the benefits of repairing without any cost. For example: additions or subtractions with immediate operands can be combined with additions, subtractions and comparison instructions with an immediate operand or with memory instructions; negations can be combined with additions or subtractions. Figure 4 shows an example, where the scheduler moves an sw instruction down.

In comparison with rematerialization, repairing results in less register pressure in the worst case: Both extend the live ranges of the values necessary for the reconstruction down to the instruction performing the reconstruction. But

		addu $5, $4, 8	addu $5, $4, 8
addu $5, $4, 8	⇒	addu $4, ...	addu $4, ...
sw $3, 4($4)	repairing	...	⇒ combining ...
addu $4, ...		subu $6, $5, 8	sw $3, -4($5)
		sw $3, 4($6)	

Fig. 4. Repairing used with combining (MIPS assembly)

rematerialization can extend them down all the way from the instruction that computed the value to be rematerialized originally, whereas repairing can extend one (a in Figure 3) down from the invertible instruction (which uses the value to be repaired and is therefore later than the instruction that computed that value) and the other down from the last instruction that uses the value computed by the invertible instruction (y in Figure 3), which is even later. In particular, repairing is guaranteed to be profitable (with respect to register pressure), if the repairing instruction needs only one register operand, whereas rematerialization is not always profitable for the analogous case.

In the preceding discussion we always wrote about "extending live ranges". Of course, repairing and rematerialization can be applied to these live ranges, too, where appropriate; still, on average, a longer live range will cause higher cost, be it register pressure, reconstruction or move instructions, or loop unrolling.

The most important application of repairing will be compiler-based speculative execution. Global code reordering techniques like trace scheduling and software pipelining move instructions up before branches. This is only legal, if the destination register of the moved instruction is dead on the other path. However, by inserting repair code in the other path the compiler can lift this restriction (see Figure 5). Note that instruction 2 need not reside in front of the branch from the beginning—it may have moved up, too.

The actual algorithm for repairing depends on the scheduling framework. E.g, a trace scheduling [Ell85] compiler would first schedule a trace without restrictions from anti dependences, then (in the bookkeeping phase) it would determine the applicability and profitability of renaming, repairing and rematerialization for each anti dependence, and apply the least costly applicable transformation, and finally it would allocate the registers.

4   Example

We demonstrate the advantages of repairing with a small example. Figure 6 shows the C function strlen, which computes the length of a zero-terminated string. Figure 7 shows the assembly language output of a compiler for the MIPS R3000. We have changed the register names to make the program more readable.

Figure 8 shows a version of the loop that is software-pipelined using register

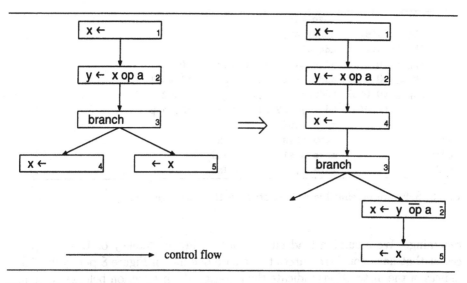

Fig. 5. Repairing applied to speculative execution (control flow graph)

```
int strlen(char *s) {
  char *t = s;
  while (*s != '\0')
    s++;
  return s-t;
}
```

Fig. 6. The C function strlen

```
#   1     int strlen(char *s) {
strlen:
#   2     char *t = s;
          move    t,s           # t=s
#   3     while (*s != '\0')
          lb      t0,0(s)        # t0=*s
          beqz    t0,end         # while (t0 != '\0')
loop:
#   4       s++;
          addu    s,s,1          # s++
          lb      t0,0(s)        # t0=*s
          bnez    t0,loop        # while (t0 != '\0')
end:
#   5     return s-t;
          subu    v0,s,t         # return_value = s-t
          j       ra             # return
```

Fig. 7. MIPS R3000 assembly language source of strlen

```
                       move t,s
        lb₀ t0,0(s)    addu₁ s1,s,1
        lb₁ t1,0(s1)   addu₂ s2,s1,1
loop:   lbₙ t2,0(s2)   adduₙ₊₁ s3,s2,1 beqzₙ₋₂ t0,end
        lbₙ₊₁ t3,0(s3) adduₙ₊₂ s,s3,1  beqzₙ₋₁ t1,end1
        lbₙ₊₂ t0,0(s)  adduₙ₊₃ s1,s,1  beqzₙ  t2,end2
        lbₙ₊₃ t1,0(s1) adduₙ₊₄ s2,s1,1 bnezₙ₊₁ t3,loop
                       move s,s3
end:                   subu v0,s,t   j ra
end1:                  move s,s1     b end
end2:                  move s,s2     b end
```

Fig. 8. Software pipelined version of strlen with register renaming

renaming.[2] We assume a load latency of 2, a branch latency of 1, and a processor that has enough resources to execute one line of Figure 8 per cycle. The indices of the instructions indicate the iteration the instruction belongs to. This example nicely demonstrates the disadvantages of register renaming. The addus are executed speculatively three iterations in advance and therefore their results live four cycles (they are used in the off-loop arms). Therefore the number of different registers necessary for s and the loop unrolling factor is $\lceil l/s \rceil = 4$. The result of the lb lives for only three cycles, but since the unrolling factor is four, we must give four registers to it, too[3]. At the exit of the loop move instructions have been generated to reunite the s values into one register.

```
                       move t,s
        lb₀ t0,0(s)    addu₁ s,s,1
        lb₁ t1,0(s)    addu₂ s,s,1
loop:   lbₙ t2,0(s)    adduₙ₊₁ s,s,1 beqzₙ₋₂ t0,end
        lbₙ₊₁ t0,0(s)  adduₙ₊₂ s,s,1 beqzₙ₋₁ t1,end
        lbₙ₊₂ t1,0(s)  adduₙ₊₃ s,s,1 bnezₙ  t2,loop
end:                   subu s,s,3
                       subu v0,s,t   j ra
```

Fig. 9. Software pipelined version of strlen with repair code

Figure 9 shows another version of the loop, this time software-pipelined with repairing and register renaming. s satisfies the conditions for repairing with the inverse operation and can safely be destroyed by incrementing it. Therefore s needs only one register. It does not pay off to destroy and repair the results of the lbs, so we have to use register renaming in this case. Since these results live for three cycles, the loop is unrolled three times. At the off-loop path, s has to

---

[2] For simplicity, we assume that the loads cannot have exceptions. Speculative execution of trapping instructions is discussed in, e.g., [EK94].

[3] We could have saved the one register by unrolling $\mathrm{lcm}(4,3) = 12$ times [Lam88].

be repaired to its proper value. s has been destroyed by incrementing thrice. Therefore the repair code consists of three decrements that have been combined into one decrement by three. In summary, repairing saves four registers (44%), one loop iteration (25%) and some other code as well.

5 Potential

This section shows how important repairing is for real-world programs. We produced traces (up to 100,000,000 instructions) of various applications and counted the antidependences in them and how many of them can be removed with various forms of repairing.

This trace-based method has some disadvantages: it does not see all antidependences that the compiler has to consider (in particular, it does not see antidependences to off-trace instructions), and it treats all antidependences equal, no matter how important or unimportant they are for the compiler. The advantage of this method is that it is independent from the compiler; if, in contrast, we implemented repairing in a compiler and presented empirical data based on experiments with this compiler, the results would strongly depend on the scheduler and on the register allocator of that compiler. Note that the results we present do not depend much on the compiler; although the compilers we used performed register allocation, this has little influence, because almost every use of a value causes an antidependence, independent of the register allocator, and the uses themselves are also quite independent of the register allocator (as long as moves and spilling are minor factors). Our empirical data supports this view: you cannot tell from the data which compiler produced the code.

The applications used are: abalone, a board game; agrep, an approximate pattern matcher; dvips, a filter used in typesetting; gcc-cc1, a part of the GNU C compiler; gzip, a compression program; and sicstus, a Prolog interpreter. All programs were compiled for the Alpha architecture under OSF/1, either with gcc-2.7.0 (abalone, gcc-cc1, sicstus) or with cc-3.1.1 (the other programs).

Figure 10 shows the results. The column *instructions* displays the trace length, *anti dep/inst.* the number of anti dependences per instruction, and the next three columns display what portion of these anti dependences can be eliminated with various forms of repairing: *repairing* comprises all forms of repairing, *one reg. operand* are those forms of repairing that are guaranteed to be profitable with respect to register pressure, and *combinable* are those cases where the repairing code can be combined with the instruction that uses the repaired value (and therefore repairing is for free, in addition to being profitable).

18%–34% of all antidependences can be removed with repairing. Only about half of them (8.6%–16.6%) are guaranteed to be profitable with respect to register pressure according to our simple one-register-operand criterion, so it is probably a good idea to invest a little more in profitability analysis. 4.1%–12.6% of the anti dependences can be repaired for free, providing the benefits of repairing without any cost.

program	instructions	anti dep./ inst.	one reg. repairable	operand	combinable
abalone	100,000,000	1.25	30.1%	15.8%	8.1%
agrep	29,251,288	1.35	34.0%	8.6%	4.2%
dvips	51,155,896	1.22	18.2%	10.9%	4.1%
gcc-cc1	100,000,000	1.17	25.7%	16.6%	12.6%
gzip	100,000,000	1.37	27.2%	14.1%	4.8%
sicstus	91,433,314	1.16	31.8%	15.8%	10.7%

Fig. 10. Portion of anti dependences that can be removed with various forms of repairing

Compilers for register-starved architectures (in particular, the 386 architecture) can employ repairing of combinable instructions now to reduce the register pressure. For other architectures, there are probably still a few years left until register pressure becomes a significant problem. The large amount of parallel units available by then will make any form of repairing attractive that reduces register pressure.

6 Conclusions

We have introduced repairing, a compiler technique that can remove anti dependences and reduce register pressure: If an instruction writing to a register is moved up across an instruction reading from that register, repairing reconstructs the destroyed value from derived values using the inverse operation.

Repairing often has advantages over other techniques for removing anti dependences: Repairing produces less register pressure and it produces shorter live ranges, requiring less loop unrolling or fewer move instructions.

18%–34% of all anti dependences can be removed by repairing, about half of them are guaranteed to reduce register pressure (others may be profitable, too), and 4.1%–12.6% of antidependences can be removed in a way that reduces register pressure without increasing the number of executed instructions.

References

[BC94] Preston Briggs and Keith D. Cooper. Effective partial redundancy elimination. In *SIGPLAN '94 Conference on Programming Language Design and Implementation*, pages 159–170, 1994.

[BCT92] Preston Briggs, Keith D. Cooper, and Linda Torczon. Rematerialization. In *SIGPLAN '92 Conference on Programming Language Design and Implementation*, pages 311–321, 1992.

[CAC+81] Gregory J. Chaitin, Marc A. Auslander, Ashok K. Chandra, John Cocke, Martin E. Hopkins, and Peter W. Markstein. Register allocation via coloring. *Computer Languages*, 6(1):45–57, 1981. Reprinted in [Sta90].

[EK92]   M. Anton Ertl and Andreas Krall.   Instruction scheduling for complex pipelines. In *Compiler Construction (CC'92)*, pages 207–218, Paderborn, 1992. Springer LNCS 641.

[EK94]   M. Anton Ertl and Andreas Krall. Delayed exceptions — speculative execution of trapping instructions. In *Compiler Construction (CC '94)*, pages 158–171, Edinburgh, April 1994. Springer LNCS 786.

[Ell85]   John R. Ellis. *Bulldog: A Compiler for VLIW Architectures*. MIT Press, 1985.

[Fis81]   Joseph A. Fisher. Trace scheduling: A technique for global microcode compaction. *IEEE Transactions on Computers*, 30(7):478–490, July 1981.

[GM86]   Phillip B. Gibbons and Steve S. Muchnick. Efficient instruction scheduling for a pipelined architecture. In *SIGPLAN '86 Symposium on Compiler Construction*, pages 11–16, 1986.

[HG83]   John Hennessy and Thomas Gross. Postpass code optimization of pipeline constraints. *ACM Transactions on Programming Languages and Systems*, 5(3):422–448, July 1983.

[KRS94]   Jens Knoop, Oliver Rüthing, and Bernhard Steffen. Partial dead code elimination. In *SIGPLAN '94 Conference on Programming Language Design and Implementation*, pages 147–158, 1994.

[Lam88]   Monica Lam. Software pipelining: An effective scheduling technique for VLIW machines. In *SIGPLAN '88 Conference on Programming Language Design and Implementation*, pages 318–328, 1988.

[LDSM80] David Landskov, Scott Davidson, Bruce Shriver, and Pattrick W. Mallet. Local microcode compaction techniques. *ACM Computing Surveys*, 12(3):261–294, September 1980.

[NE89]   Toshio Nakatani and Kemal Ebcioğlu. "Combining" as a compilation technique for VLIW architectures. In *22nd Annual International Workshop on Microprogramming and Microarchitecture (MICRO-22)*, pages 43–55, 1989.

[PHS85]   Yale N. Patt, Wen-mei Hwu, and Michael Shebanow. HPS, a new microarchitecture: Rationale and introduction. In *The 18th Annual Workshop on Microprogramming (MICRO-18)*, pages 103–108, 1985.

[PW86]   David A. Padua and Michael J. Wolfe. Advanced compiler optimizations for supercomputers. *Communications of the ACM*, 29(12):1184–1201, December 1986.

[Rau94]   B. Ramakrishna Rau. Iterative modulo scheduling: An algorithm for software pipelining. In *International Symposium on Microarchitecture (MICRO-27)*, pages 63–74, 1994.

[RG81]   B. R. Rau and C. D. Glaeser. Some scheduling techgniques and an easily schedulable horizontal architecture for high performance scientific computing. In *14th Annual Microprogramming Workshop (MICRO-14)*, pages 183–198, 1981.

[Soh90]   Gurindar S. Sohi. Instruction issue logic for high-performance, interruptable, multiple functional unit, pipelined processors. *IEEE Transactions on Computers*, 39(3):349–359, March 1990.

[Sta90]   William Stallings, editor. *Reduced Instruction Set Computers*. IEEE Computer Society Press, second edition, 1990.

[Tho64]   J. E. Thornton. Parallel operation in Control Data 6600. In *AFIPS Fall Joint Computer Conference*, pages 33–40, 1964.

[Tom67]   R. M. Tomasulo. An efficient algorithm for exploiting multiple arithmetic units. *IBM Journal of Research and Development*, 11(1):25–33, 1967.

Controlled Node Splitting

Johan Janssen and Henk Corporaal

Delft University of Technology
Department of Electrical Engineering
Section Computer Architecture and Digital Systems
P.O. Box 5031, 2600 GA Delft, The Netherlands

Abstract. To exploit instruction level parallelism in programs over multiple basic blocks, programs should have reducible control flow graphs. However not all programs satisfy this property. A new method, called Controlled Node Splitting (CNS), for transforming irreducible control flow graphs to reducible control flow graphs is presented. CNS duplicates nodes of the control flow graph to obtain reducible control flow graphs. CNS results in a minimum number of splits and a minimum number of duplicates. Since the computation time to find the optimal split sequence is large, a heuristic has been developed. The results of this heuristic are close to the optimum. Straightforward application of node splitting may result in an average code size increase of 235%. CNS with the heuristic limits the increase to only 3%.

Keywords: control flow graphs, reducibility, irreducibility, node splitting, compilation, instruction level parallelism.

1 Introduction

In current computer architectures improvements can be obtained by the exploitation of instruction level parallelism (ILP). ILP is made possible due to higher transistor densities which allows the duplication of function units and data paths. Exploitation of ILP consists of mapping the ILP of the application onto the ILP of the target architecture as efficient as possible. This mapping is used for Very Long Instruction Word (VLIW) and superscalar architectures. The latter are used in most workstations. These architectures issue multiple instructions (or operations) simultaneously. It is the responsibility of the compiler to order these instructions as efficiently as possible. This process is called scheduling.

Problem Statement: In order to find sufficient ILP to justify the cost of multiple function units and data paths, a scheduler should have a larger scope than a single basic block at a time. A basic block is a sequence of consecutive statements in which the flow of control enters at the beginning and leaves always at the end. Several scheduling scopes can be found which go beyond the basic block level [1]. The most general scope currently used is called a *region* [2]. This is a set of basic blocks that corresponds to the body of a *natural* loop. Since loops can be nested, regions can also be nested in each other. Like natural loops, regions have a single entry point (the loop header) and may have multiple exits [2]. In [1] a speedup over 40% is reported using region scheduling instead of basic block scheduling. The problem of region scheduling is that it requires loops in the control flow graph with a single entry point. These flow graphs are called reducible flow graphs. Fortunately most control flow graphs are reducible, nevertheless the problem of irreducible flow graphs cannot be ignored. To exploit the benefits of region scheduling, irreducible control flow graphs should be converted to reducible control flow graphs.

Exploiting ILP also requires efficient memory disambiguation. To accomplish this the nesting of loops must be determined. Since in an irreducible flow graph the nesting of loops is not clear, memory disambiguation techniques cannot directly be applied to these loops. To exploit the benefits of memory disambiguation, irreducible control flow graphs should be converted to reducible control flow graphs as well. Another pleasant property of reducible control flow graphs is the fact that data flow analysis, that is an essential part of any compiler, can be done more efficiently [3].

Related Work: The problem of converting irreducible flow graphs to reducible flow graphs can be tackled at the front-end or at the back-end of the compiler. In [4] and [5] methods for normalizing the control flow graph of a program at the front-end are given. These methods rewrite an intermediate program in a normalized form. During normalization irreducible flow graphs are converted to reducible ones. To make a graph reducible, code has to be duplicated, which results in a larger code size. Since the front-end is unaware of the precise number of machine instructions needed to translate a piece of code, it is difficult to minimize the growth of the code size.

Another approach is to convert irreducible flow graphs at the back-end. The advantage is that when selecting what (machine)code to duplicate one can take the resulting code size into account. Solutions for solving the problem at the back-end are given in [6, 7, 8, 9]. The solution given by Cocke and Miller [6, 9] is very time complex and it does not try to minimize the resulting code size. The method described by Hecht *et al.* [7, 8] is even more inefficient in the sense of minimizing the code size, but it requires less analysis. In this paper a new method for converting irreducible flow graphs at the back-end is given which is very efficient in terms of the resulting code size.

Paper Overview: In Sect. 2 reducible and irreducible flow graphs are defined and a method for the detection of irreducible flow graphs is discussed. The principle of node splitting and the conversion method described by Hecht *et al.*, which is a straightforward application of node splitting, are given in Sect. 3. Our approach, Controlled Node Splitting (CNS), is described in Sect. 4. All known conversion methods convert irreducible flow graphs without minimizing the number of copies. With CNS it is possible to minimize the number of copies. Unfortunately this method requires much CPU time; therefore we developed a heuristic that reduces the CPU time but still performs close to the optimum.

The results of applying CNS to several benchmarks are given in Sect. 5. Finally the conclusions are given in Sect. 6.

2 Irreducible Flow Graphs

The control flow of a program can be described with a control flow graph. Its nodes represent sequences of operations or basic blocks, and its edges represent the flow of control.

Definition 1. The *control flow graph* of a program is a triple $G = (N, E, s)$ where (N, E) is a finite directed graph, with N the collection of nodes and E the collection of edges. From the initial node $s \in N$ there is a path to every node of the graph.

Figure 1 shows a control flow graph with nodes $N = \{s, a, b, c, d, e, f\}$, edges $E = \{(s, a), (a, b), (a, c), (b, c), (c, d), (d, e), (d, f), (c, a), (e, c)\}$ and initial node s.

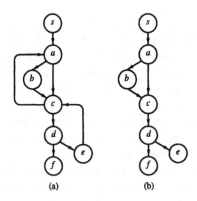

(a)   (b)

Fig. 1. a) A reducible control flow graph, b) the graph $G = (N, FE, s)$

As stated in the introduction finding sufficient ILP requires as input a reducible flow graph. Many definitions for reducible flow graphs are proposed. The one we adopt is given in [8] and is based on the partitioning of the edges of a control flow graph G into two disjoint sets:

1. The set of *back edges* BE consist of all edges whose heads dominate their tails.
2. The set of *forward edges* FE consists of all edges which are not back edges, thus $FE = E - BE$.

A node u of a flow graph dominates node v, if every path from the initial node s of the flow graph to v goes through u. Therefore $BE = \{(c, a), (e, c)\}$ and $FE = \{(s, a), (a, b), (a, c), (b, c), (c, d), (d, e), (d, f)\}$. The definition of a reducible flow graph is:

Definition 2. A flow graph G is *reducible* if and only if $G = (N, FE, s)$ is acyclic and every node $n \in N$ can be reached from the initial node s.

The control flow graph of Fig. 1 is reducible since $G = (N, FE, s)$ is acyclic. The control flow graph of Fig. 2 however is *irreducible*. The set of back edges is empty, because neither node a nor node b, dominates the other. FE is equal to $\{(s, a), (s, b), (a, b), (b, a)\}$, and $G = (N, FE, s)$ is not acyclic.

From Definition 2 we can derive that if a control flow graph G is irreducible then the graph $G = (N, FE, s)$ contains at least one loop. These loops are called irreducible loops. To remove irreducible loops, they must be detected first. There are several methods for doing this. One of them is to use interval analysis [10, 11]. The method used here is the Hecht-Ullman T1-T2 analysis [12, 3]. This method is based on two transformations T1 and T2. These transformations are illustrated in Fig. 3 and are defined as:

Definition 3. Let $G = (N, E, s)$ be a control flow graph and let $u \in N$. The *T1 transformation* removes the edge $(u, u) \in E$, which is a self-loop, if this edge exists. The derived graph becomes $G' = T1(G) = (N, E - \{(u, u)\}, s)$. In short $G \stackrel{T1(u)}{\Rightarrow} G'$.

Fig.2. The basic irreducible flow graph

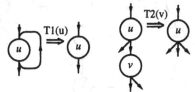

Fig.3. The T1 and T2 transformation

Definition 4. Let $G = (N, E, s)$ be a control flow graph and let node $v \neq s$ have a single predecessor u. The *T2 transformation* is the consumption of node v by node u. The successor edges of node v become successor edges of node u. The original successor edges of node u are preserved except for the edge to node v. If I is the set of successor nodes of v then the derived graph becomes $G' = T2(G) = (N - \{v\}, (E - \{(v, n) \mid n \in I\} - \{(u, v)\}) \cup \{(u, n) \mid n \in I\}, s)$. In short $G \stackrel{T2(v)}{\Rightarrow} G'$.

Definition 5. The graph that results when applying the T1 and T2 transformations in any possible order to a flow graph, until a flow graph results for which no application of T1 or T2 is possible is called the *limit flow graph*.

In [7] it is proven that the limit flow graph is unique and independent of the order in which the transformations are applied.

Theorem 6. *A flow graph is reducible if and only if after repeatedly applying T1 and T2 transformations in any particular order the flow graph can be reduced into a single node.*

The proof of this theorem can be found in [12]. An example of the application of the T1 and T2 transformations is given in Fig. 4. The flow graph from Fig. 1 is reduced to a single node, so we can conclude that this flow graph is reducible.

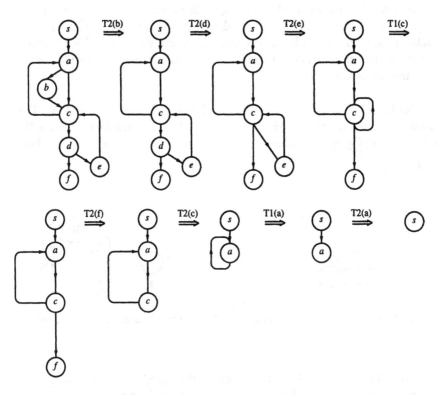

Fig. 4. An example of application of the T1 and T2 transformations

If after applying T1 and T2 transformations the resulting flow graph consists of multiple nodes, the graph is irreducible. The transformations T1 and T2 not only detect irreducibility but they also detect the nodes that causes the irreducibility. Examples of irreducible graphs are given in Fig. 5. From Theorem 6 it follows that we can alternatively define irreducibility by:

Corollary 7. *A flow graph is irreducible if and only if the limit flow graph is not a single node[1].*

---

[1] Another definition, which is more intuitive, is that a flow graph is irreducible if it has at least one loop with multiple loop entries [12].

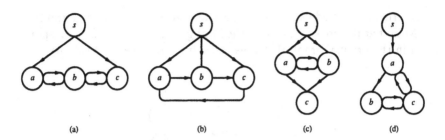

Fig. 5. Examples of extensions of the basic irreducible control flow graph of Fig. 2

3 Flow Graph Transformation

If a control flow graph occurs to be irreducible, a graph transformation technique can be used to obtain a reducible control flow graph. In the past some methods are given to solve this problem [6, 7, 8]. Most methods for converting an irreducible control flow graph are based on a technique called node splitting. In Sect. 3.1 explains the node splitting technique. Section 3.2 shows how node splitting can be applied straightforwardly to reduce an irreducible graph.

3.1 Node Splitting

Node Splitting is a technique that converts a graph G_1 to an equivalent graph G_2. We assign a label to each node of a graph; the label of node x_i is denoted $label(x_i)$. Duplication of a node creates a new node with the same label. An equivalence relation between two flow graphs is derived from Hecht [7] and given below.

Definition 8. If $P = (x_1, \dots, x_k)$ is a path in a flow graph, then define $Labels(P)$ to be a sequence of labels corresponding to this path; that is, $Labels(P) = (label(x_1), \dots, label(x_k))$. Two flow graphs G_1 and G_2 are *equivalent* if and only if, for each path P in G_1, there is a path Q in G_2 such that $Labels(P) = Labels(Q)$, and conversely.

According to this definition the two flow graphs of Fig. 6 are equivalent. Node splitting is defined as:

Definition 9. *Node splitting* is a transformation of a graph $G_1 = (N, E, s)$ into a graph $G_2 = (N', E', s)$ such that a node $n \in N$, having multiple predecessors p_i is split; for any incoming edge (p_i, n) a duplicate n_i of n is made, having one incoming edge (p_i, n_i) and the same outgoing edges as n. If node n has $K \geq 2$ predecessors and $L \geq 0$ successors then N' is defined as $N' = N \cup \{n_i \mid 2 \leq i \leq K\} - \{n\}$ and $E' = E - \{(p_i, n), (n, r_j) \mid 2 \leq i \leq K \wedge 0 \leq j \leq L\} \cup \{(p_i, n_i)(n_i, r_j) \mid 2 \leq i \leq K \wedge 0 \leq j \leq L\}$, where r_j is a successor node of n. This transformation is denoted as $G_1 \overset{S(n)}{\Rightarrow} G_2$, where $S(n)$ is the splitting of node $n \in N$.

The principle of node splitting is illustrated in Fig. 6; node a of graph G_1 is split. Note that if a node n is split in the limit graph, then it is the corresponding node n in the original graph that must be split to remove irreducibility.

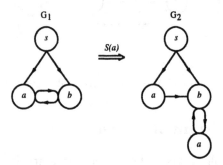

Fig. 6. A simple example of applying node splitting to node a

The name node splitting is deceptive because it suggests that the node is split in different parts but in fact the node is duplicated.

3.2 Uncontrolled Node Splitting

The transformation technique node splitting can be used to convert an irreducible control flow graph into a reducible control flow graph. From Hecht [7] we adopt Theorem 10.

Theorem 10. *Let S denote the splitting of a node, and let T denote some graph reduction transformation (e.g. $T = (T1^* \, T2^*)^*$). Then any control flow graph can be transformed into a single node by the transformation represented by the regular expression $T \, (ST)^*$.*

The proof of the theorem is given in [7].

Hecht *et al.* describe a straightforward application of node splitting to reduce irreducible control flow graphs. This method selects a node for splitting from the limit graph if the node has multiple predecessors. The selected node is split into several identical copies, one for each entering edge. This approach has the advantage that it is rather simple, but it has the disadvantage that it can select nodes that did not have to be split to make a graph reducible. In Fig. 7a we see that the nodes a, b, c and d are candidate nodes for splitting. In Fig. 7b node d is split, the number of nodes reduces after the application of two T2 transformations, but the graph is still irreducible. Splitting of node a neither makes the graph reducible, see Fig. 7c. Only splitting of node b or c converts the graph into a reducible control flow graph, see Fig. 7d.

Although this method does inefficient node splitting, it does transform an irreducible control flow graph eventually in a reducible one. The consequence of this uncontrolled node splitting is that the number of duplications becomes unnecessarily large.

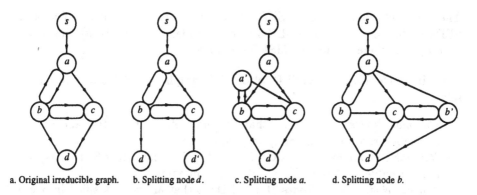

a. Original irreducible graph.　　b. Splitting node d.　　c. Splitting node a.　　d. Splitting node b.

Fig. 7. Examples of node splitting

4　Presentation of Controlled Node Splitting

The problem of existing methods is that the resulting code size after converting an irreducible graph can grow uncontrolled. Controlled Node Splitting (CNS) controls the amount of copies which results in a smaller growth of the code size. CNS restricts the set of candidate nodes for splitting. First we introduce the necessary terminology:

Definition 11. A *loop* in a flow graph is a path $(n_1, ..., n_k)$ where n_1 is an immediate successor of n_k. The set of nodes contained in the loop is called a *loop-set*.

In Fig. 7a $\{a, b\}$, $\{b, c\}$ and $\{a, b, c\}$ are loop-sets.

Definition 12. An *immediate dominator* of a node u, $\mathrm{ID}(u)$, is the last node on any path from the initial node s of a graph to u, excluding node u itself, which dominates u.

In Fig. 7a node s dominates the nodes s, a, b, c, and d, but it immediate dominates only node a.

Definition 13. A *Shared External Dominator set* (SED-set) is a subset of a loop-set L with the properties that it contains only elements that share the same immediate dominator and the immediate dominator is not part of the loop-set L. The SED-set of a loop-set L is defined as:

$$\text{SED-set}(L) = \{n_i \in L | ID(n_i) = d, d \notin L\} \qquad (1)$$

Definition 14. A *Maximal Shared External Dominator set* (MSED-set) K is defined as:

$$\text{SED-set K is maximal} \Leftrightarrow \nexists \text{ SED-set M}, K \subset M$$

The definition says that an MSED-set cannot be a proper subset of another SED-set. In Fig. 5a multiple SED-sets can be identified like $\{a, b\}$, $\{b, c\}$ and $\{a, b, c\}$. But there is only one MSED-set: $\{a, b, c\}$.

Definition 15. Nodes in an SED-set of a flow graph can be classified into three sets:

- *Common Nodes* (CN): Nodes that dominate other SED-set(s) and are not reachable from the SED-set(s) they dominate.
- *Reachable Common nodes* (RC): Nodes that dominate other SED-set(s) and are reachable from the SED-set(s) they dominate.
- *Normal Nodes* (NN): Nodes of an SED-set that are not classified in one of the above classes. These nodes dominate no other SED-sets.

In the initial graph of Fig. 8a we can identify the MSED-sets $\{a, b\}$ and $\{c, d\}$. The nodes a, c and d are elements of the set NN and node b is an element of the set RC. If the edge (c, b) was not present then node b would be an element of the set CN. Note that the nodes of loop (b, c) do not form a SED-set.

In Sect. 4.1 a description of CNS is given. It treats a method for minimizing the number of nodes to split. Section 4.2 gives a method for minimizing the amount of copies. The number of copies is not equal to the number of splits because a split creates for every entering edge a copy. If a node has n entering edges then one split creates $n - 1$ copies. To speed up the process for minimizing the amount of copies a heuristic is given.

4.1 Controlled Node Splitting

All nodes of an irreducible limit graph, except the initial node s of the graph, are possible candidates for node splitting since they have at least two predecessors. However splitting of some nodes is not efficient; see Sect. 3.2. CNS minimizes the number of splits. To accomplish this, two restrictions are made to the set of candidate nodes. These restrictions are:

1. Only nodes that are elements of an SED-set are candidates for splitting.
2. Nodes that are elements of RC are not candidates for splitting.

The first restriction prevents the splitting of nodes that are not in an SED-set. Splitting such a node is inefficient and unnecessary, as was demonstrated by Fig. 7b. These nodes are automatically reduced when all SED-sets are reduced to single nodes.

The second restriction is more complicated. The impact of this restriction is illustrated in Fig. 8. This figure shows two different sequences of node splitting. The initial graph of the figure is a graph on which T has been applied. In Fig. 8a three splits are needed and in Fig. 8b only two. In Fig. 8a node b is split; this node however is an element of the set RC. The second restriction prevents a splitting sequence as the one in Fig. 8a. Splitting an RC node merges the nodes of the MSED-set to which node RC belongs and the nodes of the MSED-set that is dominated by the RC node into a single MSED-set. In [13] it is proven that splitting an RC node, and thus merging of MSED-sets, always leads to more splits.

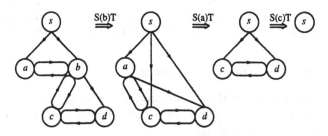

a. Node splitting sequence of three nodes.

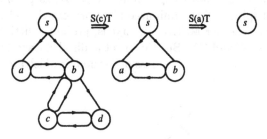

b. Node splitting sequence of two nodes.

Fig. 8. Graph with two different split graphs

Node splitting with above restrictions, alternated with T1 and T2 transformations, will eventually result in a single node. This can be seen easily. Every time a node that is an element of an SED-set is split, it is reduced by the T2 transformation and the number of nodes involved in SED-sets decreases with one. Since we are considering flow graphs with a finite number of nodes, a single node eventually remains.

Theorem 16. *A MSED-set(L) has one node ⇔ The corresponding loop L has a single header and is reducible.*

The proof of this theorem can be derived from [7].

Theorem 17. *The minimum number of splits needed to reduce an MSED-set with k nodes is given by:*

$$T_{splits} = k - 1. \tag{2}$$

Theorem 18. *The minimum number of splits needed to convert an irreducible graph, with n MSED-sets, into a reducible graph is given by:*

$$T_{splits} = \sum_{i=1}^{n}(k_i - 1) \tag{3}$$

where T_{splits} is the total number of splits, and k_i is the number of nodes of MSED-set i.

The proofs of both theorems are given in [13]; it is also shown that this minimum can be reached by obeying above restrictions. In Fig. 8 the MSED-sets $\{a, b\}$ and $\{c, d\}$ can be identified. They have both two nodes. This results in a minimal number of $(2 - 1) + (2 - 1) = 2$ splits to reduce the graph.

4.2 Minimizing the Amount of Copies

In the previous section we saw that the algorithm minimizes the number of splits, but this does not result in a minimum number of copies. Two conditions must be satisfied to achieve this minimum:

1. The freedom of selecting nodes to split must be as big as possible. Notice that the number of splits is also minimized if we prevent the splitting of all nodes that dominate another MSED-set, that is, prevent splitting of nodes that are elements of RC and CN. But this has the disadvantage that we lose some freedom in selecting nodes. This loss of freedom is illustrated in Fig. 9.

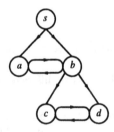

Fig. 9. A graph that has a common node that is not in the set RC

Suppose that the nodes contain a number of instructions and that we want to minimize the total resulting code size, which means that we would like to copy as few instructions as possible. The number of copied instructions if we prevent splitting nodes that are elements of RC and CN is: $a + \min(c, d)$. If we only prevent the splitting of nodes that are element of RC the number of copied instructions is: $\min(a, b) + \min(c, d)$. If the number of instructions in node b is less than in node a then the number of copied instructions is less in the latter case. Thus keeping the set of candidate nodes as big as possible pays off if one would like to minimize the amount of copies.

2. The sequence of splitting nodes must be chosen optimal. There exists multiple split sequences to solve an irreducible graph. A tree can be build to discover them all. A flow graph and its tree with all possible split sequences is drawn in Fig. 10. The nodes of the tree indicate how many copies are introduced by the split. The edges give the split sequence. The number of copies

can be found by following a path from the root to a leaf and adding the quantities of the nodes. Suppose that each node contains a number of instructions and that we want to minimize the total resulting code size, which means that we would like to copy as few instructions as possible, then we can choose from 6 different split sequences with 5 different numbers of copies. The minimum number of copied instructions is: $\min(a+c, 2a+b, a+3b, 3b+c, b+2c)$. The problem is to pick a split sequence that minimizes the number of copied instructions.

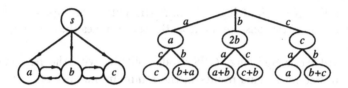

Fig. 10. An irreducible graph with its copy tree

The quantity chosen to minimize in the above is the number of instructions, but it can also be interesting to minimize another quantity, for example the number of basic blocks. In the following the quantity to minimize is denoted with Q, $Q(n)$ means the quantity of node n, $Q(G)$ is the quantity of a graph G and is defined as:

$$Q(G) = \sum_{n \in N} Q(n)$$

The purpose of CNS is to minimize $Q(G^*)$, where G^* is the transformation of G into a single node using some sequence of transformations and splits, more formally $G^* = T(G)(S(G)T(G))^*$.

Theorem 19. *Minimizing the resulting $Q(G^*)$ of an irreducible graph that is converted to a reducible graph requires a minimum number of splits, where G^* is a single node; that is the totally reduced graph. In short:*

$$Q(G^*) \text{ is minimal} \Rightarrow \# \text{ splits to produce } G^* \text{ is minimal.}$$

The proof of this theorem is given in [13].

As one can easily see, the more nodes in MSED-sets the larger the tree and the number of possible split sequences increases. It takes much computation time to compute all possibilities, therefore a heuristic is constructed which picks a node n_i to split with the smallest $H(n_i)$ as defined by:

$$H(n_i) = Q(n_i) * (\# \text{ predecessor nodes} - 1) \tag{4}$$

for every candidate node. This heuristic picks the node which results in the fewest copies. One can easily see that fewer predecessors nodes lead to fewer instructions to copy. The results of this heuristic, compared to the best possible split sequence, are given in Sect. 5.

5 Results

The goal of our experiments is to measure the quality of controlled node splitting in the sense of minimizing the amount of copies. In the experiments four methods for node splitting are used:

- Optimal Node Splitting, *ONS*. This method computes the best possible node split sequence with respect to the quantity to minimize. This algorithm however requires a lot of computation time (up to several days on a HP735 workstation).
- Uncontrolled Node Splitting, *UCNS*. A straightforward application of node splitting, no restrictions are made to the set of nodes that are candidate for splitting.
- Controlled Node Splitting, *CNS*. Node splitting with the restrictions discussed in Sect. 4.1. This results in the minimum number of splits, but not in the minimum number of copied instructions.
- Controlled Node Splitting with Heuristic, *CNSH*. The same method as CNS but now a heuristic is used to select a node from the set of candidate nodes.

The algorithms are applied to a selective group of benchmarks. These benchmarks are procedures with an irreducible control flow graph and are obtained from the real world programs: a68, bison, expand, gawk, gs, gzip, sed, tr. The programs are compiled with the GCC compiler which is ported to a RISC architecture[2]. The number of copied instructions are listed in Table 1. The reported results of the methods UCNS, CNS and CNSH are the averages of all possible split sequences.

The first column in the Table 1 lists the procedure name, with the program name in parentheses. The second column gives the number of instructions of the procedure before an algorithm is applied. The other columns give the number of copied instructions that result from the algorithms. The absolute number of copies is given and a percentage that indicates the growth in code size with respect to the original number of instructions.

From the results of the ONS method we can conclude that node splitting does not have to lead to an excessive number of copies. Furthermore we can conclude that CNS outperforms UCNS. UCNS can lead to an enormous amount of copies, the average percentage of growth in code size is 235.5%. CNS performs better, a growth of 30.1% for the number of instruction, but there is still a big gap with the optimal case. When using the heuristic, controlled node splitting performs very close to the optimum. The average growth in code size for both methods CNSH and ONS is 2.9%. Comparing the results of ONS and CNSH lead to the conclusion that CNSH performs very close to the optimum. In our experiments there was only one procedure (re_search_2) with a very small difference. The execution time of CNSH is only slightly longer than for UCNS.

---

[2] We used a RISC like MOVE architecture. The MOVE project [14, 1] researches the generation of application specific processors (ASPs) by means of Transport Triggered Architectures (TTA).

Table 1. The number of copied instructions

Procedure(Progr.)	#insn	ONS		UCNS		CNS		CNSH	
atof_generic(a68)	550	2	(0%)	186.2	(34%)	10.5	(2%)	2.0	(0%)
equals(a68)	84	1	(1%)	37.5	(45%)	37.5	(45%)	1.0	(1%)
lex(bison)	529	18	(3%)	577.3	(109%)	94.0	(18%)	18.0	(3%)
output_program(bison)	59	9	(15%)	41.5	(70%)	41.5	(70%)	9.0	(15%)
copy_definition(bison)	539	9	(2%)	1870.0	(347%)	122.5	(23%)	9.0	(2%)
copy_guard(bison)	880	18	(2%)	10408.2	(1183%)	603.3	(69%)	18.0	(2%)
copy_action(bison)	858	9	(1%)	2961.4	(345%)	122.5	(14%)	9.0	(1%)
next_file(expand)	64	1	(2%)	16.5	(26%)	16.5	(26%)	1.0	(2%)
re_compile_pattern(gawk)	2746	1	(0%)	4106.9	(150%)	218.5	(8%)	1.0	(0%)
interp(gs)	969	20	(2%)	588.1	(61%)	442.5	(46%)	20.0	(2%)
sreadhex(gs)	150	47	(31%)	79.7	(53%)	58.0	(39%)	47.0	(31%)
gs_type1_interpret(gs)	1175	19	(2%)	1063.8	(90%)	1063.8	(90%)	19.0	(2%)
s_LZWD_read_buf(gs)	228	62	(27%)	95.0	(42%)	95.0	(42%)	62.0	(27%)
copy_block(gzip)	88	4	(5%)	7.5	(9%)	7.5	(9%)	4.0	(5%)
compile_program(sed)	693	2	(0%)	391.4	(56%)	267.5	(39%)	2.0	(0%)
re_search_2(sed)	1857	91	(5%)	4803.7	(259%)	227.5	(12%)	93.0	(5%)
squeeze_filter(tr)	119	22	(18%)	57.0	(48%)	55.5	(47%)	22.0	(18%)
total	11588	335(2.9%)		27291.7(235.5%)		3484.1(30.1%)		337(2.9%)	

6 Conclusions

A method has been given which transforms an irreducible control flow graph to a reducible control flow graph. This gives us the opportunity to exploit ILP over a larger scope than a single basic block for any program. The method is based on node splitting. To achieve the minimum number of splits the set of possible candidate nodes is limited to nodes with specific properties. Since splitting of these nodes can result in a minimum resulting code size the algorithm can be used to prevent uncontrolled growth of the code size. Because the computation time to determine the optimum split sequence is (very) large, a heuristic has been developed.

The method with the heuristic is called *controlled node splitting with heuristic*. This method is compared with other methods, these methods are uncontrolled node splitting and controlled node splitting. From our experiments it follows that uncontrolled node splitting can lead to an enormous number of copies; the average growth in code size is 235.5%. Controlled node splitting performs better (32.2%) but there is still a big gap with the optimal case. We observed that the average number of copies when using controlled node splitting with heuristic is very close to that of the optimum; the average growth in code size for both methods is 2.9%.

References

1. Jan Hoogerbrugge and Henk Corporaal. Transport-triggering vs. operation-triggering. In *Lecture Notes in Computer Science 786, Compiler Construction*, pages 435–449. Springer-Verlag, 1994.
2. D. Bernstein and M. Rodeh. Global instruction scheduling for superscalar machines. In *Proc. of the ACM SIGPLAN 1991 conference on Programming Language Design and Implementation*, pages 241–255, June 1991.
3. Barbara G. Ryder and Marvin C. Paull. Elimination algorithms for data flow analysis. *ACM Computing Surveys*, 18(3):277–316, September 1986.
4. Ana M. Erosa and Laurie J. Hendren. Taming control flow: A structured approach to eliminating goto statements. In *Proceedings of the 1994 International Conference on Computer Languages*, pages 229–240, Toulouse, France, May 1994.
5. Zahira Ammarguellat. A control-flow normalization algorithm and its complexity. *IEEE Transaction on software engineering*, 18(3):237–251, March 1992.
6. John Cocke and Raymond E. Miller. Some analysis techniques for optimizing computer programs. In *Proceedings of 2nd Hawaii Conference on System Sciences*, pages 143–146, 1969.
7. Matthew S. Hecht. *Flow Analysis of Computer Programs*. Programming Languages Series. Elsevier North-Holland, 1977.
8. Alfred V. Aho, Ravi Sethi, and Jeffrey D. Ullman. *Compilers: Principles, Techniques and Tools*. Addison-Wesley Series in Computer Science. Addison-Wesley Publishing Company, 1988.
9. J. Cocke. On certain graph-theoretic properties of programs. Technical Report Research Report RC-3391, T.J. Watson Research Center, 1971.
10. F.E. Allen. A basis for program optimization. In *Proceedings of 1971 IFIP Congress*, pages 385–390, Amsterdam, 1971. IEEE, North Holland Publ.
11. F.E. Allen and J. Cocke. A program data flow analysis procedure. *Commun. ACM*, 19(3):137–147, March 1976.
12. M.S. Hecht and J.D. Ullman. Flow graph reducibility. *SIAM J. Computing*, 1(2):188–202, 1972.
13. Johan Janssen and Henk Corporaal. Making graphs reducible with controlled node splitting. Technical Report JJ-9501, Delft University of Technology, Department of Electrical Engineering, 1995.
14. Henk Corporaal and Hans (J.M.) Mulder. MOVE: A framework for high-performance processor design. In *Supercomputing-91*, pages 692–701, Albuquerque, November 1991.

Aggressive Loop Unrolling in a Retargetable, Optimizing Compiler

JACK W. DAVIDSON and SANJAY JINTURKAR

{jwd,sj3e}@virginia.edu

Department of Computer Science, Thornton Hall

University of Virginia,

Charlottesville, VA 22903 U. S. A.

Abstract

A well-known code transformation for improving the run-time performance of a program is loop unrolling. The most obvious benefit of unrolling a loop is that the transformed loop usually requires fewer instruction executions than the original loop. The reduction in instruction executions comes from two sources: the number of branch instructions executed is reduced, and the control variable is modified fewer times. In addition, for architectures with features designed to exploit instruction-level parallelism, loop unrolling can expose greater levels of instruction-level parallelism. Loop unrolling is an effective code transformation often improving the execution performance of programs that spend much of their execution time in loops by 10 to 30 percent. Possibly because of the effectiveness of a simple application of loop unrolling, it has not been studied as extensively as other code improvements such as register allocation or common subexpression elimination. The result is that many compilers employ simplistic loop unrolling algorithms that miss many opportunities for improving run-time performance. This paper describes how aggressive loop unrolling is done in a retargetable optimizing compiler. Using a set of 32 benchmark programs, the effectiveness of this more aggressive approach to loop unrolling is evaluated. The results show that aggressive loop unrolling can yield additional performance increase of 10 to 20 percent over the simple, naive approaches employed by many production compilers.

Keywords: Loop unrolling, Compiler optimizations, Code improving transformations, Loop transformations.

1 Introduction

A well known programming rule of thumb is that programs spend roughly 90% of their time executing in 10% of the code [Henn90]. Any code transformation which can reduce the time spent in these small, critical portions is likely to have a measurable, observable impact on the overall execution time of the program. This critical 10% of the code frequently consists of loops. Therefore, code improvement techniques that speed up the execution of loops are important. One such technique is *loop unrolling*. Loop unrolling replicates the original loop body multiple times and adjusts the loop termination code. The primary effect is a reduction in the total number of instructions executed by the CPU when the loop is executed. The reduction in instructions executed comes from two sources: the number of branch instructions executed is reduced, and the number of increments of the control variable is reduced. In addition, loop unrolling, in conjunction with other code optimizations, can increase instruction-level parallelism and improve memory hierarchy locality [Alex93, Baco94, Davi94, Davi95a, Mahl92].

When implementing this transformation in a production compiler, three questions regarding the way to do loop unrolling most effectively arise: when should it be done, how should it be done, and what kinds of code bodies should it be applied to? Although loop unrolling is a well-known code improvement technique [Dong79, Weiss87], there has not been a thorough study that provides definitive answers to these questions.

Possibly because of the lack of definitive answers, many production compilers use simplistic approaches when applying loop unrolling. We examined how loop unrolling was performed by various compilers on seven current architectures. The architectures were the DECstation 5000/125 (MIPS R3000 chipset), SGI RealityEngine (MIPS R4000 chipset) [Kane89], the DEC 3000 (Alpha 21064 chipset) [Digi92], the IBM model 540 (IBM RS6000 chipset) [IBM90], the SUN SPARCStation IPC (LSISIc0010 chip) [Sun87] and the SUN SPARCServer (Sun SuperSparc chipset). For each platform, we examined how the native C compiler and the GNU C compiler performed loop unrolling.

The native compilers on the R4000 (ELF 32-bit executable version 1), R2000 (version 2.1), SuperSparc (ELF 32-bit executable version 1) and the Alpha (3.11-6) unroll for loops which have a single basic block and do not have any function calls. These compilers do not unroll loops with complex control flow. They do not unroll loops formed using while and goto statements also. Unfortunately, as this study shows, loops with complex control flow form a sizable percentage of the loops. Consequently these compilers forgo many opportunities for producing better code. The native compiler on the RS6000 (version 3.1) does unroll loops with complex control flow. However, after unrolling it fails to eliminate redundant loop branch instructions from an unrolled while loop. Furthermore, the compiler does not unroll loops formed using goto statements. The native compiler on the SUN IPC (Version 1.143) does not unroll loops. The GNU C compiler (versions 2.2.2, 2.4.5, 2.6.3) has the same limitations as the native compiler on the RS6000. Furthermore, it does not eliminate redundant loop branch instructions from an unrolled counting for loop with a negative stride. The above survey of current technology indicates that the approach of existing optimizing compilers to loop unrolling is not uniform.

The lack of a thorough study of unrolling and the uneven application of unrolling in production compilers motivated us to thoroughly analyze loop unrolling and examine the issues involved. This paper presents the results of a thorough compile- and run-time analysis of loop unrolling on a set of 32 benchmarks programs. The results of the analysis show that loop unrolling algorithms that only handle loops which consist of a single basic block and whose iteration count can be determined only at compile time miss many opportunities for creating more efficient loops. Using the benchmark programs, we analyzed the effectiveness of aggressive loop unrolling on run-time performance. Our measurements show that aggressive loop unrolling can yield performance increases of 10 to 20 percent for some sets of benchmarks over the simple, naive approaches employed by many production compilers, and that for some programs increases in performance by as much as 40 to 50 percent are achieved.

2 Terminology

This section defines the frequently used terms in this paper.

Loop branch: The loop code instruction(s) that check the loop control variable and decide if control should exit the loop. The number of instructions comprising the loop branch can vary. The basic block containing these instructions is called the *loop branch block*.

Loop body: The loop code minus the loop branch instruction(s). A loop body may contain several basic blocks.

Counting loop: A loop whose iteration count can be determined either at compile time or at execution time prior to the entry into the loop code.

Compile-time counting loop: A counting loop whose iteration count is trivially known at compile time.

Execution-time counting loop: A counting loop whose iteration count is not trivially known at compile time.

Unrolled loop: A loop whose loop body consists of multiple copies of the loop body of a rolled loop. A loop unrolled n times consists of $(n + 1)$ copies of the loop body of a rolled loop. The unroll factor is n.

Prologue(Epilogue) code: If the iteration count of a rolled loop is not an integral multiple of the *unroll factor + 1*, then as many as *unroll factor* iterations are executed separately. These iterations are called leftover iterations. The code which executes these iterations is called the *Prologue (Epilogue) code*.

Candidates for unrolling: All innermost counting loops are candidates for unrolling.

3 How and When to Unroll

An optimizing compiler is likely to apply loop unrolling in conjunction with other code optimizations. The question is *how* and *when* should loop unrolling be applied?

Automatic unrolling can be done on source code, early on the unoptimized intermediate representation, or very late on an optimized, low-level representation of the program. If it is done at the source-code level, then typically only counting loops formed using for statements are unrolled. Unrolling loops formed using other control constructs is difficult since the loop count is not obvious. If automatic unrolling is applied at the intermediate-code level, then a sophisticated system to perform loop analysis is required to identify anything beyond counting loops containing more than one basic block. Introducing such a system at this level is a wasteful duplication of effort, because recent research has shown that loop optimizations are more beneficial if they are done in the compiler back end [Beni94]. Additionally, performing unrolling early has a greater impact on compilation time because more code must be processed by subsequent phases of the compiler.

Another important question concerning the implementation of loop unrolling is how many times a loop should be unrolled. Most of the benefits from unrolling are due to the elimination of branches. If loops are unrolled 15 times, then 93.75% of the branches are eliminated. Therefore, an unroll factor of 15 is sufficient to extract most of the benefits. Increasing the unroll factor further yields marginal improvement in performance. However, unconstrained unrolling can have an adverse impact on the performance if the transformed loop overflows the instruction cache [Dong79, Weis87]. The performance degradation depends on the size, organization, and replacement policy of the cache. To make sure that the unrolled loop does not overflow the instruction cache, it is necessary for the compiler to determine the size of the unrolled loop code in terms of machine-language instructions.

Another important issue concerns register allocation and assignment. If loop unrolling is done prior to register allocation and assignment, the register allocator may overcommit the registers to the unrolled code. Consequently, there may not be enough registers available to apply other useful optimizations such as strength reduction and induction variable elimination to the code. This may lead to degradation in performance, instead of improvement.

The above issues are addressed if unrolling is applied to a low-level representation of the program late in the optimization process after other traditional code optimizations have been done. With this approach, not all phases of the optimizer need to be reapplied to the larger unrolled loop bodies which reduces the increase in compilation time. Furthermore, back ends of optimizing compilers contain sophisticated loop detection mechanisms. These mechanisms can easily detect both structured and unstructured loops. Also, at this stage the size of the loop code is closer to its final size. This along with the use of a low-level representation (i.e., machine code) allows the most appropriate unroll factor to be determined. Also, since unrolling is applied after register allocation has been done, the register pressure will not increase. Any artificial dependencies introduced by this approach can be eliminated by applying register renaming [Davi95b].

4   What to Unroll

An analysis of loops in 32 benchmarks was performed at compile time to determine the complexity and size of loop bodies and the nature of their loop bounds. These benchmarks are a mix of Unix utilities, user codes, synthetic benchmarks, numerical benchmarks and the C portion of the SPEC benchmark [SPEC89] suite. The benchmarks are listed in Table 1.

The compile-time study consists of two parts. The first part classifies loops on the basis of whether they are compile-time counting loops or execution-time counting loops. The second part of the study classifies loops on the basis of the complexity of the loop body. These parts of the study give an indication of the sophistication required of the unrolling mechanism in the compiler. For each study, the percentages given are a percentage of the loops in that benchmark that are candidates for unrolling.

4.1   Loop bounds analysis

Our experience is that the iteration count of the majority of loops is difficult, and sometimes impossible to determine at compile time. An iteration count often cannot be determined at compile time because the loop bounds are passed as arguments to the function containing the loop. While interprocedural analysis provides some help, loop bounds are often based on problem size which are supplied as external inputs to the program. In these cases, the iteration count cannot be determined at compile time.

Type	Program	Description	Type	Program	Description
SYNTHETIC	arraymerge	Merges two sorted arrays	UNIX UTILITIES	banner	Draws a banner
	bubblesort	Sorting algorithm		cal	Prints out a calender
	puzzle	Test recursion		cb	C beautifier
	queens	Eight queens problem		compact	Compresses text files
	quicksort	Sorting algorithm		diff	Prints differences
	shellsort	Sorting algorithm		grep	Searches for a string
	sieve	Sieve of eratosthenes		nroff	Document formatter
USER	cache	Cache simulation		od	Prints octal dump
	encode	Encodes vpo's files		sort	Sorting utility
	sa-tsp	Trav. salesman problem		wc	Word count
NUMERICAL	ll3	Livermore kernel 3	SPEC	eqntott	PLA optimizer
	ll4	Livermore kernel 4		xlisp	LISP interpreter
	ll5	Livermore kernel 5		espresso	Boolean expr. translation
	ll6	Livermore kernel 16		gcc	Optimizing compiler
	linpack	Floating-point benchmark			
	s006	Kernel by Kuck and assoc.			
	s008	Kernel by Kuck and assoc.			
	s011	Kernel by Kuck and assoc.			

Table 1: Description of benchmarks

Type	Candidates for unrolling (percentage)	Execution-time counting loops (percentage)
User	46	89
Unix	9	35
Synthetic	54	69
Numerical	79	73
SPEC	15	84

Table 2: Distribution of loops based on loop bounds

To determine how important it is for a loop unrolling algorithm to handle execution-time counting loops, we measured the percentage of loops that are execution-time counting loops. Table 2 contains the results. Column 2 is the average percentage of loops which are candidates for unrolling in each benchmark in the five categories. As expected, numerical benchmarks have a high percentage of loops which can be unrolled. On the other hand, Unix utilities have a low percentage of loops which can be unrolled. On the other hand, Unix utilities have a low percentage of loops which can be unrolled. Column 3 contains the percentage of candidate loops which are execution-time counting loops. Thus, in user codes, on an average 46 percent of loops in each benchmark are candidates for unrolling and 89 percent of these candidates are execution-time counting loops. These statistics clearly indicate that algorithms that only handle compile-time counting loops miss many opportunities for producing more efficient code.

4.2 Control-flow complexity analysis

For the analysis of the control-flow complexity of loops, we developed a scheme for classifying the innermost counting loops based on the complexity of their loop bodies. The classification scheme has six categories and is cumulative in nature[†]. Figure 1 shows this classification. The first category contains loops which have a single basic

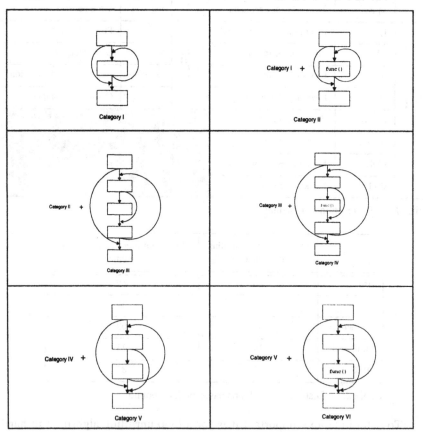

Fig: 1.   Categories of loops.

block and no function calls. The second category contains loops which have a single

---

[†]That is, category n contains all the loops in category $n - 1$.

basic block and function calls. The third category includes loops which have internal branches[†] but no function calls. The fourth category permits function calls also. The fifth category permits loops which have multiple exits, but have no function calls. The sixth category allows function calls also.

Table 3 shows the statistics related to this classification. Column 1 contains the type of benchmark. Columns 2 indicates the average percentage of loops in each benchmark in a benchmark category which are candidates for unrolling. Columns 3 through 8 show the average distribution of loops which can be unrolled in the various categories. All measurements are percentages.

From this table, it is apparent that benchmarks in all the categories have a sizable percentage of loops which have more than one basic block. This indicates that if loops with only a single basic block are unrolled, a high percentage of loops will not be considered. Consequently, unrolling loops consisting of a single basic block only limits the effectiveness of loop unrolling.

Type	Candidates for unrolling (Percentage)	Category (Percentages)					
		I	II	III	IV	V	VI
User	46	39	67	78	78	100	100
Unix	9	38	52	53	72	98	100
Synthetic	54	42	74	83	98	100	100
Numerical	79	75	76	94	100	100	100
SPEC	15	29	37	52	66	89	100

Table 3: Distribution of loops based on control-flow complexity.

5 Results

To measure the impact of aggressive unrolling, we implemented an aggressive loop unroller in *vpo*, a highly optimizing back end that has been used to implement a variety of imperative languages such as Ada, C, PL/I, and Pascal. *vpo* has two characteristics that make it an ideal framework for implementing and evaluating aggressive loop unrolling algorithms. First, *vpo* performs all code improvements on a single, low-level representation called RTLs (register transfer lists) [Beni94, Davi81]. Within *vpo*'s framework, loop unrolling can be applied late in the compilation process after many other code improving transformations have been applied and detailed information about loops has been gathered by *vpo*'s analysis phase. In addition, the late application of loop unrolling and the low-level representation allows *vpo* to accurately estimate the size of loops and choose the largest unroll factor that will not cause the loop to exceed the size of the machine's instruction cache. It also means that not all phases of *vpo* need to process the larger loop bodies which minimizes the increase in compilation time. Second, *vpo*'s internal program representation and organization permits optimizations

---

†The targets of all conditional and unconditional branches lie inside the loop.

to be reapplied as needed. Because of this, the implementation of loop unrolling is simplified as we can rely on these phases to remove any inefficiencies introduced by unrolling.

Figure 2 contains a diagram of the organization of *vpo*. Vertical columns

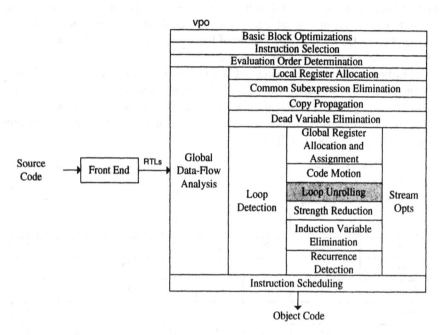

Fig: 2.   Schematic of *vpo*-based C compiler.

represent logical phases which operate serially. Columns that are divided horizontally into rows indicate that the sub-phases of the column may be executed in an arbitrary order. For example, instruction selection may be performed at any time during the optimization process. Global data-flow analysis, on the other hand, is done after the basic block optimizations, instruction selection, and evaluation order determination, but before local register assignment, common subexpression elimination, etc.

To determine the impact of aggressive loop unrolling, we measured the increase in performance due to unrolling. We measured both execution cycles/dynamic instruction counts and actual CPU time. While measures of execution cycles/dynamic instruction counts are useful in understanding the effects of code improvements, they do not take into account other system effects such as memory traffic, cache performance, and pipeline stalls which can effect overall execution time. Furthermore, most users are concerned with how much faster their program runs when a code improvement is applied. Consequently, we felt it important to collect both types of measurements.

We gathered our measurements on a R3000-based DECstation Model 5000/125 and Motorola 68020 based Sun-3/200 [Moto84]. These two architectures were chosen because they represent two ends of the computer architecture spectrum: the DECstation is a RISC architecture while the Sun-3 is a CISC architecture. The measurements for the performance increase in execution cycles were taken only on DECstation, while the measurements of the performance increase in CPU times have been taken on the DECstation as well as the Sun-3.

As described in Section 3, our loop unrolling algorithm automatically determines the best unroll factor n, where $0 \leq n \leq 15$, to use for each loop. For the DECstation 5000, all loops were unrolled fifteen times. On the Sun-3, however, the small instruction cache size (64 words) limited the amount of unrolling possible.

5.1 Performance increase

5.1.1 Reduction in cycle count

Measurements of execution cycles of all benchmarks except *xlisp*, *espresso* and *gcc* were taken using *pixie*[†], an architecture evaluation tool for MIPS processors [Kane89]. The unit of measurement is cycles. Performance of benchmarks *gcc*, *espresso* and *xlisp* were measured using *ease* [Davi90], a tool to evaluate architectures. One of the measures provided by *ease* is dynamic instruction counts. It works at the assembly language level, and therefore, does not count no-ops.[††]

To determine whether handling execution-time counting loops is important, we measured the performance increase of the benchmarks when only compile-time loops were unrolled and when both compile-time and execution-time loops were unrolled. Figure 3 contains the graph showing the percentage increase using each approach. The graph shows that unrolling algorithms that only handle compile-time counting loops are much less effective than algorithms that also handle execution-time counting loops.

A second set of measurements was performed to determine the benefits of handling loops with complex control flow. Using the categories described in Figure 1, we measured the percentage increase in performance for each set of benchmarks as loops with increasingly complex control-flow are handled. Figure 4 shows the percentage performance increase for each set of benchmarks and average performance increase across benchmark categories. We measured performance increase for each benchmark set because we were interested to see if the percentage increase depended on the type of benchmark.

In user codes, the benchmarks *encode* and *cache* slow down due to unrolling. This is because the unrolled loops in the two benchmarks are not executed enough number of times to amortize the cost of loop unrolling. *Encode* has an execution-time counting loop whose iteration count is less than sixteen. Since the unroll factor used on the DECstation is 15, only the epilogue code is executed, and the unrolled portion of the code is not executed at all. The overhead incurred in computing the iteration count of the unrolled loop slows down the benchmark. If the unroll factor had been lower, then the unrolled loop would have been executed, yielding benefits. Thus, increasing the unroll factor can have a negative impact on the performance. The benchmark *cache* slows down when loops with a single basic block and function calls are unrolled because the unrolled loop is not executed enough times to amortize the cost of

---

†The code breaks if compiled with *pixie*.
††On R2000, scheduling is done by the assembler, and therefore, no-ops are inserted by it.

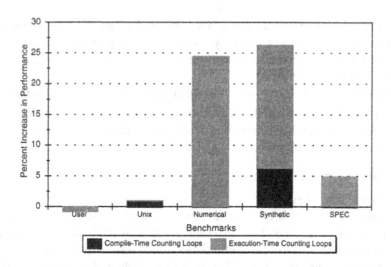

Fig: 3. Performance increase due to unrolling compile-time counting loops and execution-time counting loops on MIPS R2000.

calculating the loop iteration count and the extra conditional branch. In Unix utilities, the performance of *cal, diff* and *nroff* improves because of unrolling. The performance of other utilities does not improve because they spend a majority of their execution time in non-counting loops.

For numerical benchmarks and synthetic benchmarks, substantial performance increase occurs from unrolling loops with internal branches and multiple exits. For instance, the performance of bubblesort improves by approximately 50% when loops with complex control-flow are unrolled. Similarly, the performance of the benchmark *s008* increases by over 50% when loops with internal branches are unrolled. If loops with complex control-flow are not unrolled, these benefits would not be attained.

For SPEC benchmarks, the performance of benchmark *eqntott* improves by approximately 19% when loops with multiple exits and internal branches are unrolled. This improvement would not have been obtained if only the loops with a single basic block were to be unrolled. The performance of benchmark *espresso* is marginally better if loops with multiple basic blocks are not unrolled. This is because this benchmark contains a number of execution-time counting loops with multiple basic blocks which have an iteration count of zero or one and the overhead incurred to execute the unrolled loop is not amortized. Benchmark *xlisp* has no improvement since the execution of this benchmarks is dominated by non-counting loops, while *gcc* improves by about 0.7 percent.

The combined result shows that while unrolling loops with a single basic block is very beneficial, unrolling loops with complex control-flow is even more beneficial. The performance of numerical and synthetic benchmarks increases by an additional

12% and 17% respectively, when loops with internal branches are unrolled. The performance of SPEC benchmarks increases by about 3% when loops with multiple exits are unrolled. Clearly, unrolling loops with complex control-flow increases performance for various benchmarks.

5.1.2 Reduction in execution times

This section presents the increase in performance computed using execution times on the DECstation and the 68020-based Sun-3. To measure execution time, the Unix

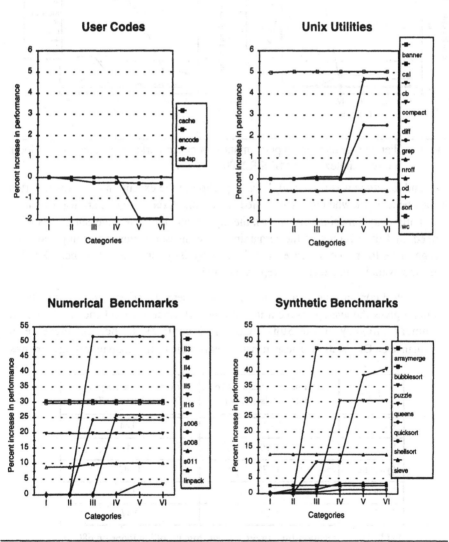

Fig: 4. Percentage increase in performance for benchmarks in all categories by loop body complexity on MIPS R2000.

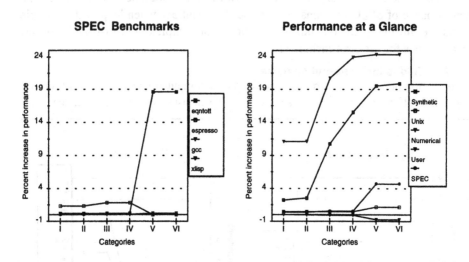

Fig: 4. Percentage increase in performance for benchmarks in all categories by loop body complexity on MIPS R2000.

command */bin/time* was used, and the *user* portion of the execution time was reported for each benchmark when loops are rolled and unrolled. Each benchmark was executed on a lightly loaded machine five times, the highest and the lowest measurements were dropped, and the average of the remaining three measurements was computed. The average of performance increase in each category is reported in this paper. Detailed results are available in a technical report [Davi95b].

Table 3 contains the measurements of the percentage increase in execution time. Column 2 gives the average percent increase in performance for a benchmark in each benchmark category on the Sun-3. Column 3 contains the percent increase in performance on DECstation. These measurements indicate that loop unrolling increases

Type	Performance increase (%) on M68020 (User Time)	Performance increase (%) on DEC R2000 (User Time)
User	-0.74	-0.44
Unix	0.90	0.47
Synthetic	15.75	17.42
Numerical	2.61	21.44
SPEC	0.07	3.47

Table 4: Execution-time improvement from unrolling loops on 68020 and MIPS R2000.

performance of benchmarks on the DECstation and the Sun-3. The performance increase is comparable for non-numerical benchmarks on both the machines. For numerical benchmarks, which perform floating-point computations, the benefits are higher on the DECstation. Loop unrolling eliminates conditional branch instructions and redundant increments to the induction variable. As a side effect, the unrolled loop has an extra counter which is required by the loop which executes the leftover iterations. The combined cost of these instructions is significant when compared to the total cost of floating-point instructions inside the loops in numerical benchmarks on the DECstation. On the other hand, the cost of conditional branches and associated instructions required to maintain the loop is not significant when compared to the floating-point instructions inside the loops on the Sun-3[†]. Therefore, the benefits from the elimination of branch instructions and redundant increments is higher on the DECstation. Loop unrolling will result in larger performance increase on the DECstation (a RISC architecture) if register renaming is applied along with it because the instruction pipeline will be better utilized [Davi95b]. In general, the benefits from loop unrolling, to a large extent, are contingent on the cost of branch instructions to other instructions inside the loop body.

From the data presented in the above sections, it is clear loop unrolling can be a very effective code improvement. Furthermore, to be most effective, loop unrolling algorithms must handle loops with complex control flow and loops whose the iteration count is not known at compile time. For some programs, performance improvements as high as 20 to 50 percent can be achieved when loops are unrolled aggressively. Also, loop unrolling does not result in excessive increase in the size of executable code [Davi95b].

Thus, loop unrolling is similar to many other code improvements, which affects only a subset of the programs to which it is applied. It is most beneficial when it is applied aggressively to unroll execution-time counting loops and loops with complex control-flow.

6   Previous Work

Many researchers have presented loop unrolling as a way of decreasing loop overhead. Dongarra suggested manual replication of the code body for loops written in FORTRAN [Dong79]. Array subscripts and loop increments are adjusted to reflect that the loop has been unrolled. Weiss discussed loop unrolling from the perspective of automatic scheduling by the compiler [Weis87]. His study considers only Livermore loops. This study also discussed the effect of loop unrolling on instruction buffer size and register pressure within the loop.

Mahlke discussed optimizations which can increase instruction-level parallelism for supercomputers [Mahl92]. Loop unrolling is one of them. By analyzing loops with known bounds, they showed that if register renaming is applied after loop unrolling, the execution time of the loop decreases. In trace-scheduling and global compaction methodology [Fish83, Freu94], loop unrolling is a key feature. Freudenberger discussed the effect of loop unrolling on SPEC benchmarks and the way in which it facilitates global scheduling and insertion of the compensation code [Freu94].

[†]The relative cost of a floating-point instruction, when compared to a conditional branch instruction, is higher on Sun-3 than on the DECstation.

7 Summary

While loop unrolling is a well-known code improvement, there has been little discussion in the literature of the issues that must be addressed to perform loop unrolling most effectively. This paper addresses this deficiency. Through extensive compile- and run-time analyses of a set of 32 benchmark programs the paper analyzes the loop characteristics that are important when considering loop unrolling. One factor analyzed was the importance of handling loops where the loop bounds are not known at compile time. The analysis shows that most loops that are candidates for unrolling have bounds that are not known at compile time (i.e., execution-time counting loops). Consequently, an effective loop unrolling algorithm must handle execution-time counting loops. Another factor analyzed was the control-flow complexity of loops that are candidates for unrolling. The analysis shows that unrolling loops with complex control-flow is as important as unrolling execution-time counting loops. For some benchmark programs significant improvements can be gained if loops with complex control flow are unrolled. Because handling such loops does not significantly impact compilation time or unduly complicate the loop unrolling algorithms, our conclusion is that an aggressive compiler should unroll such loops.

Using the benchmark programs and a C compiler that implements the algorithms for loop unrolling, the effectiveness of the code transformation at improving run-time efficiency was measured. Our measurements show that aggressive loop unrolling can yield run-time performance increases of 10 to 20 percent for some sets of benchmarks over a simple and naive approach, and that for some programs increases in performance by as much as 40 to 50 percent are achieved.

Acknowledgements

This work was supported in part by National Science Foundation grants CCR-9214904 and MIP-9307626. We also thank Mark Bailey and Bruce Childers for their feedback.

References

[Alex93]   Alexander, M. J., Bailey, M. W., Childers, B. R., Davidson, J. W., and Jinturkar, S., "Memory Bandwidth Optimizations for Wide-Bus Machines", *Proceedings of the 25th Hawaii International Conference on System Sciences*, Maui, HA, January 1993, pp. 466-475.

[Baco94]   Bacon, D. F., Graham, S. L., and Sharp, O. J., "Compiler Transformations for High-Performance Computing", *ACM Computing Surveys*, **26**(4), Dec. 1994, pp. 345-420.

[Beni94]   Benitez, M. E. and Davidson, J. W., "The Advantages of Machine-Dependent Global Optimizations", *Proceedings of the Conference on Programming Languages and System Architecture*, Springer Verlag Lecture Notes in Computer Science, Zurich, Switzerland, March 1994, pp. 105-124.

[Davi81]   Davidson, J. W., and Fraser, C. W., "The Design and Application of a Retargetable Peephole Optimizer", *ACM Transactions on Programming Languages and Systems*, **2**(2), April 1980, pp. 191-202.

[Davi90]   Davidson, J. W. and Whalley, D. B., "Ease: An Environment for Architecture Study and Experimentation", *Proceedings of the 1990 ACM Sig-*

metrics Conference on Measurement and Modelling of Computer Systems, Boulder, CO, May 1990, pp. 259-260.

[Davi94]   Davidson, J. W. and Jinturkar, S., "Memory Access Coalescing: A Technique for Eliminating Redundant Memory Accesses", *Proceedings of SIGPLAN '94 Conference on Programming Language Design and Implementation*, Orlando, FL, June 1994, pp 186-195.

[Davi95a]   Davidson, J. W. and Jinturkar, S., "An Aggressive approach to Loop Unrolling", available as University of Virginia Technical Report # CS-95-26.

[Davi95b]   Davidson, J. W. and Jinturkar, S., "Improving Instruction-level Parallelism by Loop Unrolling and Dynamic Memory Disambiguation", *Proceedings of the 28th International Symposium on Microarchitecture,* Ann Arbor, MI, Nov 1995, pp 125-134.

[Digi92]   *Alpha Architecture Handbook*, Digital Equipment Corporation, Boston, MA, 1992.

[Dong79]   Dongarra, J.J. and Hinds, A. R., "Unrolling Loops in Fortran", *Software-Practice and Experience*, **9**(3), Mar. 1979, pp. 219-226.

[Fish84]   Fisher, J. A., Ellis, J. R., Ruttenberg, J. C. and Nicolau, A., "Parallel Processing: A Smart Compiler and a Dumb Machine", *Proceedings of the SIGPLAN'84 Symposium on Compiler Construction*, Montreal, Canada, June 1984, pp. 37-47.

[Freu94]   Freudenberger, S. M., Gross, T. R. and Lowney, P. G., "Avoidance and Suppression of Compensation Code in a Trace Scheduling Compiler", *ACM Transactions on Programming Languages and Systems*, **16**(4), July 1994, pp. 1156-1214.

[Henn90]   Hennessy, J. L. and Patterson, D. A., *Computer Architecture: A Quantitative Approach*, Morgan Kaufmann Publishers, Inc, San Mateo, CA, 1990.

[IBM90]   IBM RISC System/6000 Technology, Austin, TX, 1990.

[Kane89]   Kane, G., "MIPS RISC Architecture", Prentice-Hall, Englewood Cliffs, NJ, 1992.

[Mahl92]   Mahlke, S. A., Chen, W. Y., Gyllenhaal, J. C. and Hwu, W. W., "Compiler Code Transformations for Superscalar-Based High-Performance Systems", *Proceedings of Supercomputing '92*, Portland, OR, Nov. 1992, pp. 808-817.

[Moto84]   *MC68020 32-Bit Microprocessor User's Manual*, Prentice-Hall, Englewood Cliffs, N.J.

[Stal89]   Stallman, R. M., *Using and Porting GNU CC*, Free Software Foundation, Cambridge, MA, 1989.

[Sun87]   *The SPARC Architecture Manual*, Version 7, Sun Microsystems Corporation, Mountain View, CA, 1987.

[Weis87]   Weiss, S, and Smith, J. E., "A Study of Scalar Compilation Techniques for Pipelined Supercomputers", *Proceedings of Second International Conference on Architectural Support for Programming Languages and Operating Systems"*, Palo Alto, CA, Oct. 1987, pp. 105-109.

Generalized Constant Propagation
A Study in C

Clark Verbrugge* and Phong Co and Laurie Hendren**

{clump, phaedrus, hendren}@cs.mcgill.ca
School of Computer Science
McGill University
Montréal, Québec, Canada H3A 2A7

Abstract. Generalized Constant Propagation (GCP) statically estimates the ranges of variables throughout a program. GCP is a top-down compositional compiler analysis in the style of abstract intepretation. In this paper we present an implementation of both intraprocedural and interprocedural GCP within the context of the C language. We compare the accuracy and utility of GCP information for several versions of GCP using experimental results from an actual implementation.

1 Introduction

Generalized Constant Propagation (GCP) is a top-down compositional compiler analysis based on the style of abstract interpretation [CC77]. A GCP analysis statically approximates the possible values each variable could take at each point in the program. As an extension of constant propagation (CP), GCP estimates *ranges* for variables rather than their precise value: each variable at each point is associated with a minimum and maximum value.

We have implemented GCP for the full C language, in both intraprocedural and interprocedural forms. We have tested the accuracy of our method both by assessing the quality of GCP information, and by measuring the amount of information which could be useful to subsequent analyses. Our experiments have show GCP to be efficient and viable; programs with many procedures obviously benefit more from an interprocedural analysis, but surprisingly high accuracy can be achieved with just an intraprocedural analysis. The use of read/write sets and points-to analysis also enhance the accuracy of GCP, particularly when constants cross procedure calls.

GCP information has several uses. Since it is an extension of CP, the same reasons for using it apply: elimination of dead code, arithmetic optimizations, static range-checking, etc. Naturally, GCP will tend to be more powerful in these respects; the value of a variable may not be constant, but its range might still allow a conditional to be statically evaluated. Ranges can also be useful for subsequent analyses, such as various loop transformations. However, it is also true that GCP locates more exact constants than CP, making GCP valuable even if range information is not needed.

---

* Research supported in part by an NSERC Graduate Fellowship and FCAR.
** Research supported in part by NSERC and FCAR

In examining the ouput of GCP analysis, we also noticed that the information could be useful for program understanding. For example, variables determined by GCP to be bounded can also be transformed to more tightly typed variables, such as booleans or subranges. This information could be added to the program, making the program easier to understand and simplifying further analyses.

1.1 Related Work

Constant propagation is a popular analysis that has appeared in numerous forms over the years [CCKT86, CH95, GT93, MS93, WZ91]. Generalized constant propagation, however, has not enjoyed as much attention: Harrison's [Har77] article on the *range propagation* problem is one of the few papers to address this type of analysis, albeit in a more 'traditional' setting based on precomputation of control-flow diagrams and *def* and *use* sets. GCP information also bears some resemblance to the attempts by software engineers to produce provably correct programs. Analyses developed for this goal propagate symbolic information in an attempt to establish loop and/or program invariants, either for annotation, or mechanical verification [DM81]. This is a large body of literature with very different methods, but GCP can in some sense be considered a spawn of such efforts. In fact, a paper by Bourdoncle [Bou93] describes a method called *abstract debugging*, which propagates range information top-down and bottom-up in order to locate potential program bugs.

More recently, Patterson described an analysis similar to GCP used for static branch prediction [Pat95]. Here, ranges are augmented with a probability that the actual value lies uniformly distributed within that range, and sometimes with symbolic information as well; this allows the results of conditionals to be estimated with greater accurracy. As with Wegman and Zadeck's constant propagation, this is based on a Static Single Assignment (SSA) representation.

In any range analysis, computing the values within loops will tend to be expensive —the domain of ranges tends to be quite large, and it can take a long time for ranges to converge. Patterson deals with this problem by heuristically matching templates to loop carried expressions, resorting to brute force for the unrecognized cases. The approach we develop in section 3.3 is the notion of *stepping*, or artificially moving the range up in the domain. This has also been addressed by Bourdoncle, and is similar to the *widening/narrowing* tactic of Cousot and Cousot [CC92].

1.2 Overview

Our analysis relies on an *Abstract Syntax Tree* intermediate representation of the program. In Sect. 2 we describe this structure, and how we can augment it to support interprocedural analyses as well as intraprocedural ones. Section 3 explains the semantic basis for our analysis and gives rules for the intraprocedural version. Using the framework of Sect. 2, we extend our analysis to a full interprocedural GCP in Sect. 4. We then give experimental results in Sect. 5, comparing GCP with CP and contrasting the effects of intraprocedural GCP, GCP with Read/Write sets, and the complete interprocedural GCP.

2 Background and Setting

The GCP analysis has been implemented within the context of the McCAT optimizing/parallelizing compiler[HDE+92]. As illustrated in Fig. 1, the first phase of the compiler takes multiple C files as input and creates a SIMPLE intermediate representation of the complete program[Sri92]. This phase consists of a symbolic linker that combines all of the input C files into one complete representation of the program, a simplification phase that translates the higher-level intermediate representation to SIMPLE, and a restructuring phase that eliminates goto statements[EH94]. The overall objective is to create an intermediate form that is structured and simple to analyze. Typical transformations performed in the simplification phase include: compiling complex statements into a series of basic statements, simplifying all conditional expressions in if and while statements to simple expressions with no side-effects, structuring switch statements, simplifying procedure arguments to either constants or variable names, and moving variable initializations from declarations to statements in the body of the appropriate procedure. Fig. 2(a) gives an example C program, while Fig. 2(b) gives the equivalent simplified program.

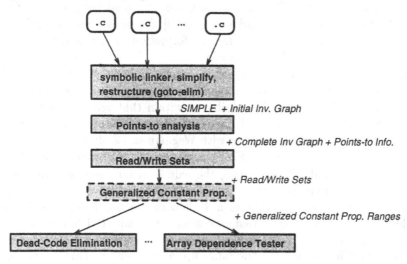

Fig. 1. Overview

GCP analysis also uses the output of points-to analysis and read/write set analysis. Points-to analysis is a context-sensitive interprocedural analysis that approximates the points-to relationships at each program point [EGH94]. For each indirection of the form *x, points-to information can be used to find the set of named locations pointed-to by x. Named locations include globals, parameters, locals, and special symbolic names that represent names that are not visible within the scope of a function, but are accessible via pointers. An example of a symbolic name is the name[3] 1-x that is used to represent the location accessed via *x in the procedure incr in Fig. 2(b).

---

[3] We use 1-x to denote the first dereference of x, 2-x for the second dereference, etc.

```
int g1,g2;

void init_glob()
{ g1 = 1; }

void incr(int *x, int delta)
{ *x = *x + delta; }

main()
{ int a,b=3,c=4;
  g2 = 2;
  init_glob();
  scanf("%d",&a);
  incr(&a,c);
  incr(&b,g1);
  printf("%d %d %d %d %d \n",
          a,b,c,g1,g2);
}
```

(a) Example C Program

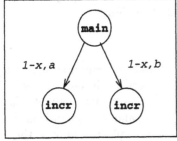

(c) invocation graph and mapping information

```
int g1,g2;

void init_glob()
{ g1 = 1; }            {g1}

void incr(int *x, int delta)
{ int t0;
  t0 = *x;             {t0}
  *x = t0 + delta;     {1-x}
}          t0:[-oo..oo] delta:[1..4]

main()
{ int a,b,c,*t1,*t2,*t3;
  b = 3;               {b}
  c = 4;               {c}
  g2 = 2;              {g2}
  init_glob();         {g1}
  t1 = &a;             {t1}
  scanf("%d",t1);      {a}
  t2 = &a;             {t2}
  incr(t2,c);c:[4..4]  {a}
  t3 = &b;             {t2}
  incr(t3,g1);g1:[1..1] {b}

  printf("%d %d %d %d %d \n",
          a,b,c,g1,g2);    {}
}       a:[-oo..oo] b:[4..4] c:[4..4]
            g1:[1..1] g2:[2..2]
```

(b) SIMPLE represenation with Write Sets
and interprocedural GCP ranges

Fig. 2. Example Program, Write Sets and Invocation Graph

Points-to analysis also computes a complete invocation graph which captures all invocation contexts and the mapping information that is used to map location names in calling context to location names in called contexts. Fig. 2(c) shows the invocation graph for the example program. The root of the invocation graph is always main, and all calling chains are explicitly represented.[4] This is completely general; in the case of recursion (even mutual recursion), implicit cycles are introduced between matching *recursive* node and *approximate* nodes for the same function in order to represent all possible unwindings of the recursion; in the case of indirect function calls via function pointers, the list of functions pointed-to by the function pointer is given. Note that calls to library functions such as scanf and printf are not included in the invocation graph. The arcs in the invocation graph store the mapping information that was computed by points-to analysis. In our example, the first invocation of incr is represented

---

[4] There are several strategies for reducing the actual size of the invocation graph by sharing subtrees. However, it is conceptually simpler to think of the full unfolding of the invocation graph.

by left arc, and the mapping information indicates that the location name a in main corresponds to the symbolic name 1-x in incr. Whereas, in the second invocation (right arc), the name b in main corresponds to 1-x in incr. This mapping allows us to use one name within incr without losing the context-specific information from each invocation site. A more detailed description of the interprocedural environment, including the invocation graph can be found in [HEGV93].

Read/write set analysis uses the points-to information to calculate the locations read and written by each basic and compositional statement.[5] For the purposes of GCP, we only use the write sets calculated for procedure calls. Note that read/write sets include all local, symbolic, and global locations written by a procedure call.[6] Figure 2(b) gives the **write** set for each statement in our example program (shown in bold italics). Note that the second assignment in incr shows that the symbolic location 1-x is written. Also note that the write sets for procedure calls are quite precise as both points-to and read/write set analysis are context-sensitive interprocedural analyses.

Figure 2(b) also gives the range information that is collected for the program. Each direct use of a variable has been decorated with the appropriate GCP information as computed by our interprocedural algorithm.

3 Intraprocedural GCP

Within a procedure, GCP is a straightforward top-down semantic analysis of the SIMPLE AST. The semantic domain is first specified; in our case we will be concerned with the domain of scalar *ranges*. A corresponding semantic function is then developed for every possible type of node, and the semantic analysis proceeds by pattern matching on the AST node type and branching to the appropriate function. This is complicated somewhat by the presence of indirection; whenever a pointer is dereferenced, the ranges for every possible target variable have to be merged. Information is further diluted by function calls, which can side-effect not just global variables, but local ones indirectly referred to by pointers. The success of GCP would thus seem to hinge on the accuracy of how it handles procedure calls, and on the accuracy of the points-to analysis.

3.1 Semantic Domains

GCP estimates the value(s) a variable can assume at each point in the program by estimating the minimum and maximum values each variable can reach. Our semantic domain is then the domain of *ranges*: closed (scalar) intervals, partially-ordered by inclusion with both a smallest element ($\bot = []$, the empty range) and a largest ($\top = [-\infty \ldots \infty]$, where by ∞ we mean the largest machine representable scalar). Note that most every data type in C fits comfortably into this paradigm; chars, shorts, ints, longs (signed and unsigned) of course, but also floats and doubles, as discrete approximations to real numbers, structs

---

[5] This is similar to MOD/REF analysis.
[6] The actual sets calculated are divided into the *definite* write set for those locations definitely written and the *possible* write set for those locations which may be written.

as aggregate scalars, and even pointers as unsigned integers. Arrays are approximated as the merge of their contents.

Ranges form a nice semantic domain. If $[a, b]$ and $[c, d]$ are (inclusive, closed) ranges, one can consider $[a, b] \sqsubseteq [c, d]$ if $a \geq c$ and $b \leq d$. The meet of two ranges $[a, b]$ and $[c, d]$ is then the range which includes them both: $[\min(a, c), \max(b, d)]$.

Our ranges are also discrete, even for the representation of real numbers; every element is finite, and there exist least upper bounds for arbitrary sets of elements. In other words, the domain is a Scott Domain. The existence of fixed-points for monotonic functions, and closure under cross-product are then guaranteed.

This domain does have one unpleasant property—it is quite 'tall,' i.e., one can form very long chains. This will have implications for how fixed points are computed during the analysis of loops and recursion, as will be seen later.

3.2 Semantic Functions

As mentioned, every type of statement in the SIMPLE AST (both expression and control) needs a semantic analogue; we need separate methods for determining how GCP information is altered by assignments, the various arithmetic operations, sequencing, conditionals, loops, ...etc. In order to ensure convergence, it is also necessary that each semantic function be monotonic in its domain.

We cannot describe all the semantic functions here, but in Figs. 3 and 4 we show the semantic operations corresponding to a few different kinds of statements in a compositional form. We hope that this will give the reader some idea of the flavour of the effort. Note that the structured nature of our SIMPLE representation lends itself to concise and relatively compact analysis rules.

Most of these functions are quite obvious; assignment requires locating the range for the right hand side value, and storing it as the range for the left hand side variable (the effect of pointers is discussed below). Semantic plus is paradigmatic of most arithmetic functions. The largest range which could result from the operation being applied to any combination of values in the operand ranges is computed and returned as the result.

Most semantic functions dilute information, due to the necessity of being conservative. Conditionals, though, can generate information. When control passes through a conditional, it is necessary that the condition be satisfied (then-part), or unsatisfiable (else-part), and this can be reflected in the range sets passed into the corresponding statements. For example, a statement such as if(i<0) implies that i must be less than 0 when entering the affirmative branch, and that i must be at least 0 within the negative branch. Every conditional we encounter therefore splits the input into two constrained sets (line 13, Fig. 4), which must be merged after the conditional is completed.

3.3 Loops and Stepping

Loops in a semantic analysis require the computation of a fixed point in the semantic domain. The process is illustrated starting from line 27 in Fig. 4 (other loop structures are similar); the GCP information coming out of the body of the loop is merged with the information entering the loop, and the process is

```
/* Given statement S, an input GCP set, returns the output GCP set */
fun process_stmt (S,Input) =
 if basic_stmt(S)
   return(process_basic_stmt(S,Input))
 else
   case S of
     < SEQ(S1,S2) > =>
       return(process_stmt(S2,process_stmt(S1,Input)))
     < IF(cond,thenS,elseS) > =>
       return(process_if(cond,thenS,elseS,Input))                    10
     < WHILE(cond,bodyS) > =>
       return(process_while(cond,bodyS,Input))
     ...


fun process_basic_stmt(S,Input) =
 case S of
   < x = y > =>
     /* RangeOf returns the range for the given variable in the given input set */
     return(Input − x:RangeOf(x,Input) + x:RangeOf(y,Input))
   < x = *y > =>                                                     20
     /* MergeRanges returns the smallest range ⊒ every range in a given list.
        Dereference returns a list of variables pointed to by the given variable
        at the given statement. RangesOf is the list−version of RangeOf */
     [a..b] = MergeRanges(RangesOf(Dereference(y,S)),Input)
     return(Input − x:RangeOf(x,Input) + x:[a..b])
     /* Merge pair−wise merges two lists of ranges for the same set of variables.
        DefinitelyPointsTo returns true if the given variables have definite points-to
        relationship at the given program point */
   < *x = y > =>
     derefx = Dereference(x,S)                                       30
     if (DefinitelyPointsTo(x,derefx,S))
       return(Input − derefx:RangeOf(derefx,Input) + derefx:RangeOf(y,Input))
     /* If x does not definitely point to a single variable, then the
        strategy is to merge the range from the right−hand−side of the
        statement with the range of all variables x can possibly point to */
     foreach temp in derefx
       Input = Input − temp:Rangeof(temp,Input) +
                     temp:Merge(RangeOf(temp,Input),Rangeof(y,Input))
     return(Input)
   < x = y + z > =>                                                  40
     [a..b] = semantic_plus(RangeOf(y,Input),RangeOf(z,Input))
     return(Input − x:RangeOf(x,Input) + x:[a..b])
     ...
```

Fig. 3. Compositional intraprocedural rules for GCP (continued on next figure)

```
fun semantic_plus([a..b],[c..d]) =
  if (a+c < −∞) e = −∞ else e = a+c
  if (b+d > ∞) f = ∞ else f = b+d
  return([e..f])

  /* Given a simple conditional cond, the statements in the then and
     else part, and GCP input, return the gcp output set. */
fun process_if(cond,thenS,elseS,Input) =
  /* ConstrainConditional splits the input set into two sets; one consistent
     with the conditional (to serve as input to the then statement), and one      10
     inconsistent (for the else statement). If either set is empty, then
     the input is such that the conditional can only have one possible outcome */
  (consistentInput,inconsistentInput) = ConstrainConditional(cond,Input)
  /* Do not process the then statement if we've determined that it
     cannot be executed! */
  if (consistentInput != {})
    thenOutput = process_stmt(thenS,consistentInput)
  else
    thenOutput = {}
  if (inconsistentInput != {})                                                    20
    elseOutput = process_stmt(elseS,inconsistentInput)
  else
    elseOutput = {}
  return(Merge(thenOutput,elseOutput))

fun process_while(cond,bodyS,Input) =
  iterations = 0
  Output = oldBodyInput = bodyOutput = {}
  do
    Input = Merge(Input,bodyOutput)                                               30
    (consistentInput,inconsistentInput) = ConstrainConditional(cond,Input)
    converged = (consistentInput == oldBodyInput)
    if (not converged and iterations > maxiterations)
      /* StepUp artificially moves a non−converging range up in the
         semantic domain */
      StepUp(consistentInput,oldBodyInput)
      iterations = 0
    oldBodyInput = consistentInput
    bodyOutput = process_stmt(bodyS,consistentInput)
    Output = Merge(Output,inconsistentInput)                                      40
    iterations = iterations + 1
  while (not converged)
  return(Output)
```

Fig. 4. Compositional intraprocedural rules for GCP (continued from previous figure)

repeated until convergence. The output of the loop is gathered as the merged result of all sets of ranges which do not satisfy the conditional; in the actual implementation we also merge the results of **break** and **continue** statements with the Output and Input sets respectively.

Our semantic functions are all monotonic in their individual range-domains, so we will reach a fixed point eventually. Unfortunately, the domain of ranges can be quite "tall;" there are monotonic chains of *very* long length: e.g., $[0..0] \leq [0..1] \leq \ldots \leq [-\infty..\infty]$ where ∞ is typically 2^{31}. In the worst case then, our monotonicity requirement only ensures convergence after 2^{32} steps per variable, which is clearly unacceptable.

We can, however, speed up this process by sacrificing the quality of information. Ranges for variables that refuse to converge after some fixed number of iterations can be artificially "stepped up" (raised in the semantic domain). If each range can be stepped only so many times before reaching $[-\infty..\infty]$, then the monotonicity of our semantic operations guarantees convergence in much less time. By using some heuristics to guide the choice of which variable to step (e.g., choosing the loop index first), we can achieve a reasonable compromise between efficiency and accuracy. In our implementation, for instance, we have 2 non-converging iterations for each stepping operation. The first four steppings individually push the non-converging ends of the variables in the loop conditional to the loop bounds (if known), or to ∞ (or $-\infty$). The next step is to push some ($n = 40$ in our case) and then all the non-converging ends of all variables to ∞, then stepping all non-converging ranges to $[-\infty, \infty]$, and finally stepping all variables to $[-\infty, \infty]$. Thus, each fixed-point requires at most $14 + 2n$ iterations.

3.4 Considerations for C

Almost all languages have loops, and the difficulties they present to semantic analyses are not unique to C. The C language though does have two distinct features which greatly impact the efficacy of GCP: pointers and an abundance of procedure calls.

Pointers. Whenever a dereferenced pointer is encountered in the code, it is essential to know which variables might be accessed in order to compute the correct range information. When a dereferenced pointer appears on the right hand side of an expression, as an *R-value*, the semantic function computes the least upper-bound of all ranges which might be referred to as the result of the dereference (see the semantic $x = *y$ in Fig. 3). No matter which variable is actually accessed during runtime, it is then guaranteed to be included in the range GCP reports for the dereference. When a dereference occurs on the left hand side of an assignment, as an *L-value*, correctness requires that the range to be stored be merged with the existing range values for every variable which might be indicated by the dereference (see $*x = y$ in Fig. 3). This sort of conservative estimation can result in very poor information. If the set of variables accessed by an arbitrary pointer dereference is not known, all referenced variables must be assumed accessible.

Points-to analysis limits this sort of conservative dilution. By identifying target variables for each dereference, it is possible to restrict the number of ranges which have to be merged, or merged into. In a language like C, where pointers are ubiquitous, this sort of information is essential for reasonable accuracy.

Procedure Calls. Each time a procedure call is encountered, intraprocedural GCP must discard all information about any variable which might be altered by the function call. In the absence of information about where pointers might be directed, the most naive conservative approach is just to push every range up to T; a slightly more clever tactic is to just raise all globals and any local variable which has had its address taken.

Points-to information allows GCP to more precisely determine which variables could be accessed by a function call. By computing the transitive closure of the possibly-points-to relation starting from the function call parameters and globals, the set of all variables which could be accessed can be determined.

Even with points-to this is still overly conservative. Pointers are often passed in C procedures to avoid copying information onto the stack, and not just to facilitate side-effects; pushing all accessible variables to T is clearly overkill. If read/write sets are available, though, it is possible to identify which variables might actually be written to during a function call. By just raising the variables in this latter·set, the number of variables needlessly raised to T can be reduced.

4 Interprocedural GCP

The approximations used for intraprocedural GCP information over procedure calls are clearly suboptimal; in order to be surely correct, we seem to be forced to throw away a great deal of information. Even with the more accurate identification of altered or aliased variables possible with points-to and read/write sets, we still have to discard all information about the range of an altered variable. We cannot know exactly what the function does to the variables it changes, so it is necessary to assume the variables could be anything after a call.

An interprocedural analysis does not suffer from this limitation. By knowing the effect of each call on both local and global variables, we can determine, for instance, that a given procedure simply increments its value rather than computing an arbitrary function. Moreover, by using the invocation graph framework developed in section 2, we can compute interprocedural information in a context-sensitive way, avoiding the generalizations (and hence dilution of information) produced by the *calling context problem*.

4.1 Using the Invocation Graph

Making GCP interprocedural requires just two functions, *map* and *unmap*. As each function call is recursively traversed, the actual parameters passed to the callee are mapped to the formal parameters. The mapping information calculated by points-to·analysis is used to map between names in the caller and symbolic names in the callee. As the function body is processed, the ranges computed from the current input set are merged with the existing ranges imbedded in the program from previous calls to the same function. Once the input set has completed the body, the values it contains are unmapped back to the caller's variables using the original map information. The ranges stored within the callee will then represent the merged input of all calls to that function, while the ranges returned after processing a function call represent the result of the call given the current input set from the caller (i.e. these values are context-sensitive). The process is shown functionally in Fig. 5 as a three-way branch on the invocation graph node (**ign**) type; non-recursive computations are illustrated in the first case, and map and unmap rules for GCP are shown in Fig. 6.

In the absence of recursion, this process is straighforward. When a recursive call appears, however, we are required to compute a fixed-point for the call representing all possible unrollings for the recursive call. This is indicated in our traversal of the invocation graph by a matching recursive and approximate node pair (linked by a backedge).

At each recursive node we store an input, an output, and a list of pending inputs. The input and output pair can be thought of as approximating the effect of the call associated with the recursive function (let us call it **f**), and the pending list accumulates input information which has not yet been propagated through the function. The fixed-point computation generalizes the stored input until it finds an input that summarizes all invocations of **f** in any unrolled call tree starting at the recursive node for **f**. Similarly, the output is generalized to find a summary for the output for any unrolling of the call tree starting in the recursive node for **f**. The generalizations of the input and output may alternate, with a new generalization of the output causing the input to change.

Consider the rule for the approximate node in Fig. 5; in this case, the current input is compared to the the stored input of the matching recursive node. If the current input is contained in the stored input, then we use the stored output as the result. Otherwise, the result is not yet known for this input, so the input is put on the pending list, and bottom ($\perp$) is returned as the result. Note that an approximate node never evaluates the body of a function, it either uses the stored result, or returns $\perp$.

Now consider the recursive rule. In this case we have an iteration that only terminates when the input is sufficiently generalized (the pending list of inputs is empty) and the output is sufficiently generalized (the result of evaluating the call doesn't add any new information to the stored output).

5   Experimental Results

In order to examine the relative merits of the different flavours of GCP, we need a qualitative way of measuring the GCP information produced. This is provided by dividing the ranges GCP can produce into four categories, according to their potential utility: **Exact,** an actual constant, like [3..3]; **Bounded,** a finite subrange, like [1...10]; **Half-open,** one end of the range is a number, but the other is infinite, like [1..∞]; and **Total,** the range is $\top$, like [$-\infty$..∞].

We have counted the number of ranges falling into each of the four categories, for each of three different variations on GCP:

Naive: Intraprocedural GCP only. No points-to information; a pointer dereference returns all variables which have had their address taken. A function
call causes all globals and all variables which have had their address taken
to be set to $\top$.

```
/* Given a list of input ranges, parameters (actuals and formals), an invocation
   graph node for the function, the function body, and mapping information,
   returns the list of ranges resulting from the function call */
fun process_call(Input,actualList,formalList,ign,funcBody,mapInfo) =
  funcInput = gcp_map(Input,formalList,actualList,mapInfo)
  case ign of
    < Ordinary > =>
      funcOutput = process_stmt(funcBody,funcInput)
      return(gcp_unmap(Input,funcOutput,mapInfo))
                                                                          10
    < Approximate > =>
      recIgn = ign.backEdge /* get partner recursive node in invoc. graph */
      /* if this input is contained in  stored input, use stored ouput */
      if isSubsetOf(funcInput,recIgn.storedInput)
        return(gcp_unmap(Input,recIgn.storedOutput,mapInfo))
      else /* put this input in the pending list, and return Bottom */
        addToPendingList(funcInput,recIgn.pendingList)
        return Bottom

    < Recursive > =>                                                      20
      ign.storedInput  = funcInput  /* initial input estimate */
      ign.storedOutput = Bottom     /* initial output estimate */
      ign.pendingList  = {}         /* no unresolved inputs pending */
      done = false
      do
        /* process the body */
        funcOutput = process_stmt(funcBody,ign.storedInput)
        /* if there are unresolved inputs, merge inputs and restart */
        if (ign.pendingList != {})
          ign.storedInput = Merge(ign.storedInput,ign.pendingList)       30
          ign.pendingList = {}
          ign.storedOutput = Bottom
        /* check to see if the new output is included in old output */
        else if isSubsetOf(funcOutput,ign.storedOutput)
          done = true;
        else /* merge outputs and try again */
          ign.storedOutput = Merge(ign.storedOutput,funcOutput)
      while (not done)
      /* return the fixed-point after unmapping */
      return(gcp_unmap(Input,ign.storedOutput,mapInfo))                  40
```

Fig. 5. Compositional interprocedural rules for GCP

```
fun gcp_map(Input,formalList,actualList,mapInfo) =
  funcInput = {}
  foreach formalI in (formalList) /* formals inherit the range from actuals */
    funcInput = funcInput + formalI:RangeOf(actualI,Input)
  foreach globalI in (globalVarList) /* the range of globals remains the same */
    funcInput = funcInput + globalI:RangeOf(globalI,Input)
  foreach x in (SymbolicVars(mapInfo))
    mappedVars = getMappedVars(x,mapInfo)
    funcInput = funcInput + x:MergeRanges(RangesOf(mappedVars,Input))
    /* symbolic vars receive the merged range of the variables they represent */   10
  return(funcInput)  ·

fun gcp_unmap(Input,funcOutput,mapInfo) =
  Output = Input /* initialize the Output of the call to its Input */
  foreach globalI in (globalVarList)
    Output = (Output − globalI:RangeOf(globalI,Input) +
        globalI:RangeOf(globalI,funcOutput))
    /* each global gets the new range from the called function */
  foreach x in (SymbolicVars(mapInfo))
    mappedVars = getMappedVars(x,mapInfo)                                          20
    foreach var in (mappedVars)
      Output = (Output − var:RangeOf(var,Input) + var:RangeOf(x,funcOutput))
        /* each variable represented by a symbolic variable in
            the called function gets the range of the symbolic variable */
  return (Output)
```

Fig. 6. Map and unmap functions for interprocedural GCP

R/W: Intraprocedural GCP that uses interprocedural points-to information, and read/write sets. Pointer dereferences return just the variables indicated by points-to. Function calls set all variables in the write set of the call to $\top$.

I-R/W Interprocedural GCP that uses interprocedural points-to information, and read/write sets. Pointer dereferences return just the variables indicated by points-to. Calls to user functions are evaluated using the using our context-sensitive ˙strategy, and calls to library functions are approximated using read/write sets to set all variables in the write set of the call to $\top$.

In each case we only count the "relevant" ranges, by which we mean ranges for references to non-pointer variables appearing on the right hand side of assignments, as arguments to a function call, or as expressions in a loop or conditional. These are the ranges which could be of interest to a subsequent analysis. Since each analysis is run on the same program, each of our three cases gives the same total number of relevant ranges. The only difference is in how many ranges fall into each of our four categories.

Figure 2(b) indicates the ranges that we would count for our example program under the **I-R/W** strategy. In this case there are 9 uses of non-pointer variables, so there is a total of 9 relevant ranges, of which 6 are exact, 1 is bounded and 2 are total. Note how the context-sensitive nature of our interprocedural analysis keeps the two different calls to `incr` distinct, while still merging the values of `delta` within the procedure. The results for this program under the **Naive** and **R/W** strategies are much less precise. With **Naive** there are only 2 exact ranges corresponding to the 2 uses of the local variable c. With the **R/W** strategy one more exact range is found for the use of the global **g2**. In this case the R/W sets are used to determine that no procedure call kills the constant value generated by the assignment **g2 = 2**.

We have run the three kinds of GCP on the following benchmark set:

Asuite: Compiler test suite from Argonne National Labs.

Chomp: Solves a simple board game.

Circle: An $O(n^4)$ minimum spanning circle algorithm.

Clinpack: Numerical test routines.

Cluster: Two greedy graph clustering algorithms.

Dhrystone: Standard timing benchmark.

Frac: Computes rational representation of a real number.

Mersenne: Computes n digits of $2^p - 1$ for a given p and n.

Nrcode2-4: Another test suite for vectorizing C compilers.

Numerical: Complex number routines – zroots, laguer.

Stanford: Baby benchmarks suite – 10 small programs.

Tomcatv: A standard Fortran benchmark, ported to C.

Of course the data GCP collects will be greatly influenced by many factors. In the left columns of Table 1, we show the number of SIMPLE statements in the program, function definitions, function calls (includes calls to library functions), global variables, maximum loop nesting and total number of loops. It should be expected that programs having more functions, calls and globals will benefit more from using read/write sets, and from using an interprocedural GCP.

Benchmark	Stmts	Funcs	Calls	Globals	Nest	Loops	F-Ps	Avg iter	Intra(s)	Inter(s)
Asuite	1841	93	299	23	3	218	623	8.10	16.08	20.39
*Chomp	439	20	54	5	2	22	259	6.33	0.89	7.07
Circle	251	4	5	12	4	8	266	6.59	58.91	57.75
Clinpack	909	11	53	23	2	33	1701	8.56	11.13	96.16
Cluster	599	20	63	18	3	53	565	6.08	21.24	28.54
Dhrystone	242	14	20	65	2	7	71	17.30	9.98	55.81
Frac	103	2	3	0	2	3	9	7.00	0.33	0.50
Mersenne	117	8	17	3	2	7	102	7.52	0.18	1.87
Nrcode2-4	405	3	36	28	2	44	82	9.16	6.33	6.44
Numerical	319	11	18	11	2	11	33	3.97	1.29	5.70
*Stanford	998	47	84	67	3	88	4058	5.46	26.93	456.88
Tomcatv	333	2	15	7	3	19	310	4.89	46.09	50.24

Table 1. Benchmarks descriptions. Dynamic measurements are I-R/W. An "*" indicates the presence of recursion.

In Fig. 7, we illustrate the relative quality of the analyses based on how ranges are divided up into the four different kinds, and the relative quality of regular constant propagation as well. The length of the black bars show the percentage of exact ranges as found by GCP and CP, and the length of the dark gray bars shows the extra constants found just by GCP. The total length of the bars show the percentage of ranges that give at least some information (exact, bounded, or open). It is interesting to note that a suprisingly large fraction of ranges contain at least some useful information, and that in several cases (stanford, mersenne, dhrystone, and marginally clinpack and asuite) GCP locates more constants than CP. These extra constants are the result of merged information being subsequently reduced to a constant, such as a boolean (b=[0..1]) within "if(b) {...}." In comparing the effectiveness of **naive** versus **R/W** and **I-R/W**, however, the results seem to depend very much on the style of the benchmark under analysis.

The **naive** analyses of circle, cluster. numerical and tomcatv2 give almost the same results as the more expensive **R/W** and **I-R/W** analyses. For the latter, there is only one large main function, all scalars are local variables, and there are no pointers to local variables. Thus, the **naive** scheme does not make any overly conservative assumptions, and the results are quite accurate. In the three former cases, there are almost no constants to speak of, regardless of the form of the analysis.

Most of the remaining benchmarks show improved results for the **I-R/W** method. In these cases constants are propagated through parameters, and so interprocedural results are substantially better. However, dhrystone, nrcode and clinpack all show benefits from using R/W sets; here, the reduced kill-sets provided by the R/W analysis (particularly with respect to library functions) allow more constants to be carried across procedure calls.

GCP is a semantic analysis on a tall domain, so the amount of time needed by GCP is important to consider. In Table 1 we also show dynamic measurements of the number of loop fixed-points, the average number of iterations for each fixed-point, and the total time (user time in seconds, on a Sun Sparc 20) consumed by both **R/W GCP** and **I-R/W GCP**. Note that these times are for our unoptimized code; a reduction in time by a constant factor would be easy to achieve with a less naive implementation of range sets, and, particularly in the **I-R/W** case, by including memoization. Relative relationships, however, are valid. Intraprocedural GCP takes time roughly proportional to nesting, but interprocedural GCP can take much longer due to procedure calls imbedded in loops, and recursion. Also note that, due to the stepping heuristics, the computation of each fixed-point actually requires very few iterations.

6 Conclusions and Further Work

We have demonstrated the efficacy of GCP in the context of the full C language. Moreover, we have shown that while a full interprocedural analysis certainly improves information for programs with constants passed via parameters, reasonable accuracy can be achieved with just a straightforward intraprocedural analysis for programs with simpler control structure. GCP also tends to locate more exact constants than CP.

A common criticism leveled at analyses based on abstract interpretation is the exponential cost of computing fixed points. GCP has also shown itself to

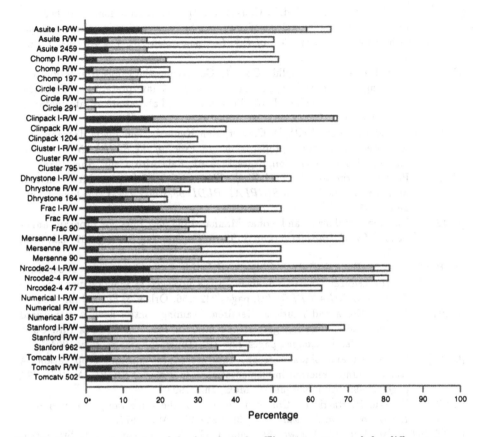

Fig. 7. Relevant ranges found for benchmarks. The percentages of the different types of ranges are show; black and dark gray are for exact constants (regular CP and extras found by GCP), light gray is bounded, and white for half-open. The remaining ranges are total. The number next to each benchmark name is the actual total number of relevant ranges in the program.

be quite reasonable in this respect; by stepping ranges that do not converge, fixed-points can be calculated in just a few iterations per loop. The inclusion of a simple heuristic, such as stepping the variable involved in the loop conditional first, permits rapid convergence without overly sacrificing quality of information.

We are also considering the effects of a few simple heuristics to enhance intraprocedural GCP. It should be possible to improve **naive** GCP by identifying the more common situations where GCP unnecessarily discards information in order to be safe, such as over selected library calls. The use of stepping also requires further examination; perhaps accuracy or speed can be improved with different heuristics. The effect of GCP on other analyses that use GCP information also remains to be examined: how often are ranges actually useful?

References

[Bou93]   François Bourdoncle. Abstract debugging of higher-order imperative languages. In *Proc. of SIGPLAN PLDI '93*, pages 46–55, Albuquerque, N. Mex., Jun. 1993.

[CC77]   Patrick Cousot and Radhia Cousot. Abstract interpretation: A unified lattice model for static analysis of programs by construction of approximations of fixpoints. In *Conf. Rec. of POPL-4*, pages 238–252, Los Angeles, Calif., Jan. 1977.

[CC92]   Patrick Cousot and Radhia Cousot. Comparing the galois connection and widening / narrowing approaches to abstract interpretation. Technical Report LIX/RR/92/09, Ecole Polytechnique Laboratoire d'Informatique, 91128 Palaiseau Cedex, France, Juin 1992.

[CCKT86] David Callahan, Keith D. Cooper, Ken Kennedy, and Linda Torczon. Interprocedural constant propagation. In *Proc. of the SIGPLAN '86 Symp. on Compiler Construction*, pages 152–161, Palo Alto, Calif., Jun. 1986.

[CH95]   Paul R. Carini and Michael Hind. Flow-sensitive interprocedural constant propagation. In *Proc. of SIGPLAN PLDI '95*, pages 23–31, La Jolla, Calif., Jun. 1995.

[DM81]   Nachum Dershowitz and Zohar Manna. Inference rules for program annotation. *IEEE Transactions on Software Engineering*, SE-7(2):207–222, Mar. 1981.

[EGH94]   Maryam Emami, Rakesh Ghiya, and Laurie J. Hendren. Context-sensitive interprocedural points-to analysis in the presence of function pointers. In *Proc. of SIGPLAN PLDI '94*, pages 242–256, Orlando, Flor., Jun. 1994.

[EH94]   Ana M. Erosa and Laurie J. Hendren. Taming control flow: A structured approach to eliminating goto statements. In *Proc. of the 1994 Intl. Conf. on Computer Languages*, pages 229–240, Toulouse, France, May 1994.

[GT93]   Dan Grove and Linda Torczon. Interprocedural constant propagation: A study of jump function implementations. In *Proc. of SIGPLAN PLDI '93*, pages 90–99, Albuquerque, N. Mex., Jun. 1993.

[Har77]   William H. Harrison. Compiler analysis of the value ranges for variables. *IEEE Trans. on Software Eng.*, 3(3):243–250, May 1977.

[HDE+92] L. Hendren, C. Donawa, M. Emami, G. Gao, Justiani, and B. Sridharan. Designing the McCAT compiler based on a family of structured intermediate representations. In *Proc. of the 5th Intl. Work. on Languages and Compilers for Parallel Computing*, number 757 in LNCS, pages 406–420, New Haven, Conn., Aug. 1992. Springer-Verlag. Publ. in 1993.

[HEGV93] Laurie J. Hendren, Maryam Emami, Rakesh Ghiya, and Clark Verbrugge. A practical context-sensitive interprocedural analysis framework for C compilers. ACAPS Tech. Memo 72, Sch. of Comp. Sci., McGill U., Montréal, Qué., Jul. 1993. In ftp://ftp-acaps.cs.mcgill.ca/pub/doc/memos.

[MS93]   Robert Metzer and Sean Stroud. Interprocedural constant propagation: An empirical study. *ACM Letters on Programming Languages and Systems*, 2(1–4):213–232, 1993.

[Pat95]   Jason R. C. Patterson. Accurate static branch prediction by value range propagation. In *Proc. of SIGPLAN PLDI '95*, pages 67–78, La Jolla, Calif., Jun. 1995.

[Sri92]   Bhama Sridharan. An analysis framework for the McCAT compiler. Master's thesis, McGill U., Montréal, Qué., Sep. 1992.

[WZ91]   Mark N. Wegman and F. Kenneth Zadeck. Constant propagation with conditional branches. *ACM Trans. on Programming Languages and Systems*, 13(2):181–210, Apr. 1991.

Structuring Decompiled Graphs

Cristina Cifuentes*

Department of Computer Science, University of Tasmania
GPO Box 252C, Hobart, Tas 7001, Australia
Email: C.N.Cifuentes@cs.utas.edu.au

Abstract. A structuring algorithm for arbitrary control flow graphs is presented. Graphs are structured into functional, semantical and structural equivalent graphs, without code replication or introduction of new variables. The algorithm makes use of a set of generic high-level language structures that includes different types of loops and conditionals. Gotos are used only when the graph cannot be structured with the structures in the generic set.

This algorithm is adequate for the control flow analysis required when decompiling programs, given that a pure binary program does not contain information on the high-level structures used by the initial high-level language program (i.e. before compilation). The algorithm has been implemented as part of the *dcc* decompiler, an i80286 decompiler of DOS binary programs, and has proved successful in its aim of structuring decompiled graphs.

1 Introduction

A decompiler is a software tool that reverses the compilation process by translating a pure binary input program to an equivalent high-level language (HLL) target program. The input program does not have symbolic information within it, and the HLL used to compile this binary program need not be the same as the target HLL produced by the decompiler.

Although decompilers have not been greatly studied in the literature, there are a variety of applications that could benefit from them, including the obvious maintenance of old code and recovery of lost source code, but also the debugging of binary programs, migration of applications to a new hardware environment [26], verification of generated code by the compiler [23], and translation of code written in an obsolete language.

When binary programs are decompiled, the control flow graph of the program is constructed and analyzed for data and control flow. Data flow analysis transforms the intermediate representation of the binary program into a higher level representation that resembles a high-level language. Control flow analysis determines the underlying structure of the program; that is, the high-level control structures used in each subroutine.

* This work was done while with the Queensland University of Technology in Brisbane, Australia. This research was partly funded by Australian Research Council (ARC) grant No. A49130261.

A structured control flow graph is a graph that can be decomposed into subgraphs that represent control structures of a high-level language. These subgraphs always have one entry point and one exit point. Unstructured graphs are generated by the use of goto statements in a program, such that the transfer of control leads to subgraphs with two or more entry points, division of the subgraphs representing a control structure due to an entry into the middle of the structure, or tail-recursive calls in languages such as Lisp [21] and Scheme [16]. Unstructured graphs can also be introduced by the optimizer phase of the compiler, when code motion is used. It is not hard to demonstrate that structured high-level languages that do not make use of the goto statement generate reducible graphs [18, 14].

During decompilation, a generic set of high-level control structures needs to be defined first in order to decompose a program's control flow graph into these fixed set of structures. The generic set of high-level structures should be general enough to cater for different control structures available in commonly used languages such as C, Pascal, Modula-2 and Fortran. Generic control structures will always include loops and conditionals. We distinguish different types of loops: pre-test loop (while()), post-test loop (repeat..until()), and infinite loop (endless loop). The for loop is a special case of the while() loop, so it is not considered a generic structure. Different types of conditionals must also be identified: 2-way conditionals are represented by if..then and if..then..else structures, and n-way conditionals are represented by case control structures. Goto statements are used only when the graph cannot be structured using the previous set of generic structures. This means that multiexit loops are structured as a loop with one real exit, and all other exits will make use of goto exits. As a general rule of thumb, it is always desirable to structure abnormal loops as multiexit loops rather than multientry loops. This is due to the fact that multientry loops are harder to understand and can produce irreducible graphs.

The rest of this paper is presented in the following way: §2 gives a brief introduction to the intermediate representation used in the *dcc* decompiler, §3 describes the order of application of the loop and conditional algorithms, §4 describes an algorithm to structure loops, §5 describes an algorithm to structure 2-way conditionals, §6 briefly mentions how code generation is done based on structured graphs, §7 mentions previous work done in the area and compares this approach to others, and §8 gives the summary and conclusions of this work.

2 Intermediate Representation of dcc

The intermediate representation of a binary program in *dcc* is in the form of a call graph with a control flow graph for each subroutine, and an intermediate language which has two levels: a low-level stage which is used initially when the program has not been analyzed, and a high-level stage that resembles a HLL [11]. The data flow analysis phase of the decompiler analyzes intermediate instructions to remove all references to low-level concepts such as condition codes and registers, and re-introduces high-level concepts such as expressions and parameter passing. The high-level instructions that are generated by this analysis are: asgn (assign), jcond (conditional jump), jmp (unconditional jump), call (subroutine call), and ret (subroutine return). No control structure instructions are restored by this phase. This phase preceeds the control flow analysis phase and is described in [10]. This paper concentrates on the control flow analysis phase.

We present a sample control flow graph in Fig. 1 with intermediate instruction information. The intermediate code has been analyzed by the data flow analysis phase, and without loss of generality, all variables have been given names for ease of understanding (names are normally given by the code generator). From observation of Fig. 1, there are several control structures: there is a nested **repeat** loop inside a **while()** loop, several 2-way conditionals (some belong to loops, others stand alone), and a short-circuit evaluated expression. This graph is used throughout the paper to illustrate the structuring algorithms. The convention used in all graphs with 2-way conditional nodes is the following: the right arrow is the true branch and the left arrow is the false branch.

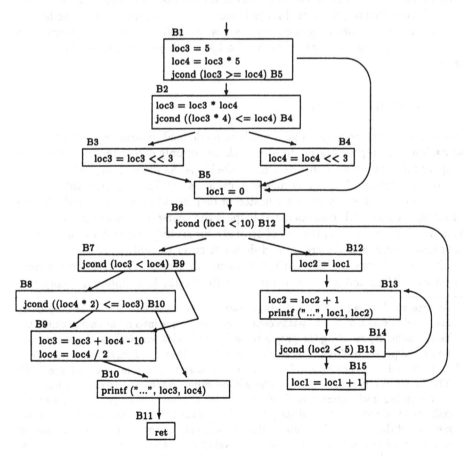

Fig. 1. Sample Control Flow Graph

3 Application Order

The structuring algorithms presented in the next sections determine the header, follow and latching nodes of subgraphs that represent high-level loops and 2-way structures. The header node is the entry node of a structure. The follow node is the first node that is executed after a possibly nested structure has finished. In the case of non-properly nested structures, the follow node is the one after the last execution of a nested structure. The latching node is the last node in a loop; the one that takes as immediate successor the header of a loop.

The algorithms presented in the next sections cannot be applied in a random order since they do not form a finite Church-Rosser system. For example, if node B6 in Fig. 1 is structured first as the header of a 2-way conditional, an if..then..else structure would be flagged for this node, and node B15 would have to use a goto jump to node B6 as it cannot be part of a loop (the header node of this loop would already belong to another structure, and hence it cannot belong to two different structures at the same nesting level). Therefore, loops are structured before 2-way conditionals to ensure the boolean condition that forms part of pre-tested or post-tested loops is part of the loop, rather than the header of a 2-way conditional subgraph. Once a 2-way conditional has been marked as being in the header or latching node of a loop, it is not considered for further structuring.

4 Structuring Loops

In order to structure loops, a loop needs to be defined in terms of a graph representation. This representation must be able to not only determine the extent of a loop, but also provide a nesting order for the loops. As pointed out by Hecht [14], the representation of a loop by means of cycles is too fine a representation since loops are not necessarily properly nested or disjoint. On the other hand, the use of strongly connected components as loops is too coarse a representation as there is no nesting order. Also, the use of strongly connected regions does not provide a unique coverage of the graph, and does not cover the entire graph.

Interval[2] theory and the derived sequence of graphs[3] $G^1 \ldots G^n$ was formulated by F.Allen and J.Cocke in the early 1970's [12, 1, 4]. Interval theory was

---

[2] An interval $I(h)$ is the maximal, single-entry subgraph in which h is the only entry node and in which all closed paths contain h. The unique interval node h is called the header node. By selecting the proper set of header nodes, graph G can be partitioned into a unique set of disjoint intervals $\mathcal{I} = \{I(h_1), I(h_2), \ldots, I(h_n)\}$, for some $n \geq 1$.

[3] The derived sequence of graphs, $G^1 \ldots G^n$ is based on the intervals of graph G. The first order graph, G^1, is G. The second order graph, G^2, is derived from G^1 by collapsing each interval in G^1 into a node. The immediate predecessors of the collapsed node are the immediate predecessors of the original header node which are not part of the interval. The immediate successors are all the immediate, non-interval successors of the original exit nodes. Intervals for G^2 are found and the process is repeated until a limit flow graph G^n is found. G^n has the property of being a single node or an irreducible graph.

used as an optimization technique for data flow analysis [2, 3, 5]. However, the use of intervals does provide a representation that satisfies the abovementioned conditions for loops: one loop per interval, and a nesting order provided by the derived sequence of graphs. This was first pointed out by Housel [15].

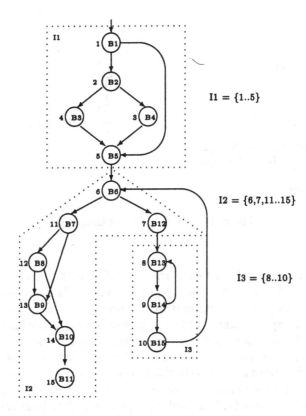

Fig. 2. Intervals of the Control Flow Graph of Fig. 1

Given an interval $I(h_j)$ with header h_j, there is a loop rooted at h_j if there is a back-edge to the header node h_j from a latching node $n_k \in I(h_j)$. Consider the graph in Fig. 2, which is the same graph from Fig. 1 without intermediate instruction information, and with intervals delimitered by dotted lines; nodes are numbered in reverse postorder. There are 3 intervals: I_1 rooted at basic block B1, I_2 rooted at node B6, and I_3 rooted at node B13.

In this graph, interval I_3 contains the loop (B14,B13) in its entirety, and interval I_2 contains the header of the loop (B15,B6), but its latching node is in interval I_3. If each of the intervals are collapsed into individual nodes, and the intervals of that new graph are found, the loop that was between intervals I_3 and I_2 must now belong to the same interval. Consider the derived sequence of graphs $G^2 \dots G^4$ in Fig. 3. In graph G^2, the loop between nodes I_3 and I_2 is in interval I_5 in its entirety. This loop represents the corresponding loop of nodes (B15,B6) in the initial graph. It is also noted that there are no more loops in these graphs, and that the initial graph is reducible since the trivial graph G^4 was derived by this process. It is noted that the length of the derived sequence is proportional to the maximum depth of nested loops in the initial graph.

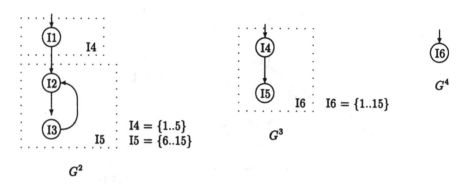

Fig. 3. Derived Sequence of Graphs $G^2 \ldots G^4$

Once a loop has been found, the type of loop (e.g. pre-tested, post-tested, endless) is determined by the type of header and latching nodes of the loop. A while() loop is characterized by a 2-way header node and a 1-way latching node, a repeat..until() is characterized by a 2-way latching node and a non-conditional header node, and a endless loop loop is characterized by a 1-way latching node and a non-conditional header node. Heuristics are used when other combinations of header/latching nodes are used. In our example, the loop (B15,B6) has a 2-way header node and a 1-way latching node, hence the loop is equivalent to a while(). In a similar way, the loop (B14,B13) has a 1-way header node and a 2-way latching node, hence it is equivalent to a repeat..until(). The nodes that belong to the loop are also flagged as being in a loop, in order to prevent nodes from belonging to two different loops; such as in overlapping, or multientry loops. In the case of nested loops, a node will be marked as belonging to the most nested loop it belongs to.

Finally, the follow of the loop, that is, the first node that is reached from the exit of the loop is determined. In the case of a while(), the follow node is the target node of the header that does not form part of the loop. In a repeat..until(), the follow node is the target node of the latching node that is not a back-edge. And in an endless loop, there could be no follow node if there are no exits from the loop, otherwise, the follow is the closest node to the loop (i.e. the smallest node in reverse postorder numbering).

Given a control flow graph $G = G^1$ with interval information, the derived sequence of graphs $G^1, \ldots, G^n$ of G, and the set of intervals of these graphs, $\mathcal{I}^1 \ldots \mathcal{I}^n$, an algorithm to find loops is as follows: each header of an interval in G^1 is checked for having a back-edge from a latching node that belongs to the same interval. If this happens, a loop has been found, so its type is determined, and the nodes that belong to it are marked. Next, the intervals of G^2, $\mathcal{I}^2$ are checked for loops, and the process is repeated until intervals in $\mathcal{I}^n$ have been checked. Whenever there is a potential loop (i.e. a header of an interval that has a predecessor with a back-edge) that has its header or latching node marked as belonging to another loop, the loop is disregarded as it belongs to an unstructured loop. These loops always generate goto jumps during code generation. In this algorithm no goto jumps and target labels are determined as this is done during the traversal of the graph during code generation. The complete algorithm is given in Fig. 4. This algorithm finds the loops in the appropriate nesting level, from innermost to outermost loop. The loop follow node is the first node that is reached once the loop is terminated. This node is determined during the loop analysis and used during code generation to traverse the tree of structures.

5 Structuring 2-way Conditionals

Both a single branch conditional (i.e. if..then) and an if..then..else conditional subgraph have a common follow node that has the property of being immediately dominated by the 2-way header node. Whenever these subgraphs are nested, they can have different follow nodes or share the same common follow node. Consider the graph in Fig. 5, which is the same graph from Fig. 1 without intermediate instruction information, and with immediate dominator[4] information. The nodes are numbered in reverse postorder.

In this graph there are six 2-way conditional nodes; namely, nodes 1, 2, 6, 9, 11, and 12. As seen during loop structuring (§4), a 2-way node that belongs to either the header or the latching node of a loop is marked as being part of the loop, and must therefore not be processed during 2-way conditional structuring. Hence, nodes 6 and 9 in Fig. 5 are not considered in this analysis. Whenever two or more conditionals are nested, it is always desirable to analyze the innermost nested conditional first, and then the outer ones. In the case of the conditionals at nodes 1 and 2, node 2 must be analyzed first than node 1 since it is nested in the subgraph headed by 1; in other words, the node that has a greater reverse postorder numbering needs to be analyzed first since it was last visited first in the depth first search traversal that numbered the nodes. In this example, both subgraphs share the common follow node 5; therefore, there is no node that is immediately dominated by node 2 (i.e. the inner conditional), but 5 is immediately dominated by 1 (i.e. the outer conditional), and this node is the follow node for both conditionals. Once the follow node has been determined, the type of the conditional can be known by checking whether one of the branches of the 2-way header node is the follow node; in which case, the subgraph is a single branching conditional, otherwise it is an if..then..else. In the case of nodes

---

[4] A node n_i dominates n_k if n_i is on every path from the header of the graph to n_k. It is said that n_i immediately dominates n_k if it is the closest dominator to n_k.

```
procedure loopStruct (G = (N, E, h))
/* Pre:  G¹ ... Gⁿ has been constructed.
 *       I¹ ... Iⁿ has been determined.
 *       ∀j ∈ {1...n} • Iⁱ = {I₁ⁱ(h_{j1}), ..., I_m^i(h_{jm})}
 *       ∀i,j • I_j^i(h_{ij}) is the jth interval of Gⁱ with header h_{ij}.
 * Post: all nodes of G that belong to a loop are marked.
 *       all loop header nodes have information on the type of loop and the
 *       latching node. */

for (Gⁱ := G¹ ... Gⁿ)
    for (all I_j^i(h_{ij}) ∈ Iⁱ)
        /* find latching node x */
        if ((∃x ∈ Nⁱ • (x, h_{ij}) ∈ Eⁱ) ∧ (inLoop(x) == False))
            for (all n ∈ loop (x, h_{ij}))
                inLoop(n) = True
            end for
            /* determine loop type */
            if (nodeType(x) == 2-way)
                if (nodeType(h_{ij}) == 1-way)
                    loopType(h_{ij}) = Post-tested
                else /* 2-way header node */
                    use heuristics to determine best type of loop
            else /* 1-way latching node */
                if (nodeType(h_{ij}) == 2-way)
                    loopType(h_{ij}) = Pre-Tested
                else
                    loopType(h_{ij}) = Endless
            end if
            /* determine loop follow */
            case (loopType(h_{ij}))
            Pre-Tested:
                if (inLoop(successor(h_{ij},1)))
                    loopFollow(h_{ij}) = successor(h_{ij},2)
                else
                    loopFollow(h_{ij}) = successor(h_{ij},1)
            Post-Tested:
                if (inLoop(successor(x,1)))
                    loopFollow(h_{ij}) = successor(x,2)
                else
                    loopFollow(h_{ij}) = successor(x,1)
            Endless:
                determine follow node (if any) by traversing all nodes in the loop
            end case
        end if
    end for
end for
end procedure
```

Fig. 4. Loop Structuring Algorithm

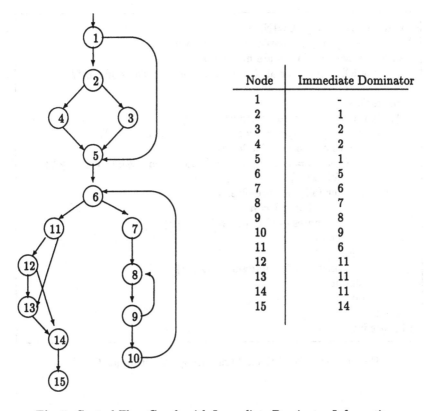

Node	Immediate Dominator
1	-
2	1
3	2
4	2
5	1
6	5
7	6
8	7
9	8
10	9
11	6
12	11
13	11
14	11
15	14

Fig. 5. Control Flow Graph with Immediate Dominator Information

11 and 12, node 12 is analyzed first and no follow node is determined since no node takes it as immediate dominator. This node is left in a list of unresolved nodes, because it can be nested in another conditional structure (whether fully nested or not). When node 11 is analyzed, nodes 12, 13, and 14 are possible candidates for follow node, since nodes 12 and 13 reach node 14; this last node is taken as the follow (i.e. the node that encloses the most number of nodes in a subgraph; the largest node, given that the subgraphs at nodes 11 and 12 are not properly nested). Node 12, that is in the list of unresolved follow nodes, is also marked as having a follow node of 14. It is seen from the graph that these two conditionals are not properly nested, and a goto jump can be used during code generation. A generalization of this example provides the algorithm to structure conditionals, and it is shown in Fig. 6.

N-way conditionals are structured in a similar way to 2-way conditionals. Nodes are traversed from bottom to top of the graph in order to find nested n-way conditionals first, followed by the outer ones. For each n-way node, a follow node is determined. This node will optimally have n in-edges coming from a path from the n succesor nodes of the n-way header node, and be immediately

```
procedure struct2Way (G=(N,E,h))
/* Pre: G is a graph numbered in reverse postorder.
 * Post: 2-way conditionals are marked in G.
 *       the follow node for all 2-way conditionals is determined. */

    unresolved = {}
    for (all nodes m ∈ N in descending order)
        if ((nodeType(m) == 2-way) ∧ (¬ isLoopHeader(m)) ∧
            (¬ isLoopLatchingNode(m)))
        if (∃ n • n = max{i | immedDom(i) = m ∧ #inEdges(i) ≥ 2})
            follow(m) = n
            for (all x ∈ unresolved)
                follow(x) = n
                unresolved = unresolved - {x}
            end for
        else
            unresolved = unresolved ∪ {m}
        end if
        end if
    end for
end procedure
```

Fig. 6. 2-way Conditional Structuring Algorithm for Graph G

dominated by such header node. The method is slightly more complex given the existance of more nodes in the structure. For more information refer to [9].

5.1 Compound Conditions

When structuring graphs in decompilation, not only the structure of the underlying structures is to be considered, but also the underlying intermediate instructions information. Most high-level languages allow for short-circuit evaluation of compound boolean conditions. In these languages, the generated control flow graphs for these conditional expressions become unstructured since an exit can be performed as soon as enough conditions have been checked and determined the expression is true or false as a whole. For example, if the expression x and y is compiled with short-circuit evaluation, and expression x is false, the whole expression becomes false as soon as x is evaluated and therefore the expression y is not evaluated. In a similar way, an x or y expression is partially evaluated if the expression x is true. Figure 7 shows the four different subgraph sets that arise from compound conditions during compilation. The top graphs represent the logical condition that is under consideration, and the bottom graphs represent the short-circuit evaluated graphs for each compound condition. In these graphs, t stands for the *then* node and e stands for the *else* node.

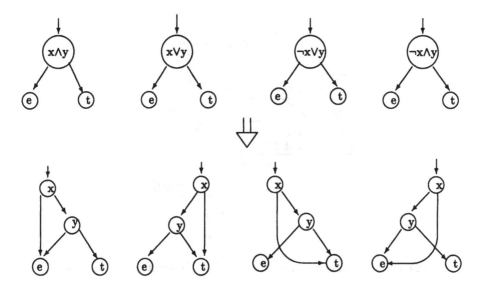

Fig. 7. Compound Conditional Graphs

During decompilation, whenever a subgraph of the form of the short-circuit evaluated graphs is found, it is checked for the following properties:

1. Nodes x and y are 2-way nodes.
2. Node y has only 1 in-edge.
3. Node y has a unique instruction; a conditional jump (jcond) high-level instruction.
4. Nodes x and y must branch to a common t or e node.

The first, second, and fourth properties are required in order to have an isomorphic subgraph to the bottom graphs given in Fig. 7, and the third property is required to determine that the graph represents a compound condition, rather than an abnormal conditional graph. Consider the subgraph of Fig. 1, in Fig. 8, with intermediate instruction information. Nodes B7 and B8 are 2-way nodes, node B8 has 1 in-edge, node B8 has a unique instruction (a jcond), and both the true branch of node B7 and the false branch of node B8 reach node B9; i.e. this subgraph is of the form ¬x ∧ y in Fig. 7.

The algorithm to structure compound conditionals makes use of a traversal from top to bottom of the graph, as the first condition in a compound conditional expression is higher up in the graph (i.e. it is tested first). For all 2-way nodes that are not a header or latching node of a loop, the **then** and **else** nodes are checked for a 2-way condition. If either of these nodes represents one high-level conditional instruction (jcond), and the node has no other entries (i.e. the only in-edge to this node comes from the header 2-way node), and the node forms one of the bottom 4 subgraphs illustrated in Fig. 7, these two nodes are merged into

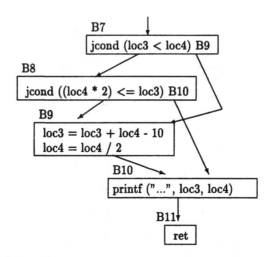

Fig. 8. Subgraph of Fig. 1 with Intermediate Instruction Information

a unique node that has the equivalent semantic meaning of the compound condition (i.e. depends on the structure of the subgraph), and the node is removed from the graph. This process is repeated until no more compound conditions are found (i.e. there could be 3 or more compound **ands** and **ors**, so the process is repeated with the same 2-way node until no more conditionals are found). The algorithm is omitted in this paper and is described in [9].

6 Code Generation from Structured Graphs

The code generation phase of a decompiler generates high-level language code from the intermediate representation of the program. Each procedure's graph is traversed according to the type of basic block and the control structures available in the graph. Basic blocks are checked for being the header of a control structure, in which case, appropriate code is generated for that structure, followed by a depth-first traversal of the nodes associated with the structure; that is, until the follow node is reached. Once code has been generated for the subgraph of a structure, the generation of code is continued with the follow node of the structure. Within a basic block, code is generated sequentially for each statement of the intermediate representation. Once code has been generated for a basic block, the block is marked as having been visited. If during code generation a marked node is reached again, the code for this node is not repeated (i.e. no code replication is used), but a unique label is placed on the first statement of this block, and a **goto** statement is used to reach it. In this way, **goto**s are generated only by the code generator, and no labels are placed on the graph on the earlier control flow analysis phase.

7 Previous Work

Most structuring algorithms have concentrated on the removal of goto statements from control flow graphs at the expense of introduction of new boolean variables [8, 29, 22, 28, 6, 13], code replication [17, 27, 29], the use of multilevel exits [7, 24], or the use of a set of high-level structures not available in commonly used languages [25]. None of these methods are applicable to a decompiler because: the introduction of new boolean variables modifies the semantics of the underlying program, as these variables did not form part of the original program; code replication modifies the structure of the program, as code that was written only once gets replicated one or more times; and the use of multilevel exits or high-level structures that are not available in most languages restricts the generality of the method and the number of languages in which the structured version of the program can be written in.

Lichtblau [19] presented a series of transformation rules to transform a control flow graph into a trivial graph by identifying subgraphs that represent high-level control structures; such as 2-way conditionals, sequence, loops, and multiexit loops. Whenever no rules were applicable to the graph, an edge was removed from the graph and a goto was generated in its place. This transformation system was proved to be finite Church-Rosser, thus the transformations can be applied in any order and the same final answer is reached. Lichtblau formalized the transformation system by introducing context-free flowgraph grammars, which are context-free grammars defined by production rules that transform one graph into another [20]. He proved that given a rooted context-free flowgraph grammar GG, it is possible to determine whether a flowgraph g can be derived from GG. Although the detection of control structures by means of graph transformations does not modify the semantics or functionality of the underlying program, Lichtblau's transformations do not take into account graphs generated from short-circuit evaluation languages, where the operands of a compound boolean condition are not all necessarily evaluated, and thus generate unstructured graphs according to this methodology.

In contrast, the structuring algorithms presented in this paper transform an arbitrary control flow graph into a functional, semantical and structural equivalent flow graph that is structured under a set of generic control structures available in most commonly used high-level languages, and that makes use of goto jumps whenever the graph cannot be structured with the generic structures. These algorithms take into account graphs generated by short-circuit evaluation, and thus do not generate unnecessary goto jumps for these subgraphs.

8 Summary and Conclusions

This paper describes a set of structuring algorithms for transforming arbitrary graphs generated by any imperative programming language, into functional, semantical and structural equivalent graphs, without the introduction of new variables or code replication. The algorithm is adequate for the analysis needed in the control flow analysis phase of a decompiler, and has been implemented as part of the *dcc* decompiler; a decompiler for the i286 and the DOS operating system [9]. This set of algorithms are shown to be non Church-Rosser with a counter example.

Structured graphs contain high-level language control structures. Unstructured graphs are introduced by the use of `gotos`, tail-recursion calls and by optimizations produced by the compiler. In a binary program, it is unknown what type of language or compiler was used on the original source program. This means that we cannot determine whether the graph is structured or not, and therefore we assume the general case of unstructured graphs.

The generic control structures that are considered by this structuring algorithm are: `if..then`, `if..then..else`, `case`, `while()`, `repeat..until()` and endless `loop` loops. Gotos are used only when the graph cannot be structured with any of the above structures. All other structures available in high-level languages (e.g. `for`, multiexit loops) can be modelled by a second structuring stage that is targeted at the language-specific control structures.

Acknowledgements and Future Work

I would like to thank Vishv Malhotra and the anonymous referees for suggestions on improving the presentation of this paper.

The *dcc* decompiler is being ported to the SPARC architecture and is supported by Sun Microsystems Laboratories and the Centre for Software Maintenance at the University of Queensland. For information on the status of the *dcc* decompiler, check: `http://crg.cs.utas.edu.au/dcc.html`

References

1. F.E. Allen. Control flow analysis. *SIGPLAN Notices*, 5(7):1–19, July 1970.
2. F.E. Allen. A basis for program optimization. In *Proc. IFIP Congress*, pages 385–390, Amsterdam, Holland, 1972. North-Holland Pub.Co.
3. F.E. Allen. Interprocedural data flow analysis. In *Proc. IFIP Congress*, pages 398–402, Amsterdam, Holland, 1974. North-Holland Pub.Co.
4. F.E. Allen and J. Cocke. Graph theoretic constructs for program control flow analysis. Technical Report RC 3923 (No. 17789), IBM, Thomas J. Watson Research Center, Yorktown Heights, New York, July 1972.
5. F.E. Allen and J. Cocke. A program data flow analysis procedure. *Communications of the ACM*, 19(3):137–147, March 1976.
6. Z. Ammarguellat. A control-flow normalization algorithm and its complexity. *IEEE Transactions on Software Engineering*, 18(3):237–251, March 1992.
7. B.S. Baker. An algorithm for structuring flowgraphs. *Journal of the ACM*, 24(1):98–120, January 1977.
8. C. Böhm and G. Jacopini. Flow diagrams, Turing machines and languages with only two formation rules. *Communications of the ACM*, 9(5):366–371, May 1966.
9. C. Cifuentes. *Reverse Compilation Techniques*. PhD dissertation, Queensland University of Technology, School of Computing Science, July 1994.

10. C. Cifuentes. Interprocedural dataflow decompilation. In print: Journal of Programming Languages, 1996.

11. C. Cifuentes and K.J. Gough. Decompilation of binary programs. *Software – Practice and Experience*, 25(7):811–829, July 1995.

12. J. Cocke. Global common subexpression elimination. *SIGPLAN Notices*, 5(7):20–25, July 1970.

13. A.M. Erosa and L.J. Hendren. Taming control flow: A structured approach to eliminating goto statements. In *Proceedings of the International Conference on Computer Languages*, Université Paul Sabatier, Toulouse, France, May 1994. IEEE Computer Society.

14. M.S. Hecht. *Flow Analysis of Computer Programs*. Elsevier North-Holland, Inc, 52 Vanderbilt Avenue, New York, New York 10017, 1977.

15. B.C. Housel. *A Study of Decompiling Machine Languages into High-Level Machine Independent Languages*. PhD dissertation, Purdue University, Computer Science, August 1973.

16. G.L. Steele Jr. and G.J. Sussman. Design of a LISP-based microprocessor. *Communications of the ACM*, 23(11):628–645, November 1980.

17. D.E. Knuth and R.W. Floyd. Notes on avoiding go to statements. *Information Processing Letters*, 1(1):23–31, 1971.

18. S.R. Kosaraju. Analysis of structured programs. *Journal of Computer and System Sciences*, 9(3):232–255, 1974.

19. U. Lichtblau. Decompilation of control structures by means of graph transformations. In *Proceedings of the International Joint Conference on Theory and Practice of Software Development (TAPSOFT)*, Berlin, 1985.

20. U. Lichtblau. Recognizing rooted context-free flowgraph languages in polynomial time. In G. Rozenberg H. Ehrig, H.J. Kreowski, editor, *Graph Grammars and their application to Computer Science*, number 532 in Lecture Notes in Computer Science, pages 538–548. Springer-Verlag, 1991.

21. J. McCarthy. Recursive functions of symbolic expressions and their computation by machine, part I. *Communications of the ACM*, 3(4):184–195, April 1960.

22. G. Oulsnam. Unravelling unstructured programs. *The Computer Journal*, 25(3):379–387, 1982.

23. D.J. Pavey and L.A. Winsborrow. Demonstrating equivalence of source code and PROM contents. *The Computer Language*, 36(7):654–667, 1993.

24. L. Ramshaw. Eliminating go to's while preserving program structure. *Journal of the ACM*, 35(4):893–920, October 1988.

25. M. Sharir. Structural analysis: A new approach to flow analysis in optimizing compilers. *Computer Languages*, 5:141–153, 1980.

26. R.L. Sites, A. Chernoff, M.B. Kirk, M.P. Marks, and S.G. Robinson. Binary translation. *Communications of the ACM*, 36(2):69–81, February 1993.

27. M.H. Williams. Generating structured flow diagrams: the nature of unstructuredness. *The Computer Journal*, 20(1):45–50, 1977.

28. M.H. Williams and G.Chen. Restructuring Pascal programs containing goto statements. *The Computer Journal*, 28(2):134–137, 1985.

29. M.H. Williams and H.L. Ossher. Conversion of unstructured flow diagrams to structured form. *The Computer Journal*, 21(2):161–167, 1978.

Non-monotone Fixpoint Iterations
to Resolve Second Order Effects

Alfons Geser[1], Jens Knoop[1], Gerald Lüttgen[2] *,
Oliver Rüthing[3], and Bernhard Steffen[1]

[1] Fakultät für Mathematik und Informatik, Universität Passau,
Innstraße 33, D–94032 Passau, Germany
[2] Dept. of Computer Science, N.C. State University, Raleigh, NC 27695-8206, USA
[3] Institut für Informatik und Praktische Mathematik, Christian-Albrechts-Universität,
Preußerstraße 1–9, D–24105 Kiel, Germany

Abstract. We present a new *fixpoint theorem* which guarantees the existence and the finite computability of the least common solution of a countable system of recursive equations over a *wellfounded* domain. The functions are only required to be *increasing* and *delay-monotone*, the latter being a property much weaker than monotonicity. We hold that wellfoundedness is a natural condition as it guarantees termination of every fixpoint computation algorithm. Our fixpoint theorem covers, under the wellfoundedness condition, all the known 'synchronous' versions of fixpoint theorems. To demonstrate its power and versatility we contrast an application in *data flow analysis*, where known versions are applicable as well, to a practically relevant application in *program optimization*, which due to its second order effects, requires the full strength of our new theorem. In fact, the new theorem is central for establishing the optimality of the *partial dead code elimination* algorithm considered, which is implemented in the new release of the Sun SPARCompiler[4] language systems.

1 Motivation and Related Work

Many practically relevant problems in computer science can be characterized by means of the least common solution of a system of *recursive equations*

$$x = f_1(x)$$
$$\vdots$$
$$x = f_n(x)$$

where $\mathcal{F} =_{df} \{f_k : D \to D \mid 1 \leq k \leq n\}$ is a family of *monotone* functions on a *wellfounded partial order* $\langle D; \sqsubseteq \rangle$. Solving this system of equations is equivalent to the computation of a fixpoint of $\mathcal{F}$, i.e. a *common fixpoint* $x = f_k(x)$ of all f_k. A typical

---

* The author is supported by the German Academic Exchange Service under grant D/95/09026 (Doktorandenstipendium HSP II/ AUFE).

[4] SPARCompiler is a registered trademark of SPARC International, Inc., and is licensed exclusively to Sun Microsystems, Inc.

iteration algorithm starts with the initial value $\perp$, the smallest element of D, and successively updates the value of x applying the functions f_k in an arbitrary order, so as to approximate the least fixpoint of $\mathcal{F}$. People speak of a *chaotic iteration*.

The origin of fixpoint theorems in computer science dates back to the fundamental work of Tarski [Tar55]. Tarski's theorem considers a monotone function and guarantees the existence of its least fixpoint with respect to a complete partial order. This setup, however, turned out to be too restrictive for a lot of practically relevant applications which led to a number of generalizations. See [LNS82] for a survey of the history of fixpoint theory.

Vector iteration [Rob76] provides such a generalization, where one computes the least fixpoint $\mathbf{x} = (x^1, \ldots, x^m) \in D^m$ of a monotone vector function $\mathbf{f} = (f^1, \ldots, f^m)$. Liberalizing Tarski's iteration $\mathbf{x}_0 = \perp, \mathbf{x}_1 = \mathbf{f}(\mathbf{x}_0), \mathbf{x}_2 = \mathbf{f}(\mathbf{x}_1), \ldots$, where $\mathbf{x}_i$ denotes the value of $\mathbf{x}$ after the i-th iteration, one may choose $\mathbf{x}_0 = \perp, \mathbf{x}_1 = \mathbf{f}_{J_0}(\mathbf{x}_0), \mathbf{x}_2 = \mathbf{f}_{J_1}(\mathbf{x}_1), \ldots$, where $J_i \subseteq \{1, \ldots, n\}$ and the k-th component $\mathbf{f}_{J_i}(\mathbf{x}_i)^k$ of $\mathbf{f}_{J_i}(\mathbf{x}_i)$ is $f^k(\mathbf{x}_i)$ if $k \in J_i$ and $\mathbf{x}_i^k$ otherwise. Intuitively, at each step i the set J_i denotes the indices k of the components which are updated. It is known that a *fairness condition* for the J_i is mandatory. Considering the vectors $\mathbf{x}$ as objects and the update operations $\mathbf{f}_J$ as functions, we have a clear instance of the chaotic iteration above (see also Section 3). Recent contributions to fixpoint theory provide efficient strategies for vector iteration, e.g. by using demand driven evaluation strategies (cf. [VWL94, Jør94]).

The vector approach has been further generalized towards *asynchronous iterations* [Bau78, Cou77, ÜD89, Wei93], where $\mathbf{f}_{J_i}$ may use components of a choice of earlier vectors $\mathbf{x}_j$, with $j \le i$, of the iteration.

Despite its power the vector iteration approach turns out too restrictive in two aspects. First, the functions involved in the fixpoint iteration may be such that they cannot be regarded as components of a single function f. To our knowledge, the only serious attack to this problem has been made by the Cousots [CC79]. The common fixpoints of a family $\mathcal{F} =_{df} (f_k)_{k \in N}$ of monotonic functions are described by iterations, given that each pair f_k, $f_{k'}$ commutes: $f_k(f_{k'}(x)) = f_{k'}(f_k(x))$ for all $x \in D$.

Second, and even worse, program transformations may have what Rosen, Wegman and Zadeck [RWZ88] call *second order effects*. Typically, program transformations are not idempotent; one transformation may have a strong impact on the profitability of another transformation; often the transformation functions involved are no longer monotone. Then none of the known fixpoint theorems apply.

In this paper we offer a new fixpoint theorem which does without monotonicity. Given $d \sqsubseteq d'$, monotonicity amounts to show $f_k(d) \sqsubseteq f_k(d')$. Instead, we allow that the expression $f_k(d')$ may be replaced by $f_j(d')$ for any j, and even by some *arbitrary composition* of functions applied to d'. If the functions are increasing, this task becomes the easier to solve, the longer the compositions are.

We require only two very weak conditions for technical convenience. First, we require that the underlying domain is *wellfounded*, a condition which is reasonable in practice, because it means termination of the iteration. In fact we are confident that wellfoundedness is not essential if one can afford nontermination. Second, we require that all functions in $\mathcal{F}$ are *increasing*, i.e. $x \sqsubseteq f_k(x)$ holds for all $k \in \mathbb{N}$. This condition is not really restrictive, as we will show (cf. Section 2 and 3).

Our fixpoint theorem is applicable to an arbitrary countable *family of functions* $\mathcal{F} =_{df} \{f_k : D \to D \mid k \in \mathbb{N}\}$ on a wellfounded partial order $\langle D; \sqsubseteq \rangle$: Under the above mentioned premises our theorem guarantees the existence of a least common fixpoint of $\mathcal{F}$, which is reached eventually by any *fair* chaotic iteration.

The remainder of the paper is structured as follows. We present the new fixpoint theorem in Section 2. In Section 3 we show that *vector iterations* are a special case of chaotic iterations. Section 4 demonstrates the power of our theorem by giving a classical application in terms of a data flow analysis algorithm, and by treating a problem beyond the scope of classical fixpoint theorems: the proof of the optimality of a program optimization for *partial dead code elimination* (cf. [KRS94b]), which is composed of program transformations with second order effects. This algorithm is implemented in Version 4.0 of the Sun SPARCompiler language systems to be released at the end of 1995, which underlines the practical relevance of the new fixpoint theorem. Section 5 contains our conclusions and directions to future work.

Appendix A finally contains all technical proofs of the paper.

2   The Fixpoint Theorem

In this section we present our new fixpoint theorem guaranteeing that a family of functions, $\mathcal{F} =_{df} (f_k)_{k \in \mathbb{N}}$, has a least common fixpoint $\mu\mathcal{F}$, together with a corresponding 'generic' terminating algorithm. This requires the following basic notions.

A *partial order* $\langle D; \sqsubseteq \rangle$ is a set D together with a reflexive, antisymmetric, and transitive binary relation $\sqsubseteq \subseteq D \times D$. A sequence $(d_i)_{i \in \mathbb{N}}$ of elements $d_i \in D$ is called an *(ascending) chain* if $\forall i \in \mathbb{N}.\ d_i \sqsubseteq d_{i+1}$. A chain $T =_{df} (d_i)_{i \in \mathbb{N}}$ is *stationary* if $\{d_i \mid i \in \mathbb{N}\}$ is finite. The partial order relation $\sqsubseteq$ is called *wellfounded* if every chain is stationary. A function $f : D \to D$ on D is *increasing* if $d \sqsubseteq f(d)$ for all $d \in D$, and *monotone* if $\forall d, d' \in D.\ d \sqsubseteq d' \Rightarrow f(d) \sqsubseteq f(d')$. If $\mathcal{F} =_{df} (f_k)_{k \in \mathbb{N}}$ is a family of functions and $s = (s_1, \dots, s_n) \in \mathbb{N}^*$ then f_s is defined by the composition $f_s =_{df} f_{s_n} \circ \cdots \circ f_{s_1}$.

The following notions are central for dealing with fixpoint iterations of a family of functions.

Definition 1 Strategy, Chaotic Iteration Sequence and Fairness. Let $\langle D; \sqsubseteq \rangle$ be a partial order and $\mathcal{F} =_{df} (f_k)_{k \in \mathbb{N}}$ be a family of increasing functions $f_k : D \to D$. A *strategy* is any function $\gamma : \mathbb{N} \to \mathbb{N}$. A strategy γ and an element $d \in D$ induce a *chaotic iteration* $f_\gamma(d) = (d_i)_{i \in \mathbb{N}}$ of elements $d_i \in D$ inductively defined by $d_0 = d$ and $d_{i+1} = f_{\gamma(i)}(d_i)$. A strategy γ is called *fair* iff

$$\forall i, k \in \mathbb{N}.\ (f_k(d_i) \neq d_i \text{ implies } \exists j > i.\ d_j \neq d_i)$$

Fixpoint theorems usually require that the considered functions are monotone. In practice, however, functions are often *not* monotone, but satisfy the following weaker notion.

Definition 2 Delay-Monotonicity. Let $\langle D; \sqsubseteq \rangle$ be a partial order and $\mathcal{F} =_{df} (f_k)_{k \in \mathbb{N}}$ be a family of functions $f_k : D \to D$. Then $\mathcal{F}$ is called *delay-monotone*, if for all $k \in \mathbb{N}$:

$$d \sqsubseteq d' \text{ implies } \exists s \in \mathbb{N}^* . f_k(d) \sqsubseteq f_s(d')$$

If every f_k is a *monotone* function in the usual sense, then $\mathcal{F}$ is delay-monotone. But note that delay-monotonicity in general does *not* carry over to proper subsets of $\mathcal{F}$.

Now we are prepared for our main result, which, in particular, yields that $\bigsqcup f_\gamma(\perp)$ is independent of the choice of γ.

Theorem 3 Chaotic Fixpoint Iterations. *Let $\langle D; \sqsubseteq \rangle$ be a wellfounded partial order with least element $\perp$, $\mathcal{F} =_{df} (f_k)_{k \in \mathbb{N}}$ a delay-monotone family of increasing functions, and $\gamma : \mathbb{N} \to \mathbb{N}$ a fair strategy. Then the least common fixpoint $\mu\mathcal{F}$ of $\mathcal{F}$ exists and is given by $\bigsqcup f_\gamma(\perp)$. In particular, $\mu\mathcal{F}$ is always reached within a finite number of iteration steps.*

Note that the following counterexample shows that "increasing" is essential. Let $\perp \sqsubseteq a$, and $f_1(\perp) = f_1(a) = \perp$, $f_2(\perp) = f_2(a) = a$, both monotone, but f_1 not increasing. Indeed, f_1 and f_2 have no common fixpoints.

Theorem 3 suggests an iterative strategy for computing the least fixpoint of $\mathcal{F}$. One defines $\gamma(i)$ at step i during the run of the algorithm. Whenever d_i is not yet a fixpoint of $\mathcal{F}$, i.e. there is some $k \in \mathbb{N}$ where $f_k(d_i)$ is strictly greater than d_i, one chooses $\gamma(i) = k$ for an arbitrary such k. This idea is illustrated in the nondeterministic skeleton algorithm presented in Figure 1.

```
d := ⊥;
while ∃ k ∈ IN. d ≠ f_k(d) do
    choose k ∈ IN where d ⊏ f_k(d) in
        d := f_k(d)
    ni
od
```

Fig. 1. The Nondeterministic Skeleton Algorithm

3 Special Case: Vector Iterations

Let $\langle C; \sqsubseteq_C \rangle$ be a wellfounded partial order and $D = C^n$ for some $n \in \mathbb{N}$, ordered by the pointwise extension $\sqsubseteq$ of $\sqsubseteq_C$. Now let $f : D \to D$ be a monotone function. Instead of iterating $d_1 = f(\perp), d_2 = f(d_1), \ldots$ according to Tarski's theorem, one may pass over to a dissection of f to its components, f^k, i.e. $f(d) = (f^1(d), \ldots, f^n(d))$ and perform selective updates. Here and in the sequel we use an upper index i at a vector of length n to select its i-th component. A *vector iteration* is an iteration of the form $d_1 = f_{J_0}(\perp), d_2 = f_{J_1}(d_1), \ldots$, where $J_i \subseteq \{1, \ldots, n\}$ and

$$f_J(d)^i =_{df} \begin{cases} f^i(d) & \text{if } i \in J \\ d^i & \text{otherwise} \end{cases}$$

performs a selective update of the components specified by J. The set of common fixpoints of the function family $\mathcal{F} =_{df} \{f_J \mid J \subseteq \{1, \dots, n\}\}$ is equal to the set of fixpoints of f. Note that each f_J is monotone since f is monotone.

Now let us demonstrate that the vector approach is modelled conveniently in our setting. To this end, we generalize the notion of a *strategy* to that of a *set strategy*. A *set strategy* is any function $\gamma : \mathbb{N} \to \mathfrak{P}(\{1, \dots, n\})$. The intended meaning being that $\gamma(i)$ yields a set J_i of indices in $\{1, \dots, n\}$ of components to be updated at step i. A set strategy is called *fair*, iff

$$\forall i \in \mathbb{N}, J \subseteq \mathbb{N}.(f_J(d_i) \neq d_i \text{ implies } \exists j > i.\, d_j \neq d_i)$$

The following result shows that for a *monotone* vector function f, every chaotic iteration sequence is a chain.

Lemma 4 Vector Iterations. *Let $\langle C; \sqsubseteq_C \rangle$ be a wellfounded partial order with least element $\perp_C$, let $n \in \mathbb{N}$, and let $D = C^n$ be ordered by the pointwise extension $\sqsubseteq$ of $\sqsubseteq_C$. Let $f = (f^1, \dots, f^n)$ be a monotone function on D, and let $\mathcal{F} =_{df} \{f_J \mid J \subseteq \{1, \dots, n\}\}$ with functions $f_J : D \to D$ as defined above and $\gamma : \mathbb{N} \to \mathfrak{P}(\{1, \dots, n\})$ be a set strategy. Then every chaotic iteration $f_\gamma(\perp)$ is a chain.*

Without loss of generality we may assume that D is the smallest set that contains $\perp$ and is closed under $\mathcal{F}$ and $\bigsqcup$. Then increasingness means exactly that every iteration yields a chain. In other words, for vector iterations the increasingness property is no real restriction.

The following corollary is a special case of Theorem 3 for vector iterations and a consequence of Lemma 4. In particular, if $|\mathcal{F}| = 1$ our corollary reduces to Tarski's theorem in the case of wellfounded partial orders.

Corollary 5 Chaotic Vector Iterations. *Let $\langle C; \sqsubseteq_C \rangle$ be a wellfounded partial order with least element $\perp_C$, let $n \in \mathbb{N}$, and let $D = C^n$ be ordered by the pointwise extension $\sqsubseteq$ of $\sqsubseteq_C$. Let $f = (f^1, \dots, f^n)$ be a monotone function on D, and let $\mathcal{F} =_{df} \{f_J \mid J \subseteq \{1, \dots, n\}\}$, and γ be a fair set strategy. Then $\bigsqcup f_\gamma(\perp)$ is the least fixpoint $\mu\mathcal{F}$ of $\mathcal{F}$. In particular, $\mu\mathcal{F} = \mu f$, and it is always reached within a finite number of iteration steps.*

4 Applications

In this section we demonstrate our Fixpoint Theorem 3 by proving the correctness and termination of a workset algorithm for *data flow analysis*, and by establishing terminating optimal *program optimization* on the basis of program transformations with second order effects. Whereas the first application can already be handled by Corollary 5, which reflects the scope of classical vector iteration approaches as they are common in practice, the second application requires the full strength of our main Theorem 3, as the component transformations of the optimization, the algorithm for *partial dead code elimination* of [KRS94b], are not even monotone on the relevant domain. Here, the new theorem is central for establishing the optimality of this algorithm, which is implemented in Version 4.0 of the Sun SPARCompiler language systems to be released at the end of 1995.

4.1 Data Flow Analysis: Workset Algorithms

Data flow analysis (DFA) is concerned with the static analysis of programs in order to support the generation of efficient object code by "optimizing" compilers (cf. [Hec77, MJ81]). For imperative languages, it provides information about the program states that may occur at a given program point during execution. Usually, this information is computed by means of some iterative workset algorithm, which can elegantly be modelled by the vector iteration approach.

In DFA and program optimization (cf. Section 4.2) it is common to represent programs as *directed flow graphs* $G = (N, E, \mathbf{s}, \mathbf{e})$ with node set N and edge set E. Nodes $n \in N$ represent the statements, edges $(n, m) \in E$ the nondeterministic branching structure of the program under consideration, and $\mathbf{s}$ and $\mathbf{e}$ the unique *start node* and *end node* of G, which are assumed to possess no predecessors and successors, respectively. Moreover, $pred_G(n) =_{df} \{ m \mid (m, n) \in E \}$ and $succ_G(n) =_{df} \{ m \mid (n, m) \in E \}$ denote the set of all immediate predecessors and successors of a node n, respectively. Finally, every node $n \in N$ is assumed to lie on a path from $\mathbf{s}$ to $\mathbf{e}$, i.e. every node $n \in N$ is reachable from $\mathbf{s}$, and $\mathbf{e}$ is reachable from every node $n \in N$.

Theoretically wellfounded are DFAs that are based on *abstract interpretation* (cf. [CC77, Mar93]). The point of this approach is to replace the "full" semantics of a program by a simpler more abstract version, which is tailored to deal with a specific problem. Usually, the abstract semantics is specified by means of a *local semantic functional*

$$[\ ] : N \to (\mathcal{C} \to \mathcal{C})$$

which gives abstract meaning to every program statement in terms of a monotone (or even continuous) transformation function on a wellfounded partial order $\langle \mathcal{C}; \sqsubseteq \rangle$ with least element $\bot$, whose elements express the DFA-information of interest.

Given a program G and a local abstract semantics $[\ ]$, the goal of DFA is to annotate the program points of G with DFA-information that properly reflect the run-time behaviour of G with respect to the problem under consideration. Formally, this annotation is defined by the least solution of Equation System 6 which specifies the consistency between pre-conditions of the statements of G expressed in terms of $\mathcal{C}$ with respect to some start information $c_0 \in \mathcal{C}$. This annotation is known as the solution of the *minimal fixpoint (MFP)* approach in the sense of Kam and Ullman [KU77].

Equation System 6.

$$\mathbf{pre}(n) = \begin{cases} c_0 & \text{if } n = \mathbf{s} \\ \bigsqcup \{ [\, m\,](\mathbf{pre}(m)) \mid m \in pred_G(n) \} & \text{otherwise} \end{cases}$$

In practice the *MFP*-solution, which we denote by $\mathbf{pre}_{c_0}$, is computed by means of some iterative workset algorithm (see Figure 2).

We will see that termination and correctness in this approach are a consequence of Corollary 5. To begin with, let $G = (N, E, \mathbf{s}, \mathbf{e})$ be the flow graph under consideration, and let $[\ ] : N \to (\mathcal{C} \to \mathcal{C})$ be a local abstract semantics, such that all semantic functions are monotone. Without loss of generality we identify in the following the

```
pre[s] := c₀;
forall n ∈ N\{s} do pre[n] := ⊥ od;
workset := N;
while workset ≠ ∅ do
    choose n ∈ workset in
        workset := workset\{ n };
        new := pre[n] ⊔ ⊔{[ m ](pre[m]) | m ∈ pred_G(n)};
        if new ⊐ pre[n] then
            pre[n] := new;
            workset := workset ∪ succ_G(n)
        fi
    ni
od
```

Fig. 2. A Workset Algorithm

set of nodes of N with the set of natural numbers $\{1, \ldots, n\}$, where n denotes the number of nodes of N.

Now let us define $D =_{df} C^n$ equipped with the pointwise extension of $\sqsubseteq$. One easily verifies that D is a wellfounded partial order. A value $d = (d^1, \ldots, d^n)$ represents an annotation of the flow graph where the value d^k is assigned to node k.

For every node k of the flow graph we define a function $f^k : D \to C$ by

$$f^k(d^1, \ldots, d^n) =_{df} d'^k$$

where

$$d'^k = d^k \sqcup \bigsqcup \{[m](d^m) \mid m \in pred_G(k)\}$$

Intuitively, f^k describes the effect of a computation of the local semantics at node k. The following lemma states that the DFA problem is modelled correctly.

Lemma 7. *For all $d \in D$ we have: d is a solution of Equation System 6 if and only if d is a fixpoint of $f =_{df} (f^1, \ldots, f^n)$.*

The workset algorithm of Figure 2 follows the general pattern of the nondeterministic skeleton algorithm of Figure 1 with $\mathcal{F} = \{f_{\{k\}} \mid 1 \leq k \leq n\}$. It profits from a set *workset* of indices which satisfies the invariant: *workset* $\supseteq \{k \mid f_{\{k\}}(d) \neq d\}$. One easily verifies that f is monotone. Hence the premises of Corollary 5 are satisfied and we obtain the following theorem.

Theorem 8 Correctness and Termination. *Every run of the workset algorithm terminates with the MFP-solution pre_{c_0}.*

4.2 Program Optimization: Partial Dead Code Elimination

In this section we demonstrate an application of the Chaotic Fixpoint Iteration Theorem 3 in program optimization by proving the optimality of the *partial dead code elimination* algorithm of [KRS94b]. Intuitively, an assignment in a program is *dead* if its left hand side variable is dead immediately after its execution, i.e., if on every program continuation reaching the end of the program the first use of this variable is preceded by a redefinition of it. Correspondingly, an assignment is *partially dead*, if it is dead along some program paths reaching the end of the program.

Conceptually, the elimination of partially dead occurrences of an assignment pattern α (for short: partially dead α-occurrences) can be decomposed into two steps. First, moving them as far as possible in the direction of the control flow, and second, removing all dead α-occurrences. In order to preserve the program semantics, both the sinking and the elimination steps must be *admissible*. This is defined in full detail in [KRS94b]. So, we here restrict the presentation to those parts that are essential for Theorem 3.

The relevance of Theorem 3 for partial dead code elimination stems from the fact that assignment sinking and elimination steps in general have *second order effects*, i.e. they usually enable assignment sinking and elimination steps for other assignment patterns. For example, eliminating the partially dead occurrences of some assignment pattern is often the premise that occurrences of other assignment patterns can be eliminated at all. In [KRS94b] this is taken care of by repeatedly applying admissible assignment sinking and elimination steps to the assignment patterns of the argument program until the program stabilizes, i.e. until a fixpoint is reached. The correctness of this iterative approach is a consequence of Theorem 3, as we are going to show in the remainder of this section, where we consider an arbitrary, but fixed program G.

For a program G', we will write $G' \vdash_{se} G''$ if the flow graph G'' results from G' by applying an admissible assignment sinking or elimination transformation. We denote the set of all admissible assignment sinking and dead code elimination functions by S and $\mathcal{E}$, respectively. Additionally, we abbreviate $S \cup \mathcal{E}$ by $\mathcal{T}$. It consists of all functions $f_{G_1,G_2} : \mathcal{G} \rightarrow \mathcal{G}$ defined by

$$\forall G' \in \mathcal{G}. \; f_{G_1,G_2}(G') =_{df} \begin{cases} G_2 & \text{if } G' = G_1 \\ G' & \text{otherwise} \end{cases}$$

where $G_1, G_2 \in \mathcal{G}$ and $G_1 \vdash_{se} G_2$. Alternatively to $f(G') = G''$ we will also write $G' \vdash_{se}^{f} G''$. Then,

$$\mathcal{G} =_{df} \{ G' \mid G \vdash_{se}^{*} G' \}$$

denotes the *universe* of programs resulting from G by partial dead code elimination.

In order to compare the quality of different programs in $\mathcal{G}$, we introduce the relation "better" between programs of $\mathcal{G}$. Note that this relation is reflexive. In fact, *at least as good* would be the more precise but uglier notion.

Definition 9 Optimality.

1. Let $G', G'' \in \mathcal{G}$. Then G' is *better* than G'', in signs $G'' \sqsubseteq G'$, if and only if for every assignment pattern α and every program path p leading from the start node to the end node of the argument program there are at most as many occurrences of α in G' as in G''.[5]

2. $G^* \in \mathcal{G}$ is *optimal* if and only if G^* is better than any other program in $\mathcal{G}$.

---

[5] Partial dead code elimination preserves the branching structure of the argument program. Hence, starting from a path in G, we can easily identify corresponding paths in G' and G''.

It is easy to check that the relation $\lesssim$ is reflexive, transitive, and wellfounded. Unfortunately, it is not antisymmetric. Hence, there may be several programs being optimal in the sense of Definition 9. In order to apply Theorem 3, we thus consider the partial order $\vdash_{se}^*$ instead of $\lesssim$, but we are going to reconsider relation $\lesssim$ subsequently (cf. Theorem 18).

In addition to S and $\mathcal{E}$, we define the set of maximal assignment sinkings and eliminations, which are the functions involved in the partial dead code elimination algorithm of [KRS94b]. A function $f_{G_1,G_2} \in S$ $(\mathcal{E})$ is called *maximal*, if for all functions $f_{G_1,G_3} \in S$ $(\mathcal{E})$ there is a function $f_{G_3,G_2} \in \mathcal{T}$ with $f_{G_1,G_2} = f_{G_3,G_2} \circ f_{G_1,G_3}$. The set of all maximal sinking and elimination functions are denoted by S^{max} and $\mathcal{E}^{max}$, respectively, and $\mathcal{T}^{max} \subseteq \mathcal{T}$ denotes the union of S^{max} and $\mathcal{E}^{max}$. Finally, we denote the set of (maximal) admissible assignment sinkings and eliminations with respect to an assignment pattern α by $\mathcal{T}_\alpha$ and $\mathcal{T}_\alpha^{max}$. As a first result we then obtain the Dominance Lemma 10, which follows immediately from the definitions of $\mathcal{T}_\alpha^{max}$ and $\mathcal{T}_\alpha$.

Lemma 10 Dominance. *Let $G_1 \in \mathcal{G}$, let $f \in \mathcal{T}_\alpha^{max}$ and $g \in \mathcal{T}_\alpha$ be corresponding functions, i.e. both sinking or both elimination functions, let $G_1 \vdash_{se}^g G_2$, and $G_1 \vdash_{se}^f G_3$. Then we have: $G_2 \vdash_{se} G_3$. In particular: $G_3 \neq G_1$ if $G_2 \neq G_1$.*

The next lemma can be proven by a straightforward induction on the length of a derivation sequence. The point for proving the induction step is that a program resulting from a transformation of $\mathcal{T}$ is at least as good as its argument with respect to $\lesssim$. It is in the same equivalence class after sinking and trivial elimination steps, i.e., elimination steps, where no assignment occurrence has been eliminated; and it is better otherwise. This follows immediately from the constraints that are satisfied by admissible assignment sinkings and eliminations.

Lemma 11. *We have: $G' \vdash_{se}^* G'' \Rightarrow G' \lesssim G''$*

In other words, Lemma 11 says $\vdash_{se}^* \subseteq \lesssim$. From the wellfoundedness of $\lesssim$ and the definitions of $\vdash_{se}$ and $\mathcal{T}^{max}$ we immediately conclude:

Lemma 12 Wellfoundedness and Increasingness.

1. *The relation $\vdash_{se}^*$ is wellfounded.*
2. *All functions $f \in \mathcal{T}^{max}$ are increasing.*

Next we are going to show that $\mathcal{T}$ is delay-monotone. This proof is supported by the following lemma, whose first part is a consequence of the fact that eliminating dead assignment occurrences does not reanimate other dead assignment occurrences, and whose second part is a consequence of the admissibility of g and a simple program transformation supposed in [KRS94b] which is typical for code motion transformations (cf. [DRZ92, KRS92, KRS94a, RWZ88]), namely to insert in every edge leading from a node with more than one successor to a node with more than one predecessor a new 'synthetic' node.

Lemma 13. *Let $G_1, G_2, G_3 \in \mathcal{G}$, and $g, h \in \mathcal{T}$ with $G_1 \vdash_{se}^g G_2$ and $G_1 \vdash_{se}^h G_3$.*

1. If $g \in \mathcal{E}_\alpha$, and occ an α-occurrence occurring both in G_1 and G_2, then we have: If occ is dead in G_1, then it is dead in G_2.

2. If $g, h \in S_\alpha$, occ an α-occurrence that has been moved by g into a node n of G_2 with more than one predecessor, and occ' an α-occurrence that has been moved by h into a predecessor m of n, then we have: occ is dead in n iff occ' is dead in m.

Additionally, we have:

Lemma 14. Let $G_1, G_2 \in \mathcal{G}$, let $g \in \mathcal{T}$, $f \in \mathcal{T}^{max}$, and let $\alpha, \beta \in \mathcal{AP}$ be two different assignment patterns. Then we have:

1. If $f, g \in \mathcal{E}$, then there are transformations $f', g' \in \mathcal{E}$ such that the diagram in Figure 3 commutes.
2. If $f, g \in S$, then there are transformations $f', g' \in S$ such that the diagram in Figure 3 commutes.
3. If $g \in \mathcal{E}_\alpha$ and $f \in S_\beta$, then there are transformations $g' \in \mathcal{E}_\alpha$ and $f' \in S_\beta$ such that the diagram in Figure 3 commutes.
4. If $g \in S_\alpha$ and $f \in \mathcal{E}_\beta$, then there are transformations $g' \in S_\alpha$ and $f' \in \mathcal{E}_\beta$ such that the diagram in Figure 3 commutes.

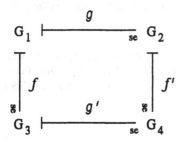

Fig. 3. Commuting Diagram

Lemma 13 and Lemma 14 allow us to establish the following lemma, which is the key for proving the delay-monotonicity of $\mathcal{T}$.

Lemma 15 Main Lemma.
$\forall g \in \mathcal{T}. \ G_1 \vdash^g_{se} G_2 \Rightarrow \forall f \in \mathcal{T} \ \exists f_1, \dots, f_n \in \mathcal{T}. \ f(G_1) \vdash^*_{se} f_n \circ \dots \circ f_1(G_2)$

The following theorem states the desired delay-monotonicity result. The reasoning closely resembles the classical Newman Lemma [New42], saying that confluence follows from local confluence if the given relation is wellfounded. Note that monotonicity does not hold.

Lemma 16 Delay-Monotonicity.
$\mathcal{T}$ is delay-monotone, i.e.,

$$\forall f \in \mathcal{T}. \ G' \vdash^*_{se} G'' \Rightarrow \exists f_1, \dots, f_n \in \mathcal{T}. \ f(G') \vdash^*_{se} f_n \circ \dots \circ f_1(G'')$$

Finally, we have to show that the set of common fixpoints of $\mathcal{T}^{max}$ and $\mathcal{T}$ coincide. Central for proving this result is the Dominance Lemma 10. Moreover, we have to check that the fixpoints of $\mathcal{T}$ are maximal in $\mathcal{G}$.

Theorem 17 Fixpoint Characterization.

1. $G' \in \mathcal{G}$ is a fixpoint of the functions of $\mathcal{T}$ if and only if G' is a fixpoint of the functions of $\mathcal{T}^{max}$.
2. $G' \in \mathcal{G}$ is a fixpoint of the functions of $\mathcal{T}$ if and only if G' is maximal in $\mathcal{G}$.

Collecting our results we have: $\vdash_{se}^*$ is a wellfounded (Lemma 12(1)) complete partial order on $\mathcal{G}$, whose least element is G itself; all functions $f \in \mathcal{T}^{max}$ are increasing (Lemma 12(2)) and $\mathcal{T}$ is delay-monotone with respect to $\vdash_{se}^*$ (Lemma 16). Hence, Theorem 3 is applicable.

Moreover, the function families $\mathcal{T}^{max}$ and $\mathcal{T}$ have the same common fixpoints (Theorem 17(1)), and all of their fixpoints are maximal in $\vdash_{se}^*$ (Theorem 17(2)).

Combining these results and applying Lemma 11 we obtain that there exists a terminating optimal program transformation [KRS94b]:

Theorem 18 Optimal Partial Dead Code Elimination.
$\mathcal{G}$ has (up to local reorderings in basic blocks) a unique optimal element (with respect to $\sqsubseteq$) which can be computed by any fair sequence of function applications from $\mathcal{T}^{max}$.

We remark that the optimality of the partial faint code elimination algorithm which is also introduced in [KRS94b] as well as the optimality of the algorithm for the uniform elimination of partially redundant expressions and assignments in [KRS95] can be proven in exactly the same fashion.

5 Conclusions

We have presented a new fixpoint theorem, which gives a sufficient condition for the existence and computability of the least common fixpoint of a family of functions on a wellfounded partial order. The point of this theorem is that for wellfounded partial orders the usual monotonicity condition can be substantially weakened. This allows us to capture a new and interesting class of practically relevant applications. To characterize this class, we discussed applications in *data flow analysis* and *program optimization*. Whereas the first application could still be treated by the known fixpoint theorems, the second application requires the generalization developed in this paper. Our new theorem is the key for proving the optimality of the partial dead code elimimation algorithm of [KRS94b], which is implemented in the new release of the Sun SPARCompiler language systems. Moreover, as our theorem only requires delay-monotonicity, a property being weaker than monoticity, algorithm designers gain greater flexibility in the construction process than in the classical setup.

References

[Bau78]   Gérard Baudet. Asynchronous iterative methods for multiprocessors. *Journal of the ACM*, 25(2):226–244, April 1978.

[CC77]   P. Cousot and R. Cousot. Abstract interpretation: A unified lattice model for static analysis of programs by construction or approximation of fixpoints. In *Conf. Record of the 4th ACM Symp. on Principles of Programming Languages*, pages 238 – 252, Los Angeles, CA, 1977.

[CC79]   P. Cousot and R. Cousot. Constructive versions of Tarski's fixed point theorems. *Pacific Journal of Mathematics*, 82(1):43–87, 1979.

[Cou77]   P. Cousot. Asynchronous iterative methods for solving a fixed point system of monotone equations in a complete lattice. Technical Report 88, Laboratoire d'Informatique, U.S.M.G., Grenoble, France, September 1977.

[DRZ92]   D. M. Dhamdhere, B. K. Rosen, and F. K. Zadeck. How to analyze large programs efficiently and informatively. In *Proc. ACM SIGPLAN Conf. on Programming Language Design and Implementation'92*, volume *27,7* of *ACM SIGPLAN Notices*, pages 212 – 223, San Francisco, CA, June 1992.

[Hec77]   M. S. Hecht. *Flow Analysis of Computer Programs*. Elsevier, North-Holland, 1977.

[Jør94]   N. Jørgensen. Finding fixpoints in finite function spaces using needeness analysis and chaotic iteration. In *First International Static Analysis Symposium(SAS'94)*, Lecture Notes in Computer Science 864, pages 329–345, Namur, Belgium, 1994. Springer-Verlag.

[KRS92]   J. Knoop, O. Rüthing, and B. Steffen. Lazy code motion. In *Proc. ACM SIGPLAN Conf. on Programming Language Design and Implementation'92*, volume *27,7* of *ACM SIGPLAN Notices*, pages 224 – 234, San Francisco, CA, June 1992.

[KRS94a]   J. Knoop, O. Rüthing, and B. Steffen. Optimal code motion: Theory and practice. *ACM Transactions on Programming Languages and Systems*, 16(4):1117–1155, 1994.

[KRS94b]   J. Knoop, O. Rüthing, and B. Steffen. Partial dead code elimination. In *Proc. ACM SIGPLAN Conf. on Programming Language Design and Implementation'94*, volume *29,6* of *ACM SIGPLAN Notices*, pages 147 – 158, Orlando, FL, June 1994.

[KRS95]   J. Knoop, O. Rüthing, and B. Steffen. The power of assignment motion. In *Proc. ACM SIGPLAN Conf. on Programming Language Design and Implementation'95*, volume *30,6* of *ACM SIGPLAN Notices*, pages 233 – 245, La Jolla, CA, June 1995.

[KU77]   J. B. Kam and J. D. Ullman. Monotone data flow analysis frameworks. *Acta Informatica*, 7:309 – 317, 1977.

[LNS82]   J.-L. Lassez, V.L. Nguyen, and E.A. Sonnenberg. Fixed point theorems and semantics: A folk tale. *Information Processing Letters*, 14(3):112–116, 1982.

[Mar93]   K. Marriot. Frameworks for abstract interpretation. *Acta Informatica*, 30:103 – 129, 1993.

[MJ81]   S. S. Muchnick and N. D. Jones, editors. *Program Flow Analysis: Theory and Applications*. Prentice Hall, Englewood Cliffs, NJ, 1981.

[New42]   M.H.A. Newman. On theories with a combinatorial definition of equivalence. *Annals of Math.*, 43,2:223–243, 1942.

[Rob76]   F. Robert. Convergence locale d'itérations chaotiques non linéaires. Technical Report 58, Laboratoire d'Informatique, U.S.M.G., Grenoble, France, December 1976.

[RWZ88] B. K. Rosen, M. N. Wegman, and F. K. Zadeck. Global value numbers and redundant computations. In *Conf. Record of the 15th ACM Symp. on Principles of Programming Languages*, pages 12 – 27, San Diego, CA, 1988.

[Tar55] A. Tarski. A lattice-theoretical fixpoint theorem and its applications. *Pacific Journal of Mathematics*, 5:285–309, 1955.

[ÜD89] Aydin Üresin and Michel Dubois. Sufficient conditions for the convergence of asynchronous iterations. *Parallel Computing*, 10:83–92, 1989.

[VWL94] B. Vergauwen, J. Wauman, and J. Lewi. Efficient fixpoint computation. In *First International Static Analysis Symposium(SAS'94)*, Lecture Notes in Computer Science 864, pages 314–328, Namur, Belgium, 1994. Springer-Verlag.

[Wei93] Jiawang Wei. Parallel asynchronous iterations of least fixed points. *Parallel Computing*, 19:887–895, 1993.

A Proofs

Proof of the New Fixpoint Theorem 3

The *wellfoundedness* of $\sqsubseteq$, the *increasingness* of the functions of $\mathcal{F}$, and the *fairness* of the strategy directly imply that $\bigsqcup f_\gamma(\bot)$ is a fixpoint and that it is reached in a finite number of iteration steps. Thus, we are left with showing that $\bigsqcup f_\gamma(\bot)$ is a lower bound for every common fixpoint of $\mathcal{F}$. Let δ be an arbitrary fixed point of $\mathcal{F}$, i.e. $f_k(\delta) = \delta$ for all $f_k \in \mathcal{F}$ and as a consequence $f_s(\delta) = \delta$ for all $s \in \mathbb{N}^*$. For $(d_i)_{i \in \mathbb{N}} = f_\gamma(\bot)$ we show $d_i \sqsubseteq \delta$ for all $i \in \mathbb{N}$ by induction on i. For $i = 0$, we have $d_0 = \bot \sqsubseteq \delta$. The induction step, $d_{i+1} = f_{\gamma(i)}(d_i) \sqsubseteq f_s(\delta) = \delta$ for some $s \in \mathbb{N}^*$, then follows from the induction hypothesis $d_i \sqsubseteq \delta$ and delay-monotonicity. Hence $d_i \sqsubseteq \delta$ for all i and so $\bigsqcup f_\gamma(\bot) \sqsubseteq \delta$ by definition of $\bigsqcup$. $\qquad\square$

Proof of Lemma 4

Let γ be an arbitrary set strategy on $\{1, \ldots, n\}$, and $(d_i)_{i \in \mathbb{N}}$ be its induced chaotic iteration, starting from $\bot =_{df} (\bot_C, \ldots, \bot_C)$. We have to show

$$\forall i \in \mathbb{N}. \; d_i \sqsubseteq d_{i+1}$$

The proof is by induction on i. Let $J =_{df} \gamma(i)$. By definition of f_J the property

$$\forall k \in \{1, \ldots, n\} \backslash J \; \forall d \in D. \; f_J(d)^k = d^k$$

holds. Therefore, it suffices to show $d_i^k \sqsubseteq_C f_k(d_i)^k$ for all $k \in J$. The case $d_i^k = \bot_C$ is trivial. Otherwise, d_i^k must have been updated in an earlier step. More precisely, $d_i^k = f_{\gamma(j)}(d_j)^k$ where j is the greatest index $j < i$ such that $k \in \gamma(j)$. By induction hypothesis for each $j' = j, \ldots, i - 1$, we obtain $d_{j'} \sqsubseteq d_{j'+1}$, from which $d_j \sqsubseteq d_i$ follows by transitivity of $\sqsubseteq$. By monotonicity of $f_{\gamma(j)}$ then, $d_i^k = f_{\gamma(j)}(d_j)^k \sqsubseteq_C f_{\gamma(j)}(d_i)^k = f_k(d_i) = f_J(d_i)^k = d_{i+1}^k$ follows, and the proof is done. $\qquad\square$

Proof of Lemma 14

For $f \in \mathcal{E}_\alpha$, let $elim_\alpha(f, G')$ denote the set of α-occurrences in G' that are eliminated by f. Then, the first part of Lemma 14 is proven by investigating two cases: (1a) $g, f \in \mathcal{E}_\alpha$, (1b) $g \in \mathcal{E}_\alpha$, $f \in \mathcal{E}_\beta$

In case (1a), the maximality of f guarantees: $elim_\alpha(g, G_1) \subseteq elim_\alpha(f, G_1)$. Applying Lemma 13(1) we obtain that all α-occurrences in $elim_\alpha(f, G_1) \backslash elim_\alpha(g, G_1)$

are dead in G_2. Hence, there is a transformation in $\mathcal{E}$, which eliminates all α-occurrences in $elim_\alpha(f, G_1) \backslash elim_\alpha(g, G_1)$ in G_2. Choosing this transformation as f', and an arbitrary function of $\mathcal{T}^{max}$ leaving G_3 invariant as g', we get:

$$G_2 \vdash_{se}^{f'} G_4$$

and therefore as desired:

$$G_3 \vdash_{se}^{g'} G_3 = G_4$$

In case (1b) Lemma 13(1) yields that $elim_\alpha(g, G_1)$ and $elim_\beta(f, G_1)$ are subsets of the sets of dead α- and β-occurrences in G_3 and G_2, respectively. Hence, there are transformations in $\mathcal{E}$ which eliminate all α-occurrences of $elim_\alpha(g, G_1)$ in G_3 and all β-occurrences of $elim_\beta(f, G_1)$ in G_2. Choosing these transformations as g' and f', respectively, we obtain as desired

$$G_2 \vdash_{se}^{f'} G_4 \quad \text{and} \quad G_3 \vdash_{se}^{g'} G_4$$

Similarly to the proof of the first part of Lemma 14, two cases must also be considered in the proof of its second part: (2a) $g, f \in S_\alpha$, (2b) $g \in S_\alpha$, $f \in S_\beta$

In case (2a) the Dominance Lemma 10 yields the existence of an admissible assignment sinking $f' \in S$, which directly transforms G_2 into G_3. Thus, by choosing an arbitrary function of $\mathcal{T}^{max}$ leaving G_3 invariant as g', we succeed in this case.

In order to prove case (2b) consider the program G_2', which results from G_2 by reinserting all α-occurrences that have been moved by g. Let G_4' be the program which results from the maximal β-sinking to G_2', i.e., $G_2' \vdash_{se}^{f} G_4'$, and let G_4 result from G_4' by eliminating the reinserted α-occurrences. Obviously, there is a transformation $f' \in S_\beta$, which directly transforms G_2 into G_4. The admissibility of g implies that G_2 and G_4 are identical except for β-occurrences. Thus, interchanging the roles of α and β and applying the same construction to G_3, we get the existence of a transformation $g' \in S_\alpha$, which transforms G_3 into G_4. This completes the proof of case (2b).

The remaining two parts of Lemma 14 can now be proven straightforward along the proof lines of part (2) by additionally applying Lemma 13(1). $\square$

Proof of the Main Lemma 15
Let $\alpha, \beta \in \mathcal{AP}$ be different assignment patterns. Then the Main Lemma 15 is proven by investigating the following cases:

1. $g, f \in \mathcal{E}$ 3. $g \in \mathcal{E}_\alpha$, $f \in S_\beta$ 5. $g \in \mathcal{E}_\alpha$, $f \in S_\alpha$
2. $g, f \in S$ 4. $g \in S_\alpha$, $f \in \mathcal{E}_\beta$ 6. $g \in S_\alpha$, $f \in \mathcal{E}_\alpha$

Applying the Dominance Lemma 10 we can assume without loss of generality that f is maximal, i.e., $f \in \mathcal{T}^{max}$. The first four cases are then immediate consequences of the corresponding parts of Lemma 14. Thus, we are left with the cases (5) and (6), which both can be proven in the same fashion. Thus, we only present the proof of case (5).

In the situation of case (5) let G_2' be the program, which results from G_2 by reinserting a labelled version of all α-occurrences that have been eliminated by g.

Due to the labelling the reinserted α-occurrences can be distinguished from the remaining ones. In G_2', we assume that only unlabelled α-occurrences can be subject to assignment sinkings; however, all α-occurrences, i.e., labelled or not, are considered to block the sinking of α-occurrences, i.e., no α-occurrence can sink across a labelled or unlabelled α-occurrence in G_2'. Now we choose the uniquely determined maximal α-sinking and α-elimination as f_1 and f_2, respectively, and denote the program resulting from the subsequent application of f_1 and f_2 to G_2' by G_4'. By eliminating all labelled α-occurrences in G_4' we obtain the program G_4. Of course, f_1 and f_2 have corresponding functions in $\mathcal{T}$ which directly transform G_2 into G_4. Thus, in order to complete the proof of case (5), it is sufficient to show that a maximal α-elimination transforms G_3 into G_4 as well. The point here is that due to the reinsertion of α-occurrences eliminated by g, G_2' has precisely the same 'α-blockades' as G_1. Hence, on join-free paths, i.e., on paths where no node has more than one predecessor, (unlabelled) α-occurrences in G_2' have precisely the same sinking potential as their corresponding occurrences in G_1. Only on paths containing join-nodes the sinking potential can be different: In G_2' an α-occurrence occ can be blocked in a predecessor n of a join-node j, because there is a brother m of n,[6] to which no α-occurrence is sinkable; in G_1, however, the same α-occurrence can successfully be sunk into j, because some of the α-occurrences eliminated by g in G_1 are sinkable to m. It is worth noting that the α-occurrence is dead in j and will never become live again. Hence, it is eliminated by the subsequent application of f_2. This, however, holds for the α-occurrence blocked in the predecessor n of j as well, since it is dead according to Lemma 13(2). Combining these results we obtain as desired that maximal α-elimination transforms G_3 into G_4. □

Proof of Lemma 17

Since (2) holds trivially, we only prove (1). The first implication, "$\Rightarrow$", is a simple consequence of $\mathcal{T}^{max} \subseteq \mathcal{T}$. The second implication, "$\Leftarrow$", is proven by showing the contrapositive. Without loss of generality, we can assume $g \in \mathcal{T}_\alpha \backslash \mathcal{T}_\alpha^{max}$ and $G' \vdash^g_{se} G''$ with $G'' \neq G'$. Let now $f \in \mathcal{T}_\alpha^{max}$ be the uniquely determined function f of $\mathcal{T}_\alpha^{max}$ corresponding to g. Then the Dominance Lemma 10 yields as desired that the program resulting from the application of f to G' is different from G'. □

---

[6] The set of brothers of a node n is given by $\bigcup \{pred(m) \mid m \in succ(n)\}$.

How to Uniformly Specify
Program Analysis and Transformation
with Graph Rewrite Systems

Uwe Aßmann

INRIA Rocquencourt
Domaine de Voluceau, BP 105, 78153 Le Chesnay Cedex, France
Uwe.Assmann@inria.fr*

Abstract. Implementing program optimizers is a task which swallows an enourmous amount of man-power. To reduce development time a simple and practial specification method is highly desirable. Such a method should comprise both program analysis and transformation. However, although several frameworks for program analysis exist, none of them can be used for analysis and transformation uniformly. This paper presents such a method. For program analysis we use a simple variant of graph rewrite systems (*edge addition rewrite systems*). For program transformation we apply more complex graph rewrite systems. Our specification method has been implemented prototypically in the optimizer generator OPTIMIX. OPTIMIX works with arbitrary intermediate languages and generates real-life program analyses and transformations. We demonstrate this by several examples and measurements.

Keywords: Program analysis, program transformation, optimization, specification, graph rewrite systems

1   Introduction

This paper presents a uniform specification method for program analysis and transformation. It is based on graph rewrite systems (Grs), can be used for arbitrary intermediate languages (also abstract syntax trees), and leads to efficiently executing optimizer parts. The major idea behind it is the insight that the intermediate representations in optimizers are *graphs* which are constructed and manipulated by *graph transformations*. Thus it is quite natural to use graph rewrite systems to specify both problems of program analysis and transformation.

With our specification method the process of writing an optimizer is divided into four phases. First a data model for the graphs — intermediate code as well

---

* This work has been supported by Esprit project No. 5399 COMPARE. Most of this work has been done while the author was at Universität Karlsruhe IPD, Vincenz-Prießnitz-Str. 3, 76128 Karlsruhe, Germany

as analysis information — has to be developed. Secondly, program analysis has to be specified by graph rewrite systems. For this we supply a special variant of graph rewrite systems, *edge addition rewrite systems* (EARS). EARS are very simple graph rewrite systems because they only allow the addition of edges to graphs and do not remove any existing parts. Thirdly, program transformations can be specified by more general graph rewrite systems which allow deletion of edges, and insertion and deletion of nodes. Finally, after having described the optimization abstractly, the representations of the graph classes can be changed in order to speed up the generated algorithms. The user also can feed the generator with assertions so that the generator can apply index structures (dictionaries). We will show that this is an essential part to achieve effiently executing optimizer parts.

The structure of the paper is shaped along this process. We will present a running example, the elimination of partial redundancies (lazy code motion) [KRS94]. It comprises syntactic equivalence of intermediate expressions (section 4.1), global data flow analysis (section 4.2), and a transformation phase (section 5). Additionally we present some figures concerning the efficiency of the generated algorithms. We conclude the paper with a section about related work.

To demonstrate the validity of the specification method the optimizer generator OPTIMIX and several optimizer parts have been developed within the compiler framework CoSy [AAvS94]. All generated components work on the *common COMPARE medium intermediate representation*, the intermediate language CCMIR. The CCMIR serves as common platform for frontends in C, Fortran-90, Modula-2, Modula-P [VH92], and soon C++ (http://www.ace.nl).

2 The method

The central idea of our specification method is to regard the optimization process as a sequence of applications of graph rewrite systems (Figure 1). We start with a graph given by the frontend which is the abstract syntax tree or the intermediate code sequence. First we have to perform program analysis. This is normally done by several EARS, executed one after the other. These may comprise one or several data-flow analyses. After that the transforming graph rewrite systems can be applied.

The advantages of this scheme are the following. First we have a uniform view on the intermediate language and the analysis information: everything is represented as graphs, and all actions are done by graph rewriting. Second, instead of describing everything with one big graph rewrite system (which could be possible) we prefer to write a sequence of smaller ones. Larger graph rewrite systems tend to loose confluence or termination. With a suitable separation one can isolate non-confluency or even resolve non-termination. Third, for smaller graph rewrite systems we know how to generate good code because smaller rewrite systems in general have a lower *order* than bigger ones: often linear or quadratic algorithms can be achieved [Aß95b]. Forth, this division breaks the optimization task down into component problems which can be solved independently. If we

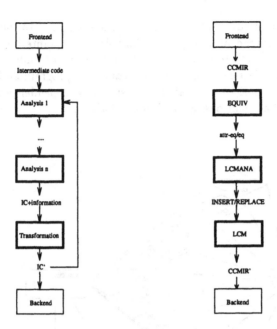

Fig. 1. Left: Optimization as a sequence of graph rewrite system applications. Thick boxes are generated phases. Right: our examples as an instance of the method

do not find a system for a certain task, or some developed system turns out to be too slow, or we can always substitute it by a hand-written algorithm. This is anyway the case for the frontend and the backend; they are implemented as usual.

In order to make this scheme work, all phases of the compiler have to use a uniform object handling package including uniform graph and set classes. In COMPARE this is solved by the data description language fSDL. It provides graph and set *functors* (template classes). From this a uniform access interface is generated [WKD94]. All hand-written and generated phases use this interface so that a uniform data access is given.

3 Designing the data model

Before developing graph rewrite systems for program analysis and transformations, we have to say how the intermediate graphs look like. This amounts to specifying a *data model* or *graph schema* [Sch90]. We have to layout the following:

1. model the graph node types: among these are intermediate code instructions such as expressions, statements, loops, procedures. Also already analyzed information can be encoded in nodes of graphs, e.g. definitions, or expression equivalence classes.

2. model the graph edge types (relations): First we have to model the information the frontend produces, e.g. expression tree pointering, or statement lists. Second we have to model all predicates we want to infer about the program, i.e. the relations among the objects of the program and the analysis. Examples are relations such as the classical flow dependencies, equvialence relations, calling relations, control flow relations.

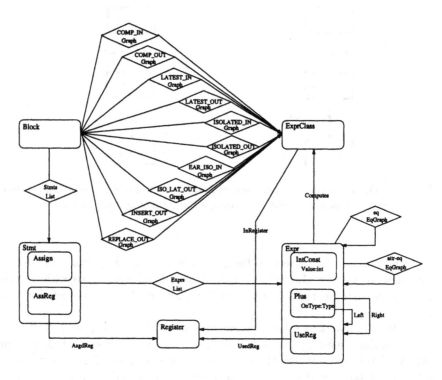

Fig. 2. Data model as higraph.

Our running example relies on the data model in figure 2. The diagram is a higraph, i.e. an extended ER-model [Har88]. Boxes denote entity types, box inclusion denotes inheritance. n:m-relations are depicted by diamond boxes, n:1-relations by simple arrows. Because we deal with directed graphs, we have to indicate source and target domains of the relations, which is done by arrows. For the example we assume some familiar object types, such as blocks, statements and expressions. Several of them are generated by the frontend (`Block`, `Assign`, `IntConst`, `Plus`) and form the basis for the optimization process. Others are generated by the optimizer: `AssReg`- and `UseReg`- objects denote assignments and uses of registers (`Register`), objects of type `ExprClass` denote syntactically equivalent expressions. Also the relations are only partially produced by the frontend (**Stmts**, **Exprs**, **Left**, **Right**). All others are the results of optimizer components, i.e. computed by graph rewrite systems.

This data model can easily be transformed into a concrete data description language such as a fSDL [WKD94]. In such a language relations must be annotated by a concrete representation class. fSDL provides two kinds of representations: bidirectional relations (such as **Graph** or **EqGraph**), and directed relations (such as **Set** or **List**). The relations in our figure carry such annotations. Note that this choice does not influence the specification, but the generated code.

4 Specifying the analysis

4.1 Local analysis

One of the central ideas of our specification method is to describe the collection of information as simple graph rewrite systems which only add edges to graphs. One example for a local program analysis is the specification of syntactic equivalence of expression trees. This is the prerequisite for lazy code motion data-flow analysis. In intermediate languages such as the CCMIR we distinguish two kinds of expressions: those with operands (non-leaf expressions) and those without (leaf expressions). Among the first there are operators such as **Plus**, among the latter there are those such as **IntConst**.

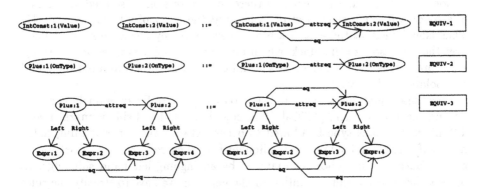

Fig. 3. EQUIV: Syntactic equivalence of expressions

Two arbitrary expressions are attribute-equivalent to each other if their attributes are the same. For **IntConst** expressions the value of the constant must be equal. For **Plus** expressions their field **OnType** must be equal. Two leaf expressions are equivalent if they are attribute-equivalent. Two non-leaf expressions are equivalent if they are attribute-equivalent and all their sons are equivalent. For **IntConst** and **Plus** these conditions are expressed by the EARS in Figure 3. For a complete specification of syntactical tree equivalence of expressions we have to add similar rules for all subtypes of expressions.

Applying the rules of EQUIV to the intermediate representation of a procedure yields a relation **eq** which is a partition of all expressions and denotes the syntactical equivalence relation over expressions. With another simple graph rewrite system we can generate for each partition a representant node **ExprClass**. This object type will be used in the global data-flow analysis. Due to the lack of space we will not show this here.

4.2 Global data-flow analysis

With EARS it is also possible to specify global data-flow analysis. If the EARS is recursive, the rules have to be applied until a fixpoint is reached. This is similar to finding a fixpoint in a distributive data-flow framework. We demonstrate this by some equations from the equation system for lazy code motion ([KRS94], p. 1138). This data-flow analysis relates the blocks of the program to its expression classes, i.e. the syntactical equivalent expressions. If we encode this with graphs, the nodes are the blocks and the expression classes, whereas the edges represent the data-flow sets. Due to the lack of space we will only present the equation system for **ISOLATED**, as well as the non-recursive equation system for **INSERT/REPLACE_OUT** which determines the places of transformations at the end of blocks (Figure 4). We also do not show the initialization of the system, which can easily be written down with graph rewrite rules, too.

The rules mean the following: an expression must be inserted at the end of a block, if is latest and not isolated there. An expression is isolated at the exit of a block if it is either earliest or isolated at the entry of all successor blocks. Thus isolatedness at the exit of a block is expressed by recursive rules, defined over the successors of the block, which makes the fixpoint evaluation necessary. An expression is to be replaced at the end of a block if it is computed there and not isolated and latest.

For these equations we have to use two extensions of EARS, namely negation and universal quantifiers [Aß95a]. If an edge in a left hand side is marked with **NOT** no edge of this type is allowed to occur between the corresponding redex nodes. If a left hand side node is allquantified, then redexes must exist for all graph nodes in a neighbor set matched by an ingoing left hand side edge. In order to achieve a sound semantics for the negation we have to stratify the rules so that they still yield a unique normal form [Aß95a]. As strata exactly the rule groups (equation systems) result which are mentioned in [KRS94]. Here they are coalesced only for the purpose of demonstration. Also the given equations relate almost one-to-one to the equations in [KRS94]. Thus, writing a specification for global data-flow analysis, and generating an executable algorithm with OPTIMIX can be done in very short time. Actually this part seems to be the most easy part of the whole optimization process: take an arbitrary equation system, and type it in.

In this paper we consider only intraprocedural analysis. For interprocedural analysis special specification or evaluation strategies have to be applied to reach

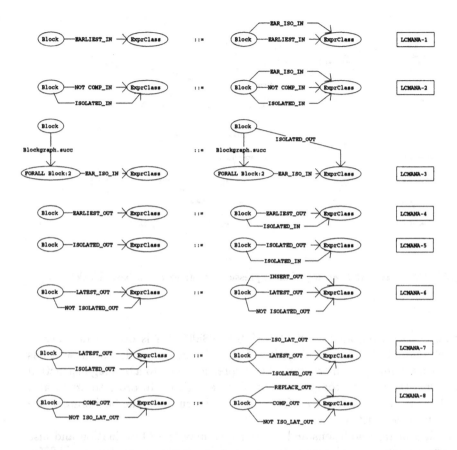

Fig. 4. LCMANA: Data-flow analysis for lazy code motion: isolatedness, earliest-ness, insert-out, replace-out. LCMANA-1 – LCMANA-5 make up the first rule group, LCMANA-6–8 the second

the same preciseness. As EARS model distributed data-flow frameworks over finite powersets there are several methods which can be applied [RHS95].

5 Specifying transformations

If we allow edge deletions, node additions, and node deletions, we can spec-ify program transformations by deleting and adding objects from and to the intermediate representation. Our running example is continued by specifying some transformation rules for lazy code motion (Figure 5). We regard only the necessary relations for transformation at the end of blocks (INSERT_OUT, REPLACE_OUT). The first rule inserts an expression at the end of a block. No nodes are deleted; only new statements for creating the expression value and

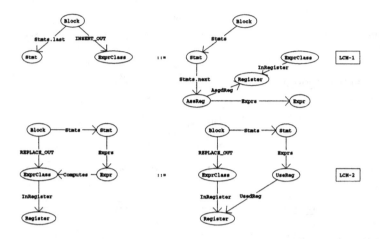

Fig. 5. LCM: Insert and replace of an expression at the exit of a basic block

storing it into a register are created. Edge **INSERT_OUT** is deleted in order to prevent that LCM-1 is applied again. LCM-2 also deletes nodes, because it has to replace a computing instruction of an expression class to a **UseReg** instruction which uses the already computed value from a register. In order to arrive at a complete lazy code motion transformation similar rules for the beginning of the blocks must be written.

With arbitrary additions and deletions we may loose termination and also (strong) confluence. Of course termination is absolutely necessary. [Aß95a] presents two termination criteria which are statically decidable:

1. Termination by *edge addition*. In the case of EARS the rewrite process stops when the added relations are complete. This can be carried over to general graph rewrite systems, if each rule adds an edge of such a *terminating relation* and no other rule is allowed to delete these edges again. Then the system terminates because the terminating relation is complete.

2. Termination by *redex deletion*: each rule deletes nodes or edges of types which are not added either. This means that although the rules may add nodes and edges of other types they do not produce any redex again. Thus after deletion of all initial redexes termination follows. This is the case for LCM: LCM-1 subtracts the edge **INSERT_OUT** and LCM-2 the edge **Computes**. Thus it terminates, although it adds statements and expressions.

These termination criteria are very useful if a graph rewrite system has to perform a finite number of actions depending on the size of the manipulated graph. This is the case for many code optimizations, especially for code motion and replacement algorithms: first they compute the places where to transform and then they transform only once.

If a graph rewrite system is not confluent, it delivers a correct, but arbitrarily selected result. LCM cannot be proved to be confluent regarding its rules. However, because the redexes in the manipulated graph do not overlap, it is in deed confluent and delivers unique results.

6 Execution

6.1 Optimix meta-code-generation

In order to understand how the specifications given so far can be executed efficiently, we will give a short overview on a special (meta-)code-generation for graph rewrite systems [Aß95b], the *order evaluation*. This technique is based on the idea that we will find all redexes of a rule if we regard all possible permutations of source nodes of left hand sides and look up the rest of the redex by traversing neighbor sets. For that the *order* of the graph rewrite system has to be calculated, which is the maximal number of source nodes in left hand sides. If a graph rewrite system has order k, we also call it GRS(k).

For order evaluation we have to compute an *edge disjoint path cover* for each left hand side. This is a set of paths which cover the left hand side such that they intersect each other only at their end points. Then the problem of finding a redex for a given set of source nodes in the manipulated graph is reduced to a join of the path problems of the edge disjoint path cover. Consider Figure 6 which contains a path cover of LCM-2. For this rule OPTIMIX generates the code in Figure 7. The outer loops (1) and (2) enumerate the path problem of path 1. The inner loops (3) and (4) enumerate path 2. The paths are joined with a nested-loop-join under the join condition $c = c2$, because we need to find the intersection of their enumerated objects.

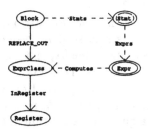

Fig. 6. A edge-disjoint path cover for LCM-2 with two paths. Path 1 is drawn with normal edges, path 2 with dotted edges

For non-recursive (recursive) graph rewrite systems the *order evaluation* has complexity $O(n^k e^{lp})(O(n^{k+2}e^{lp}))$, where l the length of the longest path of a path cover over all left hand sides, p the maximum number of paths in a path

Input: Node type Block. Relations Stmts,
Exprs, REPLACE_OUT, Computes, InRegister

Output: Modified intermediate code: expressions replaced by UseReg expressions

```
/* Enumerate path 1 */
forall b ∈ Block do (1)
    forall c ∈ b.REPLACE_OUT do (2)
        r ← c.InRegister; /* 1:1-relation */
        /* Join with path 2 */
        forall s ∈ b.Stmts do (3)
            forall e ∈ s.Exprs do (4)
                c₂ ← e.Computes; /* n:1-relation */
                /* Join condition */
                if not c = c₂ then
                    continue ;
                /* Redex (place for transformation) found. */
                .. Do the transformation ..
```

Fig. 7. Algorithm generated for LCM-2

cover, n the maximal number of nodes in a node type, and e the maximum out-degree of a node concerning an arbitrary relation. However, for concrete algorithms often better costs result because many relations are n:1 and often object domains are partitioned by graphs. Because the test for LCM-1 can be overlapped with the loops of algorithm 7, it can be used to solve LCM. LCM is non-recursive, because it does not create new redexes for itself. According to the order evaluation cost formula it has complexity $O(|\mathtt{Block}|^1 e^6)$, because $k = 1, l = 3, p = 2$. Then $\mathtt{Computes}$ and $\mathtt{InRegister}$ are n:1- and 1:1-relations, respectively. Also expressions are partitioned over the blocks, i.e. loop (3) and (4) only loop once over all expressions of a procedure. Thus the generated algorithm has cost $O(|\mathtt{Block}||\mathtt{Expr}||\mathtt{ExprClass}|)$. It is also clear that if other directions are chosen for the relations of the data model, a graph rewrite system with higher order may result. For our example we use already a reasonably good one, but in general this needs some thinking.

EQUIV has order 2, because the rules for attribute-equivalence contain isolates in the left hand sides. It is recursive. A theorem in [Aß95b] shows that because we deal with expression trees the fixpoint computation can be avoided. Also, $\mathtt{Left}$ and $\mathtt{Right}$ are n:1-relations. Thus EQUIV can be solved with order evaluation in $O(|\mathtt{Expr}|^2 e^3)$ because $l = 1, p = 3$. However, e is here much smaller than $|\mathtt{Expr}|$ because the relations $\mathtt{eq}$ and $\mathtt{attreq}$ partition $\mathtt{Expr}$. If we neglect their cardinality, we achieve a quadratic algorithm in the number of expressions.

LCMANA has order 1, because $\mathtt{Block}$ is the only source node type of all rules. Because it is recursive, we have to apply fixpoint computation. Because $l = 2, p = 2$, we have complexity $O(|\{\mathtt{Block,ExprClass}\}|^3 e^4)$. However, if we use a bitvector representation for the relations, the standard round-robin iteration for data-flow analysis results. Because bitvector union/intersection has linear effort in the number of expressions, a concrete algorithm has cost $O(|\mathtt{Block}|^2|\mathtt{ExprClass}| \times |\mathtt{Block}||\mathtt{ExprClass}|) = O(|\mathtt{Block}|^3|\mathtt{ExprClass}|^2)$. This rough estimate can be improved by taking the loop nesting of the control-flow graph into account [Hec77].

All terminating graph rewrite systems can be solved by order evaluation. For terminating and confluent systems it will deliver the unique normal form. For non-confluent systems it will deliver a correct, but arbitrarily selected result. Hence order evaluation provides a simple and uniform solution procedure for program optimization problems. Thus we are able not only to specify analysis and transformation uniformly, but also execute the specifications with a uniform execution mechanism.

6.2 Speeding up

The following sections present some numbers and shows how to speed up the execution of order evaluation. Within CoSy two optimizer configurations have been tested: a Modula-2 compiler with lazy code motion, and a C compiler with copy propagation.

Our experience is that by using graph rewrite systems the development time of an optimizer is greatly reduced. Our estimate is that about 50% savings are possible. For instance, equation systems such as LCMANA can be typed in in a few hours. If the generator generates correct code the correctness of the generated algorithm can be achieved quite quickly. Also in transformation the savings are enormous: normally it is a tedious work to write algorithms which search for the transformation places. Using graph rewriting this is automatic.

Also the relation of generated and hand-written part in the optimizers is very interesting. Because OPTIMIX does not yet implement all possible features, still some parts are hand-written. Nevertheless, the constructed optimizer components consist of about 60-80% of generated code and the hand-written parts are not critical for the runtime of the optimizers. We estimate that with an industrial-strength implementation of OPTIMIX 90% of an optimizer can be generated without problems.

6.3 Effectiveness of generated optimization phases

The lazy code motion optimizer demonstrates that graph rewriting in deed can produce effective optimizers. The following table shows the execution times in seconds of some routines of the Stanford benchmark from Henessy and Nye. The optimizer achieves up to 32% speedup, although it is a prototypical implementation. Gcc and sun-cc are much more effective here. However, the quality of the optimized program code is a matter of the quality of the specification of the optimizer components. Thus much better results are possible by improving the specification, e.g. by including better alias information.

Routine	without LCM	with LCM	speedup in %	gcc -O4	sun-cc -O4
Queens	11.9	10.9	8	4.7	5.2
MatrixMult	12.6	8.5	32	2.9	5.9
Puzzle	4.9	4.0	18	1.4	1.8
Quicksort	8.3	7.4	13	2.8	6.1
Erastothenes	32.5	24.1	25	24.7	19.5

6.4 Overall optimization speed

In order to test the compilation speed of the generated components, the two compilers were compared running with and without optimization, compiling the Stanford benchmark. The table shows that the optimizers add about factor 3-7 to the runtime of the compilers. Clearly gcc and sun-cc are faster here, although they perform more optimizations. However, for generated optimizer parts the results are very good: OPTIMIX and the specified components are quite new implementations which leave a lot of possibilities for improvements. Also the lazy code motion optimizer performs already rather a computation-intensive optimization: it computes four data-flow equation fixpoints and syntactical expression equivalence. Again, with an industrial-strength implementation the velocity of the generated optimizer parts could very well reach that of hand-written parts.

Compiling Stanford benchmark	Slowdown factor
M-2, lazy code motion	7.2
C, copy propagation	2.9
gcc -O4	2.2
sun-cc -O4	3.1

6.5 Speeding up expression equivalence

[Aß95b] shows that an index structure can be used to speed up EQUIV. This structure maps attributes to nodes and simulates virtual edges between the two isolates of EQUIV-1/EQUIV-2. With this modified production EQUIV turns into an EARS(1) and its cost changes to $O(|\mathbf{Expr}|e^3)$. If the maximum number of elements in expression classes is small compared with the number of expressions, the runtime of EQUIV will be dominated by the cubic cost factor only for very large programs.

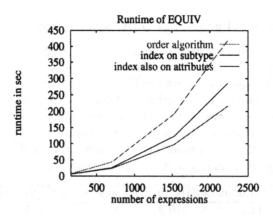

This assumption is supported by the diagram above. Here the runtime of a Modula-2 compiler including the EQUIV algorithm is measured. The upper curve shows clear quadratic runtime in the number of expressions of the program (order evaluation). The curve in the middle is measured with a hash index over the expressions; the hash index function comprises the subtypes of the expression nodes. The lower curve additionally comprises attributes of the most frequent expressions. Although the behaviour is not linear in the number of expressions the cubic factor starts to dominate the runtime only when very large procedures are compiled. Thus using a good hash function doubles the speed of the compiler: the use of index structures is very important in practice.

6.6 Graph representations

We also measured the influence of the graph representations on the runtime of the Modula-2 compiler. For that the LCMANA component was run with a list-based and a bitvector-based implementation for the data-flow sets. Both representations can be exchanged by changing the concrete class of the relations in the fSDL data specification (and of course, by adapting any non-generated code). When compiling the Stanford benchmark, the bitvector implementation is about 6 times faster than the list-based implementation. The difference lies in the implementation of the union and intersection operation of neighbor sets: on bitvectors these operations are linear and on lists they are quadratic.

This shows that it is very important which data representations are chosen for the manipulated graphs. Thus the final phase of writing an optimizer with graph rewriting consists of selecting the right data representation. Fortunately this can be done by only changing the data model; the generator adjusts its code generation automatically. This reveals a unique strength of our method: the specification is independent of the representation of the graphs.

7 Related work

Sharlit [TH92] and PAG [AM95] are two tools for generating efficient data-flow analyses. With both tools users have to supply data structures in C for the lattice elements and also for flow functions. Thus exchange of implementations is not so easy. SPARE [Ven89] follows the same approach and is additionally tied to the Synthesizer Generator. Generation of data-flow analysis from modal logic specification stems from [Ste91]. Although the powerful modal operators allow very short specifications, an application in a real-life compiler is not known. All these tools allow for the specification of more complex lattices and flow functions. However, we believe that our method is much more intuitive for the average programmer because it relies on the more familiar concept of graphs.

Only few approaches are known which integrate transformations. SPECIFY [Koc92] additionally provides a proof language but was never implemented completely. GENESIS [WS90] allows very powerful transformation specifications. Preconditions can be specified in a variant of first-order logic. However, because fixpoint computations cannot be specified, generation of data-flow analysis is not possible. Also it seems that the code generation scheme is quite ad hoc.

Also the existing tools for graph rewrite systems could be used for generation of program optimizers. PROGRES [Sch90] is the most advanced. However, it is designed for an interactive user environment and not for batch processing. Currently it does not allow for fixpoint computations and is tied to an underlying database, although it provides an excellent user interface. UBS systems [Dör95] provide a subclass of graph rewrite systems which can be handled more efficiently. However, the described implementation is still too slow for program optimization. OPTIMIX produces much faster algorithms: order evaluation of EQUIV (which only adds edges) performs at least $2300^2/400 = 13000$ redex tests/second[2]. Using an index the system is twice as fast: thus OPTIMIX should also provide one of the fastest existing tools to execute graph rewrite systems.

8   Outlook

We have presented in this paper a novel uniform specification method for program analysis and transformation. EARS can be used for analysis, terminating GRS for transformation. Both can be evaluated uniformly and efficiently with order evaluation. With this method for the first time complete optimizers can be specified. The prototypical tool OPTIMIX demonstrates that it is also possible to generate them.

EARS are equivalent to Datalog with binary predicates [Aß95a]. The idea that Datalog can been used to describe data-flow analysis has also been discovered by [Rep94]. However, the restriction to binary predicates makes it possible to use efficient graph search algorithms.

I would like to thank Jürgen Vollmer and Andreas Winter. As main implementors of the mentioned optimizer components and first users of OPTIMIX they forced me to spent a lot of nights in front of my machine; however, I believe, with nice results.

References

[Aß95a]   Uwe Aßmann. *Generierung von Programmoptimierungen mit Graphersetzungssystemen*. PhD thesis, Universität Karlsruhe, Kaiserstr. 12, 76128 Karlsruhe, Germany, July 1995.

[Aß95b]   Uwe Aßmann. On Edge Addition Rewrite Systems and Their Relevance to Program Analysis. In J. Cuny, editor, *5th Workshop on Graph Grammars and Their Application To Computer Science*, to appear in Lecture Notes in Computer Science. Springer, 1995.

[AAvS94] M. Alt, U. Aßmann, and H. van Someren. Cosy Compiler Phase Embedding with the CoSy Compiler Model. In P. A. Fritzson, editor, *Compiler Construction, Lecture Notes in Computer Science 786*, pages 278–293. Springer Verlag, April 1994.

[AM95]   M. Alt and F. Martin. Generation of efficient interprocedural analyzers with pag. In A. Mycroft, editor, *Static Analysis Symposium*, volume to appear of *Lecture Notes in Computer Science, Spinger Verlag*. Springer Verlag, 1995.

---

[2] The measurements of EQUIV comprise the runtime of the frontend. For simplification a quadratic algorithm is assumed for the number of tests. In fact even more tests are done

[Dör95]   Heiko Dörr. *Efficient Graph Rewriting and Its Implementation*, volume 922 of *Lecture Notes in Computer Science, Spinger Verlag*. Springer Verlag, 1995.

[Har88]   D. Harel. On visual formalisms. *Communications of the ACM*, 31(5):514–530, May 1988.

[Hec77]   M. S. Hecht. *Flow Analysis of Computer Programs*. Elsevier North-Holland, 1977.

[Koc92]   Gerd Kock. *Spezifikation und Verifikation von Optimierungsalgorithmen*. GMD Bericht 201, Universität Karlsruhe, 1992.

[KRS94]   J. Knoop, O. Rüthing, and B. Steffen. Optimal code motion: Theory and practice. *Transactions on Programming Languages and Systems*, 16(7), July 1994.

[Rep94]   Thomas Reps. Solving Demand Versions of Interprocedural Analysis Problems. In P.A. Fritzson, editor, *Compiler Construction*, volume 786 of *Lecture Notes in Computer Science*, pages 389–403, April 1994.

[RHS95]   T. Reps, S. Horwitz, and M. Sagiv. Precise interprocedural dataflow analysis via graph reachability. In *ACM Symposium on Principles of Programming Languages*, volume 22, pages 49–61. ACM, January 1995.

[Sch90]   A. Schürr. Introduction to PROGRES, an Attribute Graph Grammar Based Specification Language. In *Graph-Theoretic Concepts in Computer Science*, volume 541 of *Lecture Notes in Computer Science*, pages 444–458. Springer Verlag, 1990.

[Ste91]   Bernhard Steffen. Data flow analysis as model checking. In *Proceedings of Theoretical Aspects of Computer Software (TACS)*, pages 346–364, 1991.

[TH92]   S. W. K. Tjiang and J. L. Henessy. Sharlit – A tool for building optimizers. *SIGPLAN Conference on Programming Language Design and Implementation*, 1992.

[Ven89]   G. A. Venkatesh. A Framework for Construction and Evaluation of High-Level Specifications for Program Analysis Techniques. In *ACM SIGPLAN Conference on Programming Language Design and Implementation*, June 1989.

[VH92]   Jürgen Vollmer and Ralf Hoffart. Modula-P, a language for parallel programming: Definition and implementation on a transputer network. In *Proceedings of the 1992 International Conference on Computer Languages ICCL'92, Oakland, California*, pages 54–64. IEEE, IEEE Computer Society Press, April 1992.

[WKD94]   H.R. Walters, J.F.Th. Kamperman, and T.B. Dinesh. An extensible language for the generation of parallel data manipulation and control packages. In P. Fritzson, editor, *Proceedings of the Poster Session of Compiler Construction*, number LiTH-IDA-R-94-11 in PELAB Research Report. Linköping University, 1994.

[WS90]   D. Whitfield and M. L. Soffa. An approach to ordering optimizing transformations. In *ACM Conference on Principles and Practice of Parallel Programming (PPOPP)*, 1990.

Points-to Analysis by Type Inference
of Programs with Structures and Unions

Bjarne Steensgaard

Microsoft Research*

Abstract

We present an interprocedural flow-insensitive points-to analysis algorithm based on monomorphic type inference. The source language model the important features of C including pointers, pointer arithmetic, pointers to functions, structured objects, and unions. The algorithm is based on a non-standard type system where types represent nodes and edges in a storage shape graph.

This work is an extension of previous work on performing points-to analysis of C programs in almost linear time. This work makes three new contributions. The first is an extension of a type system for describing storage shape graphs to include objects with internal structure. The second is a constraint system that can deal with arbitrary use of pointers and which incorporates a two-tier domain of pointer offsets to improve the results of the analysis. The third is an efficient inference algorithm for the constraint system, leading to an algorithm that has close to linear time and space performance in practice.

Keywords: interprocedural program analysis, points-to analysis, C programs, non-standard types, constraint solving.

1 Introduction

Modern optimizing compilers and program understanding and browsing tools for pointer languages like C [Ame89, KR88] are dependent on semantic information obtained by either an alias analysis or a points-to analysis. Alias analyses compute pairs of expressions (or access paths) that may be aliased (*e.g.*, [LR92, LRZ93]). Points-to analyses compute a store model using abstract locations (*e.g.*, [CWZ90, EGH94, WL95, Ruf95]). Points-to analysis results serve no purpose in themselves, but they are a prerequisite for most other analyses and transformations for imperative programs (*e.g.*, computing use-def relations, permitted code motion, and detection of use of uninitialized variables).

Most current compilers and programming tools use only intraprocedural points-to analyses, as the polynomial time and space complexity of the common data-flow based points-to analyses prevents the use of interprocedural analyses for large programs. Interprocedural analysis is becoming increasingly important, as it is a prerequisite for whole-program optimization and various program understanding tools.

---

*Author's address: Microsoft Corporation, One Microsoft Way, Redmond, WA, USA. E-mail: rusa@research.microsoft.com

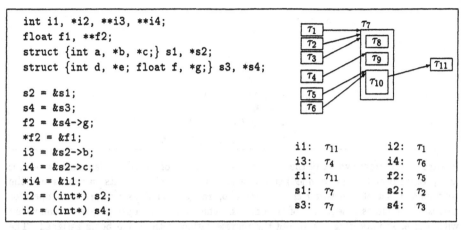

```
int i1, *i2, **i3, **i4;
float f1, **f2;
struct {int a, *b, *c;} s1, *s2;
struct {int d, *e; float f, *g;} s3, *s4;

s2 = &s1;
s4 = &s3;
f2 = &s4->g;
*f2 = &f1;
i3 = &s2->b;
i4 = &s2->c;
*i4 = &i1;
i2 = (int*) s2;
i2 = (int*) s4;
```

i1: τ_{11} i2: τ_1
i3: τ_4 i4: τ_6
f1: τ_{11} f2: τ_5
s1: τ_7 s2: τ_2
s3: τ_7 s4: τ_3

Figure 1: A small C program fragment, the storage shape graph that our algorithm builds for it out of types, and a typing of the program variables. Type τ_7 represents both structured variables in the program. The third type component, τ_{10}, of τ_7 represents structure elements s1.c, s2.f and s2.g.

We extend our previous work on flow-insensitive interprocedural points-to analysis of C programs by type inference methods [Ste96, Ste95] by enabling the algorithm to distinguish between components of structured objects, thereby increasing the precision of the analysis in the presence of structures and unions in the program to be analyzed. Other members of our research group have found this extension crucial to the value (accuracy) of some subsequent analyses (e.g., detection of use of uninitialized variables). The extended algorithm does not have the almost linear time complexity of the original algorithms, but it is exhibiting close to linear time complexity in practice (Sect. 5.3 discusses complexity).

The algorithm is based on type inference over a domain of types that can model a storage shape graph [CWZ90]. The inferred types describe the *use* of memory locations. The *declarations* of locations are irrelevant. The algorithm computes a valid typing even when memory locations are used in inconsistent ways, in contrast to ML type inference which will fail to compute a typing in that case. An example illustrating types modeling a storage shape graph for a program is shown in Fig. 1.

The computed solution is a storage shape graph that is a conservative description of the dynamic storage shape graphs for all program points simultaneously. If programmers use locations in a consistent manner throughout their programs the loss in precision by not computing separate solutions for each program point is typically small. Computing only one storage shape graph permits the algorithm to be fast for even very large programs.

We proceed by stating the source language (Sect. 2), which captures the essential parts of the C programming language, the non-standard set of types we use to model the storage use (Sect. 3), and a set of typing rules for programs (Sect. 4). Finding a typing of the program that obeys the constraints imposed by the typing rules amounts to performing a points-to analysis. We then show how to efficiently deduce the minimal typing that obeys the constraints (Sect. 5) and report on practical experience with the algorithm (Sect. 6). Finally we describe related work (Sect. 7) and present our conclusions and point out directions for future work (Sect. 8).

$$
\begin{aligned}
S \quad ::= \quad & x =_s y \\
| \quad & x =_s \&y \\
| \quad & x =_s *y \\
| \quad & x =_s \text{allocate}(y) \\
| \quad & *x =_s y \\
| \quad & x =_s \text{op}(y_1 \ldots y_n) \\
| \quad & x =_s \&y\text{->}n \\
| \quad & x =_s \text{fun}(f_1 \ldots f_n) \rightarrow (r_1 \ldots r_m) \ S^* \\
| \quad & x_1 \ldots x_m =_{s_1 \ldots s_m} p(y_1 \ldots y_n)
\end{aligned}
$$

Figure 2: Abstract syntax of the relevant statements, S, of the source language. x, y, f, r, and p range over the (unbounded) set of variable names and constants. n ranges over the (unbounded) set of structure element names. op ranges over the set of primitive operator names. S^* denotes a sequence of statements. The assignment operator, $=$, is annotated with a size, s, indicating the size of the representation of the value being assigned. The control structures of the language are irrelevant.

2 The Source Language

We describe the points-to analysis for a pointer language with structures and unions that captures the important properties of the C programming language [Ame89, KR88]. Since the analysis is flow insensitive, the control structures of the language are irrelevant. An important feature of the language is that any memory object may be accessed as a unit or as a structured object. Type casts and variable declarations as found in C are irrelevant; the source language permits inconsistent use of locations as well as the use of any memory object as a structured object without such constructs. Unions are implicit in the use of memory objects. Figure 2 shows the abstract syntax of the relevant parts of the language.

The syntax for pointer operations borrows from the C programming language. All variables are assumed to have unique names. The op(...) expression form is used to describe primitive computations like arithmetic operations. The allocate(y) expression dynamically allocates a block of memory of size y.

Functions are constant values described by the fun(...)$\rightarrow$(...)S^* expression form[1]. The f_i variables are formal parameters (sometimes called *in parameters*), and the r_i variables are return values (sometimes called *out parameters*). Function calls have call-by-value semantics [ASU86]. Both formal and return parameter variables may appear in left- and right-hand-side position in statements in the function body.

We assume that programs are as well-behaved as (mostly) portable C programs. We allow assignment of a structured value to a location supposed to hold only pointer values, and vice versa, provided the representation of the assigned value fits within the size of the representation of the object being modified. The analysis algorithm may produce wrong (unsafe) results for programs that construct pointers from scratch (*e.g.*, by bitwise duplication of pointers by control flow rather than data flow) and non-portable programs (*e.g.*, programs that rely on how a specific compiler allocates variables relative to each other). All previously described analyses suffer from the same problem. However, the analysis algorithm as presented below will deal with, *e.g.*, exclusive-or operations on pointer values, where there is a flow of values.

---

[1]We allow functions with multiple return values; a feature not found in C.

3 Types

For the purpose of performing the points-to analysis, we define a non-standard set of types to describe the store. The types are unrelated to the types normally used in C (*e.g.*, `integer`, `float`, `pointer`, `struct`). The types are used to model how storage is used in a program at runtime (a storage model). Locations of program variables and locations created by dynamic allocation are all described by types. Each type describes a set of locations as well as the possible runtime contents of those locations.

The types must be able to model both simple locations, which are only ever accessed as a whole (e.g., integer variables), structured locations, and locations that are accessed in inconsistent ways. We want to accommodate inconsistent accesses of locations with minimal information loss. We use four different kinds of types: **blank** describes locations with no access pattern, **simple** describes locations only accessed as a whole, **struct** describes locations only accessed as structured objects, and **object** describes locations accessed in ways not covered by the other three kinds of types.

Structured objects may be accessed in inconsistent ways. We want the **struct** types to be able to describe commonalities in the accesses anyway. We assume structures with a "common prefix" share layout of the common prefix elements. The **struct** types have component types describing distinguishable components of a location, where "distinguishable" means that any access of part of the memory object only accesses a single component. For the program fragment in Fig. 1, one distinguishable component describes the first element of the structured objects, another the second element, and a third the remaining components.

The size of an access is important. For example, if a pointer value may point to an integer component of a structured object and an access through the pointer is "larger" than the size of an integer, other components of the structure pointed into may be modified or retrieved. For example, if the program fragment shown in Fig. 1 were extended with a reference of "`*(long*)i3`" then the structures would only have two distinguishable components.

The type of a memory object must also describe the contents of the object. Only pointer values are relevant. We describe pointers to locations by the type representing the object(s) it pointed to or into and an offset, which may be either **zero** or **unknown**. If a pointer with an **unknown** offset is used in an indirect assignment (*e.g.*, `*x =`$_s$` y`) then we don't know what part of the referenced object is being modified, and the object must be described by an **object** type.

Functions, or rather function pointer values, are described by signature types describing the locations of the argument and result values.

The non-standard set of types used by our points-to analysis algorithm is described by the following productions:

$$
\begin{array}{llll}
\tau & ::= & \bot \mid \mathbf{simple}(\alpha, \lambda, s, p) \mid \mathbf{struct}(m, s, p) \mid & \\
      &   & \mathbf{object}(\alpha, \lambda, s, p) \mid \mathbf{blank}(s, p) & \text{(Objects)} \\
\alpha & ::= & (\tau \times o) & \text{(Pointers)} \\
o & ::= & \mathbf{zero} \mid \mathbf{unknown} & \text{(Offsets)} \\
\lambda & ::= & \bot \mid \mathbf{lam}(\tau_1 \ldots \tau_n)(\tau_{n+1} \ldots \tau_{n+m}) & \text{(Functions)} \\
s & ::= & \text{SIZE} \mid \top & \text{(Sizes)} \\
p & ::= & \mathcal{P}(\tau) \mid \top & \text{(Parents)} \\
m & ::= & (\text{element} \mapsto \tau) \text{ mapping} & \text{(Elements)}
\end{array}
$$

$$
\begin{array}{ll}
\text{i1:} & \tau_{11} = \mathbf{simple}(\bot, \bot, \top, \emptyset) \\
\text{i2:} & \tau_1 = \mathbf{simple}(\tau_7, \bot, < \mathbf{ptr} >, \emptyset) \\
\text{i3:} & \tau_4 = \mathbf{simple}(\tau_9, \bot, < \mathbf{ptr} >, \emptyset) \\
\text{i4:} & \tau_6 = \mathbf{simple}(\tau_{10}, \bot, < \mathbf{ptr} >, \emptyset) \\
\text{f1:} & \tau_{11} \\
\text{f2:} & \tau_5 = \mathbf{simple}(\tau_{10}, \bot, < \mathbf{ptr} >, \emptyset) \\
\text{s1:} & \tau_7 = \mathbf{struct}([< \mathbf{int} > \mapsto \tau_8, < \mathbf{int}, \mathbf{int} > \mapsto \tau_9, {}^* \mapsto \tau_{10}], \top, \emptyset) \\
\text{s2:} & \tau_2 = \mathbf{simple}(\tau_9, \bot, < \mathbf{ptr} >, \emptyset) \\
\text{s3:} & \tau_7 \\
\text{s4:} & \tau_3 = \mathbf{simple}(\tau_9, \bot, < \mathbf{ptr} >, \emptyset) \\
& \tau_8 = \mathbf{simple}(\bot, \bot, < \mathbf{int} >, \{\tau_7\}) \\
& \tau_9 = \mathbf{simple}(\bot, \bot, < \mathbf{int} >, \{\tau_7\}) \\
& \tau_{10} = \mathbf{object}(\tau_{11}, \bot, \top, \{\tau_7\})
\end{array}
$$

Figure 3: Typing of the program fragment of Fig. 1 in terms of the types of our analysis algorithm.

The τ types describe objects or object components, the α types describe pointers to locations, the λ types describe pointers to functions. The m type components are mappings from structure element specifiers to component types. The element specifiers can be either symbolic or numeric.

The s type components describe object or object component sizes. The sizes can be either numeric or symbolic. The $\top$ size indicates the rest of a memory object and is used in types describing objects of different sizes. The p type components describe the set of **struct** types (parents) of which a given type is a component. The $\top$ value means "no parents" and is introduced to enable a requirement that a type has no parents while allowing use of least-upper-bound operators in the inference algorithm. We assume the programmer is denied knowledge of the activation record layout and therefore do not consider parents of λ type.

Types may be recursive (the type graph may be cyclic). The types may be written out using type identifiers (type variables). Two types are equal when they are either both $\bot$ or are described by the same type identifier. Note that this is different from the usual structural equality criterion on types. We could use the structural equality criterion if we added a tag to the τ, o, and λ types.

Figure 3 shows the typing of the variables of the program fragment of Fig. 1.

4 Typing Rules

In this section we define a set of typing rules based on the set of non-standard types defined in the previous section. The typing rules specify when a program is well-typed. A well-typed program is one for which the static storage shape graph indicated by the types is a safe (conservative) description of all possible dynamic (runtime) storage configurations and which also safely describes the use of the storage.

There are three kinds of use of storage in the source language. Use via pointer indirection uses the pointer location as a whole. Computing the address of a structure element is a use of a location as a structured object. These two uses force the location being addressed to be described by at least a **simple** or **struct** type respectively in the $\trianglelefteq_s$ partial order described below. The third kind of use is by assignment of entire objects. For example, if we assign a structured value to a location that is otherwise used only as a whole the contents of the location assigned to is used in inconsistent ways. The assigned-to location must therefore be described by an **object** type, while the assigned-from location may still be described by a **struct** type.

We use the partial order $a \trianglelefteq_s b$ to describe the relationship between the type, b, of the assigned-to location, and the type, a, of the assigned-from location. The partial order is parameterized by a size, s, as the size of the representation of the assigned value must be smaller than that of (the types of) the assigned-to and the assigned-from location to avoid problems with unmodeled capture of adjacent elements in a structured object. The size constraints are trivially fulfilled if the types describe entire objects or the entire rest of objects ($s = \top$).

The $\trianglelefteq_s$ partial order uses the following hierarchy among the kinds of types:

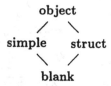

where a necessary (but not sufficient) requirement for $a \trianglelefteq_s b$ to hold is that a and b are either of the same kind or the kind of b appears above the kind of a in the hierarchy.

If the offset component of either a or b is **unknown** then we have to assume the worst about the usage of the described memory location and the memory object component should be of the **object** kind.

Since there is a flow of data from the assigned-from location to the assigned-to location, any pointer content of the assigned-from location should also be described by the content components of the assigned-to location. We describe the relationship between the assigned-from and assigned-to location contents by the $\sqsubseteq_s$ and $\sqsubseteq$ partial order between memory and function pointer component types respectively defined as follows:

$$(\tau_1 \times o_1) \sqsubseteq_s (\tau_2 \times o_2) \;\;\Leftrightarrow\;\; (\tau_1 = \bot) \vee ((\tau_1 \sqsubseteq_s \tau_2) \wedge (o_1 \sqsubseteq o_2))$$
$$\tau_1 \sqsubseteq_s \tau_2 \;\;\Leftrightarrow\;\; (\tau_1 = \tau_2) \wedge (s \sqsubseteq \mathrm{sizeof}(\tau_1))$$
$$o_1 \sqsubseteq o_2 \;\;\Leftrightarrow\;\; (o_1 = \mathbf{zero}) \vee (o_1 = o_2)$$
$$s_1 \sqsubseteq s_2 \;\;\Leftrightarrow\;\; (s_1 = s_2) \vee (s_2 = \top)$$
$$\lambda_1 \sqsubseteq \lambda_2 \;\;\Leftrightarrow\;\; (\lambda_1 = \bot) \vee (\lambda_1 = \lambda_2),$$

where "$\mathrm{sizeof}(\tau)$" denotes the size component of whatever kind of type τ is. For example, a necessary requirement for $\mathbf{simple}(\alpha_1, \lambda_1, s_1, p_1) \trianglelefteq_s \mathbf{simple}(\alpha_2, \lambda_2, s_2, p_2)$ to hold is that $\alpha_1 \sqsubseteq_s \alpha_2$ and $\lambda_1 \sqsubseteq \lambda_2$ both hold.

We could have used equality ($=$) instead of $\sqsubseteq$ ordering. The primary reason for not doing so is discussed in [Ste96]. Of particular importance to the type system used in the present paper is that use of $\sqsubseteq$ rather than $=$ permits non-pointer content of components of **struct** mappings when a value in a **struct** location is assigned to an **object** location.

$$\frac{A \vdash x : \tau_1 \qquad A \vdash y : \tau_2 \qquad (\tau_2 \times \mathbf{zero}) \trianglelefteq_s (\tau_1 \times \mathbf{zero})}{A \vdash welltyped(x =_s y)}$$

$$\frac{A \vdash x : \mathbf{sim/obj}(\alpha_1, \lambda_1, s_1, p_1) \qquad A \vdash y : \tau_2 \qquad s \sqsubseteq s_1 \qquad (\tau_2 \times \mathbf{zero}) \sqsubseteq_s \alpha_1}{A \vdash welltyped(x =_s \&y)}$$

$$\frac{A \vdash y : \mathbf{sim/obj}(\alpha_2, \lambda_2, s_2, p_2) \qquad A \vdash x : \tau_1 \qquad \alpha_2 \trianglelefteq_s (\tau_1 \times \mathbf{zero})}{A \vdash welltyped(x =_s {*}y)}$$

$$\frac{A \vdash x : \mathbf{sim/obj}((\tau_1 \times o_1), \lambda_1, s_1, p_1) \qquad \tau_1 \neq \bot \qquad s \sqsubseteq s_1}{A \vdash welltyped(x =_s allocate(y))}$$

$$\frac{A \vdash x : \mathbf{sim/obj}(\alpha_1, \lambda_1, s_1, p_1) \qquad A \vdash y : \tau_2 \qquad (\tau_2 \times \mathbf{zero}) \trianglelefteq_s \alpha_1}{A \vdash welltyped({*}x =_s y)}$$

$$\frac{A \vdash x : \tau \qquad A \vdash y_i : \tau_i \qquad \forall i \in [1 \ldots n] : (\tau_i \times \mathbf{zero}) \trianglelefteq_s (\tau \times \mathbf{zero}) \qquad \tau = \mathbf{sim/obj}((\tau' \times \mathbf{unknown}), \lambda, s', p)}{A \vdash welltyped(x =_s op(y_1 \ldots y_n))}$$

$$\frac{A \vdash x : \mathbf{sim/obj}(\alpha_1, \lambda_1, s_1, p_1) \qquad A \vdash y : \mathbf{sim/obj}((\tau_2 \times o_2), \lambda_2, s_2, p_2) \qquad \tau_2 = \mathbf{object}(\alpha_3, \lambda_3, \top, \top) \qquad s \sqsubseteq s_1 \qquad (\tau_2 \times o_2) \sqsubseteq_s \alpha_1}{A \vdash welltyped(x =_s \&y\text{->}n)}$$

$$\frac{A \vdash x : \mathbf{sim/obj}(\alpha_1, \lambda_1, s_1, p_1) \qquad A \vdash y : \mathbf{simple}((\tau_2 \times \mathbf{zero}), \lambda_2, s_2, p_2) \qquad \tau_2 = \mathbf{struct}(m_3, s_3, p_3) \qquad compatible(n, m_3) \qquad s \sqsubseteq s_1 \qquad (m_3(n) \times \mathbf{zero}) \sqsubseteq_s \alpha_1}{A \vdash welltyped(x =_s \&y\text{->}n)}$$

$$\frac{\begin{array}{c} A \vdash x : \mathbf{sim/obj}(\alpha_0, \lambda_0, s_0, p_0) \qquad \lambda_0 = \mathbf{lam}(\tau_1 \ldots \tau_n)(\tau_{n+1} \ldots \tau_{n+m}) \\ A \vdash f_i : \tau_i' \qquad A \vdash r_j : \tau_{n+j}' \\ s_i = sizeof(f_i) \qquad s_{n+j} = sizeof(r_j) \qquad s \sqsubseteq s_0 \\ \forall i \in [1 \ldots n] : (\tau_i \times \mathbf{zero}) \trianglelefteq_{s_i} (\tau_i' \times \mathbf{zero}) \\ \forall j \in [1 \ldots m] : (\tau_{n+j}' \times \mathbf{zero}) \trianglelefteq_{s_{n+j}} (\tau_{n+j} \times \mathbf{zero}) \\ \forall x \in S^* : A \vdash welltyped(x) \end{array}}{A \vdash welltyped(x =_s \mathbf{fun}(f_1 \ldots f_n) \rightarrow (r_1 \ldots r_m) \ S^*)}$$

$$\frac{\begin{array}{c} A \vdash p : \mathbf{sim/obj}(\alpha_0, \lambda_0, s_0, p_0) \\ \lambda_0 = \mathbf{lam}(\tau_1 \ldots \tau_n)(\tau_{n+1} \ldots \tau_{n+m}) \\ A \vdash x_j : \tau_{n+j}' \qquad A \vdash y_i : \tau_i' \qquad s_i = sizeof(y_i) \\ \forall i \in [1 \ldots n] : (\tau_i' \times \mathbf{zero}) \trianglelefteq_{s_i} (\tau_i \times \mathbf{zero}) \\ \forall j \in [1 \ldots m] : (\tau_{n+j} \times \mathbf{zero}) \trianglelefteq_{s_{j+n}} (\tau_{n+j}' \times \mathbf{zero}) \end{array}}{A \vdash welltyped(x_1 \ldots x_m =_{s_{n+1} \ldots s_{n+m}} p(y_1 \ldots y_n))}$$

Figure 4: Type rules for the relevant statement types of the source language. The **sim/obj** pattern matches both **simple** and **object** types. All variables are assumed to have been associated with a type in the type environment, A.

Given the $\trianglelefteq_s$ partial order, well-typedness of a simple assignment statement can be expressed as follows:

$$\frac{A \vdash x : \tau_1 \qquad A \vdash y : \tau_2 \qquad (\tau_2 \times \mathbf{zero}) \trianglelefteq_s (\tau_1 \times \mathbf{zero})}{A \vdash welltyped(x =_s y)}$$

In Fig. 4 we state the typing rules for the relevant parts of the source language. A program is well-typed under typing environment A if all the statements of the program are well-typed under A. A typing environment associates all variables with a type.

In statements of the form $x = op(y_1 \ldots y_n)$, the op operation may be a comparison, a bit-wise operation, an addition, etc. Consider a subtraction (or bitwise exclusive or) of two pointer values. The result is not a pointer value, but either of the two pointer values can be reconstituted from the result given the other pointer value[2]. The result must therefore be described by the same location type as the two input pointer values and an **unknown** offset. There are operations from which operand pointer values cannot be reconstituted from the result (*e.g.*, comparisons: $<$, $\neq$, etc.). For such

---

[2]This is true for most implementations of C even though subtraction of pointers to different objects is implementation dependent according to the ANSI C specification [Ame89].

operations, the result is not required to be described by the same type as any input pointer value. We treat all primitive operations identically.

The typing rule for dynamic allocation states that some pointer value is being assigned. The type that describes the allocated location need not be the type of any variable in the program. The type of the allocated location is then only indirectly available through the type of the variable assigned to. All locations allocated by the same statement will have the same type, but locations allocated by different allocation statements may have different types.

The typing rule for computing the address of a structure element makes use of a predicate, compatible(n,m). The details of the predicate is dependent on the choice of representation of element specifiers, but the predicate should capture that the mapping describes a structure whose prefix matches that of the structure being accessed up to and including the element n.

We have defined the typing rules under the assumption that the number of formal and actual parameters (and results) always match up. The rules are trivially extendible to handle programs where this is not the case and to handle programs with variable arguments (*e.g.*, using <stdarg.h> in C).

5 Efficient Type Inference

Performing a points-to analysis amounts to inferring a typing environment under which a program is well-typed. The typing environment we seek is the minimal solution to the well-typedness problem, *i.e.*, each location type describes as few locations as possible, and each function type describes as few functions as possible. In this section we state how to efficiently compute such a minimal solution.

The basic principle of the algorithm is that we start with the assumption that all variables are described by different types (type variables) and then proceed to unifying and merging types as necessary to ensure well-typedness of different parts of the program. Merging two types means replacing the two type variables with a single type variable throughout the typing environment. When all parts of the program has been processed, the program is well-typed.

5.1 Algorithm Stages

In the first stage of the algorithm we provide a typing environment where all program variables are described by different type variables. A type variable consists of a fast union/find structure (an equivalence class representative (ECR)) with associated type information. ECRs allows us to replace two type variables with a single type variables by a constant time "union" operation. The initial type of each program variable is blank$(s,\emptyset)$, where s is the size of the representation of the variable. We assume that name resolution has been performed and that we can encode the typing environment in the program representation and get constant time access to the type variable associated with a variable name.

In the second stage of the algorithm we process each statement of the program exactly once. Type variables are joined as necessary to ensure well-typedness of each statement (as described in the next section). When joining two type variables, the associated type information is unified by computing the least upper bound of the two types, joining component type variables as necessary. Joining two types will never make a once well-typed statement no longer be well-typed. If type variables are only joined when necessary to ensure well-typedness, the final type graph is the minimal solution we seek.

5.2 Processing Constraints

When processing a statement, we must ensure that the constraints imposed by the $\sqsubseteq$, and $\trianglelefteq$, partial orders are obeyed. This can be achieved by joining type variables and by "upgrading" **simple** and **struct** types to **object** types and **blank** types to **simple**, **struct**, or **object** types.

It may happen that the effects of a constraint cannot be determined at the time of processing the statement introducing the constraint. The algorithm uses latent constraints by annotating type variables with actions that are to be invoked if the "value" of the type variable should change.

For example, consider a partial order constraint between two function types, $\lambda_1 \sqsubseteq \lambda_2$. If λ_1 is anything other than $\perp$, then λ_1 and λ_2 must be joined to meet the constraint. However, we may not know at the time of processing the statement with the constraint whether λ_1 will be $\perp$ or something else in the final solution. Joining the two type variables will be safe, but it may be too conservative, and the final result may not be the minimal solution we seek. If λ_1 is $\perp$ at the time we encounter the constraint, we add to the set of latent actions associated with λ_1 that it should be joined with λ_2 if it ever changes value.

Figure 5 provides the precise set of rules for processing the relevant kinds of statements of a program. The processing rules follow immediately from the well-typedness rules and are straightforward to implement. Figure 6 provides the details of the join operations.

5.3 Complexity

We argue that the space and time complexity is exponential in the size of the input program using a theoretically correct (but practically meaningless) metric, is quadratic in the size of the program using a more reasonable metric, and is likely to be close to linear in the size of the program in practice.

The number of distinguishable memory locations in a program is $O(\exp N)$, where N is the size of the program. This is achievable by building a structure in the shape of a binary tree. A size N program could also populate all the "left" leaves of such a binary tree with pointers to the root of the tree. The points-to solution for such a program would be of size $O(\exp N)$. The runtime complexity of any points-to algorithm computing such a solution must therefore be exponential or worse.

While theoretically correct, expressing the algorithm complexity in terms of N is a practically meaningless metric of the complexity of the algorithm. We know of no related work using this metric; although several specify complexity in terms of N they are really using a different metric. A more reasonable metric measures the complexity of the algorithm in terms of the combined size, S, of all variables of the program.

The number of type variables created during the stages of our algorithm is $O(S)$. Any constraints not involving **struct** types can be processed in linear space and almost linear time complexity in terms of the number of type variables joined. For programs that do not use structured variables, the algorithm has a $O(S)$ space and

Figure 5 content (left column):

$x =_s y$
let $\tau_1 = \text{ecr}(x)$, $\tau_2 = \text{ecr}(y)$ in
  $\text{cjoin}(s, \tau_2, \tau_1)$

$x =_s \&y$
let $\tau_1 = \text{ecr}(x)$, $\tau_2 = \text{ecr}(y)$ in
  $\text{ensure-sim/obj}(\tau_1, s)$
  let $\text{sim/obj}(\alpha_1, \lambda_1, s_1, p_1) = \text{type}(\tau_1)$ in
  if $s \not\sqsubseteq s_1$ then $\text{expand}(\tau_1)$
  $\text{join}((\tau_2 \times \text{zero}), \alpha_1)$

$x =_s *y$
let $\tau_1 = \text{ecr}(x)$, $\tau_2 = \text{ecr}(y)$ in
  $\text{ensure-sim/obj}(\tau_2, s)$
  let $\text{sim/obj}(\alpha_2, \lambda_2, s_2, p_2) = \text{type}(\tau_2)$ in
  let $(\tau_3 \times o_3) = \alpha_2$ in $\text{unless-zero}(o_3, \tau_3)$
  $\text{cjoin}(s, \tau_3, \tau_1)$

$x =_s \text{allocate}(y)$
let $\tau = \text{ecr}(x)$ in
  $\text{ensure-sim/obj}(\tau, s)$
  let $\text{sim/obj}(\alpha_1, \lambda_1, s_1, p_1) = \text{type}(\tau)$ in
  if $s \not\sqsubseteq s_1$ then $\text{expand}(\tau)$
  let $(\tau_1 \times o_1) = \alpha_1$ in
  if $\text{type}(\tau_1) = \bot$ then
    $\text{settype}(\tau_1, \text{blank}(\top, \emptyset))$

$*x =_s y$
let $\tau_1 = \text{ecr}(x)$, $\tau_2 = \text{ecr}(y)$ in
  $\text{ensure-sim/obj}(\tau_1, s)$
  let $\text{sim/obj}(\alpha_1, \lambda_1, s_1, p_1) = \text{type}(\tau_1)$ in
  let $(\tau_3 \times o_3) = \alpha_1$ in $\text{unless-zero}(o_3, \tau_3)$
  $\text{cjoin}(s, \tau_2, \tau_3)$

$x =_s \text{fun}(f_1 \ldots f_n) \rightarrow (r_1 \ldots r_m)\ S^*$
let $\tau_0 = \text{ecr}(x)$ in
  $\text{ensure-sim/obj}(\tau_0, s)$
  let $\text{sim/obj}(\alpha_0, \lambda_0, s_0, p_0) = \text{type}(\tau_0)$ in
  if $s \not\sqsubseteq s_0$ then $\text{expand}(\tau_0)$
  if $\text{type}(\lambda_0) = \bot$ then
    let $[\tau_1 \ldots \tau_{n+m}] = \text{MakeECR}(n + m)$ in
    let $t = \text{lam}(\tau_1 \ldots \tau_n)(\tau_{n+1} \ldots \tau_{n+m})$ in
    $\text{settype}(\lambda_0, t),$
  let $\text{lam}(\tau_1 \ldots \tau_n)(\tau_{n+1} \ldots \tau_{n+m}) = \lambda_0$ in
  for $i \in [1 \ldots n]$ do
    let $s_i = \text{sizeof}(f_i)$, $\tau'_i = \text{ecr}(f_i)$ in
    $\text{cjoin}(s_i, \tau_i, \tau'_i)$
  for $j \in [1 \ldots m]$ do
    let $s_{n+j} = \text{sizeof}(r_j)$, $\tau'_{n+j} = \text{ecr}(r_j)$ in
    $\text{cjoin}(s_{n+j}, \tau'_{n+j}, \tau_{n+j})$

Figure 5 content (right column):

$x =_s \text{op}(y_1 \ldots y_n)$
let $\tau = \text{ecr}(x)$ in
  for $i \in [1 \ldots n]$ do
    let $\tau_i = \text{ecr}(y_i)$ in $\text{cjoin}(s, \tau_i, \tau)$
  $\text{ensure-sim/obj}(\tau, s)$
  let $\text{sim/obj}(\alpha', \lambda', s', p') = \text{type}(\tau)$ in
  let $(\tau' \times o') = \alpha'$ in
  if $\text{type}(o') = \text{zero}$ then
    $\text{make-unknown}(o')$

$x =_s \&y\text{->}n$
let $\tau_1 = \text{ecr}(x)$, $\tau_0 = \text{ecr}(y)$ in
  $\text{ensure-sim/obj}(\tau_1, s)$
  $\text{ensure-sim/obj}(\tau_0, \text{sizeof}(y))$
  let $\text{sim/obj}(\alpha_1, \lambda_1, s_1, p_1) = \text{type}(\tau_1)$
    $\text{sim/obj}(\alpha_2, \lambda_2, s_2, p_2) = \text{type}(\tau_0)$ in
  if $s \not\sqsubseteq s_1$ then $\text{expand}(\tau_1)$
  let $(\tau_2 \times o_2) = \alpha_2$ in
  if $\text{type}(o_2) = \text{unknown}$ then
    $\text{collapse}(\tau_2)$, $\text{join}(\alpha_2, \alpha_1)$
  else
    $\text{unless-zero}(o_2, \tau_2)$
    if $\text{type}(\tau_2) = \text{blank}(s_3, p_3)$ then
      $m_3 = [\ ]$
      $\text{settype}(\tau_2, \text{struct}(m_3, s_3, p_3))$
      $\text{make-compatible}(n, m_3)$
      $\text{join}((m_3(n) \times \text{zero}), \alpha_1)$
    elseif $\text{type}(\tau_2) = \text{struct}(m_3, s_3, p_3)$ then
      $\text{make-compatible}(n, m_3)$
      $\text{join}((m_3(n) \times \text{zero}), \alpha_1)$
    else
      $\text{promote}(\tau_2, \text{sizeof}(*y))$, $\text{join}(\alpha_2, \alpha_1)$

$x_1 \ldots x_m =_{s_{n+1} \ldots s_{n+m}} p(y_1 \ldots y_n)$
let $\tau_0 = \text{ecr}(p)$ in
  $\text{ensure-sim/obj}(\tau_0, \text{sizeof}(p))$
  let $\text{sim/obj}(\alpha_0, \lambda_0, s_0, p_0) = \text{type}(\tau_0)$ in
  if $\text{type}(\lambda_0) = \bot$ then
    let $[\tau_1 \ldots \tau_{n+m}] = \text{MakeECR}(n + m)$ in
    let $t = \text{lam}(\tau_1 \ldots \tau_n)(\tau_{n+1} \ldots \tau_{n+m})$ in
    $\text{settype}(\lambda_0, t)$
  let $\text{lam}(\tau_1 \ldots \tau_n)(\tau_{n+1} \ldots \tau_{n+m}) = \lambda_0$ in
  for $i \in [1 \ldots n]$ do
    let $s_i = \text{sizeof}(y_i)$, $\tau'_i = \text{ecr}(y_i)$ in
    $\text{cjoin}(s_i, \tau'_i, \tau_i)$
  for $j \in [1 \ldots m]$ do
    let $\tau'_{n+j} = \text{ecr}(x_j)$ in
    $\text{cjoin}(s_{n+j}, \tau_{n+j}, \tau'_{n+j})$

Figure 5: Inference rules corresponding to the typing rules given in Fig. 4. $\text{make-compatible}(n, m)$ is a side-effecting predicate that modifies mapping m to be compatible with access of structure element n (if possible and necessary) and returns a boolean value indicating the success of this modification. $\text{MakeECR}(x)$ constructs a list of x new ECRs, each associated with the bottom type, $\bot$. Figure 6 provides details of the other functions used in the above rules.

```
join((τ₁ × o₁), (τ₂ × o₂)):
    if type(o₁) = zero then
        pending(o₁) ←pending(o₂) ∪
            {<makeunknown,o₂>}
    elseif type(o₂) = zero then
        make-unknown(o₂)
    join(τ₁, τ₂)

join(e₁, e₂):
    if type(e₁) = ⊥ then
        pending(e₁) ←pending(e₁) ∪
            {<join,e₁,e₂>}
    else
        let e = ecr-union(e₁, e₂) in
        pending(e) ←
            pending(e₁) ∪ pending(e₂)
        type(e) ← type(e₁)
        settype(e, unify(e₁, e₂))

settype(e, t):
    type(e) ← t
    for a ∈ pending(e) do
        case a of
            [<join,e₁,e₂>]: join(e₁, e₂)
            [<cjoin,s,e₁,e₂>]: cjoin(s, e₁, e₂)

ensure-sim/obj(τ, s):
    case type(τ) of
        [⊥]: settype(τ, simple(⊥, ⊥, s, ∅))
        [blank(s', p)]:
            settype(τ, simple(⊥, ⊥, s', p))
            if s ⋢ s' then expand(τ)
        [simple(α, λ, s', p)]:
            if s ⋢ s' then expand(τ)
        [struct(m, s', p)]: promote(τ, s')

expand(e):
    let τ = blank(⊤, ∅) in
    settype(e, unify(type(e), τ))

promote(e, s):
    let τ = object(⊥, ⊥, s, ∅) in
    settype(e, unify(type(e), τ))

collapse(e):
    let τ = object(⊥, ⊥, ⊤, ⊤) in
    settype(e, unify(type(e), τ))

make-unknown(o):
    type(o) ← unknown
    for a ∈ pending(o) do
        case a of
            [<collapse,τ>]: collapse(τ)
            [<makeunknown,o'>]:
                make-unknown(o')
```

```
unless-zero(o, τ):
    if type(o) = zero then
        pending(o) ← {<collapse,τ>} ∪ pending(o)
    else collapse(τ)

cjoin(s, e₁, e₂):
    pending(e₁) ←{<cjoin,s,e₁,e₂>} ∪ pending(e₁)
    case type(e₁) of
        [⊥]: /* nothing */
        [blank(s₁, p₁)]:
            if s ⋢ s₁ then expand(e₁)
            elseif type(e₂) = ⊥ then
                settype(e₂, blank(s, ∅))
            elseif s ⋢ sizeof(type(e₂)) then
                expand(e₂)
        [simple(α₁, λ₁, s₁, p₁)]:
            if s ⋢ s₁ then expand(e₁)
            else
                case type(e₂) of
                    [⊥]: settype(e₂, simple(α₁, λ₁, s, ∅))
                    [blank(s₂, p₂)]:
                        settype(e₂, simple(α₁, λ₁, s₂, p₂))
                        if s ⋢ s₂ then expand(e₂)
                    [simple(α₂, λ₂, s₂, p₂)]:
                        join(α₁, α₂), join(λ₁, λ₂)
                        if s ⋢ s₂ then expand(e₂)
                    [struct(m₂, s₂, p₂)]: promote(e₂, s₂)
                    [object(α₂, λ₂, ⊤, ∅)]:
                        join(α₁, α₂), join(λ₁, λ₂)
        [struct(m₁, s₁, p₁)]:
            if s ⋢ s₁ then expand(e₁)
            else
                case type(e₂) of
                    [⊥]: settype(e₂, struct(m₁, s, ∅))
                    [blank(s₂, p₂)]:
                        settype(e₂, struct(m₁, s₂, p₂))
                        if s ⋢ s₂ then expand(e₂)
                    [simple(α₂, λ₂, s₂, p₂)]: promote(e₂, s₂)
                    [struct(m₂, s₂, p₂)]:
                        if s ⊑ s₂ ∧
                            ∀x ∈ Dom(m₁) :
                                make-compatible(x, m₂) then
                            for x ∈ Dom(m₁) do
                                cjoin(sizeof(x), m₁(x), m₂(x))
                        else expand(e₂)
                    [object(α₂, λ₂, ⊤, ∅)]:
                        for x ∈ Dom(m₁) do
                            cjoin(sizeof(x), m₁(x), e₂)
        [object(α₁, λ₁, ⊤, ∅)]:
            if type(e₂) = object(α₂, λ₂, ⊤, ∅) then
                join(α₁, α₂), join(λ₁, λ₂)
            else promote(e₂, s)
```

Figure 6: Implementation details for the function used in the inference rules in Figure 5. ecr(x) is the ECR representing the type of variable x, and type(E) is the type associated with the ECR E. join(x, y) performs the conditional ⊑ₛ join and cjoin(s, x, y) performs the conditional ⊴ₛ join of ECRs x and y. ecr-union performs a (fast union/find) join operation on its ECR arguments and returns the value of a subsequent find operation on one of them.

$O(S\alpha(S,S))$ time complexity, where α is the inverse Ackerman's function [Tar83]. The $\alpha(S,S)$ component of the time complexity is due to the use of fast union/find data structures. This complexity result is equal to that of our previous algorithm [Ste96].

Constraints involving **struct** types may require processing all the element types in addition to any joins being performed. If all structures have R or fewer elements, the algorithm has an $O(S)$ space and $O(RS\alpha(S,S))$ time complexity. While this means that the algorithm has a quadratic worst-case running time complexity in terms of S, the actual running time complexity is likely to be close to linear as R is typically a fairly small number. While R *does* grow with program size, the growth is controlled by the tendency of programmers to group structure elements in substructures when the number of elements grows large.

6 Experience

We have implemented a slightly improved version of the above algorithm in our proto-type programming system based on the Value Dependence Graph (VDG) [WCES94]. The implementation is performed in the Scheme programming language [CR91]. The implementation uses a weaker typing rule for primitive operations returning boolean values (thus leading to better results). It also uses predetermined transfer functions for calls of library functions, effectively making the type inference algorithm be poly-morphic (context-sensitive) for all direct calls of library functions.

Our implementation demonstrates that the running time of the algorithm is roughly linear in the size of the input program on our test-suite of around 50 C programs. We have performed points-to analysis of programs up to 75,000 lines of code[3]. The experience with the algorithm is very encouraging; we are considering doing an im-plementation that allows piecewise analysis of programs, thus permitting analysis of programs of a million lines of code or more.

In Table 1 we present empirical data on the performance of the algorithm on the unoptimized representation of a number of programs. The programs are a subset of the programs in William Landi's test suite, Todd Austin's test suite, the SPEC92 benchmarks, and LambdaMOO (version 1.7.1) from Xerox PARC. These programs are the same we presented results for in our previous paper [Ste96]. We have also included information on analysis of a Microsoft tool of 75,000 lines of C code.

The first column indicates running time for our implementation of the algorithm. The time is the result of a single measurement. The time includes initial setup and type inference. The runtime measurements are not directly comparable with the runtime measurements presented in [Ste96] as the old implementation was able to use a trick to reduce the number of initial type variables by 50%. The second column indicates the number of extra distinguishable elements of structured objects compared with our previous algorithm [Ste96]. An object with two distinguishable elements will thus contribute a count of one to this number. These numbers are very significant as they in most cases represent separation of distinguishable elements in central data structures. The separation has significant second-order effects on the results, but space limitations prevent us from providing details.

---

[3]This is the largest program we have represented in the VDG program representation.

Benchmark name	running time	struct count
landi:allroots	0.23/0.21s	0
landi:assembler	2.47/2.38s	10
landi:loader	0.99/0.96s	6
landi:compiler	1.17/1.16s	5
landi:simulator	2.81/2.62s	8
landi:lex315	0.50/0.49s	0
landi:football	4.34/3.51s	1
austin:anagram	0.44/0.37s	2
austin:backprop	0.30/0.28s	0
austin:bc	5.03/4.19s	11
austin:ft	0.73/0.65s	12

Benchmark name	running time	struct count
austin:ks	0.76/0.70s	4
austin:yacr2	3.40/2.45s	0
spec:compress	1.12/0.80s	0
spec:eqntott	3.05/2.30s	1
spec:espresso	30.0/22.2s	121
spec:li	8.96/6.47s	41
spec:sc	10.8/8.08s	12
spec:alvinn	0.28/0.27s	0
spec:ear	2.40/2.12s	6
LambdaMOO	25.3/19.5s	147
MS tool	95.4/58.7s	1747

Table 1: Running time (wall time and process time on a 150MHz Indigo2 running Chez Scheme) and number of extra distinguishable structure components relative to our previous algorithm [Ste96].

7 Related Work

The algorithm presented in this paper is an extension of two almost-linear points-to analysis algorithms that did not distinguish between components of structured objects [Ste96, Ste95]. William Landi independently arrived at the earliest of these algorithms [Lan95]. Barbara Ryder and Sean Zhang have independently developed an similar algorithm that distinguishes components of structured objects [Zha95]. They use a type system without a ⊥ element, substituting the ⊑ operator by the = operator, thus not being as precise as our algorithm. David Morgenthaler extended our earliest algorithm to distinguish components of structured objects [Mor95]. His algorithm also uses a type system without a ⊥ element and does not incorporate pointer offsets in the constraint system. Furthermore, his implementation is not meant to deal correctly with unions. His analysis is performed during parsing of the program.

Henglein used type inference to perform a binding time analysis in almost linear time [Hen91]. His types represent binding time values. Our points-to analysis algorithms have been inspired by Henglein's type inference algorithm.

Choi, et al., developed a flow-insensitive points-to analysis based on data flow methods [CBC93]. Their algorithm was only developed for a language with pair structures (like cons cells in Lisp). Their algorithm has worse time and space complexity than our algorithm. Burke, et al., describes an improvement of the algorithm [BCCH95]. The improved algorithm does not deal with pointers into structured objects and has worse time and space complexity than our algorithm. Both algorithms are potentially more accurate than our algorithm, as their analysis results permit a location representative to have pointers to multiple other location representatives.

Andersen defined a flow-insensitive, context-sensitive[4] points-to analysis in terms of constraints and constraint solving [And94]. The values being constrained are sets of abstract locations, the analysis being more conventional than the analysis presented in the present paper. His algorithm assumes source programs to be strictly conforming to ANSI C and may generate unsafe results for the large class of programs written by

---

[4]Andersen uses the term "inter-procedural" to mean "context-sensitive".

programmers who make "creative" assumptions about the language implementation. A context-insensitive version of Andersen's algorithm would compute results very similar to those of [BCCH95] but is likely to be faster since it is based on constraint solving rather than data flow analysis.

O'Callahan and Jackson convert C programs to ML programs and use ML type inference to compute the equivalent of points-to results [OJ95]. Not all C programs can be converted to ML by their techniques, and even then their algorithm may compute unsafe results due to type casts in the source program.

There exist many interprocedural flow-sensitive data flow analyses, e.g., [CWZ90, EGH94, WL95, Ruf95]. Both the algorithm by Chase, et al., [CWZ90] and Ruf's algorithm [Ruf95] are context-insensitive and have polynomial time complexity. The two other algorithms are context-sensitive. The algorithm by Emami, et al., [EGH94] has a exponential time complexity (in theory and in practice), as it performs a virtual unfolding of all non-recursive calls. The algorithm by Wilson and Lam [WL95] also has exponential time complexity but is likely to exhibit polynomial time complexity in practice as it uses partial transfer functions to summarize the behavior of already analyzed functions and procedures.

8 Conclusion and Future Work

We have presented a flow-insensitive, interprocedural, context-insensitive points-to analysis based on type inference methods. The algorithm is being implemented. We will have empirical evidence that the algorithm is very efficient in practice before the final version of the paper is due.

This work is part of an effort to construct very efficient points-to analysis algorithms for large programs. We have found type inference methods a very useful tool for doing so. The algorithms presented in this paper and in previous papers [Ste96, Ste95] are based on monomorphic type inference methods. We have also investigated extending the algorithm of [Ste96] to use polymorphic type inference methods. We have yet to combine the extensions to generate an context-sensitive (polymorphic) points-to algorithm that can distinguish between elements of structured objects.

Acknowledgments

Roger Crew, Michael Ernst, Erik Ruf, and Daniel Weise of the Analysts group at Microsoft Research co-developed the VDG-based programming environment without which this work would not have come into existence. Daniel Weise and the reviewers provided helpful comments. The author also enjoyed interesting discussions with David Morgenthaler, William Griswold, Barbara Ryder, Sean Zhang, and Bill Landi on performing points-to analysis by type inference methods.

References

[Ame89] American National Standards Institute, Inc. Programming language — C, December 1989.

[And94] Lars Ole Andersen. *Program Analysis and Specialization for the C Programming Language.* PhD thesis, Department of Computer Science, University of Copenhagen, May 1994.

[ASU86] Alfred V. Aho, Ravi Sethi, and Jeffrey D. Ullman. *Compilers—Principles, Techniques, and Tools.* Addison-Wesley, 1986.

[BCCH95] Michael Burke, Paul Carini, Jong-Deok Choi, and Michael Hind. Flow-insensitive interprocedural alias analysis in the presence of pointers. In *Proceedings from the 7th International Workshop on Languages and Compilers for Parallel Computing*, volume 892 of *Lecture Notes in Computer Science*, pages 234–250. Springer-Verlag, 1995. Extended version published as Research Report RC 19546, IBM T.J. Watson Research Center, September 1994.

[CBC93] Jong-Deok Choi, Michael Burke, and Paul Carini. Efficient flow-sensitive interprocedural computation of pointer-induced aliases and side effects. In *Proceedings of the Twentieth Annual ACM SIGPLAN-SIGACT Symposium on Principles of Programming Languages*, pages 232–245, January 1993.

[CR91] William Clinger and Jonathan Rees (editors). Revised[4] report on the algorithmic language Scheme, November 1991.

[CWZ90] David R. Chase, Mark Wegman, and F. Kenneth Zadeck. Analysis of pointers and structures. In *Proceedings of the SIGPLAN '90 Conference on Programming Language Design and Implementation*, pages 296–310, June 1990.

[EGH94] Maryam Emami, Rakesh Ghiya, and Laurie J. Hendren. Context-sensitive interprocedural points-to analysis in the presence of function pointers. In *SIGPLAN'94: Conference on Programming Language Design and Implementation*, pages 242–256, June 20-24 1994.

[Hen91] Fritz Henglein. Efficient type inference for higher-order binding-time analysis. In *Functional Programming and Computer Architecture*, pages 448–472, 1991.

[KR88] Brian W. Kernighan and Dennis M. Ritchie. *The C Programming Language, Second edition*. Prentice Hall, 1988.

[Lan95] William Landi. Almost linear time points-to analyses. Personal communication at POPL'95, January 1995.

[LR92] William Landi and Barbara G. Ryder. A safe approximate algorithm for interprocedural pointer aliasing. In *Proceedings of the SIGPLAN '92 Conference on Programming Language Design and Implementation*, pages 235–248, June 1992.

[LRZ93] William A. Landi, Barbara G. Ryder, and Sean Zhang. Interprocedural modification side effect analysis with pointer aliasing. In *Proceedings of the SIGPLAN '93 Conference on Programming Language Design and Implementation*, pages 56–67, June 1993.

[Mor95] David Morgenthaler. Poster presentation at PLDI'95, June 1995.

[OJ95] Robert O'Callahan and Daniel Jackson. Detecting shared representations using type inference. Technical Report CMU-CS-95-202, School of Computer Science, Carnegie Mellon University, September 1995.

[Ruf95] Erik Ruf. Context-insensitive alias analysis reconsidered. In *SIGPLAN'95 Conference on Programming Language Design and Implementation*, pages 13–22, June 1995.

[Ste95] Bjarne Steensgaard. Points-to analysis in almost linear time. Technical Report MSR-TR-95-08, Microsoft Research, March 1995.

[Ste96] Bjarne Steensgaard. Points-to analysis in almost linear time. In *Proceedings 23rd SIGPLAN-SIGACT Symposium on Principles of Programming Languages*, January 1996.

[Tar83] Robert E. Tarjan. Data structures and network flow algorithms. In *Regional Conference Series in Applied Mathematics*, volume CMBS 44. SIAM, 1983.

[WCES94] Daniel Weise, Roger F. Crew, Michael Ernst, and Bjarne Steensgaard. Value dependence graphs: Representation without taxation. In *Proceedings 21st SIGPLAN-SIGACT Symposium on Principles of Programming Languages*, pages 297–310, January 1994.

[WL95] Robert P. Wilson and Monica S. Lam. Efficient context-sensitive pointer analysis for C programs. In *SIGPLAN'95 Conference on Programming Language Design and Implementation*, pages 1–12, June 1995.

[Zha95] Sean Zhang. Poster presentation at PLDI'95, June 1995.

Compiler Construction: Craftsmanship or Engineering?

William M. Waite

William.Waite@Colorado.EDU
University of Colorado, Boulder, CO 80309-0425, USA

Abstract. Engineering is defined as the application of scientific principles to practical purposes, as the design, construction and operation of efficient and economical structures, equipment and systems. Computer science is concerned with efficient and economical systems, but what are the "scientific principles" that we apply in their design, construction and operation? Compiler construction was one of the first areas of computer science to be treated formally, and is often used as a touchstone for application of scientific principles in our field, but does formalization imply scientific principles? The issues of craftsmanship and engineering in compiler construction are bound up with the set of problems that compilers must solve and the ways in which people solve problems by computer; our positions on these issues determine our approach to compiler research.

Keywords: Problem solving, formal methods, complexity, modularity, reusability

1 Introduction

Two conferences, held under the sponsorship of the NATO Science Committee in 1968 [20] and 1969 [6], introduced the term "software engineering". This phrase "was deliberately chosen to be provocative, in implying the need for software manufacture to be based on the types of theoretical foundations and practical disciplines that are traditional in the established branches of engineering [20]."

What does software development in general and compiler construction in particular have in common with "established branches of engineering"? Our products are not manufactured in the same way as buildings and motors. Our work is based on theoretical foundations, but they involve discrete rather than continuous mathematics. We are not limited by the physical properties of matter, although space and time certainly bound what we can do. In order to see whether the analogy is useful, we need to look at it more carefully.

My dictionary defines engineering as "the application of scientific principles to practical purposes, as the design, construction and operation of efficient and economical structures, equipment and systems." We need to design, construct and operate efficient and economical systems, but what scientific principles are we applying?

Philosophers customarily divide the sciences into two main groups on the basis of the way scientists arrive at conclusions. Mathematicians justify their conclusions on the basis of deduction from some set of given axioms. Physicists justify their conclusions as generalizations of behavior observed in nature. Thus mathematics is classified as a *deductive* science and physics as an *inductive* science.

Civil and mechanical engineers apply principles from inductive sciences like physics and chemistry to create useful products. Those principles provide a framework within which the engineer operates, both guiding and constraining the engineer's efforts. Software engineers apply principles from deductive sciences that guide their efforts but do not significantly constrain them.

Section 2 summarizes some properties of deductive principles, and Sect. 3 indicates how such principles are applied in compiler development. Thus it appears that our behavior satisfies the definition of engineering, but Sect. 4 argues that we probably need to move more in that direction.

2 Scientific Principles for Compiler Construction

A system S is a nonempty set D (or possibly several such sets) of objects among which certain relationships exist [16]. When the objects of the system are known only through the relationships of the system, the system is *abstract*.

A *lattice* [26] is an example of an abstract system. The relation of the system is $\leq$, and for any $a, b, c \in D$ the following hold:

- $a \leq a$
- if $a \leq b$ and $b \leq c$ then $a \leq c$
- if $a \leq b$ and $b \leq a$ then a and b are identical

A lower bound of $X \subseteq D$ is an element a such that $a \leq x$ for all $x \in X$. The greatest lower bound of X is a lower bound c of X such that $a \leq c$ for every lower bound a of X. Upper bounds and the least upper bound are defined analogously. Every pair of elements must have a greatest lower bound and a least upper bound if the system is to be a lattice.

Only the *structure* of an abstract system is established by its definition. What the objects are, in any respects other than the way in which they fit into the structure, is left unspecified. Any further specification of what the objects are yields a *representation* of the abstract system. The representation is a system whose objects satisfy the relationships of the abstract system but have some further properties as well.

The type system of a programming language is usually a representation of a lattice [12]: Each object is a type. For any types t_1 and t_2, $t_1 \leq t_2$ if and only if values of type t_1 are coercible to values of type t_2. (One value is coercible to another if the compiler is allowed to insert a type conversion operation without explicit programmer input.)

Another representation of a lattice is the system of addressing modes used by machine instructions to obtain operands: Each object is an addressing mode, and for any modes m_1 and m_2 $m_1 \leq m_2$ if and only if operands specified by mode m_1 can also be specified by mode m_2. For example, an operand specified by a literal addressing mode can also be specified by a memory addressing mode or (after loading the value into a register) by a register addressing mode.

A computer program is inevitably an implementation of an abstract system. The computer cannot perform manipulations on the basis of representations, because it has no understanding of the world at large. Thus the task that we undertake when we write a program is to develop an abstract system that captures exactly the relationships of interest in solving the given problem. That task involves four distinct kinds of activity:

- *Understanding* the problem
- *Pondering* the problem to obtain an idea for a solution
- *Reasoning* about the idea to show that it solves the problem
- *Implementing* the idea in a programming language

Of course these activities do not proceed sequentially; there is much iteration as certain aspects of the idea turn out to be wrong, or inefficient, or irrelevant. Nevertheless, we can identify all of the individual things we do with one or another of these activities.

The term "pondering" is due to Dijkstra, who said that the purpose of pondering is to reduce the amount and complexity of the reasoning needed to show that the idea solves the problem:

The ability to "ponder" successfully is absolutely vital. When we encounter a "brilliant, elegant solution", it strikes us, because the argument, in its austere simplicity, is so shatteringly convincing. And don't think that such a vein of gold was struck by pure luck: the man who found the conclusive argument was someone who knew how to ponder well [8].

Both understanding and pondering often involve making connections with other problems and methods. In any discipline, we make progress by increasing the number of problems with known solutions [23]. Computing is not an exception: Studies have shown that the only reliable discriminator between novice and expert programmers is the number of problem and solution patterns that they can access [13].

The scientific principles of software development (and of compiler construction in particular) are therefore useful abstract systems and the deductions that can be made within them. For example, computability theory and computational complexity involve deductions within abstract systems based upon simple relationships among states and operations. They provide the only "physical limitations" on computer algorithms. They give us ways of deciding what is and is not possible, and of characterizing the behavior of an algorithm on the basis of problem size. As long as real computers are representations of those systems, the deductions will be applicable to all software we develop.

Formal languages are the abstract systems most frequently associated with compiler construction. Any interesting programming language contains an infinite number of strings, and formal language theory allows us to give finite descriptions of that infinite set. We can use the description to reason about the language, deducing such properties as expressiveness and ambiguity.

The semantics of a programming language construct are often described in terms of the semantics of the components of that construct. For example, the meaning of a conditional is described in terms of the meanings of the condition, then-part and else-part. A tree is an abstract system on whose elements the "component of" relation exists, and therefore it is also associated with compiler construction.

There are many other abstract systems that are useful in compiler construction, but I shall make no attempt to list them here because the purpose of this section is simply to characterize the nature of the scientific principles on which the question of engineering vs. craftsmanship is based.

3 Application of Scientific Principles

If we agree that the scientific principles of compiler construction constitute a set of useful abstract systems, then the application of those principles to practical purposes is the use of those abstract systems in building a compiler. For a given project, some of the abstract systems used will exist at the start and others developed during the course of the project may later come into general use as new scientific principles. Still others will be highly dependent on the particular problem and will never be seen again.

In the terms of software engineering, application of existing abstract systems by the compiler writer is *reusing* them. Initially applied to simple incorporation of code fragments, this term has more recently been applied to a wide variety of artifacts [17,21]. Here we will be concerned with only three kinds of reuse:

Code The artifact to be reused is specific source code. It may exist as a module in a library, or as a fragment of an existing program.

Generator The artifact to be reused is a solution to a class of problems that has been embodied in a tool.

Design The artifact to be reused is an explanation of how a class of problems can be solved.

Reuse is only possible when, during either the understanding or the pondering activity, we recognize the problem at hand as an instance of some problem class for which a solution is known.

A problem class is characterized by some *requirements space* that distinguishes one instance of the class from another. Code reuse requires that the developer understand only this requirements space, and be able to select the appropriate code on the basis of the portion of the requirements space that it covers. For example, a developer might select a dynamic storage manager on the basis of whether or not it provided garbage collection facilities [5].

Generator reuse requires that the developer not only understand the requirements space, but also understand how to describe a problem to the generator. For example, an attribute grammar is a formal language capable of describing the structure of a tree and relating computations to that structure. Generators that produce efficient programs to carry out the the computations described by an attribute grammar exist, but to use them the developer must understand the attribute grammar language in addition to the requirements space of tree computations.

Design reuse involves reading and understanding the appropriate literature, and then implementing the design in a manner compatible with the particular problem instance being solved.

Our ability to apply scientific principles in compiler construction rests with the availability of code fragments, generators and literature. Most of these artifacts deal with *tactics*: techniques for solving single problems that arise in the course of writing a compiler. When we try to build a compiler using these tactics, we find that very careful selection is required if they are to work smoothly together. Taken as a group, they must implement a coherent compilation *strategy*.

For example, one of the simplest strategies is the classical one-pass approach taken in many current compiler classes. If the source language is suitably defined, a program can be checked for adherence to the language definition in a single pass over the text without retaining a representation of the program in memory. Often the entire translation can be accomplished as the source program is being checked, although the quality of the generated code may leave something to be desired. The result is a fast compiler with a relatively simple structure [2,3,4].

If source language properties require that the compiler retain a representation of a portion of the program in memory for semantic analysis, then code generation tactics should be chosen to take advantage of that requirement. Thus selection of tactics for solving one subproblem of the compilation problem will depend on the characteristics of another subproblem.

4   Research Agenda

Software engineers concerned with reuse believe that the most significant reuse products involve specifications:

> Specification reuse, which offers the highest payoff of all, is a form of generative reuse [21].
>
> By focusing on a narrow domain, the code expansion in application generators can be one or more orders of magnitude greater than the code expansion in programming language compilers [17].

Compiler construction is the enabling technology for these forms of reuse. An *application generator* is a form of compiler that accepts a specification in a domain-specific language and automatically selects algorithms and data structures so that the developer can concentrate on *what* the system should do rather than *how* it is done.

Figure 1 is a summary of the characteristics of application generators, taken from Krueger's paper on software reuse [17]. It makes a strong case for the importance of application generators.

Abstraction Abstractions come directly from the application domain. These high-level abstractions are mapped directly into executable source code by the generator.

Selection Application generator libraries have not received much attention in the literature. The parallel between software schemas and application generators suggests, however, that library techniques could be used to select among a collection of application generators.

Specialization Application generators are specialized by writing an input specification for the generator. Due to the diversity in application domain abstractions, the techniques used for specialization are also widely varied. Examples include grammars, regular expressions, finite-state machines, graphical languages, templates, interactive dialog, problem-solving methods and constraints.

Integration Application generators do not require integration techniques when a single executable system is generated. In cases in which a collection of generators produce a collection of subsystems, composition is best done in terms of domain abstractions.

Pros Since high-level abstractions from an application domain are automatically mapped into executable software systems, most of the conventional software development life cycle is automated. This significantly reduces cognitive distance.

Cons Because of limited availability of application generators, many of which have narrow domain coverage, it is often difficult or impossible to find an application generator for a particular software development problem. It is difficult to build an application generator with appropriate functionality and performance for a broad range of applications.

Fig. 1. Reuse in Application Generators

The drawbacks of application generators presented in Fig. 1 are closely related. Availability is limited because they are expensive to build, and the only incentive to broaden the range of application is to spread the cost. Nevertheless, it is often cost-effective to build an application generator to generate one software system [19], and becomes more so the cheaper the application generator. Since application generators always involve specification languages, anything that reduces the cost of implementing processors for specification languages will reduce the cost of the application generator.

A specification language processor is a compiler, so in order to reduce the cost of building an application generator we need to reduce the cost of building a compiler. According to the software engineers, the best way to reduce the cost of building a compiler is to use an application generator whose application domain is compiler construction! This should not be surprising, because scanner and parser generators have been part of the compiler writer's toolbox for years [14,18]. Compare the specification of a simple expression language using these tools to early papers on expression analysis [24] to get an idea of the leverage that an application generator can provide.

Scanning and parsing only account for about 9% of the time and 11% of the code in a typical compiler, so to continue to increase our leverage we need to go to application generators that deal with larger subproblems. A key point is to begin to embody strategy as well as tactics in the generator.

We already have experience with application generators for the scanning [10,18], parsing [7,14], tree computation [15,28], and code generation [1,22] subtasks of a compiler. Several such generators have been combined under the control of an expert system to create an application generator for complete compilers [11,27]. An evaluation of such generators shows that the code they generate runs as fast as hand code, but uses more memory [25]. Additional research is needed to improve space efficiency and broaden coverage.

Creation of a more comprehensive application generator for the compiler construction domain is really just a process of making our understanding of the compilation process explicit. None of the details are left to the imagination, as they usually are in a reusable design. Many of those details involve things that everyone supposedly understands, but that are easy to do poorly. For example, the speed of a generated compiler and a hand-coded compiler were recently compared by using each to process a test suite of 471 programs [25]. The generated compiler was about 5.4% faster on average. Careful analysis of the compilation time revealed that the source text input routine was responsible for a significant part of speed differential: A carefully optimized routine was produced by the generator, but the hand coder had simply used the C library.

Complete compiler generators give tremendous leverage to the compiler expert. In order to fulfill their promise of lowering the cost of other application generators, however, they must also make the abstractions that constitute our scientific principles available to people with limited experience. That means packaging support for developing a processor design as part of the generator [9], and providing training materials covering basic compiler construction technology.

Even for the expert, it is not sufficient to have only the compiler generator. Input specifications that specialize (Fig. 1) it to analyze common programming languages and generate code for common machines are required as well. Such specifications would make it possible for (say) a person interested in optimization research to quickly and cheaply generate a program to build an appropriate representation of the code to be optimized. If they want to make extensions to the source language to convey additional information those changes can be made in specifications rather than in code. Thus the researcher obtains the necessary infrastructure cheaply and can get on with the interesting aspects of their work.

5 Conclusion

Compiler construction as a discipline can be considered engineering according to the definition given in Sect. 1. There is a set of scientific principles, and those principles are applied to practical purposes. Design reuse is practiced widely, and some generators are used. Code is also reused in specific cases.

Craftsmanship is by no means unknown, however. Optimizing compilers are usually built by craftsmen on an engineered base, and compilers for new or unusual languages involve ad-hoc solutions.

Compiler construction is an enabling technology for application generators, and in order to support this area we need to provide higher levels of automation. Such improvements would also reduce the cost of entry for compiler researchers who wish to investigate problems involving specific compiler components.

References

1. Aho, A. V., Ganapathi, M. & Tjiang, S. W. K., "Code Generation Using Tree Pattern Matching and Dynamic Programming," *ACM Transactions on Programming Languages and Systems* 11 (October 1989), 491–516.

2. Ammann, U., "The Method of Structured Programming Applied to the Development of a Compiler," in *Proceedings of the International Computing Symposium 1973*, North-Holland, Amsterdam, 1974, 94–99.

3. Ammann, U., "Die Entwicklung eines PASCAL-Compilers nach der Methode des Strukturierten Programmierens," Eidgenössischen Technischen Hochschule Zürich, Ph.D. Thesis, Zürich, 1975.

4. Ammann, U., "On Code Generation in a PASCAL Compiler," *Software - Practice & Experience* 7 (1977), 391–423.

5. Boehm, H-J. & Weiser, M., "Garbage Collection in an Uncooperative Environment," *Software - Practice & Experience* 18 (September 1988), 807–820.

6. Buxton, J. N. & Randell, B., eds., *Software Engineering Techniques*, NATO Science Committee, April 1970.

7. Dencker, P., Dürre, K. & Heuft, J., "Optimization of Parser Tables for Portable Compilers," *ACM Transactions on Programming Languages and Systems* 6 (October 1984), 546–572.

8. Dijkstra, E. W., *On the Teaching of Programming, i.e. On the Teaching of Thinking*, International Summer School on Language Hierarchies and Interfaces, Munich, 1975.

9. Fischer, G. & Nakakoji, K., "Empowering Designers with Integrated Design Environments," in *Artificial Intelligence in Design '91*, J. Gero, ed., Butterworth-Heinemann Ltd., Oxford, 1991, 191–209.

10. Gray, R. W., "A Generator for Lexical Analyzers That Programmers Can Use," *Proceedings USENIX Conference* (June 1988).

11. Gray, R. W., Heuring, V. P., Levi, S. P., Sloane, A. M. & Waite, W. M., "Eli: A Complete, Flexible Compiler Construction System," *Communications of the ACM* 35 (February 1992), 121–131.

12. Hext, J. B., "Compile-Time Type Matching," *The Computer Journal* 9 (February 1967), 365–369.

13. Jeffries, R., Turner, A. T., Polson, P. G. & Atwood, M. E., "The Processes Involved in Software Design," in *Acquisition of Cognitive Skills*, J. R. Anderson, ed., Lawrence Erlbaum Associates, Hillsdale, NJ, 1981, 254–284.

14. Johnson, S. C., "Yacc - Yet Another Compiler-Compiler," Bell Telephone Laboratories, Computer Science Technical Report 32, Murray Hill, NJ, July 1975.

15. Kastens, U., "LIGA: A Language Independent Generator for Attribute Evaluators," Universität-GH Paderborn, Bericht der Reihe Informatik Nr. 63, Paderborn, FRG, 1989.

16. Kleene, S. C., *Introduction to Metamathematics*, D. Van Nostrand Company, NYC, 1952.

17. Krueger, C. W., "Software Reuse," *ACM Computing Surveys* 24 (June 1992), 131–184.

18. Lesk, M. E., "LEX – A Lexical Analyzer Generator," Bell Telephone Laboratories, Computing Science Technical Report 39, Murray Hill, NJ, 1975.

19. Levy, L. S., "A Metaprogramming Method and its Economic Justification," *IEEE Transactions on Software Engineering* SE-12 (February 1986), 272–277.

20. Naur, P. & Randell, B., eds., *Software Engineering*, NATO Science Committee, January 1969.

21. Prieto-Díaz, R'en, "Status Report: Software Reusability," *IEEE Software* 10 (May 1993), 61–66.

22. Proebsting, T. A., "Simple and Efficient BURS Table Generation," *SIGPLAN Notices* 27 (July 1992), 331–340.

23. Shaw, M., "Larger Scale Systems Require Higher-Level Abstractions," in *Proceedings Fifth INTL Workshop on Software Specification and Design*, IEEE Computer Society, 1989, 143–146.

24. Sheridan, P. B., "The FORTRAN Arithmetic-Compiler of the IBM FORTRAN Automatic Coding System," *Communications of the ACM* 2 (February 1959), 9–.

25. Sloane, A. M., "An Evaluation of an Automatically Generated Compiler," *ACM Transactions on Programming Languages and Systems* 17 (September 1995), 691–703.

26. Stone, H. S., *Discrete Mathematical Structures and Their Applications*, Science Research Associates, Chicago, 1973.

27. Waite, W. M., Heuring, V. P. & Kastens, U., "Configuration Control in Compiler Construction," in *Proceedings of the International Workshop on Software Version and Configuration Control*, Teubner, Stuttgart, FRG, 1988.

28. Zimmermann, E., Kastens, U. & Hutt, B., *GAG: A Practical Compiler Generator*, Lecture Notes in Computer Science #141, Springer Verlag, Heidelberg, 1982.

Code Generation = A* + BURS

Albert Nymeyer*, Joost-Pieter Katoen, Ymte Westra, Henk Alblas

University of Twente, Department of Computer Science,
P.O. Box 217, 7500 AE Enschede, The Netherlands

Abstract. A system called BURS that is based on term rewrite systems and a search algorithm A* are combined to produce a code generator that generates optimal code. The theory underlying BURS is re-developed, formalised and explained in this work. The search algorithm uses a cost heuristic that is derived from the term rewrite system to direct the search. The advantage of using a search algorithm is that we need to compute only those costs that may be part of an optimal rewrite sequence.

Key words: compiler generators, code generation, term rewrite systems, search algorithms, formal techniques

Compiler building is a time-consuming and error-prone activity. Building the front-end (i.e. scanner, parser and intermediate-code generator) is straightforward—the theory is well established, and there is ample tool support. The main problem lies with the back-end, namely the code generator and optimiser—there is little theory and even less tool support. Generating a code generator from an abstract specification, also called automatic code generation, remains a very difficult problem.

Pattern matching and selection is a general class of code-generation technique that has been studied in many forms. The most successful form uses a code generator that works predominantly bottom-up; a so-called *bottom-up pattern matcher* (BUPM). A variation of this technique is based on term rewrite systems. This technique, popularised under the name BURS, and developed by Pelegrí-Llopart and Graham [30], has arguably been considered the state of the art in automatic code generation. BURS, which stands for *bottom-up rewrite system*, has an underlying theory that is poorly understood. The theory has received virtually no attention in the literature since its initial publication [29]. The only research that has been carried out in this technique has been on improved table-compression methods. Many researchers who claim to use BURS theory (e.g. [31, 14]) generally use 'weaker' tree grammars instead of term rewrite systems, or equate BURS with a system that does a static cost analysis (e.g. [13]). We argue that a static cost analysis is neither necessary nor sufficient to warrant a BURS label, and that a system that is based on tree grammars cannot be a BURS.

In this work we present an outline of formal BURS theory. Due to space restrictions, we present the full theory in [28]. This formalisation of BURS contrasts with the semi-formal work of Pelegrí-Llopart and Graham. But there are other important differences in our work. We do not, for example, use instruction costs to do static pattern selection, and we do not use dynamic programming. Instead we use a *heuristic* search algorithm that only needs to dynamically compute costs for those patterns that may contribute to

---

* Contact author: e-mail address is nymeyer@cs.utwente.nl

optimal code. A result of this dynamic approach is that we do not require involved table-compression techniques. Note that we do not address register allocation in this work; we are only interested in pattern matching and selection, and optimal code generation.

We begin in the following section with a brief survey of the literature. In Section 2 we derive the *input* and *output* sets of an expression tree. These sets contain the patterns that match the given expression tree. The patterns are selected by the heuristic search algorithm A*. This algorithm, described in Section 3, is all-purpose—it can be used to solve all kinds of 'shortest-path' problems. In our case the search graph consists of all possible reductions of an expression tree, and we wish to find the least expensive. The A* algorithm uses a *successor function* (*algorithm*) to select patterns and apply rewrite rules. In this sense, the successor function marries A* to BURS. The successor function is presented in Section 4. In the implementation, the algorithm that generates input and output sets, and the successor function, are modules that can be simply 'plugged' into A* to produce a code generator. The implementation is also briefly described in Section 4. Finally, in Section 5, we present our conclusions.

1 Other work

Kron [25], Hoffmann and O'Donnell [23], and Chase [7] have laid the foundations of the BUPM technique. Chase [7] implemented a BUPM by specifying patterns using a *regular tree grammar* (RTG). An RTG is a context-free grammar with prefix notation on the right-hand sides of the productions representing trees. Chase found that the tables generated by the pattern matcher were enormous, requiring extensive use of compression techniques. A formalisation of Chase's table-compression technique can be found in Hemerik and Katoen [18]. An asymptotic improvement in both space and time to Chase's algorithm is given by Cai *et al* [3].

Hatcher and Christopher [17] went further than Chase and built a complete BUPM for a VAX-11. Their work was a milestone in that they carried out *static* cost analysis, which is a cost analysis carried out at code-generator generation time. In a *dynamic* cost analysis, the code generator itself performs the cost analysis. This is a space-time trade-off. Static cost-analysis makes the code-generator generator more complex and requires a lot of space for tables. In effect, pattern selection is encoded into the tables. The resulting code generator, however, is simple and fast. In both the static and dynamic BUPMs, the cost analysis is usually carried out using *dynamic programming* [1, 8, 32]. For a comparison of the performance of static and dynamic BUPMs, see Henry and Damron [22, 21] and Henry [19, 20]. Two notable attempts to improve the efficiency of the dynamic (BUPM) code generator have been Emmelmann *et al* [11], who developed the BEG system, and more recently Fraser *et al* [13] with the IBURG system.

In 1990, Balachandran *et al* [2] used a RTG and techniques based on the work of Chase, Hatcher and Christopher to build a static BUPM. Very recently, Ferdinand *et al* [12] reformulated the (static) bottom-up pattern-matching algorithms (based on RTGs) in terms of finite tree automata. A subset-construction algorithm is developed that does a static cost analysis, and generalises the table-compression technique of Chase.

Pelegrí-Llopart and Graham [29, 30] combined the static cost analysis concept from Hatcher and Christopher, the pattern-matching and table-compression techniques from

Chase, and, most importantly, term rewrite systems (rather than tree grammars) to develop a system called BURS. A BURS is, in fact, a generalisation of a BUPM, and is more powerful. The term rewrite system in a BURS consists of rewrite rules that define transformations between *terms*. A term, which is represented by a tree, consists of operators and operands (which are analogous to nonterminals and terminals in context-free grammars). However, *variables* that can match any tree are also allowed. The advantage of using a term rewrite system is that, as well as the usual rewrite rules that reduce the expression tree, we can use rules that transform the expression tree. Algebraic properties of terms can therefore be incorporated into the code-generation process. The 'theory' that Pelegrí-Llopart and Graham develop is quite complex, however. They also compare the performance of a BURS with other techniques. They find that the tables are smaller and the code generator much faster.

Mainly theoretical research into the role of term rewrite systems in code generation has been carried out by Emmelmann [10] and Giegerich [16, 15].

In 1992, Fraser, Henry and Proebsting [14] presented a new implementation of 'BURS technology'. Their system, called BURG, accepts a tree grammar (and not a term rewrite system) and generates a 'BURS'. The algorithm for generating the 'BURS' tables is described by Proebsting in [31].

The only serious application of heuristic search techniques to code generation has been the PQCC (Production-Quality Compiler-Compiler) Project [33]. The construction of the code generator and the code-generator generator in PQCC are reported by Cattell in [4, 5, 6]. Cattell uses a means-ends analysis to determine an optimal code match. This involves selecting a set of instruction templates that are *semantically close* to a given pattern in the input expression tree. The heuristic *semantic closeness* means that either the root operators of the pattern and a particular template match, or that there is a rewrite rule that rewrites the root operator of the template into the root operator of the pattern. For performance reasons, the search procedure is done mostly statically, using a set of heuristically generated pattern trees.

2   An Outline of BURS Theory

In this section we describe how the sets of patterns that match a given expression tree are computed. We will only outline the formal approach that has been used—for a full treatment, the reader is referred to [28]. For more information on term rewrite systems see [9].

A *ranked alphabet* Σ is a pair (S, r) with S a finite set of symbols and $r \in S \to \mathbb{N}$, where $\mathbb{N}$ denotes the set of natural numbers. If a is a symbol in S, then $r(a)$ is its rank. Symbols with rank 0 are called *constants*. The set of symbols with rank n, denoted Σ_n, is $\{ a \in S \mid r(a) = n \}$.

For Σ a ranked alphabet and V a set of variable symbols, the set of terms $T_\Sigma(V)$ consists of constants, variables and $a(t_1, \ldots, t_n)$, where $a \in \Sigma_n$, and $t_1, \ldots, t_n \in T_\Sigma(V), n \geq 1$. For term t, $\mathrm{Var}(t)$ denotes the set of variables in t. The terms t for which $\mathrm{Var}(t) = \emptyset$ are called *ground terms*.

The position of a sub-term of a term t can be indicated by a path from the root of t to the root of the sub-term. A position is represented as a string of positive naturals, separated by dots. For example, the position of the first child of the root is 1, and the second child 2. The position of the first grandchild of the root is $1 \cdot 1$. The root is at position ε. We define $Pos(t)$ as the set of positions of all nodes in t. The sub-term of a term t at position $p \in Pos(t)$ is denoted $t|_p$. We are now able to define a term rewrite system with costs.

Definition 2.1 *Costed term rewrite system*

A *costed term rewrite system* (CTRS) is a triple $((\Sigma, V), R, C)$ with
- Σ, a non-empty ranked alphabet
- V, a finite set of variables
- R, a non-empty, finite subset of $T_\Sigma(V) \times T_\Sigma(V)$
- $C \in R \to \mathbb{R}^+ \cup \{0\}$, a cost function

such that, for all $(t, t') \in R$, $t' \neq t$, $t \notin V$ and $Var(t') \subseteq Var(t)$. $\qquad \square$

Note that $\mathbb{R}$ denotes the set of real numbers. Elements of R, identified as r_1, r_2, and so on, are called *rewrite rules*. An element $(t, t') \in R$ is usually written as $t \longrightarrow t'$. The cost function C assigns to each rewrite rule a non-negative cost. This cost reflects the cost of the instruction associated with the rewrite rule and may take into account, for instance, the number of instruction cycles, or the number of memory accesses. When C is irrelevant it is omitted from the CTRS. A term rewrite system (TRS) is in that case a tuple $((\Sigma, V), R)$.

The CTRS defined in the following example is a modified version of an example taken from Pelegrí-Llopart and Graham [30], and will be used as a running example throughout this section.

Example 2.2 Let $((\Sigma, V), R, C)$ be a CTRS, where $\Sigma = (S, r)$, $S = \{+, c, a, r, 0\}$, $r(+) = 2, r(c) = r(r) = r(a) = r(0) = 0, V = \{x, y\}$, and R defined as follows:

$$R = \{ \begin{array}{lll} (r_1) + (x, y) \longrightarrow +(y, x), & (r_2) + (x, 0) \longrightarrow x, & (r_3) + (a, a) \longrightarrow r, \\ (r_4) + (c, r) \longrightarrow a, & (r_5)\, 0 \longrightarrow c, & (r_6)\, c \longrightarrow a, \\ (r_7)\, a \longrightarrow r, & (r_8)\, r \longrightarrow a \} \end{array}$$

The cost function C is defined by $C(r_1) = C(r_2) = C(r_5) = 0$, $C(r_3) = C(r_6) = 3$, $C(r_4) = 5$ and $C(r_7) = C(r_8) = 1$. Some example terms are $+(0, +(c, c))$, a, and $+(x, +(0, +(c, y)))$. For $t = +(x, +(0, +(c, y)))$ we have that $Pos(t) = \{\varepsilon, 1, 2, 2 \cdot 1, 2 \cdot 2, 2 \cdot 2 \cdot 1, 2 \cdot 2 \cdot 2\}$. Some sub-terms of t are $t|_\varepsilon = t$, $t|_1 = x$, and $t|_{2 \cdot 2} = +(c, y)$. $\square$

Variables in a term t can be substituted by some term. The substitution $\sigma \in V \to T_\Sigma(V)$ in a term t is written t^σ. Rewrite rules $r_1 : t_1 \longrightarrow t_1'$ and $r_2 : t_2 \longrightarrow t_2'$ are *equivalent* if and only if there is a bijection $\sigma \in Var(t_1) \to Var(t_2)$ such that $t_1^\sigma = t_2$ and $t_1'^\sigma = t_2'$. Thus, rewrite rules that are identical, except for variable symbols, are considered equivalent.

A rewrite rule and substitution are used to define a *rewrite step*. In a rewrite step $t_1 \xrightarrow{\langle r, p \rangle} t_2$, where $t_1, t_2 \in T_\Sigma(V)$, $r : t \longrightarrow t' \in R$ and $p \in Pos(t_1)$, the result term t_2 is obtained from t_1 by replacing $t_1|_p$ by t'^σ in t_1 and using substitution σ with $t^\sigma = t_1|_p$. We can also write $\langle r, p \rangle\, t_1 = t_2$. A rewrite rule r that is applied at the root position, i.e. $\langle r, \varepsilon \rangle$, is usually abbreviated to r.

A sequence of rewrite steps that are applied one after another is called a *rewrite sequence*. A rewrite step is a rewrite sequence of length 1. We write $t \xrightarrow{\langle r_1, p_1 \rangle \ldots \langle r_n, p_n \rangle} t'$ if and only if $\exists t_1, \ldots, t_{n-1} : t \xrightarrow{\langle r_1, p_1 \rangle} t_1 \xrightarrow{\langle r_2, p_2 \rangle} \ldots t_{n-1} \xrightarrow{\langle r_n, p_n \rangle} t'$. We can also let $S(t) = \langle r_1, p_1 \rangle \ldots \langle r_n, p_n \rangle$, and write $S(t) t = t'$. We sometimes denote a rewrite sequence $S(t)$ by τ.

The cost of a rewrite sequence τ is defined as the sum of the costs of the rewrite rules in τ. The length of τ is denoted $|\tau|$ and indicates the number of rewrite rules in τ. If a rewrite rule r occurs in a rewrite sequence τ, then we write $r \in \tau$. We assume that all rewrite sequences are acyclic.

Two rewrite sequences may also be *permutations* of each other. Permuted rewrite sequences will, of course, have the same cost, but note that corresponding rules in the two sequences may not be applied at the same positions.

Example 2.3 Consider the CTRS shown in Example 2.2, and let $t = +(0, +(r, c))$. We can write $t \xrightarrow{\langle r_1, 2 \rangle} t'$, with $t' = +(0, +(c, r))$. We can also write $\langle r_1, 2 \rangle t = t'$. The term t' is obtained from t by replacing $t|_2$ by $+(y, x)^\sigma$ in t, using substitution σ with $\sigma(x) = r$ and $\sigma(y) = c$ such that $(x, y)^\sigma = t|_2$. Two derivations starting with t' are:

1. $+(0, +(c, r)) \xrightarrow{\langle r_4, 2 \rangle} +(0, a) \xrightarrow{\langle r_7, 2 \rangle} +(0, r) \xrightarrow{\langle r_1, \varepsilon \rangle} +(r, 0) \xrightarrow{\langle r_2, \varepsilon \rangle} r$

2. $+(0, +(c, r)) \xrightarrow{\langle r_4, 2 \rangle} +(0, a) \xrightarrow{\langle r_1, \varepsilon \rangle} +(a, 0) \xrightarrow{\langle r_7, 1 \rangle} +(r, 0) \xrightarrow{\langle r_2, \varepsilon \rangle} r$

These rewrite sequences are permutations of each other and both have cost 6. □

Given a CTRS $((\Sigma, V), R, C)$ and 2 ground terms $t, t' \in T_\Sigma$, we now wish to determine a rewrite sequence τ such that $t \xRightarrow{\tau} t'$ with minimal cost. In practice, term rewrite systems in code generation will allow many different rewrite sequences to transform t into t'. Fortunately, optimisations are possible so that we only need to consider relatively few of these rewrite sequences.

The first optimisation is based on an equivalence relation on rewrite sequences. The equivalence relation is based on the observation that rewrite sequences can be transformed into permuted sequences of a certain form, called *normal form*. Permuted rewrite sequences yield the same result for all terms t. Hence we only need to consider rewrite sequences in normal form. It is a stipulation for our approach, and a property of a BURS, that permuted sequences also have the same cost. If a cost function does not satisfy this property (for example, if the cost of an instruction includes the number of registers that are free at a given moment), then the reduction that we obtain by only considering the normal form will lead to legal rewrite sequences being discarded.

We can label, or decorate, each node in a term with a rewrite sequence. Such a rewrite sequence is called a *local rewrite sequence*, and is denoted by $L(t|_p)$, where $t|_p$ is the sub-term of t at position p at which the local rewrite sequence occurs. Of course, p may be ε (denoting the root). A term t in which each sub-term is labelled by a (possibly empty) local rewrite sequence is called a *decorated term*, or *decoration*, and is denoted by $D(t)$. We can usually decorate a given term in many ways. If we wish to differentiate between the rewrite sequences in different decorations, then we use the notation $L_D(t|_p)$.

Given a decoration $D(t)$ of a term t, the corresponding rewrite sequence $S_D(t)$ can be obtained by a post-order traversal of t. The rewrite sequence $S_D(t)$ corresponding to a decoration $D(t)$ is defined as:

$$S_D(t) = \begin{cases} L_D(t|_\varepsilon), & \text{if } t \in \Sigma_0 \\ (1 \cdot S_D(t_1) \ldots n \cdot S_D(t_n)) L_D(t|_\varepsilon), & \text{if } t = a(t_1, \ldots, t_n) \end{cases}$$

Here, $n \cdot \tau$ for rewrite sequence τ and (positive) natural number n denotes τ where each position p_i in τ is prefixed with $n\cdot$. Decorations are considered to be equivalent if and only if their corresponding rewrite sequences are permutations of each other.

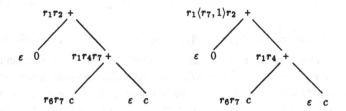

Fig. 1. Equivalent decorations $D(t)$ and $D'(t)$ of a term t

Example 2.4   Consider the CTRS shown in Example 2.2 and let $t = +(0, +(c, c))$. Two decorations $D(t)$ and $D'(t)$ of t are depicted in Figure 1, on the left and right, respectively. The corresponding rewrite sequences are:

$$S_D(t) = \langle r_6, 2 \cdot 1 \rangle \langle r_7, 2 \cdot 1 \rangle \langle r_1, 2 \rangle \langle r_4, 2 \rangle \langle r_7, 2 \rangle \langle r_1, \varepsilon \rangle \langle r_2, \varepsilon \rangle$$
$$S_{D'}(t) = \langle r_6, 2 \cdot 1 \rangle \langle r_7, 2 \cdot 1 \rangle \langle r_1, 2 \rangle \langle r_4, 2 \rangle \langle r_1, \varepsilon \rangle \langle r_7, 1 \rangle \langle r_2, \varepsilon \rangle$$

The decorations $D(t)$ and $D'(t)$ are equivalent because $S_D(t)$ is a permutation of $S_{D'}(t)$. □

We can define an ordering relation $\prec$ on equivalent decorations. The intuitive idea behind this ordering is that $D(t) \prec D'(t)$ for equivalent decorations $D(t)$ and $D'(t)$ if their associated local rewrite sequences for t are identical, except for one rewrite rule r that can be moved from a higher position q in $D'(t)$ to a lower position p in $D(t)$.

The transitive closure of $\prec$ is denoted $\prec^+$. The minimal decorations under $\prec^+$ are said to be in normal form. Normal forms need not be unique as $\prec^+$ does not need to have a least element. We let $NF(t)$ denote the set of decorations of t that are in normal form. In [28] we prove that, given a term t and a rewrite sequence τ such that $t \xrightarrow{\tau} t'$, a normal-form decoration of t always exists.

Example 2.5   In Example 2.4 we have $D(t) \prec D'(t)$ because rewrite rule r_7 associated with the root position of t in $D'(t)$ can be moved to a lower position of t in $D(t)$. As all local rewrite rules in $D(t)$ are applied to the root position of the sub-term with which they are associated, they cannot be moved any lower, hence $D(t)$ is in normal form. □

In a second optimisation, we reduce the number of decorations that we need to consider still further by restricting the class of normal-form decorations to *strong normal form*. Local rewrite sequences in this restricted class contain rewrite rules that are only applied to positions that have not previously been substituted for a variable. We say that each position in a term is either *rewriteable* or *non-rewriteable*. If a term is rewritten using a rewrite rule that does not contain a variable, then the writeability of the positions in the rewritten term do not change. If the rewrite rule does contain a variable, then the positions in the term substituted for the variable become non-rewriteable.

Let $RP_t(\tau)$ be the set of rewriteable positions in the term resulting from applying τ to t. Initially, all positions in t are rewriteable, so $RP_t(\varepsilon) = Pos(t|_\varepsilon)$. For rewrite sequence $\tau\langle t_1 \longrightarrow t_2, p\rangle$ we define:

$$RP_t(\tau\langle t_1 \longrightarrow t_2, p\rangle) = (RP_t(\tau) - Pos(t'|_p)) \cup Pos(t''|_p) - \{Pos(t''|_{p \cdot q}) \mid q \in VP(t_2)\}$$

where $t \stackrel{\tau}{\Longrightarrow} t' \stackrel{\langle t_1 \longrightarrow t_2, p\rangle}{\Longrightarrow} t''$, and $VP(t)$ is the set of positions in t at which a variable occurs. In the definition above, we see that the set of rewriteable positions in t'' consists of the rewriteable positions in t' (i.e. $RP_t(\tau)$), minus the positions in the sub-term that has been matched by t_1 ($Pos(t'|_p)$), plus the positions in the sub-term t_2 that replaced t_1 ($Pos(t''|_p)$), and minus the positions in the sub-terms that are substituted for the variables (if any) in t_2 ($\{Pos(t''|_{p \cdot q}) \mid q \in VP(t_2)\}$). Given a normal-form decoration, we prove in [28] that a strong-normal form always exists.

Example 2.6 We are given a TRS with $S = \{*, +, c, r, 2\}$, corresponding ranks $\{2, 2, 0, 0, 0\}$, $V = \{x\}$ and R defined as follows:

$$R = \{ (r_1) \ *(2, x) \longrightarrow +(x, x), \quad (r_2) \ +(c, c) \longrightarrow r, \quad (r_3) \ +(r, r) \longrightarrow r \}$$

Assume that we have some term $t = *(2, +(c, c))$. Initially, the rewriteable positions in t are given by $RP_t(\varepsilon) = \{\varepsilon, 1, 2, 2 \cdot 1, 2 \cdot 2\}$. If we now apply the rewrite rule $\langle r_2, 2\rangle$ (note that this rule does not contain a variable), then we generate the term $t'' = *(2, r)$ with rewriteable positions:

$$
\begin{aligned}
RP_t(\langle r_2, 2\rangle) &= (RP_t(\varepsilon) - Pos(t|_2)) \cup Pos(t''|_2) - \emptyset \\
&= \{\varepsilon, 1, 2, 2 \cdot 1, 2 \cdot 2\} - \{2, 2 \cdot 1, 2 \cdot 2\} \cup \{2\} \\
&= \{\varepsilon, 1, 2\}
\end{aligned}
$$

We now apply the rewrite rule $\langle r_1, \varepsilon\rangle$ and generate $t'' = +(r, r)$. We are allowed to do this because the position ε is rewriteable. The rewriteable positions in this new term are:

$$
\begin{aligned}
RP_t(\langle r_2, 2\rangle\langle r_1, \varepsilon\rangle) &= (RP_t(\langle r_2, 2\rangle) - Pos(t'|_\varepsilon)) \cup Pos(t''|_\varepsilon) \\
&\quad - \{Pos(t''|_q) \mid q = 1, 2\} \\
&= \{\varepsilon, 1, 2\} - \{\varepsilon, 1, 2\} \cup \{\varepsilon, 1, 2\} - \{1, 2\} \\
&= \{\varepsilon\}
\end{aligned}
$$

Because the root position in the term $+(r, r)$ is rewriteable, we can now apply the rewrite rule $\langle r_3, \varepsilon\rangle$ and generate the goal term r. □

A normal-form decoration $D(t)$ is in *strong normal form* if all rewrite rules r in local rewrite sequences $L_D(t|_p)$ are applied at rewriteable positions p, for all $p \in Pos(t)$. We let $SNF(t)$ denote the set of decorations of t that are in strong normal form.

Example 2.7 Let $((\Sigma, V), R)$ be a TRS with $S = \{*, a, b, c, d, e, f\}$, $r(*) = 2$ and all others with rank 0, $V = \{x\}$, and R defined as follows:

$$R = \{ (r_1) \ *(a, b) \longrightarrow *(c, d), \quad (r_2) \ *(c, x) \longrightarrow *(e, x), \quad (r_3) \ d \longrightarrow f \}$$

Let $t = *(a, b)$, and define a decoration $D(t)$ by local rewrite sequences $L_D(t) = r_1 r_2 \langle r_3, 2 \rangle$ and $L_D(t|_1) = L_D(t|_2) = \varepsilon$. The decoration $D(t)$ is in normal form, but not in strong normal form, because r_2 makes position 2 non-rewriteable (r_3 may therefore not be applied to this position). The decoration $D'(t)$ defined by $L_{D'}(t) = r_1 \langle r_3, 2 \rangle r_2$ and $L_{D'}(t|_1) = L_{D'}(t|_2) = \varepsilon$ is, however, in strong normal form. Note that the rewrite step $\langle r_3, 2 \rangle$ is applied at the root in both decorations. □

We now use the strong normal-form decorations of a term to compute the *input* and *output sets*. These sets define the patterns that match the expression tree. Given the strong-normal-form decoration $D(t)$ such that $t \xRightarrow{S_D(t)} g$ for some given goal term g, then we define the possible inputs for each sub-term t' of t, denoted $I_D(t')$, and outputs, denoted $O_D(t')$, as follows:

$$I_D(t) = \begin{cases} t, & \text{if } t \in \Sigma_0 \\ a(t'_1, \ldots, t'_n), & \text{if } t = a(t_1, \ldots, t_n) \end{cases}$$

$$\text{where } I_D(t_i) \xRightarrow{L_D(t_i)} t'_i \text{ for } 1 \le i \le n$$

$$O_D(t) = t' \text{ where } I_D(t) \xRightarrow{L_D(t)} t'$$

Using the inputs and outputs, we can now define the *input set* and *output set* of a term t for some goal term g. The input set $IS_g(t)$ is the union of all possible inputs for all strong normal-form decorations of t. Similarly for the output set $OS_g(t)$.

$$IS_g(t) = \{ I_D(t) \mid D(t) \in SNF(t) \wedge t \xRightarrow{S_D(t)} g \}$$

$$OS_g(t) = \{ O_D(t) \mid D(t) \in SNF(t) \wedge t \xRightarrow{S_D(t)} g \}$$

Note that the sets are computed for a specific goal term g.

Example 2.8 Consider again our running example and the term t given by $+(0, +(c, c))$. A normal-form decoration $D(t)$ for this term is shown on the left in Figure 1. This decoration is also in strong normal form. The inputs $I_D(t)$ and outputs $O_D(t)$ of this decoration for goal term r are depicted on the left in Figure 2, where the inputs and outputs are given on the left and right side (resp.) of each node. The input sets $IS_r(t)$ and output sets $OS_r(t)$ of this term t for goal term r are shown on the right in Figure 2. □

An algorithm to calculate input and output sets for terms t and g, and the corresponding local rewrite sequences, consists of 2 passes. In the first, bottom-up pass, sets of *triples* are computed for all possible goal terms. A triple, written $\langle t, \tau, t' \rangle$, consists of an input t, rewrite sequence τ, and output t' such that $t \xRightarrow{\tau} t'$. In the second, top-down pass, these sets of triples are 'trimmed' using the given goal term g. These trimmed sets of triples, denoted by $V(t)$, consist of the input and output sets, and the associated local rewrite sequences. For space reasons, the algorithm to compute $V(t)$ is not shown, but can be found in [28].

Example 2.9 Below we show the set of triples $V(t)$ for our running example with expression tree $t = +(0, +(c, c))$.

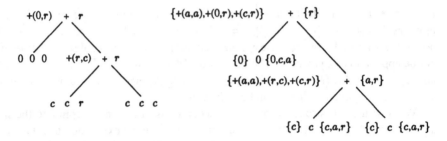

Fig. 2. The inputs, outputs, input sets and output sets of the term $+(0, +(c, c))$

$$t|_\varepsilon = \{ \langle +(a,a), r_3, r\rangle, \langle +(0,r), r_1 r_2, r\rangle, \langle +(c,r), r_4 r_7, r\rangle \}$$
$$t|_1 = \{ \langle 0, \varepsilon, 0\rangle, \langle 0, r_5, c\rangle, \langle 0, r_5 r_6, a\rangle \}$$
$$t|_2 = \{ \langle +(a,a), r_3, r\rangle, \langle +(a,a), r_3 r_8, a\rangle, \langle +(r,c), r_1 r_4, a\rangle, \langle +(r,c), r_1 r_4 r_7, r\rangle,$$
$$\langle +(c,r), r_4, a\rangle, \langle +(c,r), r_4 r_7, r\rangle \}$$
$$t|_{2\cdot 1} = \{ \langle c, \varepsilon, c\rangle, \langle c, r_6, a\rangle, \langle c, r_6 r_7, r\rangle \}$$
$$t|_{2\cdot 2} = \{ \langle c, \varepsilon, c\rangle, \langle c, r_6, a\rangle, \langle c, r_6 r_7, r\rangle \}$$

Note that all rewrite rules are applied at the root. □

To guarantee termination of this algorithm the length of each local rewrite sequence must be bounded. That is, for all $t \in T_\Sigma(V)$ and $D(t) \in SNF(t)$ there exists some natural number k such that $\forall p \in Pos(t) : | L_D(t|_p) | \leq k$. This is referred to as the *BURS property*. The BURS property is necessary because we can have terms that contain variables on the right-hand side of rewrite rules in our rewrite system. Rewrite sequences can therefore continue indefinitely, and terms can 'explode' if the property does not hold. Our running example, by the way, is BURS with $k = 3$.

The work of Pelegrí-Llopart and Graham

Pelegrí-Llopart and Graham[30] (PLG) first define a normal-form rewrite sequence, and then a local rewrite sequence and assignment. We have reversed this order, and we have been more formal. For example, we characterise normal-form decorations by using the ordering relation $\prec$. Our rewriteable positions are related to PLG's *touched positions*, which PLG define only informally and unclearly. PLG do not explicitly define a strong normal form. While we directly encode the inputs, outputs and local rewrite sequences into the expression tree, PLG use *local rewrite graphs* for each sub-term of the given expression tree. These graphs represent the local rewrite sequences of all 'normal-form rewrite sequences' that are applicable.

3 Heuristic-Search Methods

Search techniques are used extensively in artificial intelligence [24, 27] where data is dynamically generated. In a search technique, we represent a given state in a system by a node. The system begins in an initial state. Under some action, the state can change—this is represented by an edge. Associated with an action (or edge) is a cost. By carrying out a sequence of actions, the system will eventually reach a certain goal state. The aim of the search technique is to find the least-cost series of actions from the initial state to one of the goal states. In most problems of practical interest, the number of states in the system is very large. The representation of the system in terms of nodes, edges and costs is called the search graph. A *search graph* G is a quadruple (N, E, n_0, N_g) with a set of nodes N, a set of directed edges $E \subseteq N \times N$, each labelled with a cost $C(n, m) \in \mathbb{R}$, $(n, m) \in E$, an initial node $n_0 \in N$, and a set of goal nodes $N_g \subseteq N$. Furthermore, G is connected, $N_g \neq \emptyset$ and $\forall (n, m) \in E : n \notin N_g$.

One of the best known search techniques is the A^* algorithm ([26, 27]). The letter 'A' here stands for 'additive' (an additive cost function is used), and the asterisk signifies that a heuristic is used in the algorithm. The A^* algorithm computes the least-cost *path* from the initial node to a goal node. The algorithm begins by initialising sets of *open* nodes $N_o \subseteq N$ to $\{n_0\}$, *closed* nodes $N_c \subseteq N$ to $\emptyset$, and the path and cost of the initial node n_0. As long as we have not found a goal node, we carry out the following procedure. We use a cost function to compute N_s, which is the set of nodes in N_o with lowest cost. If this set contains a goal node, then we are finished, and we return the path of this node. Otherwise we choose a node out of N_s, remove it from N_o, add it to N_c, and compute its successors. The *successor nodes* of a given node are those nodes that can be reached with a path of length 1 from the node. If a successor, m say, is neither in N_o nor N_c, then we add m to N_o, and compute its path and cost. If we have visited m before, and the 'new' cost of m is less than the cost on the previous visit, then we will need to 'propagate' the new cost. This involves visiting all nodes on paths emanating from m and recomputing the cost. The algorithm terminates when we find a successor node that is a goal node.

The cost of a node n, denoted $f^*(n)$, is the sum of the minimum cost of a path from n_0 to n, denoted $g(n)$, and the *estimated* cost from n to a goal node, denoted $h^*(n)$. The estimated cost is obtained by using heuristic domain knowledge. This heuristic knowledge allows us to avoid searching some unnecessary parts of the search graph. The search technique therefore needs to try fewer paths in an attempt to find a goal node. Note that the *actual* cost of reaching a goal node from n is denoted $h(n)$. The relationship between $h^*(n)$ and $h(n)$ is important. We consider the following cases:

1. $h^*(n) = 0$ If we do not use a heuristic, then the search will only be directed by the costs on the edges. This is called a *best-first* search.
2. $0 < h^*(n) < h(n)$ If we always underestimate the actual cost, then the algorithm will always find a minimal path (if there is one). A search algorithm with this property is said to be *admissible*.
3. $h^*(n) = h(n)$ If the actual and estimated costs are the same, then the algorithm will always choose correctly. As we do not need to choose between nodes, no search is necessary.
4. $h^*(n) > h(n)$ If the heuristic can overestimate the actual cost to a goal node, then the A^* algorithm may settle on a path that is not minimal.

In some applications (code generation, for example), it may not be important that we find a path that is not (quite) minimal. It may be the case, for example, that a heuristic that occasionally overestimates the actual cost has superior performance than a heuristic that always plays safe. Furthermore, a heuristic that occasionally overestimates may only generate a non-minimum path in a very small number of cases.

In our description of the A* algorithm we have used successor nodes and paths. Given a search graph $G = (N, E, n_0, N_g)$, the set of successor nodes $Successor(n) \in \mathcal{P}(N)$ of a node $n \in N$, where $\mathcal{P}(N)$ is the power set of N, can be defined as $Successor(n) = \{m \in N \mid (n, m) \in E\}$. Note that if $n \in N_g$ then $Successor(n) = \emptyset$. Furthermore, the path $Path(n) \in N^*$ to a node $n \in N$, where N^* denotes sequences of elements from N, is a string of nodes $n_0 n_1 \ldots n_k$ such that $\forall 1 \leq i \leq k : n_i \in Successor(n_{i-1}) \wedge n_k = n, k \geq 0$. Note that there may be more than 1 path that leads to a node. If $Path(n) = n_0 n_1 \ldots n_k$ and $m \in Successor(n)$ then we can append the node m to the path $Path(n)$ using the append operator $\oplus$. We write $Path(m) = Path(n) \oplus m = n_0 n_1 \ldots n_k m$.

Conceptually the A* algorithm can be quite straightforwardly applied to code generation. The transformations in code generation are specified by rewrite rules. Each rule consists of a match pattern, result pattern, cost and an associated machine instruction. A node n is an expression tree. The initial node is the given expression tree. From a given node, we can compute successor nodes by transforming sub-trees that are matched by match patterns. If a match occurs, we rewrite the matched sub-tree by the corresponding result pattern. The aim is to rewrite the expression tree (node) into a goal using the least-expensive sequence of rules. The associated sequence of machine instructions forms the code that corresponds to the expression tree.

4 Coupling A* to BURS

In practice, the major problem in coupling A* and BURS is determining the successor nodes of a given node (in the search graph). In other words, given some term (expression tree), at what positions may we apply rewrite rules? We note that all rewrite rules that we apply must be *correct*, of course. A rewrite rule is correct if there is a path in the search graph from the resulting term (node) to a goal term (node). In this section we describe how a search graph for a BURS is initialised, and how successor nodes are computed.

The search graph $G = (N, E, n_0, N_g)$ consists of a set of nodes N, edges E and goal nodes N_g, and an initial node n_0. A node represents a state of the system, and is denoted by a quadruple (t, p, τ, t') where t is the current term, p is the current position in that term, τ the local rewrite sequence applied at p, and t' the (chosen) input tree at p.

The initial node n_0 is given by the quadruple $(t_I, p_0, \epsilon, t_I|_{p_0})$. The term t_I is the input expression tree for which we want to generate code. The initial position p_0 is the lowest left-most position in this tree, and is of the form $1 \cdot 1 \cdot \ldots$.

Example 4.1 Consider our running example (Example 2.2). The initial node is the quadruple $(+(0, +(c, c)), 1, \epsilon, 0)$. The lowest left-most position in $t_I = +(0, +(c, c))$ is 1, and $t_I|_1$ is 0. The set of goal terms is the singleton set $\{r\}$. $\square$

To determine the search graph, we need to compute the successor nodes of a given node. This is carried out by the function *Successor*, which is shown in Figure 3. In this function we use the functions *Next*, *Parent* and *Child* to position ourselves in the search graph. Given a position $p \in Pos(t) \setminus \{\epsilon\}$ in a term t, $Next(p, t) \in \mathbb{N}_+^*$ is the next position in a post-order traversal of t. Note $\mathbb{N}_+$ is $\mathbb{N} \setminus \{0\}$. The function $Parent(p, t) \in \mathbb{N}_+^*$ is the position of the parent of p in t, and $Child(p, t) \in \mathbb{N}_+$ is the child-number of p in t. If a position p in tree t has children $p \cdot 1, \ldots, p \cdot n$ then the *child-number* of position $p \cdot i$ is i. Further, $Parent(\epsilon, t) = Child(\epsilon, t) = \epsilon$, but $Next(\epsilon, t)$ is undefined, for any t. Note that $p = Parent(p, t) \cdot Child(p, t)$.

Example 4.2 In the term $t = +(0, +(c, c))$, we have $Next(1, t) = 2 \cdot 1$, $Next(2 \cdot 1, t) = 2 \cdot 2$, $Next(2 \cdot 2, t) = 2$ and $Next(2, t) = \epsilon$. Furthermore, $Parent(2 \cdot 1, t) = 2$ and $Child(2 \cdot 1, t) = 1$. □

$\|$ **con** $((\Sigma, V), R) : \text{TRS};$
    $t, g : T_\Sigma;$
    $V(t) : \mathcal{P}(T_\Sigma \times (R \times \mathbf{N}_+^*)^* \times T_\Sigma);$

func $Successor\,(t : T_\Sigma, \; p : \mathbf{N}_+^*, \; \tau : (R \times \mathbf{N}_+^*)^*, \; it : T_\Sigma)$
                $: \mathcal{P}(T_\Sigma \times \mathbf{N}_+^* \times (R \times \mathbf{N}_+^*)^* \times T_\Sigma)$
$\|$ **var** $S : \mathcal{P}(T_\Sigma \times \mathbf{N}_+^* \times (R \times \mathbf{N}_+^*)^* \times T_\Sigma);$

  func $Match(p' : \mathbf{N}_+^*, \; t' : T_\Sigma) : boolean$
  $\|$ **var** $Z : \mathcal{P}(T_\Sigma);$
        $it' : T_\Sigma;$
        $b : boolean;$
    $b := (p' = \epsilon);$
    $Z(t) := \{ it \mid \langle it, \tau, ot \rangle \in V(t|_{Parent(p')}) \; \wedge \; it|_{Child(p')} = t' \};$
    do $Z \neq \emptyset \wedge \neg b \longrightarrow \|$ **choose** $it' \in Z;$
                    $Z := Z \setminus \{it'\};$
                    $b := (\forall\, 1 \leq i < Child(p') : it'|_i = t|_{Parent(p') \cdot i})$
             $\|$
    od;
    return b
  $\|;$

  if $(p = \epsilon) \vee \neg Match(p, t|_p) \longrightarrow S := \emptyset$
  $\mid (p \neq \epsilon) \wedge Match(p, t|_p) \longrightarrow S := Successor(t, \; Next(p), \; \epsilon, \; t|_{Next(p)})$
  fi ;
  for all $r \in R$
  do for all $p' \in Pos(it)$
    do for all $\langle it, \tau \langle r, p' \rangle \tau', \; ot \rangle \in V(t|_p)$ (* this is a loop over τ' and ot *)
      do if $\neg Match(p, ot) \longrightarrow$ **skip**
        $\mid Match(p, ot) \longrightarrow S := S \cup \{\, (\langle r, p' \rangle t, \; p, \; \tau \langle r, p' \rangle, \; it) \,\}$
        fi
      od
    od
  od;
  return S
$\|$
$\|.$

Fig. 3. The successor function that computes a set of new search nodes.

The basic idea behind the successor function is the following. If we can add a rewrite step ($\langle r, p' \rangle$ in the algorithm) to a local rewrite sequence (τ) at the current position (p), and there exists a rewrite sequence ($\tau \langle r, p' \rangle \tau'$) whose output tree ($ot$) matches a corresponding child of an input tree (it') of the parent (of p), and all the 'younger' siblings of the current position also match corresponding children of the same input tree, then we have found a successor node. The function *Successor* is called recursively, using the next post-order position, for as long as the sub-term at the current position, and all the 'younger' siblings of the current position, match corresponding children of an input tree of the parent. The function *Match* carries out the task of matching a node (sub-tree) and its siblings with the children of an input tree of the parent.

When the algorithm reaches the root position, $p = \epsilon$, the recursion will stop, and the function *Match* will always yield true. The algorithm will return with the empty set when it reaches the root position and the term $t \in N_g$.

Example 4.3 Consider our running example again. Let us compute the successor nodes of the initial node, i.e. we compute $Successor(+(0, +(c, c)), 1, \epsilon, 0)$. Because $p \neq \epsilon$ and $Match(1, t|_1)$ = *true*, we recursively call the function again with the next position, $p = 2 \cdot 1$. That is, we call $Successor(+(0, +(c, c)), 2 \cdot 1, \epsilon, c)$. Again, because $p \neq \epsilon$ and $Match(2 \cdot 1, t|_{2 \cdot 1})$ = *true*, we recursively call $Successor(+(0, +(c, c)), 2 \cdot 2, \epsilon, c)$. The recursion now stops because $Match(2 \cdot 2, t|_{2 \cdot 2})$ = *false*. We therefore let $S := \emptyset$, and inspect all the triples of $V(t|_{2 \cdot 2})$ (see Example 2.9). The triple $\langle c, r_6 r_7, r \rangle$ satisfies the loop condition, and since $Match(2 \cdot 2, r)$ = *true*, we generate the search node $(+(0, +(c, a)), 2 \cdot 2, r_6, c)$. The call of *Successor* for $p = 2 \cdot 2$ is now complete, so we need to inspect the triples associated with the previous position, $V(t|_{2 \cdot 1})$. The triple $\langle c, r_6 r_7, r \rangle$ (again) satisfies the loop condition, $Match(2 \cdot 1, r)$ = *true*, and we generate the search node $(+(0, +(a, c)), 2 \cdot 1, r_6, c)$. The call of *Successor* for $p = 2 \cdot 1$ is also now complete. Inspecting the triples associated with the initial position, $V(t|_1)$, we find that triple $\langle 0, r_5 r_6, a \rangle$ satisfies the loop condition, and that $Match(1, a)$ = *true*. We therefore generate the search node $(+(c, +(c, c)), 1, r_5, 0)$. The result of the above computations is that we have generated 3 new search nodes from the initial node, namely:

$$\{(+(0, +(c, a)), 2 \cdot 2, r_6, c), (+(0, +(a, c)), 2 \cdot 1, r_6, c), (+(c, +(c, c)), 1, r_5, 0)\}$$

We can continue computing successors until all the goal nodes have been found. In Figure 4 we see the search graph for the expression tree $+(0, +(c, c))$. The nodes in the graph are the expression trees, and the edges are labelled with the rewrite steps and the positions at which they are applied. Note that there are a total of 11 paths leading from the initial node (the root node) to a goal node in Figure 4. □

In the example above, we have shown how the successor function shown in Figure 3 can be used to compute the complete search graph. However, calling the successor function for each and every newly created node can result in a very large tree, and is wasteful as we only wish to find one least-cost path. The A* algorithm will compute successors of *only* those nodes that potentially lie on a least-cost path from the initial node to a goal node. The cost $g(n)$ of a node n is simply the sum of the costs of the rewrite rules applied along the path to n. But what is the value of the heuristic cost $h^*(n)$? In principle, of course, we cannot predict how much it will cost to rewrite a given node to a goal node. However, we can provide an (under) estimate of the cost.

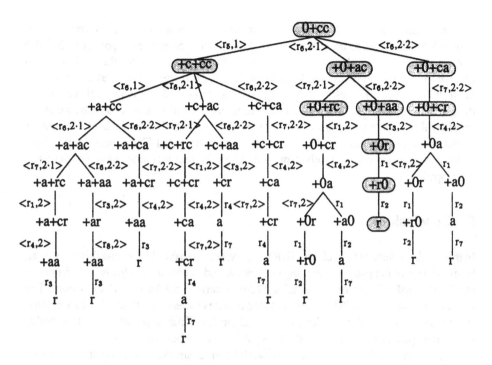

Fig. 4. A complete search graph, and heuristic search graph (in shaded boxes)

Example 4.4 The heuristic function that we use to 'predict' the cost for our running example is:

$$h^*(n) = 3 * (|+(x,y)|_t + |c|_t), \quad x \neq 0, \quad y \neq 0$$

where $n = (t, p, \tau, t')$, and $|s|_t$ denotes the number of sub-terms in t that match s. This heuristic function, which we obtain by inspection, predicts a cost that under-estimates, or is equal to, the actual cost. For example, $h^* = 0$ for $t = a$ (the actual cost is 1), $h^* = 3$ for $t = +(0, c)$ (actual cost 4) and $h^* = 6$ for $t = +(c, a)$ (actual cost 6). ☐

Example 4.5 We now apply the A* search algorithm with the cost function $f^*(n) = g(n) + h^*(n)$ to our running example. We begin by generating the (3) successors of the initial node, as shown in Example 4.3. The costs of these nodes are $0 + 15$, $3 + 6$ and $3 + 6$ (resp.). The second and third nodes are the cheapest; we choose the second, and compute its successors using the successor function. This results in $+(0, +(r, c))$ and $+(0, +(a, a))$, using rewrite steps $\langle r_7, 2 \cdot 1 \rangle$ and $\langle r_6, 2 \cdot 2 \rangle$. These nodes have costs $4 + 6$ and $6 + 3$. Continuing on in this way we find a goal node in just 6 steps, having visited (computed) just 10 nodes in total. The resulting *heuristic* search graph is shown using shaded boxes in Figure 4. The cost of the path to the goal node is 9. ☐

Implementation

The A* algorithm was straightforward to implement. The pattern-matching and successor-function algorithms proved more difficult, requiring many intricate tree-manipulation routines to be written. In total, the system comprises approximately 3000 lines of C code. The implementation has revealed the 'strength' of the theory. For example, we saw in Example 2.9 that there are only 3 local rewrite sequences at the root of the term $+(0, +(c, c))$. Before trimming, there are in fact 101 sequences. If we remove the restriction that sequences must be in strong normal form (in other words, we allow rewrite rules to be applied at all positions, not just rewriteable ones), then the number of (untrimmed) sequences is too large ($\gg 10^6$) to be computed. The strong-normal-form restriction is therefore extremely powerful. TRSs for real machines have not yet been developed.

5 Conclusions

In this work we have reformulated BURS theory, and we have shown how this theory can be used to solve the pattern-matching problem in code generation. This is our first major result. The task of selecting optimal patterns is carried out by the A^* algorithm. The interface between the BURS algorithm that generates patterns, and the A^* algorithm that selects them, is provided by the successor algorithm. This important algorithm builds the search space. Combining BURS theory A^* is our second major result.

Term rewrite systems are a more powerful formalism than the popular regular tree grammars on which most code-generator-generator systems are based. The term rewrite system that underlies the BURS system is used to deduce a heuristic cost function. This cost function speeds up the search process. Optimality is guaranteed if the cost heuristic never over-estimates the actual cost of generating code.

Future work will be mainly concerned with the development of term rewrite systems that describe real machines, and a systematic technique to construct the heuristic cost function.

Acknowledgements: Gert Veldhuyzen van Zanten contributed many formative ideas.

References

1. A. V. Aho, M. Ganapathi, and S. W. K. Tjiang. Code generation using tree matching and dynamic programming. *ACM Transactions on Programming Languages and Systems*, 11(4):491–516, October 1989.

2. A. Balachandran, D. M. Dhamdhere, and S. Biswas. Efficient retargetable code generation using bottom-up tree pattern matching. *Computer Languages*, 15(3):127–140, 1990.

3. J. Cai, R. Paige, and R. Tarjan. More efficient bottom-up multi-pattern matching in trees. *Theoretical Computer Science*, 106:21–60, 1992.

4. R. G. G. Cattell. Code generation in a machine-independent compiler. *Proceedings of the ACM SIGPLAN 1979 Symposium on Compiler Construction, ACM SIGPLAN Notices*, 14(8):65–75, August 1979.

5. R. G. G. Cattell. Automatic derivation of code generators from machine descriptions. *ACM Transactions on Programming Languages and Systems*, 2(2):173–190, April 1980.

6. R. G. G. Cattell. *Formalization and Automatic Derivation of Code Generators*. UMI Research Press, Ann Arbor, Michigan, 1982.

7. D. R. Chase. An improvement to bottom-up tree pattern matching. In *Proceedings of the Fourteenth Annual ACM Symposium on Principles of Programming Languages*, pages 168–177, Munich, Germany, January 1987.

8. T. W. Christopher, P. J. Hatcher, and R. C. Kukuk. Using dynamic programming to generate optimised code in a Graham-Glanville style code generator. *Proceedings of the ACM SIG-PLAN 1984 Symposium on Compiler Construction, ACM SIGPLAN Notices*, 19(6):25–36, June 1984.

9. N. Dershowitz and J.-P. Jouannaud. Rewrite systems. In J. van Leeuwen, editor, *Handbook of Theoretical Computer Science (Vol. B: Formal Models and Semantics)*, chapter 6, pages 245–320. Elsevier Science Publishers B.V., 1990.

10. H. Emmelmann. Code selection by regularly controlled term rewriting. In R. Giegerich and S. L. Graham, editors, *Code generation—concepts, tools, techniques*, Workshops in Computing Series, pages 3–29. Springer-Verlag, New York–Heidelberg–Berlin, 1991.

11. H. Emmelmann, F. W. Schröer, and R. Landwehr. BEG—a generator for efficient back ends. *ACM SIGPLAN Notices*, 24(7):246–257, July 1989.

12. C. Ferdinand, H. Seidl, and R. Wilhelm. Tree automata for code selection. *Acta Informatica*, 31(8):741–760, 1994.

13. C. W. Fraser, D. R. Hanson, and T. A. Proebsting. Engineering a simple, efficient code-generator generator. *ACM Letters on Programming Languages and Systems*, 1(3):213–226, September 1992.

14. C. W. Fraser, R. R. Henry, and T. A. Proebsting. BURG—fast optimal instruction selection and tree parsing. *ACM SIGPLAN Notices*, 27(4):68–76, July 1992.

15. R. Giegerich. Code selection by inversion of order-sorted derivors. *Theoretical Computer Science*, 73:177–211, 1990.

16. R. Giegerich and K. Schmal. Code selection techniques: pattern matching, tree parsing, and inversion of derivors. In H. Ganzinger, editor, *Proc. 2nd European Symp. on Programming*, volume 300 of *Lecture Notes in Computer Science*, pages 247–268. Springer-Verlag, New York–Heidelberg–Berlin, 1988.

17. P. J. Hatcher and T. W. Christopher. High-quality code generation via bottom-up tree pattern matching. In *Proceedings of the Thirteenth Annual ACM Symposium on Principles of Programming Languages*, pages 119–130, Tampa Bay, Florida, January 1986.

18. C. Hemerik and J.-P. Katoen. Bottom-up tree acceptors. *Science of Computer Programming*, 13:51–72, January 1990.

19. R. R. Henry. The codegen user's manual. Technical report 87-08-04, Computer Science Department, University of Washington, Seattle, Washington, October 1988.

20. R. R. Henry. Encoding optimal pattern selection in a table-driven bottom-up tree-pattern matcher. Technical report 89-02-04, Computer Science Department, University of Washington, Seattle, Washington, February 1989.

21. R. R. Henry and P. C. Damron. Algorithms for table-driven generators using tree-pattern matching. Technical report 89-02-03, Computer Science Department, University of Washington, Seattle, Washington, February 1989.

22. R. R. Henry and P. C. Damron. Performance of table-driven code generators using tree-pattern matching. Technical report 89-02-02, Computer Science Department, University of Washington, Seattle, Washington, February 1989.

23. C. M. Hoffmann and M. J. O'Donnell. Pattern matching in trees. *Journal of the ACM*, 29(1):68–95, January 1982.

24. L. Kanal and V. Kumar, editors. *Search in Artificial Intelligence*. Springer, 1988.

25. H. Kron. *Tree Templates and Subtree Transformational Grammars*. PhD thesis, Information Sciences Department, University of California, Santa Cruz, CA, 1975.

26. N. J. Nilsson. *Problem-solving methods in artificial intelligence.* McGraw-Hill, New York, 1971.

27. N. J. Nilsson. *Principles of artificial intelligence.* Morgan Kaufmann Publishers, Palo Alto, CA, 1980.

28. A. Nymeyer and J.-P. Katoen. Code generation based on formal BURS theory and heuristic search. Technical report 95–42, Department of Computer Science, University of Twente, Enschede, The Netherlands, November 1995.

29. E. Pelegrí-Llopart. *Rewrite systems, pattern matching, and code generation.* PhD thesis, University of California, Berkeley, December 1987. (Also as Technical Report CSD-88-423).

30. E. Pelegrí-Llopart and S. L. Graham. Optimal code generation for expression trees: An application of BURS theory. In *Proceedings of the Fifteenth Annual ACM Symposium on Principles of Programming Languages*, pages 294–308, San Diego, CA, January 1988.

31. T. A. Proebsting. BURS automata generation. *ACM Transactions on Programming Languages and Systems*, 3(17):461–486, 1995.

32. B. Weisgerber and R. Wilhelm. Two tree pattern matchers for code selection. In D. Hammer, editor, *Compiler compilers and high speed compilation*, volume 371 of *Lecture Notes in Computer Science*, pages 215–229. Springer-Verlag, New York–Heidelberg–Berlin, October 1989.

33. W. A. Wulf, B. W. Leverett, R. G. G. Cattell, S. O. Hobbs, J. M. Newcomer, A. H. Reiner, and B. R. Schatz. An overview of the production-quality compiler compiler project. *IEEE Computer*, 13(8):38–49, August 1980.

A Compiler for Natural Semantics

Mikael Pettersson

Department of Computer and Information Science
Linköping University, S-581 83 Linköping, Sweden
E-mail: mpe@ida.liu.se

Abstract. Natural semantics is a formalism used for specifying both semantics and implementations of programming languages. Until recently, no practical implementation of the formalism existed. We have defined the Relational Meta-Language, RML, as an executable specification language for natural semantics. After a brief outline of the language, we describe the compilation strategy used by our rml2c compiler: transformations are applied to minimize non-determinism, and a continuation-passing style form is produced and simplified. Finally the CPS is emitted as low-level C code, using an efficient technique for implementing tailcalls. We also present performance measurements that support our choice of compilation strategy.

Keywords: natural semantics, determinacy, continuations, tailcalls.

1 Introduction

Natural Semantics is a successor to Structural Operational Semantics that has become a popular tool for specifying type systems, dynamic (interpretive) semantics, and compilation [9, 18, 20, 25]. Until recently, the only implementation of the formalism was the Typol language in the Centaur programming environment [10, 17]. However, that implementation is both very inefficient, and does not support stand-alone executables.

We have a defined a meta-language for Natural Semantics, RML, with the intention of producing a practical compiler for it. Efficient code was the foremost goal, followed by the ability to produce code that could be combined with other code, hand-written or generated, to form stand-alone applications.

In this paper we describe the main aspects of the rml2c compiler, which compiles RML to efficient C code. Our contributions are:

- We outline the features of Natural Semantics and the RML specification language.
- We describe a reasonably straightforward compilation strategy for RML that has proven to be very effective for several non-trivial specifications.
- Compiling tailcalls to C code is a problem faced by many compilers for high-level languages; we describe a new strategy that is both correct and efficient.

Section 2 starts by giving a brief overview of natural semantics and RML. Section 3 then discusses the compilation strategy, and some alternatives, followed in section 4 by a description of the high-level transformations employed in the first compilation phase. Then follows section 5 with a brief discussion of the continuation-passing style intermediate representation used. The back-end emits low-level C code, but in doing so needs to emulate *tailcalls*. Section 6 starts with a brief overview of known techniques, before detailing a new solution we have developed. Then follows a summary of our benchmark results in section 7. Section 8 compares this with related work, and section 9 concludes.

2 Overview of Natural Semantics and RML

Natural semantics is a formalism frequently used to specify programming languages in general, type systems, special properties, and transformations between representations [9, 18, 20]. Specifications consist of three parts: declarations of the types of objects involved (typically in the form of abstract syntax), declarations of the judgements (logical formulas) involved, and axioms and inference rules defining those judgements. The end result is a Gentzen-style natural deduction system (a *sequent calculus* [12]) for an application-specific logic.

The Relational Meta-Language, RML, is a straightforward realization of the description above. Data type declarations are identical to those found in Standard ML, and 'relations' (our terminology for groups of related inference rules) are written textually almost as they are on paper. An ML-like polymorphic type system is present for static type checking. The operational interpretation of specifications is roughly as in Prolog. To prove a judgement, a top-down search through the program is performed to find a relevant inference rule. Then a left-right execution of the premises of that rule is done, after which the judgement is considered 'proved'. As in Prolog, we refer to relations as *procedures* when taking an operational view.

In contrast to Prolog, the search rule is defined to be *determinate*, which means that once a proof is found for a judgement, no attempts will be made to find alternative proofs. The full power of backtracking is still present *during* proof construction.

A small example specification is listed in figure 1. It contains type declarations for *expressions* and *environments*, and a relation eval(*env*, *exp*) => *int* describing the relationship between environments, expressions, and values. Pragmatically, we use the relation to *evaluate* expressions in order to retrieve their values.

3 Implementation Strategy

The compilation process is a multi-stage pipeline, with appropriate optimizations applied at each level:

1. Source code is translated to a form reminiscent of first-order logic, FOL. A left-factoring transformation is applied to reduce the usually enormous amount of non-determinism present in specifications.

```
datatype Exp = INT of int
             | VAR of string
             | ADD1 of Exp
             | IF of Exp * Exp * Exp

type Env = (string * int) list
relation lookup =
  (* rules defining lookup(env,var) => val *)
end

relation eval =                    (* eval(env, exp) => int *)
  axiom eval(env, INT i) => i

  rule  lookup(env, x) => i
        ----------------
        eval(env, VAR x) => i

  rule  eval(env, exp) => i &
        int_add(i, 1) => i'
        ----------------
        eval(env, ADD1 exp) => i'

  rule  eval(env, cond) => 1 &  (* if-true *)
        eval(env, then) => v
        ----------------
        eval(env, IF(cond,then,else)) => v

  rule  eval(env, cond) => 0 &  (* if-false *)
        eval(env, else) => v
        ----------------
        eval(env, IF(cond,then,else)) => v
end
```

Fig. 1. Small RML example

2. Then the FOL form is translated to a continuation-passing style functional form, CPS. Inlining of procedures and continuations is performed, as is constant propagation and other simple optimizations.
3. A low-level *Code* representation is produced in which continuations are replaced by concrete data structures, and data structure creation is made explicit. A *copy-propagation* optimization is applied to remove some redundancies introduced by the code to pass parameters when tailcalls are emulated.
4. The final step prints the low-level form as C code, compiles it, and links with a small ($\approx$ 2600 lines) runtime system.

The compiler is written in 11569 lines of Standard ML.

Absent from this description is any mention of Warren's Abstract Machine (WAM) [2], which is a standard starting point for logic programming language implementations. There are two reasons for this. First, its instructions are very low-level, which means that high-level optimizations would be difficult to express for it, and it is not certain that they would be effective. Second, the instructions are complex, hiding many smaller operations inside. This in turn prevents useful *low-level* optimizations.

In an earlier paper [22], we showed that a continuation-passing style denotational semantics for RML has operational properties that correspond closely to the WAM. In essence, we make use of a WAM-like model of the control and trail stacks, but ignore its instruction set.

4   Improving Determinacy

Many natural semantics specifications describe deterministic processes, e.g. type checking, evaluation, or translation. However, neither the formalism nor RML has local control-flow operators such as conditionals. Choices have to be expressed as separate inference rules.

Consider for instance the expression evaluator in figure 1, in particular the two rules defining IF-expressions. Interpreted naively, the first rule calls for the pattern-matching of the arguments, followed by evaluation of the predicate. If the predicate is not true (1), the first rule fails, backtracking takes us to the next rule, and the pattern-matching and evaluation is done all over. Obviously, this can be very inefficient.

While rules like these can be rewritten to be more efficient, this is not something we want specification writers to have to deal with. Instead, the compiler performs a *left-factoring* transformation that converts these rules into the obvious conditional.

4.1   Left-factoring

We call this transformation left-factoring because execution of relations is much like top-down parsing, and the transformation is similar to left-factoring of context-free grammars.

After type checking, relations are translated into a form that is a disjunctive-normal form of a kind of first-order logic; we call it FOL. First, every inference rule becomes a conjunction of its explicit and implicit goals. For instance, the first rule for the conditional above would become (we use Lisp-like notation for these forms):

```
(and (match [(arg1 env)
             (arg2 (IF cond then else))])
     (and (call eval [env cond] [result1])
          (and (match [(result1 1)])
               (and (call eval [env then] [result2])
                    (and (match [(result2 v)])
                         (return v))))))
```

I.e., the arguments are pattern-matched, a call is performed, the result is pattern-matched, a new call is done and its result is pattern-matched, and finally a single value is returned. The second rule would be similar. Then the disjunction of all these conjunctions is formed.

Left-factoring attempts to perform the following transformations:

- Consider a disjunction of the form:

$$(A \wedge B) \vee (A \wedge C)$$

If the left A succeeds, but either B fails, or failure occurs later, then the right A will be executed during backtracking. This second execution is clearly redundant[1]. On the other hand, should the left A fail, then there is no point in trying to execute the right A. Therefore, this form is rewritten to:

$$A \wedge (B \vee C)$$

This is reminiscent of both one of the basic laws of logic and the familiar left-factoring of context-free grammars.

- In a disjunction of the form:

$$(A \wedge B) \vee (\neg A \wedge C)$$

the two disjuncts are mutually exclusive: if the left one succeeds, the right one cannot possibly succeed. This form is rewritten to use a logical if-then-else operator:

if A **then** B **else** C

- Match operators are introduced to make implicit pattern-matching operations explicit[2]. If both parts of a disjunction $(M \wedge A) \vee (M' \wedge B)$ start by using the **match** operator on the same variables, then the two matches are combined into a larger **case** construct. The branches of the **case** are the remainders of the disjuncts, i.e. A and B.

For example, after left-factoring, the two rules for the conditional would have been rewritten to:

```
(case [arg1 arg2]
  [([env (IF cond then else)]
    (and (call eval [env cond] [result1])
         (case [result1]
           [([1]
             (and (call eval [env then] [result2])
                  (and (match [(result2 v)])
                       (return v))))
            ([0]
             (and (call eval [env else] [result2])
                  (and (match [(result2 v)])
                       (return v))))])))])
```

---

[1] In a declarative language, that is.

[2] But they are not 'compiled' to simple code; that is done in the translation to CPS.

This form no longer contains any explicit disjunctions. Later on, the pattern-match compiler will discover that there is no overlap between the cases in the inner **case**, so the implicit disjunction there is also eliminated. The result is completely deterministic code.

4.2 Implementation

Our compiler uses a term-rewriting system with 17 rules to specify these and related transformations. Of the rules, 11 perform useful work, while the remaining ones make sure the terms are in a right-linear form recognizable by the useful rules.

The code, which is only 105 lines of Standard ML, also includes support for a limited form of higher-order unification. Some rules need to compare terms for equality, but equality must ignore the actual names of bound variables. Hence renamings must be performed on-the-fly.

4.3 Limitations

As indicated by the performance evaluation presented later, the left-factoring phase is very effective in removing unnecessary non-determinism. However, the purely syntactic nature of the transformations causes some cases to be missed.

Some primitive language operators are known to be mutually exclusive. For instance, two rules, one containing $x < y$ and one containing $x \geq y$, must be mutually exclusive. The current implementation knows nothing of primitive operators, and so will not be able to introduce a conditional in this case. This problem, while not frequent, does occur occasionally.

Also, even if two user-defined relations happen to be mutually exclusive, the compiler will not notice this since it never inspects the definitions of called relations. Luckily, typical specifications do not seem to suffer from this.

5 Intermediate Code

After the left-factoring optimizations, the FOL representation is translated into a continuation-passing style (CPS) representation. At the same time, a pattern-match compiler [21] is used to expand pattern-matching constructs into appropriate combinations of data structure inspections and tests.

Since RML has backtracking, the CPS transformation introduces *two* kinds of continuations, success and failure continuations. The former are used for normal calls and returns, while the latter are introduced at disjunctions as handles for backtracking [22]. Apart from this, the CPS representation is fairly conventional.

Our reasons for using CPS are several:

1. We obviously need to model and optimize both ordinary calls and returns, and backtracking. Continuations provide us with an easy way to do so.

2. CPS has nice pragmatic features for compiler writers. It has a simple structure, and, being a λ-calculus, makes some optimizations (inlinings, constant and copy propagations) easy. Other lower-level optimizations can be left for the back-end, which in our case is a C compiler.

3. Although CPS is high-level, it has a simple interpretation in terms of machine resources. This makes the final translation to low-level code straightforward.

Our compiler only applies simple optimizations to its CPS representation, mainly constant propagation, copy propagation, and inlining of those continuations and procedures that have single unique invocation points. No static analysis is performed, except a simple per-module reference count analysis.

We refer the reader to the literature for further details concerning the practical issues involved [3, 19, 22, 27, 28].

6 Tailcalls in C

Implementations of high-level languages must often deal with *tailcalls*. A tailcall is a function call that occurs as the last action (the 'tail') in a function body. An implementation is *properly tail-recursive* if tailcalls do not cause net growth in stack usage. In effect, tailcalls are gotos that pass arguments.

Functional and logic languages typically have no primitive iteration constructs: instead recursive procedures and tailcalls are used to *synthesize* a variety of iteration schemes.

Some compilers, including rml2c, use a continuation-passing style representation of programs. In this representation, *all* non-local control transfers are tailcalls.

In both of these cases, it is important to implement tailcalls both efficiently and correctly, i.e. properly tail-recursively.

For portability reasons, many compilers choose to compile to low-level C code instead of machine code. This causes problems, since C's function calls are not guaranteed to be implemented tail-recursively[3].

6.1 Earlier solutions

A number of techniques for implementing tailcalls have been proposed over the years, especially in the functional and logic programming communities; we summarize them below. We do not concern ourselves with approaches that do not guarantee proper tail-recursion.

In this section the term *module* is often used. By this we mean *an individual compilation unit*, usually just a single file with a set of declarations. In RML, a module is a language construct which simultaneously defines a number of types and relations, and declares the externally visible interface.

---

[3] Some C compilers recognize trivial cases, but the great majority never do anything special about tailcalls.

In the plain dispatching technique, every label becomes a single function. When a label terminates with a tailcall, it returns the label to which control is to be transferred. A dispatcher is given an initial label. It calls the label, receives as the return value the next label to call, and loops ad infinitum. While this preserves tail-recursion, parameter passing cannot be done in a natural way. Instead, global variables are used to communicate arguments from caller to callee. This technique has been used many times [24, 27, 28].

To eliminate the high overhead for parameter passing and control flow in the previous scheme, some compilers collect *all* code into a single C function [13]. This allows parameters to be located in local C function variables, perhaps even registers, and known control transfers become simple gotos. For unknown control transfers, a big switch statement is used[4]. This scheme is not really practical though, since it makes separate compilation impossible. Also, gathering all code into a single function makes that function extremely large, which in turn negatively affects compilation times and the C compiler's ability to perform register allocation.

Some use the first-class labels in the Gnu C compiler to goto from one function to another, e.g. the Erlang and Mercury compilers [15, 26]. All code for a module is collected into a single C function. Known calls within this module use ordinary gotos. A label is exported by exporting its address (a GCC extension). To branch to *any* unknown label, a goto is done to the address of that label (a GCC extension). Unfortunately, to make this work, severe restrictions have to placed on the generated C code. In particular, local C variables are banned: all computations must use only global variables. This has a very negative effect on the performance of the code.

The wamcc Prolog-to-C compiler [7] uses an idea similar to the previous one, but without being GCC-specific. On some RISC processors, calling a function does not in itself cause stack growth. Rather, it is the callee that extends the stack in its function prologue. The wamcc approach is to insert an assembly label at the start of every function body, and then declare a C function of that name. A function call to this label will therefore bypass the prologue, and hence not cause stack growth. Unfortunately, this elegant idea only works on some systems; on many others, the wamcc compiler has to insert system-dependent assembly code, making the idea inherently non-portable.

Baker [5] has proposed that tailcalls *should* be implemented by actual recursion. To prevent unbounded stack growth, the stack size is checked at the start of every function. When it has grown to some limit, a non-local goto (longjmp) is performed to back the stack up to an earlier point, then the aborted function is re-invoked. Also, since the C stack actually behaves like the allocation arena of a garbage collector, memory allocation can be performed simply by declaring local C variables of appropriate types. When the stack overflows, the garbage collector copies live data to a 'proper' heap. Unfortunately, the performance of this elegant scheme is *extremely* sensitive to the chosen stack size. Also, our measurements have indicated that it is slower than other schemes.

---

[4] The first-class labels of GCC allow this to be implemented by a jump table.

6.2 Our solution: 'dispatching switches'

One disadvantage of the plain dispatching technique is that *all* calls go through the dispatcher loop, even when the target is known to be in the same module as the caller.

It is possible to compile all code in a module to a single function, and only use the dispatcher when going from one module to another, this is called 'block compilation'. Although this allows known intramodular calls to be very fast, no system we know of [6, 11] tries to make *unknown* intramodular calls efficient. Source-level 'returns' are one common source of unknown calls. In the code generated by rml2c, about 40% of all calls are unknown intramodular.

Our contribution here is a technique for efficiently testing whether an unknown call is intra- or intermodular.

First suppose that each module is compiled into a single C function. A label is represented as a record containing two fields: a pointer to the C function, and an integer tag. The C function takes the tag as an argument, and branches to the corresponding piece of code using a switch statement.

One strategy is to compile an unknown tailcall into a test, followed by separate code sequences for the intra- and intermodular cases. This has two problems: code size increase, and the fact that the test itself takes time. The test can be implemented either by comparing the function pointer of the target label with the current function, or by requiring different modules to use disjoint ranges of tags. The first problem can be avoided, but the test remains a bottleneck.

Our technique is the following: Let each module have a private *bitmask* variable. When the module is entered, its bitmask is set to all-ones, and when it is exited, the bitmask is set to zero. Also let label records have a third field, which is a pointer to its module's bitmask.

Recall that the labels are given integer tags, and that a switch is used to branch to the code when the module is entered. We reserve tag zero as a kind of *trap handler*. To perform an unknown tailcall, arguments are evaluated as if it was a known intramodular call, then the switch is used to branch to the bitwise 'and' of the label's tag and its bitmask variable. The code below exemplifies:

```
struct label {
    struct label *(*module)(unsigned);
    unsigned tag;
    unsigned *bitmask;
};

/* my_module.c */
static unsigned my_bitmask = 0;
struct label *my_module(unsigned); /*forward*/
struct label my_label_N = { my_module, N, &my_bitmask };
struct label *my_module(unsigned tag)
{
    struct label *label;
```

```
    my_bitmask = ~0; /* we are active */
dispatch:
    switch(tag) {
    case 0: break;    /* intermodular; leave module */
    ...
    case K:
        /* make an unknown call: */
        label = <expr>;
        tag = label->tag & *(label->bitmask);
        goto dispatch;
    ...
    case N:
    ...
    }
    my_bitmask = 0;   /* we are not active */
    return label;
}
```

If the unknown call was intramodular, the bitmask is all-ones, and so the switch will branch to the correct label. The overhead compared to a *known* intramodular call is two memory loads, one 'and', and the switch[5]. If the call was intermodular, case zero is invoked, and the module can move parameters to global variables and return the label to the dispatcher.

This scheme has the advantage of allowing both known and unknown intramodular calls to be efficient. This is important, because of the high frequency of these cases.

6.3   Copy-propagation

As a consequence of tailcall emulation, global variables are used for parameter passing between modules. Even though our intermediate CPS representation is assignment-free, assignments are introduced in the translation to low-level code.

It turns out that in many label bodies, when they tailcall some other label, one or more of the outgoing (global) argument variables will have the same values as they had on entry to the label. A simple *copy-propagation* [1] optimization can discover when this happens, and eliminate some of the unnecessary loads and stores. (A C compiler can in general not do this optimization, since any recursive call, say to a runtime primitive, may modify any global location.)

7   Evaluation

To evaluate the rml2c compiler, we have performed a large number of benchmarks on several combinations of machines and C compilers [23].

---

[5] Usually implemented by a jump table if GCC is used.

Our benchmark suite consisted of three RML specifications: an interpreter for a normal-order functional language applied to a prime numbers program (mf), a type checker for most of the Standard ML core language applied to a number of function definitions and a pathological expression with more than 4000 schematic type variables (miniml), and a multi-stage translator for a Pascal-like language to low-level C applied to a 2300 line program (petrol). These specifications represent three common application areas for natural semantics.

We have implemented four different strategies for tailcalls in rml2c. In table 1, 'switch' is our dispatching switches strategy, 'plain' is the plain dispatching strategy, 'pushy' is Baker's recursive scheme, and 'warped' is the Erlang/Mercury use of GCC's labels. In the other dimension is listed the machines we used. Most of these are standard Unix workstations, using either their vendor's standard compiler or gcc 2.7.0/2.6.3. The 'ppc' target is a single PowerPC 601 processor in a 128-processor Parsytec GC/PP.

To do these comparisons, we had to allow the size of the 'pushy' scheme's stack buffer to vary, because of its great sensitivity to this parameter. To be fair, we also varied the size of the allocation arena used by the other schemes. In table 1, the size was varied from 1K to 128K words, each benchmark was run at each step, and the sum of the execution times was computed for each tailcall scheme. Then these times were normalized with respect to the 'switch' entry.

As is evident from table 1, our dispatching switches scheme is a clear winner on all machines we have used. It is also clear that the 'pushy' scheme loses big, because of its sensitivity of the size of the stack. (Space restrictions do not allow us to report all results from this benchmark. However, our 'switch' scheme *always* won, and 'plain' always beat both 'pushy' and 'warped'.)

To evaluate the effectiveness of the optimizations implemented in rml2c, we re-ran the benchmarks but with some optimizations turned off. Tables 2, 3, and 4 list the results. In the Oall column, all optimizations are enabled. In the no-Ofol column, the FOL optimizations are disabled, and in the no-Ocps column, no optimizations were applied to the CPS level. In the last column, no-Ocode, the low-level copy propagation optimization was not performed. It is clear that optimizations applied to higher level representations, earlier in the compiler, are significantly more important for good performance than are lower-level optimizations.

To compare rml2c with the obvious alternatives, Typol and Prolog, we wrote Typol and Prolog versions of one of the benchmarks, viz. the mf interpreter for the normal-order functional language. In table 5 we see that Typol's performance is several orders of magnitude worse than rml2c's. Typol obviously was not implemented with efficiency in mind.

In table 6, we compare the same benchmark against two popular commercial Prolog compilers (both in native-code mode). rml2c generates code that is about ten times faster than that produced by these Prolog compilers.

The petrol compiler is a natural semantics specification of a language that has been used in our department's undergraduate compiler course. We compared the performance of our rml2c generated compiler with the existing one, which

	switch	plain	pushy	warped
alpha-cc	1.00	1.17	3.40	n/a
alpha-gcc	1.00	1.34	3.00	1.62
hp-cc	1.00	1.56	1.95	n/a
hp-gcc	1.00	1.59	2.03	1.62
i586-cc	1.00	1.18	2.07	n/a
mips-cc	1.00	1.13	1.45	n/a
mips-gcc	1.00	1.15	1.30	1.54
ppc-cc	1.00	1.27	1.97	n/a
ppc-gcc	1.00	1.27	1.88	1.40
sparc-cc	1.00	1.17	3.20	n/a
sparc-gcc	1.00	1.20	1.50	1.41
average	1.00	1.28	2.16	1.52

Table 1. Normalized time as a function of tailcall strategy

Oall	no-Ofol	no-Ocps	no-Ocode
1.00	2.93	1.35	1.06

Table 2. Normalized time as a function of optimization level

is written in Sun Pascal. As table 7 shows, even though the Pascal version was compiled with all optimizations enabled, it is actually 39% *slower* than the generated compiler.

8 Related Work

There are extremely few implementations of compilers for natural semantics specifications. We have already mentioned the most well-known one, the Typol compiler in the Centaur programming environment. This compiler works by translating Typol to Prolog. As our benchmarks have shown, this implementation is not efficient enough for practical use.

Oall	no-Ofol	no-Ocps
1.00	2.25	2.08

Table 3. Normalized #calls as a function of optimization level

Oall	no-Ofol	no-Ocps
1.00	2.00	1.51

Table 4. Normalized max stack as a function of optimization level

primes	RML	TYPOL	T/R
3	0.0026	13	5000
4	0.0037	72	19459
5	0.0063	1130	179365

Table 5. MF, RML vs. TYPOL, time in seconds

Recently, Attali and Parigot [4] have described a system that translates a sub-class of natural semantics into strongly non-circular attribute grammars. By then using the FNC-2 system's compiler for this class, they are able to improve performance by a factor of 10 compared to Typol.

A description of an early prototype of rml2c was published in [22]. At that time, the language had a full Prolog-like search rule, but no attempts were made to reduce non-determinism. Both the left-factoring transformations and the new implementation technique for tailcalls are later extensions.

Transformations similar to our left-factoring ones have been described before, e.g. by da Silva [8], Hannan [14], and others. As far as we know, no one has made use of them in an actual implementation before.

9 Conclusion

We have described a simple yet very effective compilation strategy for natural semantics. We have shown the great importance of applying high-level determinacy-improving optimizations early in the compiling process.

We have also shown that using a continuation-passing style intermediate

primes	RML	SICStus	S/R	Quintus	Q/R	machine
18	0.45	5.0	11.1	4.5	10.0	Sun 4/470
18	0.22	2.20	10.0			Sun 10/40
30	0.87	11.20	12.9			Sun 10/40

Table 6. MF, RML vs. Prolog, time in seconds

RML	Pascal	P/R
1.06	1.47	1.39

Table 7. Petrol, RML vs. Pascal, time in seconds

representation can be both practical and effective in a compiler for a logic-programming language.

A new technique, 'dispatching switches', for compiling tailcalls to efficient C code has been described. Our benchmarks indicate that this technique is better than several known portable and non-portable alternatives.

Our benchmarks show that rml2c generates much better code than some commercial Prolog compilers, and even better code than one commercial Pascal compiler. This clearly supports our choice of compilation strategy.

References

1. A. V. Aho, R. Sethi, and J. D. Ullman. *Compilers Principles, Techniques, and Tools.* Addison-Wesley, 1986.
2. Hassan Aït-Kaci. *Warren's Abstract Machine: A Tutorial Reconstruction.* The MIT Press, 1991.
3. Andrew W. Appel. *Compiling with Continuations.* Cambridge University Press, 1992.
4. Isabelle Attali and Didier Parigot. Integrating natural semantics and attribute grammars: the Minotaur system. Research report N° 2339, INRIA, September 1994.
5. Henry G. Baker. CONS should not CONS its arguments, part II: Cheney on the M.T.A. *ACM SIGPLAN Notices*, 30(9):17–20, September 1995.
6. Takashi Chikayama, Tetsuro Fujise, and Daigo Sekita. A portable and efficient implementation of KL1. In Hermenegildo and Penjam [16], pages 25–39.
7. Philippe Codognet and Daniel Diaz. wamcc: Compiling Prolog to C. In Leon Sterling, editor, *Proceedings of the Twelfth International Conference on Logic Programming*, pages 317–331, Tokyo, Japan, 1995. The MIT Press.
8. Fabio Q. B. da Silva. Towards a formal framework for evaluation of operational semantics. Technical Report ECS-LFCS-90-126, University of Edinburgh, 1990.
9. Joëlle Despeyroux. Proof of translation in natural semantics. In *Proceedings of the 1st Symposium on Logic in Computer Science, LICS'86*, pages 193–205. IEEE, 1986.
10. Thierry Despeyroux. Executable specification of static semantics. In Gilles Kahn, editor, *Semantics of Data Types*, volume 173 of *LNCS*, pages 215–233. Springer-Verlag, 1984.
11. Marc Feeley. Gambit-C version 2.2. Available by anonymous ftp from ftp.iro.umontreal.ca, May 1995.
12. Jean H. Gallier. *Logic for Computer Science.* John Wiley & Sons, 1987.
13. David Gudeman, Koenraad De Bosschere, and Saumya K. Debray. jc: An efficient and portable sequential implementation of Janus. In Krzysztof Apt, editor,

Proceedings of the Joint International Conference and Symposium on Logic Programming, pages 399–413, Washington, USA, 1992. The MIT Press.

14. John Hannan. Investigating a proof-theoretic meta-language for functional programs. Report 91/1, DIKU Copenhagen, 1991. PhD thesis.

15. Bogumił Hausman. Turbo Erlang: Approaching the speed of C. In E. Tick and G. Succi, editors, *Implementations of Logic Programming Systems*, pages 119–135. Kluwer Academic Publishers, 1994.

16. M. Hermenegildo and J. Penjam, editors. *Proceedings of the 6th International Symposium on Programming Language Implementation and Logic Programming, PLILP'94*, volume 844 of *LNCS*. Springer-Verlag, 1994.

17. I. Jacobs. *The Centaur 1.2 Manual*, 1992. Available from INRIA – Sophia Antipolis.

18. Gilles Kahn. Natural semantics. In F. J. Brandenburg, G. Vidal-Naquet, and M. Wirsing, editors, *Proceedings of the Symposium on Theoretical Aspects of Computer Science, STACS'87*, volume 247 of *LNCS*, pages 22–39. Springer-Verlag, 1987.

19. David Kranz, Richard Kelsey, Jonathan A. Rees, Paul Hudak, James Philbin, and Norman I. Adams. Orbit: an optimizing compiler for Scheme. In *Proceedings of the ACM SIGPLAN '86 Symposium on Compiler Construction*, pages 219–233. ACM Press, 1986.

20. Robin Milner, Mads Tofte, and Robert Harper. *The Definition of Standard ML*. The MIT Press, 1990.

21. Mikael Pettersson. A term pattern-match compiler inspired by finite automata theory. In U. Kastens and P. Pfahler, editors, *Compiler Construction, 4th International Conference, CC'92*, volume 641 of *LNCS*, pages 258–270. Springer-Verlag, October 1992.

22. Mikael Pettersson. RML – a new language and implementation for natural semantics. In Hermenegildo and Penjam [16], pages 117–131.

23. Mikael Pettersson. *Compiling Natural Semantics*. PhD thesis, Department of Computer and Information Science, Linköping University, December 1995.

24. Simon L. Peyton Jones. Implementing lazy functional languages on stock hardware: the spineless tagless G-machine. *Journal of Functional Programming*, 2(2):127–202, April 1992.

25. Gordon D. Plotkin. A structural approach to operational semantics. Report DAIMI FN-19, Computer Science Department, Aarhus University, Denmark, September 1981.

26. Zoltan Somogyi, Fergus James Henderson, and Thomas Charles Conway. The implementation of Mercury, an efficient purely declarative logic programming language. In Koen De Bosschere, Bart Demoen, and Paul Tarau, editors, *ILPS'94 Post-Conference Workshop on Implementation Techniques for Logic Programming Language*, pages 31–58, 1994.

27. Guy L. Steele Jr. Rabbit: a compiler for Scheme (a study in compiler optimization). MIT AI Memo 474, Massachusetts Institute of Technology, May 1978. Master's Thesis.

28. David R. Tarditi, Peter Lee, and Anurag Acharya. No assembly required: Compiling Standard ML to C. *ACM LOPLAS*, 1(2):161–177, June 1992.

Abstract Compilation: A New Implementation Paradigm for Static Analysis

Dominique Boucher and Marc Feeley

Département d'informatique et de recherche opérationnelle (IRO)
Université de Montréal
C.P. 6128, succ. centre-ville, Montréal, Québec, Canada H3C 3J7
E-mail: {boucherd,feeley}@iro.umontreal.ca

Abstract. For large programs, static analysis can be one of the most time-consuming phases of the whole compilation process. We propose a new paradigm for the implementation of static analyses that is inspired by partial evaluation techniques. Our paradigm does not reduce the complexity of these analyses, but it allows an efficient implementation. We illustrate this paradigm by its application to the problem of control flow analysis of functional programs. We show that the analysis can be sped up by a factor of 2 over the usual abstract interpretation method.

Keywords: Abstract interpretation, static analysis, partial evaluation, compilation, control flow analysis.

1 Introduction

As the trend in designing higher level languages continues, it is increasingly becoming important to design compilation techniques to implement them efficiently. Optimizing compilers for such languages must typically perform a variety of static analyses to apply their optimizations. Most of these analyses are very time-consuming. It is therefore essential to perform them as efficiently as possible. Speed of analysis is the issue addressed in this paper.

For the class of first-order imperative languages, several techniques for static analysis have been designed and are now well established [1, 6]. Static analysis of higher-order functional languages is more difficult because the control flow graph (call graph) is not known at compile-time. Nevertheless, several kinds of analyses have been designed [2, 7, 15] and some have been successfully integrated in real compilers [13, 15].

1.1 A New Paradigm

A popular approach for implementing static analyses is non-standard interpretation. Even traditional data-flow analysis can be viewed as an interpretation layer, the flow graph being the abstract program to be "executed". The more recent analyses, devised in the abstract interpretation framework, are implemented as true interpreters (for example, see [13]).

But interpretation is costly because it adds a layer of abstraction to the analysis process. We propose to go one step further and perform what we call *abstract compilation*. This new paradigm is based on a simple idea: instead of interpreting (in some sense) the source program, we compile it into a program which computes the desired analysis when it is executed.

More formally, suppose we want to compute some static analysis S. S can be viewed as a function of two arguments. The first is the program p we want to analyze. The second is an initial abstract environment σ_0 that depends on the analysis to be performed. The result of the analysis, $S(p, \sigma_0)$, is an abstract environment which contains the desired information. The *abstract compilation* of p, $C(p)$, would then be a function of one argument such that:

$$C(p)(\sigma_0) = S(p, \sigma_0).$$

Essentially, C is nothing more than a curried version of S. But, as we will see, only the "real computational part" of $S(p, \sigma_0)$ can be kept in the code of $C(p)$. For instance, there is no traversal of the abstract syntax tree of p in $C(p)$. This way, all the overhead of interpretation is eliminated. The abstract compilation process is really a kind of *ad hoc* partial evaluation. In fact, the abstract compiler C can be seen as a partial evaluator specialized for the static analysis S.

Devising C directly made us aware of several interesting optimizations that can be performed to further speed up the analysis. Our results show that, using the technique of abstract compilation, the analysis can be sped up by over a factor of 2.

1.2 Overview

In this paper, we demonstrate our paradigm by showing how the control flow analysis (**cfa**) of higher-order functional programs can be compiled. We first describe the analysis and the language we want to analyze. Then, two different compilation strategies are presented. The first compiles the analysis into a textual program which is then executed using a general interpretation procedure. The second shows how we can use closures to produce a more efficient analysis program. Finally, we compare our results with more conventional implementations of the **cfa**.

Throughout the text, the Scheme programming language is used, mainly for our examples. But note that the compilation algorithms presented here do not rely on any particular language although they use some Lisp-like notation.

2 Control Flow Analysis

In higher-order functional languages, functions are first-class objects, i.e. they can be passed as arguments to other functions, returned as the result of functions, stored in data structures, and so on. It is thus more difficult to predict at compile-time the behavior of programs making heavy use of higher-order functions. One way to do so is the control flow analysis (**cfa**), of which there exists several variants [2, 8, 12]. The *0cfa* [15] computes, for each call site (α ...) of a program, the set of functions that could be bound to α at runtime.

To appreciate the usefulness of *0cfa*, consider the Scheme program of Fig. 1. The *0cfa* would find that in the **map** function, the only function that can be bound to **f** results from the evaluation of **(lambda (y) (+ y x))** (the result of applying **adder** to the value 1 or 2). Knowing this, the compiler can optimize the runtime representation of the closure and the call to **f**. Rather than being a record with a code pointer and environment, the "closure" could simply be the value of **x** (1 or 2) and the call to **f** can be replaced by a jump to the body of the **lambda** expression with **x** as an argument.

```
(define (adder x) (lambda (y) (+ y x))

(define (map f l)
  (if (null? l)
      '()
      (cons (f (car l)) (map f (cdr l)))))

(let ((lst '(1 2 3 4 5 6)))
  (append (map (adder 1) lst)
          (map (adder 2) lst)))
```

Fig. 1. A small program

$\Pi \in$ Prog
$C \in$ Call
$L \in$ Lam
$F \in$ Fun
$A \in$ Arg
$V \in$ Var
$K \in$ Const
$P \in$ Prim (primitive functions: if, +, etc.)

$\Pi ::= C$
$C ::= (F \ A_1 \ ... \ A_n)$
$\quad | \ (\text{letrec} \ ((F_1 \ L_1) \ \cdots \ (F_n \ L_n)) \ C)$
$L ::= (\lambda \ (V_1 \ ... \ V_n) \ C)$
$F ::= L \ | \ V \ | \ P$
$A ::= K \ | \ V \ | \ L$

Fig. 2. Abstract syntax

We will now see how we can compute this **cfa**. Figure 2 describes the abstract syntax of our source language. It is a continuation passing style (*CPS*) λ-language. We assume that all programs are fully alpha-converted. We use CPS to simplify the analysis. Special forms like if can then be considered as primitive functions and all intermediate results are given names. Since only lambda-expressions, variables, and primitives can appear in the operator position of a call site, the *0cfa* problem is equivalent to the one of finding, for each variable v occurring in the program, the set of functions that can be bound to v. Our use of CPS carries no loss of generality since any non-CPS program can be easily converted to an equivalent CPS program.

Figure 3 gives the functionalities of the abstract interpretation algorithm[1] for *0cfa* shown in Fig. 4. The following terminology is assumed. First, $l \downarrow_{formals_i}$ stands for the ith formal parameter of procedure l. Similarly, $l \downarrow_{body}$ is the body of procedure l (a call site). The abstract environments are functions from syntactic domain Var and deliver results in domain 2^{Lam}. The empty environment is denoted σ_0 ($\sigma_0(v) = \emptyset$ for all v) and $[v \mapsto S]$ stands for the environment σ such that $\sigma(x)$ is S if $x = v$ and $\emptyset$ otherwise. Finally, environments can be joined using the $\sqcup$ operator, defined by $(\sigma \sqcup \sigma')(v) = \sigma(v) \cup \sigma'(v)$.

$$
\begin{aligned}
\text{0cfa-program} \;&: \; \text{Prog} \times \widehat{\text{Env}} \to \widehat{\text{Env}} \\
\text{0cfa-call} \;&: \; \text{Call} \times \widehat{\text{Env}} \to \widehat{\text{Env}} \\
\text{0cfa-app} \;&: \; \text{Fun} \times \text{Arg}^* \times \widehat{\text{Env}} \to \widehat{\text{Env}} \\
\text{0cfa-abstract-app} \;&: \; 2^{\text{Lam}} \times \text{Arg}^* \times \widehat{\text{Env}} \to \widehat{\text{Env}} \\
\text{0cfa-args} \;&: \; \text{Arg}^* \times \widehat{\text{Env}} \to \widehat{\text{Env}} \\
\text{0cfa-prim} \;&: \; \text{Prim} \times \text{Arg}^* \times \widehat{\text{Env}} \to \widehat{\text{Env}} \\
\text{lookup} \;&: \; \text{Arg} \times \widehat{\text{Env}} \to \widehat{\text{Env}}
\end{aligned}
$$

$$
\widehat{\text{Env}} = \text{Var} \to 2^{\text{Lam}}
$$

Fig. 3. Functionalities

The *0cfa* of a program p is computed by finding an environment σ such that $\sigma = \textit{0cfa-program}(p, \sigma)$. This can be done iteratively by successive approximation, starting with σ_0. It can easily be shown that this process eventually terminates. The approximations $\sigma_0, \sigma_1, \ldots$ form an ascending chain (taking $\sigma \sqsubseteq \sigma'$ to mean $\sigma(v) \subseteq \sigma'(v)$ for all v), since we only add elements to the environment. Also, since every program is finite, $\sigma(v)$ must be finite for all v. Thus our algorithm will find σ in a finite number of steps.

This is the usual way the *0cfa* is implemented. For example, [13] describes the analysis performed in the Bigloo compiler [14]. It is essentially the same as the one we have presented. It is also very close to the one presented by Shivers

---

[1] For the sake of simplicity, we do not include any error-detection mechanism to the *0cfa*. We thus assume that all programs are syntactically valid.

Ocfa-program$(p, \sigma) = $ Ocfa-call(p, σ)

Ocfa-call$([\![(f\ a_1 \ldots a_n)]\!], \sigma) =$
$\qquad$ Ocfa-app$(f, \langle a_1, \ldots, a_n \rangle,$ Ocfa-args$(\langle a_1, \ldots, a_n \rangle, \sigma))$
Ocfa-call$([\![(\texttt{letrec}\ ((f_1\ l_1)\ \cdots\ (f_n\ l_n))\ c)]\!], \sigma) =$
$\qquad$ Ocfa-call$(c, \sigma \sqcup [f_1 \mapsto \{l_1\}] \sqcup \cdots \sqcup [f_n \mapsto \{l_n\}])$

Ocfa-app$(f, \langle a_1, \ldots, a_n \rangle, \sigma) =$
$\qquad$ **cond**
$\qquad\qquad$ *isVar*(f) :
$\qquad\qquad\qquad$ Ocfa-abstract-app$(\sigma(f), \langle a_1, \ldots, a_n \rangle, \sigma)$
$\qquad\qquad$ *isPrim*(f) :
$\qquad\qquad\qquad$ Ocfa-prim$(f, \langle a_1, \ldots, a_n \rangle, \sigma)$
$\qquad\qquad$ *isLam*(f) :
$\qquad\qquad\qquad$ **let** $\sigma' = \sigma \sqcup [f \downarrow_{\text{formals}_1} \mapsto \text{lookup}(a_1, \sigma)] \sqcup \cdots$
$\qquad\qquad\qquad\qquad\qquad \cdots \sqcup [f \downarrow_{\text{formals}_n} \mapsto \text{lookup}(a_n, \sigma)]$
$\qquad\qquad\qquad$ **in** Ocfa-call$(f \downarrow_{\text{body}}, \sigma')$

Ocfa-abstract-app$(\emptyset, \langle a_1, \ldots, a_n \rangle, \sigma) = \sigma$
Ocfa-abstract-app$(S, \langle a_1, \ldots, a_n \rangle, \sigma) =$
$\qquad$ **let** $l = $ some member of S
$\qquad\qquad$ $\sigma' = \sigma \sqcup [l \downarrow_{\text{formals}_1} \mapsto \text{lookup}(a_1, \sigma)] \sqcup \cdots$
$\qquad\qquad\qquad\qquad \cdots \sqcup [l \downarrow_{\text{formals}_n} \mapsto \text{lookup}(a_n, \sigma)]$
$\qquad$ **in** Ocfa-abstract-app$(S - \{l\}, \langle a_1, \ldots, a_n \rangle, \sigma')$

Ocfa-args$(\langle\rangle, \sigma) = \sigma$
Ocfa-args$(\langle a_1, \ldots, a_n \rangle, \sigma) =$
$\qquad$ **let** $\sigma' = $ **if** *isLam*(a_1)
$\qquad\qquad\qquad\qquad$ **then** $\sigma \sqcup$ Ocfa-call$(a_1 \downarrow_{\text{body}}, \sigma)$
$\qquad\qquad\qquad\qquad$ **else** σ
$\qquad\qquad$ **in** Ocfa-args$(\langle a_2, \ldots, a_n \rangle, \sigma')$

Ocfa-prim$([\![+]\!], \langle a_1, \ldots, a_3 \rangle, \sigma) = $ Ocfa-args$(\langle a_1, \ldots, a_3 \rangle, \sigma)$
Ocfa-prim$([\![\texttt{if}]\!], \langle a_1, \ldots, a_3 \rangle, \sigma) = $ Ocfa-args$(\langle a_1, \ldots, a_3 \rangle, \sigma)$
$\ldots$

lookup$(e, \sigma) =$
$\qquad$ **cond**
$\qquad\qquad$ *isConst*(e) : $\emptyset$
$\qquad\qquad$ *isVar*(e) : $\sigma(e)$
$\qquad\qquad$ *isLam*(e) : $\{e\}$

Fig. 4. Ocfa abstract interpretation algorithm

in [15]. We will now show how we can compile the analysis, by extending the interpretation algorithm.

3   A First Abstract Compiler

When many iterations are needed for the algorithm to reach a fixed point, a lot of work is done which does not have a direct impact on the result of the analysis. The reason for this is that each iteration requires a traversal of the entire syntax tree, examining each node to see if it is an application, an abstraction, etc. This is the interpretation overhead. When we consider the interpretation algorithm of Fig. 4, we notice that only three functions can actually influence the result of the analysis: *0cfa-call* when applied to a `letrec` special form, *0cfa-app* when f is a λ-expression, and *0cfa-abstract-app*.

What we are interested in is a way to remember only those computations which affect the final result of the analysis. Consider the sample CPS program of Fig. 5, where each λ-expression has been numbered from 1 to 7 (we will later refer to these expressions as λ_1 to λ_7). It defines a currified version of `apply`, a function such that `((apply f) x) = (f x)`. The program then computes `((apply (apply (λ (x) (+ x 1)))) 2)`.

```
((λ1 (apply k1)
    (apply (λ2 (x1 k2)
              (+ x1 1 k2))
           (λ4 (t2)
              (apply t2 (λ5 (t3) (t3 2 k1))))))))

(λ6 (f k3)
    (k3 (λ7 (x2 k4)
            (f x2 k4))))

tl-cont)
```

Fig. 5. A small CPS program.

By carefully examining the program, we can determine the particular call sites where the control flow information will be propagated. The call $(\lambda_1\ \lambda_6$ tl-cont$)$ will add λ_6 to $\sigma(\text{apply})$ and tl-cont to $\sigma(\text{k1})$. This is the simplest case. But consider an inner call site, (t3 2 k1), in λ_5. The analysis will take each $\lambda_i \in \sigma(\text{t3})$ and will add $\sigma(\text{k1})$ to $\sigma(\lambda_i \downarrow_{\text{formals}_2})$. In constrast, the call (+ x1 1 k2) adds no information and has no impact on the final result.

Note that only the call sites where the information is propagated are useful for the computation of the analysis. One way to implement the analysis would be to first traverse the syntax tree and store the useful call sites in some data structure and then traverse it at each iteration. But again, there still remains an interpretation layer, namely the computations needed to traverse the data structure.

Compilation can overcome this layer of interpretation by replacing the data structure representing the program to analyse by the control structure of another program (the "analysis program"). The only "interpretation" that remains is at the processor level but since this is unavoidable we will not count it. Figure 6 shows a first compilation algorithm for *0cfa*. We use a Scheme-like notation for the produced code. The function *comp-program* takes as input a program p and produces p', the analysis program[2] in source form. When p' is run, it performs the analysis by finding an abstract environment such that $\sigma = p'(\sigma)$, by the technique of successive approximation.

To see how it works, consider the following program:

```
((λ₁ (f c1)
    ((λ₂ (x c2)
        (f x c2))
     2
     c1))
 (λ₃ (y c3)
    (+ y 1 c3))
 tl-cont)
```

Once compiled, we get the following analysis program:

```
    (λ (σ)
      ((λ (σ)
        ((λ (σ)
          ((λ (σ)
            ((λ (σ)
(1)           ((λ (σ) (0cfa-abstract-app σ(f) σ x c2))
(2)           σ ⊔ [x ↦ (lookup 2 σ)] ⊔ [c2 ↦ (lookup c1 σ)]))
            ((λ (σ) σ)
             σ)))
(3)       σ ⊔ [f ↦ (lookup λ₃ σ)] ⊔ [c1 ↦ (lookup tl-cont σ)]))
          ((λ (σ) σ)
           σ)))
        ((λ (σ)
          ((λ (σ)
            ((λ (σ) σ)
             ((λ (σ) σ)
              σ)))
          ((λ (σ) σ)
           σ)))
       σ)))
```

---

[2] We assume that *0cfa-abstract-app* and *lookup* can be "linked" in some way with the resulting program.

comp-program(p) = comp-call(p)

comp-call$([\![(f\ a_1 \ldots a_n)]\!])$ =
   let C_1 = comp-args$(\langle a_1, \ldots, a_n \rangle)$
      C_2 = comp-app$(f, \langle a_1, \ldots, a_n \rangle)$
   in $[\![(\lambda\ (\sigma)\ (C_2\ (C_1\ \sigma)))]\!]$

comp-call$([\![(\texttt{letrec}\ ((f_1\ l_1)\ \cdots\ (f_n\ l_n))\ c)]\!])$ =
   let C = comp-call(c)
   in $[\![(\lambda\ (\sigma)\ (C\ \sigma \sqcup [f_1 \mapsto \{l_1\}] \sqcup \cdots \sqcup [f_n \mapsto \{l_n\}]))]\!]$

comp-app$(f, \langle a_1, \ldots, a_n \rangle)$ =
   cond
     isVar(f) :
       $[\![(\lambda\ (\sigma)$
          $(\texttt{0cfa-abstract-app}\ (\sigma\ f)\ \sigma\ a_1\ \ldots\ a_n))]\!]$
     isPrim(f) :
       0cfa-prim$(f, \langle a_1, \ldots, a_n \rangle)$
     isLam(f) :
       let C = comp-call$(f \downarrow_{\text{body}})$
         in $[\![(\lambda\ (\sigma)$
            $(C\ \sigma \sqcup [f \downarrow_{\text{formals}_i} \mapsto (\texttt{lookup}\ a_i\ \sigma)]))]\!]$

comp-args$(\langle \rangle)$ = $[\![(\lambda\ (\sigma)\ \sigma)]\!]$
comp-args$(\langle a_1, \ldots, a_n \rangle)$ =
   if *isLam*(a_1)
     then let C_1 = comp-call$(a_1 \downarrow_{\text{body}})$
            C_2 = comp-args$(\langle a_2, \ldots, a_n \rangle)$
        in $[\![(\lambda\ (\sigma)\ (C_2\ (C_1\ \sigma)))]\!]$
     else comp-args$(\langle a_2, \ldots, a_n \rangle)$

comp-prim$([\![+]\!], \langle a_1, \ldots, a_3 \rangle)$ = comp-args$(\langle a_1, \ldots, a_3 \rangle)$
comp-prim$([\![\texttt{if}]\!], \langle a_1, \ldots, a_3 \rangle)$ = comp-args$(\langle a_1, \ldots, a_3 \rangle)$
$\ldots$

Fig. 6. 0cfa compilation algorithm

It is not hard to see that only lines *(1)*, *(2)*, and *(3)* will contribute to the abstract environment. We can also see that there are still a number of useless computations done by this analysis program. Two simple optimizations can further reduce the number of computations performed at each iteration.

We can first eliminate all the calls to the identity function $(\lambda\ (\sigma)\ \sigma)$ by performing η-reductions. This can be done at low cost by adding additional tests to the compilation process. For example, assuming that *Id-Funct?* is true if its argument is the code of the identity function, the *comp-call* function becomes:

```
comp-call([[(f a₁ ... aₙ)]]) =
   let C₁ = comp-args(⟨a₁,...,aₙ⟩)
       C₂ = comp-app(f,⟨a₁,...,aₙ⟩)
   in if Id-funct?(C₁)
         then C₂
         else if Id-funct?(C₂)
                 then C₁
                 else [[(λ (σ) (C₂ (C₁ σ)))]]
```

The second optimization comes from the behavior of lookup. When applied to a constant, it returns the empty set; when applied to a λ-expression, it returns the set containing only this expression. This leads to the following optimization. First, we can eliminate all the contributions of the form $[v \mapsto (\text{lookup } c\ \sigma)]$, where v is a variable and c is constant. Also, we can remove the environments of the form $[v \mapsto \{\lambda_k\}]$ and add them to the initial environment. This saves one iteration, but more importantly, it simplifies the lookup mechanism and makes each iteration faster.

When these two optimizations are added to the compilation algorithm, the compiled code for the previous example now becomes

```
(λ (σ)
  ((λ (σ)
     ((λ (σ)
        ((λ (σ)
           ((λ (σ) (0cfa-abstract-app σ(f) σ x c2))
            σ ⊔ [c2 ↦ (lookup c1 σ)]))
         σ))
      σ ⊔ [c1 ↦ (lookup t1-cont σ)]))))
```

Starting with $\sigma_0' = [\text{f} \mapsto \{\lambda_3\}]$ (as computed by the second optimization), we can find that $\sigma_1 = [\text{f} \mapsto \{\lambda_3\}]$ is a fixed point for this function in only one iteration.

This solution is not entirely satisfactory. The layer of abstraction is no longer present in the resulting code but the program must be executed in some way, thus requiring interpretation at another level. If, for example, we use a builtin interpretation procedure, like Scheme's eval, our experimentations reveal that it remains much more efficient to compute the analysis by means of abstract interpretation. But it is possible to do better.

4 Representing the Compiled Analysis with Closures

Many functional programming languages allow the user to create new functions via λ-expressions. When these expressions are evaluated, they return a **closure**, i.e. a function that remembers the current environment.

We will use closures here to overcome the interpretation overhead of the analysis program. The idea is to represent a compiled expression with a closure. When this closure is applied, it performs the analysis of the given expression.

We will thus replace the "code generation" by a "closure generation" (as in the work of Feeley and Lapalme [5]). This leads to the compilation algorithm of Fig. 7 (without the optimizations discussed above).

comp-program(p) = comp-call(p)

comp-call$(\llbracket (f\ a_1 \ldots a_n) \rrbracket)$ =
   let C_1 = comp-args$(\langle a_1, \ldots, a_n \rangle)$
      C_2 = comp-app$(f, \langle a_1, \ldots, a_n \rangle)$
   in $\lambda \sigma . C_2(C_1(\sigma))$

comp-call$(\llbracket (\texttt{letrec}\ ((f_1\ l_1) \ \cdots \ (f_n\ l_n))\ c) \rrbracket)$ =
   let C = comp-call(c)
   in $\lambda \sigma . C(\sigma \sqcup [f_1 \mapsto \{l_1\}] \sqcup \cdots \sqcup [f_n \mapsto \{l_n\}])$

comp-app$(f, \langle a_1, \ldots, a_n \rangle)$ =
  cond
    $isVar(f)$:
      $\lambda \sigma . 0$cfa-abstract-app$(\sigma(f), \sigma, \langle a_1, \ldots, a_n \rangle)$
    $isPrim(f)$:
      0cfa-prim$(f, \langle a_1, \ldots, a_n \rangle)$
    $isLam(f)$:
      let C = comp-call$(f \downarrow_{\text{body}})$
        in $\lambda \sigma . C(\sigma \sqcup [f \downarrow_{\text{formals}_i} \mapsto \text{lookup}(a_i, \sigma)])$

comp-args$(\langle \rangle)$ = $\lambda \sigma . \sigma$
comp-args$(\langle a_1, \ldots, a_n \rangle)$ =
  if $isLam(a_1)$
    then let C_1 = comp-call$(a_1 \downarrow_{\text{body}})$
            C_2 = comp-args$(\langle a_2, \ldots, a_n \rangle)$
        in $\lambda \sigma . C_2(C_1(\sigma))$
    else comp-args$(\langle a_2, \ldots, a_n \rangle)$

comp-prim$(\llbracket + \rrbracket, \langle a_1, \ldots, a_3 \rangle)$ = comp-args$(\langle a_1, \ldots, a_3 \rangle)$
comp-prim$(\llbracket \texttt{if} \rrbracket, \langle a_1, \ldots, a_3 \rangle)$ = comp-args$(\langle a_1, \ldots, a_3 \rangle)$

Fig. 7. 0cfa compilation algorithm using closures

Comp-app would thus be implemented as:

```
(define (comp-app f args)
  (cond
    ((var? f)
     (lambda (env)
       (0cfa-abstract-app (env f) env args)))
    ...
    ))
```

It may seem that this new compilation scheme is not very different from the previous one; the main difference being that the generated code is no longer textual. This change of representation has two main advantages.

First, there is no longer a need for an interpretation procedure like **eval**. Any language that provides closures can be used to implement the abstract compiler. Secondly, and more importantly, both the abstract compiler and the analysis program run much faster because all the $\lambda\sigma.E$ expressions are also compiled (we assume that the abstract compiler is itself compiled). Only closures are created in the process of abstract compilation.

5   Results

We have implemented the *0cfa* using the abstract interpretation algorithm and the compilation algorithm using closures for code generation. Our implementations handle a larger subset of Scheme than the one presented here. Imperative constructs such as **set!**, **set-car!**, **set-cdr!**, etc., are treated.

Our implementations also handle the case of functions "escaping" to memory. By this we mean functions which are stored in data-structures and that could be later fetched and applied. In order to handle this case conservatively, we introduce a special variable, $\mathcal{ESC}$, that abstracts the memory. For example, if the program to analyze contains the call (**cons x y k**), all the λ-expressions that can be bound to **x** and **y** at runtime are added to $\sigma(\mathcal{ESC})$. Conversely, a call (**car x (lambda (z)** E)) will cause $\sigma(\mathcal{ESC})$ to be added to $\sigma(\mathbf{z})$. Clearly, this approximation is very coarse, but conservative and easy to implement.

The front-end is the same for the three implementations. It performs the following operations:

1. It reads the Scheme program to analyze.
2. It performs a certain number of syntactic expansions to express the program using a minimum set of constructs (for example, **let** and **let*** special forms are expressed using only the **lambda** and **set!** special forms).
3. It CPS-converts the program.
4. It labels the λ-expressions and α-converts the program. An abstract syntax tree (AST) results from this last operation.

The *0cfa* is then computed directly from the AST.

The implementations have both been written in Scheme and they have been compiled with the Gambit-C compiler (which generates C code) on a DEC Alpha. Set operations have been implemented in C for efficiency reasons. Several representations for sets have been considered. A list representation was too costly and bit vectors consumed too much memory (typical sets contain very few elements and are very sparse). The representation we adopted consists of vectors in which the elements are sorted. Each set union operation allocates a new vector in which the elements are merged while being copied.

We ran the *0cfa* over the following set of programs:

conform A program that manipulates lattices and partial orders.
earley A parser generator for context-free languages based on Earley's
        algorithm.
interp A small interpreter implementing call-by-need semantics.
lambda A λ-calculus interpreter.
lex   A lexical analyzer generator.
link   The application linker for the Gambit-C compiler.
lll   An $LL(1)$ parser generator.
peval   A small Scheme partial evaluator.
source A parser for Scheme.

Figure 8 gives the execution times for both implementations on a 160MB DEC AXP3000 (a DEC Alpha microprocessor under OSF/1). The times are all given in seconds. The first column gives the number of lines in the program. The second column gives the number of iterations needed to reach the fixed point and the third column gives the average number of elements of $\sigma(v)$, where σ is the result of the analysis and v ranges over all the variables of the program. The interp column gives the execution time required by the abstract interpreter to perform the analysis. The closure column gives the time for the analysis programs generated by the second compilation algorithm, including all optimizations discussed. The numbers in parentheses give the speedup relative to the times given in the interp column. The last column (gen+closure) gives the time needed to generate and execute the analysis programs and to execute them. The numbers in parentheses give the speedup over interpretation.

We can see that the compilation process can speed up the analysis by a factor varying between 3 and 5 for most of these programs[3] The only exception is interp. We can observe that the average set length (in the last column) for this program is much higher than for the others (except peval) indicating that it makes heavy use of higher-order functions and/or that a larger number of functions are stored in data-structures. Since the sets contain more elements, relatively more time is spent in the set manipulation procedures compared to the time spent to traverse the syntax tree. So it is not surprising that the interpretation overhead will be less significant and the speedup lower than the other programs. Note also that even if we consider the time required to generate the analysis programs (the gen+closure column), the overall speedup is close to 2 in almost all cases.

Figure 9 shows the relative benefits of the optimizations we have discussed, namely the η-reduction and the lookup optimization. The first column gives

---

[3] We consider that the time spent in the code generation phase can be amortized if the analysis program is to be run several times. Such a situation can arise in the global analysis of separately compiled modules.

	Number of lines	Number of iterations	Average set length	Execution times		
				interp	closure	closure+gen
conform	557	3	0.59	0.0648	0.0154 (4.2)	0.0416 (1.56)
earley	648	3	0.41	0.0603	0.0117 (5.2)	0.0366 (1.65)
interp	411	9	3.02	0.1230	0.0435 (2.8)	0.0612 (2.01)
lambda	617	4	0.60	0.1050	0.0326 (3.2)	0.0634 (1.66)
lex	1133	3	0.59	0.1290	0.0266 (4.8)	0.0752 (1.72)
link	1608	6	2.22	0.4687	0.1322 (3.5)	0.2116 (2.12)
lll	613	5	0.43	0.0940	0.0226 (4.2)	0.0470 (2.00)
peval	618	5	6.80	0.1727	0.0508 (3.4)	0.0896 (1.93)
source	453	5	0.77	0.0773	0.0195 (4.0)	0.0400 (1.93)

Fig. 8. Comparison of two strategies.

the execution times (in seconds) for the analysis programs when the abstract compiler does not perform any optimization. The next two columns give the percentage of work that is saved by each optimization. The last column gives the same information when both optimizations are performed. It proves that it is worth the effort to add them to the abstract compiler.

Program	No opt.	η-reduct.	Lookup	All opt.
conform	0.0292	18.7%	28.8%	47.3%
earley	0.0274	26.4%	37.0%	57.3%
interp	0.0675	22.0%	15.7%	35.6%
lambda	0.0507	23.1%	18.6%	35.8%
lex	0.0547	21.6%	31.9%	51.4%
link	0.2137	20.6%	16.2%	38.3%
lll	0.0410	21.5%	16.9%	44.9%
peval	0.0846	20.0%	17.7%	40.0%
source	0.0370	24.7%	18.5%	47.5%

Fig. 9. Relative benefits of each optimization.

6 Related Work

Although our work is novel in the field of static analysis, it is related to a number of other works.

Our work originated from the study of abstract interpretation, a framework well-adapted for the design of static analyses. A growing interest has been shown for this framework since the pioneering work of the Cousots [4]. It has been applied to a number of interesting analyses in the area of functional programming, including strictness analysis [11], reference counting [7], and control flow analysis [15]. In [2], Ayers presents several techniques for the efficient implementation of the *0cfa*. His "initial call sites" correspond to the calls where our technique can perform the **lookup** optimization.

Although we present here a more efficient implementation of *0cfa*, our paradigm is not restricted to analyses designed in the abstract interpretation framework. In fact, it can be applied to more conventional data-flow analyses [1, 6].

In [13], Serrano describes the control flow analyses performed in the Bigloo Scheme to C compiler [14]. His results show that these analyses allow significant optimizations to be performed. But they also show that it can take 4 to 9 times longer to compile a program when all the optimizations are enabled. Since his compiler produces C code, the time spent by the analysis and optimization process is often compensated by the time saved during the C compilation (the generated C code is easier to compile).

We argue that if the Bigloo compiler was to produce native code instead of C code, the time lost would not be compensated, thus revealing the real cost of control flow analysis (which has an $O(n^3)$ worst-case complexity).

Lin and Tan [10] show how to compile the dataflow analysis of logic programs. Although they named their technique "abstract compilation", they actually compile Prolog programs into code for the Warren Abstract Machine (WAM) using a (standard) compiler and that code is passed to an abstract interpreter for the WAM which computes the dataflow analysis. So there is no concept of analysis program in this technique, the abstract interpretation is being computed from another intermediate representation of the source program. Thus, optimizations of the analysis program, as those we described here, cannot be performed.

The use of closures for code generation has previously been proposed for compilation [5]. The latter describes an approach to compiling where each compiled expression is embodied by a closure whose application performs the evaluation of the given expression. This idea of replacing "code generation" by "closure generation" is essentially the same as we used in our compilation algorithm.

Closure generation is a form of runtime code generation. Leone and Lee [9] describe a technique for runtime code generation called *deferred compilation*. Their results also show that significant speedups can be obtained. For example, multiplication of sparse matrices is sped up by a factor of 2 using their technique.

7   Future Work

The analysis programs can be much faster if we consider generating machine code instructions instead of closures. Preliminary results show that they can typically be sped up by yet another factor of 4 in almost all cases. The only drawback is that the (abstract) compilation time also increases by a factor of 10, making the overall process slower than abstract interpretation if the analysis program is run a small number of times. The Scheme-to-C interface that we use is in part responsible for this increase. Also, the creation of a closure at runtime is much faster than the generation of a relatively long sequence of machine code instructions that do the same work. Nevertheless, we believe that the efficiency of the code generation can be further improved.

Our approach is most beneficial when the analysis is performed several times. This led us to the idea that the analysis program can be stored in a file and later reloaded together with other analysis programs in order to perform global control flow analysis of separately compiled multimodule programs. We are currently working on this idea [3].

8 Conclusion

We have presented a new way of implementing static analyses. It is based on the concept of *abstract compilation*. This paradigm is attractive for several reasons. It is conceptually simple, it is not restricted to any kind of static analysis, and more importantly, it can speed up the analysis.

As an example, we have described how to compile the control flow analysis of higher-order functional languages and our results have shown that the analysis can be sped up by over a factor of 2.

References

[1]   A. V. Aho, R. Sethi and J. D. Ullman. *Compilers. Principles, Techniques, and Tools.* Addison-Wesley, 1986.

[2]   Andrew E. Ayers. *Abstract Analysis and Optimization of Scheme.* PhD thesis, MIT, September 1993.

[3]   Dominique Boucher and Marc Feeley. *Un système pour l'optimisation globale de programmes d'ordre supérieur par compilation abstraite séparée.* Technical report 992, Université de Montréal, september 1995.

[4]   Patrick Cousot and Radhia Cousot. Abstract interpretation: a unified lattice model for static analysis of programs by construction or approximation of fixed points. In *Proceedings of the 4th ACM Symposium on Principles of Programming Languages, Los Angeles,* 1977, pp. 238–252.

[5]   Marc Feeley and Guy Lapalme. Using closures for code generation. *Comput. Lang.* **12**, 47–66, 1987.

[6]   Matthew S. Hecht. *Flow Analysis of Computer Programs.* North-Holland, New York, 1979.

[7]   Paul Hudak. A Semantic Model of Reference Counting and its Abstraction (Detailed Summary). In *Proceedings of the 1986 ACM Conference on Lisp and Functional Programming,* 351–363, 1986.

[8]   David A. Kranz. *ORBIT: An Optimizing Compiler for Scheme.* Ph.D. thesis, Yale University, 1988.

[9]   Mark Leone and Peter Lee. Lightweight Run-Time Code Generation. In *Proceedings of the 1994 ACM SIGPLAN Workshop on Partial Evaluation and Semantics-Based Program Manipulation,* pp. 97–106.

[10]   I-P. Lin and J. Tan. Compiling Dataflow Analysis of Logic Programs. In *Proceedings of the 1992 ACM Conference on Programming Language Desing and Implementation,* pp. 106–115.

[11]   Alan Mycroft. *Abstract Interpretation and Optimizing Transformations for Applicative Programs.* Ph.D. thesis, University of Edinburgh, 1981.

[12] Guillermo Juan Rozas. Taming the Y operator. In *Proceedings of the 1992 ACM Conference on Lisp and Functional Programming*, 226–234, 1992.

[13] Manuel Serrano. Control Flow Analysis: a compilation paradigm for functional languages. In *Proceedings of SAC 95*.

[14] Manuel Serrano. Bigloo User's Manual. Inria-Rocquencourt. March 1994.

[15] Olin Shivers. *Control-Flow Analysis of Higher-Order Languages*. Ph.D. thesis, Carnegie Mellon University, Pittsburgh, 1991.

Using Partial Evaluation in Support of Portability, Reusability, and Maintainability

Daniel J. Salomon

Dept. of Computer Science, University of Manitoba, Winnipeg, Manitoba,
Canada R3T 2N2, E-mail: salomon@cs.UManitoba.CA

Abstract. Partial evaluation is ordinarily intended to be used to increase program efficiency. This paper shows how partial evaluation can be used in place of a preprocessor phase and of source-code templates (e.g. C++ templates or Ada generics). In this way it can be used to support portability features provided by a preprocessor, and the reusability provided by code templates, but with higher maintainability due to the simpler syntax required. The important mechanisms needed are: annotating variables and functions with an evaluation time, treating declarations as translation-time "executable" statements, treating user-defined types as translation-time variables, giving programmers control over the scope of symbols, and providing translation-time name binding. The effects of these changes on the size and complexity of a compiler are estimated. A translator for a language called "Safer_C" which supports these techniques has been implemented. Important existing C software is analyzed to evaluate the applicability of these techniques in replacing the preprocessor.

1 Introduction

Partial evaluation [2, 5] is a program transformation technique whereby program constants and input whose values are known in advance of execution are used to specialize the program for those specific values and thus obtain a faster and/or smaller program. In this paper, we show that partial evaluation can also be used in support of portability, reusability, and maintainability of programs.

One of the reasons that the languages C & C++ have been popular for **portable** programming is that their preprocessors allows the automatic tailoring of programs to particular platforms. We show how the techniques of partial evaluation can be used to eliminate the need for a preprocessor phase by providing much of the same functionality.

A motivation for the development of templates in C++ and generic procedures in Ada has been to facilitate the coding of **reusable** procedures. We also show how partial evaluation can be used to duplicate the functionality of C++ templates.

The functionality of these two features is provided with minimal changes to the syntax and semantics of the original language, and certainly with less additional syntax than is ordinarily needed to support preprocessors and templates.

The simplicity and orthogonality with which partial evaluation can replace preprocessing and templates, makes the programs more readable, and easier to manipulate with program processors such as pretty printers, structured editors, and language version updaters, thus making programs more **maintainable.** At the same time the programmer is gaining the usual efficiency benefits of partial evaluation.

This work does not attempt to present new functionality for programming languages, but rather shows how partial evaluation can provide well recognized functionality in a simpler and more consistent way.

1.1 Replacing Preprocessors

The standardization and availability of the C preprocessor, cpp, is one of the principal reasons that the C language has become so popular for the programming of portable systems. With a preprocessor, the same source program can be customized down to fine details for different target architectures and operating systems.

Despite this advantage, preprocessors have fallen into disrepute. The principal complaints against them are that:

1. They add another level to the syntax and semantics of a programming language. This causes difficulties in the description, implementation, and use of the language.
2. They usually have a different syntax and semantics from the languages they are modifying.
3. Preprocessor statements can be misused to violate the structuredness of programs by overlapping instead of nesting control constructs.

The preprocessors for the C & C++ languages have all of the above faults, but because of their advantages and widespread use, they cannot simply be discarded.

In this paper, the author proposes that the principal functionality of preprocessors can be replaced by compile-time processing. Thus the number of program processing phases will be reduced by one. This equivalent functionality is provided within a single level of syntax, and with minimal changes to the syntax of the existing language.

Although we have focused on the C & C++ languages, our belief is that other languages too would benefit from these techniques by gaining the advantages of a preprocessor phase and of templates without the disadvantages.

1.2 Replacing Templates & Generic Packages

Templates in C++ and generic packages in Ada allow a generalized version of an algorithm to be coded, and translation-time parameters to be provided that customize the source code to a specific problem. The principal reason for introducing these language features was to increase the reusability of code. The translation-time specialization of functions, however, is the trademark of partial evaluation.

By treating user-defined types as translation-time variables, partial evaluation can be extended to provide the functionality of templates and generics, while hardly increasing the size of the grammar of a carefully designed language.

1.3 The Method

In this section, we summarize the changes to the syntax and processing of a C-like language that can give the compilation phase enough computational power to allow the elimination of the preprocessor phase and provide the functionality of templates. The changes are:

1. Program entities such as variables, functions and formal parameters, can be annotated at their declaration with a designation of their evaluation time.
2. The evaluation time of program entities is propagated through a program to determine the evaluation time of expressions, and where possible, control structures.
3. Predefined types are translation-time type constants, and user-defined type names are treated as translation-time variables.
4. Control structures can be annotated with an evaluation time to assist the compiler, or to clarify the programmer's intentions.
5. Declarations are treated as compile-time "executable" statements. Thus a programmer can gain control over not only what computations are to be performed, but also over what variables and functions are to be declared. This is an essential feature if partial evaluation is to be used to replace preprocessors and templates.
6. The programmer is provided with additional control over the scope of program entities.
7. Control structures are allowed outside of any function, where only declarations are normally allowed, provided that those control structures can be evaluated at compile time and that only declarations are left as residual code.
8. A boolean operator **decl** can be used to test whether an identifier has been declared. This operator is used to provide the functionality of the C preprocessor statements #ifdef and #ifndef.
9. Translation-time name binding is provided, so that the programmer can gain control over the final names of exported program entities. Normally names for program entities are bound at coding time.

These changes are described in greater detail in subsequent sections.

1.4 Origins of This Project

The work described in this paper originated from a project to design a language called Safer_C [10], which is a modern descendant of the C language. The primary objective of the design is to produce a language that is more error-resistant than C without sacrificing any expressiveness or computational power. The plan is to continue enhancing Safer_C until it matches C++ in expressive power, but with less of the tattered syntactic baggage that C++ inherited from C.

Due mostly to the fact that it was designed over 20 years ago, the C language has many syntactic deficiencies that lead to common programming errors. Some of the best known of these errors are: using the operator = for comparison instead of ==, forgetting the closing delimiters on comments, forgetting break statements at the end of switch cases, missing or adding erroneous semicolons, erroneous type declarations, and erroneous preprocessor statements. Some of these errors can persist in a program until run time, even though they originate strictly from deficient syntax. Koenig [6] gives a readable and valuable description of most of the syntactic deficiencies of C, along with tips on how to avoid them, and they are also summarized by Salomon [10].

Except for its added compile-time functionality, Safer_C is semantically identical to C, but has most of the syntactic deficiencies eliminated by using modern conventions. The C language was chosen for modernization because, despite its flaws, it is a popular language, and is used in many important systems that would benefit substantially from greater reliability. The intention was to design Safer_C such that all existing C programs could be machine translated to Safer_C, and further maintenance of those programs could be carried out in the more-error-resistant, modern syntax.

The greatest obstacle to modernizing C that was encountered is its preprocessor phase. Since preprocessors are used to change source text, the machine translation of C programs into a new version or a different form can be blocked by even tame preprocessor statements. Sometimes the actual C program that is being manipulated cannot be known until specific values are assumed for some of the preprocessor variables, and then only the program generated by those specific values can be manipulated, not the general form of the program.

Since the existence of a preprocessor phase impedes even simple source-to-source code manipulation, it was decided that the preprocessor should be replaced early in the evolution of Safer_C so that even though the transformation of existing C programs to Safer_C would still be hard, further transformation to later versions of Safer_C would be considerably simplified.

2   Related Work

Stroustrup [11], in the design of C++, has tried to eliminate the preprocessor phase as much as possible by allowing the compiler access to the values of const variables, and by providing in-line functions. These mechanisms, however, do not provide any support for conditional declarations, and #include preprocessor statements are still acknowledged as necessary.

The PL/I language [4] provides a preprocessor language with syntax and power that is quite similar to the run-time language. The many restrictions on the preprocessor language, a few extensions over the run-time language, and scope-rule differences, however, mean that the level of evaluation-time independence is actually quite limited. Since run-time code is always treated as text by the preprocessor, the readability and maintainability of programs is impaired. PL/I also provides a separate and powerful translation-time computation ability, which results in the duplication of implementation effort for preprocessing time and translation time.

The templates of C++ and the generic packages and procedures of Ada do provide reusability of code, but do so by providing an added level of function invocation with its own fully separate syntax and semantics.

A number of other researchers have studied the applicability of partial evaluation to imperative programs. Some recent examples are: Meyer [7], Nirkhe & Pugh [8], and Baier, Glück, & Zöchling [1]. Their methods are more extensive than the ones described here in that they try to maximize the amount of computation performed before run time. The work described here relies more heavily on programmer annotations. In Safer_C, more emphasis is placed on the programmer being able to predict what computations will be done at compile time, and being able to control when computations will be performed. We concentrate on how to use partial evaluation to replace the functionality of a preprocessor and templates.

The work of Weise and Crew [12] on programmable syntax macros may seem to be similar to ours. Their method adds more programming power than text macros, but also adds a meta level of syntax, and still poses an obstacle to automatic source-to-source manipulations.

The idea of explicit control over the scope of program entities is due to Cormack [3], who also gives the benefits of such control for ordinary run-time variables.

3 Declaring the Evaluation Time of Program Entities

The mechanism used by Safer_C to replace the preprocessor phase is to provide program entities, such as types, variables, functions, and formal parameters, with an *evaluation-time* attribute. For brevity and readability in this discussion, the term "variable" will often be used to refer to all such program entities. A variable can be specified as having a translation-time evaluation by preceding its type specification with the keyword "tran," otherwise it is assumed to have run-time evaluation[1].

Sample declarations might be:

```
SIZE  :: tran int := 10
table :: [0..SIZE-1] int
WIDTH :: tran float := SIZE/14.0
```

---

[1] Actually Safer_C allows the specification of one of five evaluation times: translation, linking, loading, frame allocation, and run time, and it attempts to provide the same computation power in each of those five phases. This corresponds to the principle of evaluation-time independence described by Salomon [9]. Since translation time and run time are the only phases currently operational in Safer_C, they are the only ones discussed in this paper.

In these declarations, SIZE and WIDTH are translation-time variables, and table is a run-time variable.

4 The Evaluation Time of Expressions and Statements

Methods for propagating evaluation time through a program appear in the literature (See for instance Meyer [7] or Nirkhe and Pugh [8]), so only the elements unique to Safer_C are emphasized here.

- Arithmetic Expressions (e_1 **op** e_2, **pre_op** e_1, or e_1 **post_op**) – The evaluation time of an arithmetic expression is the latest evaluation time of any of the subexpressions or variables that comprise it.
  Referencing is an exception to this rule. A reference operation takes the evaluation time of the address of the object referenced, not of the object.
  Short-circuit boolean operators are also treated specially. Consider the expression e_1 && e_2, where "&&" is the short-circuit **and** operator in C. If e_1 has an evaluation time t_1 that is earlier than t_2 the evaluation time of e_2 then if e_1 evaluates to **true** the expression takes the evaluation time and value of the second operand, whereas if e_1 evaluates to **false** then the expression takes the value and evaluation time of e_1. A corresponding calculation of evaluation time is used for the the short-circuit **or** operator.
- Assignment (Dest_Var := Source_Expr) – The expression Source_Expr must have an evaluation time earlier or equal to that of the variable Dest_Var, otherwise an error is reported. The assignment is carried out at the evaluation time of the variable Dest_Var.
- Boolean Selection (**if** (Bool_Expr) **then** Then_Stmt **else** Else_Stmt) – The selection is carried out at the evaluation time of the boolean expression Bool_expr. Only the selected statement is processed, the other statement is ignored. The ignored statement must be syntactically correct, but need not necessarily be semantically correct. In particular, if Bool_Expr is a translation-time expression, since declarations are "executed" at translation time, the effect is that no type checking is performed on the ignored statement, and any subprograms invoked need not be made available for any of the processing phases. The selected statement may have an evaluation time later than Bool_Expr, and then would be processed as residual code.
- Case Selection (**switch** (Ord_Expr) Case_List) – The execution of case selection statements is analogous to boolean selection. There is an added provision that, for efficiency reasons, the evaluation times of the case-label expressions must be translation-time.
- While Loops (**while** (Bool_Expr) Loop_Body) – If Bool_Expr evaluates to **false** at translation time, then the body of the loop is ignored. Otherwise, the loop is considered to be a run-time loop, unless it is explicitly annotated as a translation-time loop. To mark a **while** loop as a translation-time loop it is preceded by the marker #tran#. This method of determining evaluation times is used because unbounded run-time loops are a common mechanism

in C programs, and it is not always possible to determine whether or not they can be replaced by unrolled code at translation time. Rather than attempting to make such a prediction, Safer_C unrolls **while** loops only if explicitly requested to do so by the programmer.

If Bool_Expr is a non-false translation-time expression, and the programmer requests translation-time evaluation, then the loop is unrolled until Bool_Expr becomes false at or until a **break** statement is executed.

- For loops (**for** (Init_Stmt; Test_Expr; Inc_Stmt) Loop_Body) – Safer_C **for** loops have a standard mapping into while loops, and that mapping holds for determining the evaluation time of the **for** loop as well. The mapping is the same as for the C language: the statement Init_Stmt precedes the loop, the expression Test_Expr is used as the boolean control expression of the generated while loop, and the statement Inc_Stmt is inserted as the last statement of the loop body.

- Do Loops (**do** Loop_Body **while** (Bool_Expr)) – Safer_C **do** is a post-test loop that is handled in a fashion closely analogous to the pretest **while** loop.

- Goto statements are currently allowed only for run-time evaluation.

5 The Evaluation Time of Function Invocations

In Safer_C, as in C, functions returning void are equivalent to procedures, and hence this discussion of function invocation applies equally well to procedure invocation. The number of possible strategies for partial evaluation of function invocations is large. In keeping with the overall simple implementation philosophy of the C language, Safer_C also has a fairly simple strategy. Safer_C provides three kinds of partial evaluation of functions, each described in one of the following subsections. Function invocations not processed in one of these three ways are left as ordinary run-time function invocations.

5.1 Replacement by a Result

In some situations, it is possible to replace a function invocation by a function result even if the function is declared as having run-time evaluation. This kind of partial evaluation is done if:

1. The values of all of the actual arguments and external variables accessed by the function are known at translation time,
2. Either the source code for the function is available at translation time, or the object code for the function is available and a dynamic loader is provided to the translator, and
3. The function has no side effects.

Since a programmer may want to invoke the version of a function provided on the target machine, rather than the version provided on the compilation machine, a "time-warp" notation is available to delay the execution of functions until run-time.

5.2   In-Line Expansion

A function is expanded in-line, such that the function invocation is replaced by any computations specified by the function that cannot be carried out at translation time, if:

1. The source code for the function is available at translation time, and
2. The function is declared to have translation-time evaluation.

This is the kind of partial evaluation that is normally used to replace C-preprocessor macro invocations. Care must be taken to observe the normal scope rules of function variables expanded in-line. In source-to-source translators, scope rules can be enforced by variable renaming.

5.3   Function Specialization

A specialized version of a function that assumes specific values of its formal parameters is generated if:

1. The source code for the function is available at translation time,
2. The function is declared to have run-time evaluation, and
3. Some of the formal parameters of the function are declared to have translation-time evaluation.

An aggressively optimizing partial evaluator could apply this transformation even for functions with only run-time formal parameters.

This kind of partial evaluation can be used in place of C++ templates, or Ada generics. The translation-time formal parameters play the part of translation-time template parameters. Since, in Safer_C, user-defined types are treated as translation-time variables, functions can be specialized for specific type arguments.

The Implications for Reusability. When a function is coded to be as general as possible, in order to maximize the number of applications for which it can be reused, a common result is that some part of the function will be useless for some applications. The superfluous code is often marked by superfluous formal parameters that will always take the same value for any particular application. This kind of partial evaluation permits a specialized version of the function to be instantiated with the superfluous code eliminated.

A common indicator of superfluous parameters is default values for formal parameters, which are allowed by some languages. The default values are the ones unlikely to be changed by the programmer, and hence usually add redundant generality.

Many programmers resist reusing general code written for other projects because they fear it will slow down their application. For the same reason they may resist writing reusable code themselves. Translation-time specialization can increase efficiency, thus increasing the likelihood of coding and reusing more-general code.

Implementation Strategy. When a function with translation-time formal parameters is invoked, a record is kept of the particular values used for the corresponding actual arguments, and a new name is assigned to that forthcoming instantiation of the function. Repeated use of the same values for the same translation-time parameters does not increase the size of the list of specialized functions, since functions are instantiated only once for each combination of the specializing arguments. This method is called "polyvariant" specialization [2].

Ideally the compiler should have a way of communicating the particular values of formal parameters used for each instantiation of a function to the linker, so that the same instantiation could serve even separately compiled invocations of the function. This can be done by *name mangling:* coding the fixed parameters values into the name of the specialized function.

6 Providing Translation-Time Input and Output

Safer_C strives to achieve evaluation-time independence [9], which means that the same level of computational power should be provided for calculations performed at translation-time as is provided at run time. This principle includes I/O facilities. To meet this goal, Safer_C provides I/O streams that have translation-time evaluation. In particular, the input stream "tranin" is an input stream corresponding to "stdin" that is open for input at translation time, and "tranout" is the translation-time standard output stream corresponding to "stdout" at run-time.

By allowing explicit translation-time input, Safer_C source code can be customized at translation time for a particular application, without having to edit source code. The system tailoring parameters can be input interactively at translation time, or prepared in an independent specification file. Similarly, translation-time output can be used to prompt an installer for input, and report on the progress of compilation. If installers were instead required to edit system constants directly into source code then they would need a good understanding of the implementation language, and the possibilities for installation errors would be increased. Translation-time I/O is not a new idea. It has been used for decades in operating-system generation on minicomputer systems, such as RSX-11M for the DEC PDP-11 processor.

7 Translation-Time "Executable" Declarations

In C, declarations can be included or excluded from the source program under preprocessor control. This facility provides significant programmer control over the size of task-images, and the ability to perform substantial customization of programs for specific target systems. In order to duplicate this level of program control, Safer_C treats declarations as translation-time executable statements. The "execution" of a declaration consists of inserting a new entry into the symbol table. This treatment of declarations might seem peculiar, but it is actually not much different from the way that declarations are actually implemented in existing C compilers.

Safer_C's parent, the C language, provided an unexpected advantage in this respect. In C, there are no delimiters between declaration sections and executable sections of code, and Safer_C keeps this characteristic. As a result, declarations can be enclosed and controlled by control structures as easily as other statements.

The form of a Safer_C declaration is:

$$declaration \rightarrow symbol\_list :: [eval\_time] \; type\_expr \; [:= initial\_value]$$

This notation is like Ada's declaration syntax except that Ada's colon has been replaced by a double colon, and an optional evaluation time can be specified.

As an example, a programmer may wish to select between two declarations, based on the operating system used by the target machine, by using statements similar to the following:

```
if  ( Target == System_1 )
    Field :: int
    process(&Field, 5124)
else
    Field :: float
    process(&Field, 5.124)
endif
```

8   Replacing #include Statements

One of the important uses of the C preprocessor is to insert declaration header files into a source program as requested by an #include statement. For instance, a common preprocessor statement in C programs is:

```
#include <stdio.h>
```

which inserts standard I/O declarations, macros, and function headers into the program. The concept of the #include statement—escaping to separately specified code—is similar to that of procedure invocation, and in Safer_C translation-time procedure invocation is used to take its place. The above include statement would be coded as:

```
stdio_h()
```

Both declarations and executable statements can be placed in a translation-time procedure, and it can be invoked at translation time to have the effect of inserting those statements into a program at the invocation site.

This mechanism may seem to be an extreme way of handling standard declarations as compared to the methods used by other programming languages, such as Ada or Modula-3, but few other languages allow executable statements in their declaration files.

9   Additional Control over the Scope of Program Entities

One problem with using compile-time procedures to replace #include statements is that normally each procedure starts a new scope, and the usual implicit
scope rules will result in all the declarations within the procedure becoming in-
accessible outside of the procedure. Normally the body of a function in Safer_C
is enclosed between the keywords **block** and **end**, which correspond to braces {}
in the C language. If, instead, the body of a function is enclosed by the keywords
body and **end** then no new scope will be started for the body of the function.
Thus any declarations made in the function will effectively be made at the point
where the function is invoked. A new distinct lexical scope still exists for the
formal parameters of the function.

10   Translation-Time Name Binding

An important use of the C preprocessor is to create new distinct identifiers for
external symbols. In code being ported to different operating systems, different
architectures, or different peripheral-device environments, the names of external
symbols may need to change to reflect the particular environment.

Even mathematical functions can benefit from translation-time name binding. For instance, the computation of the trigonometric functions *sin* and *cos*
could be generated from the same source with parameter rotation inserted at
translation time, and renaming of the residual function.

Safer_C supports translation-time name binding by allowing the name of a
variable or function to be taken indirectly from a translation-time string variable.
Using the notation #(tt_string)# will cause the value of the variable tt_string
to be used as an identifier. Without this feature, only coding-time name binding
and code duplication would be available.

11   Effects on Compiler Size and Complexity

Providing Safer_C with evaluation-time annotations takes up 8% of the rules of
the grammar. (The full grammar for Safer_C has only 91% of the number of rules
in the grammar for C; the decrease being mostly due to a simplification of C's
arcane declaration syntax and precedence rules.) Remember also that a grammar
for the preprocessor (not included in this comparison) has been dispensed with.

Most of the code for evaluating expressions at compile time is already present
in most C compilers, since the optimization phase usually makes provisions for
some compile-time computation and constant folding. Code added to the compiler for boolean selection is similar in size and nature to the code that exists in
the C preprocessor for the same purposes.

The translation-time evaluation of functions is not usually part of constant
folding. It is similar in nature to macro expansion done by the preprocessor,
but since the formal parameters can have types other than text strings, it is
somewhat more complex.

New code must be added for compile-time case selection and loops, but it is slightly smaller than the code for expression evaluation needed by a preprocessor. All in all, the size of the translator grows little considering the added functionality of the method.

12 The Status of the Safer_C Project

The Safer_C language has been implemented as a translator to the C language. The translation-time computations are performed and the residual code is output in C. Since the translator is written in ANSI C and generates ANSI C output, its portability between systems should be good. All the run-time functionality of C is has been implemented. Translation-time loops and arrays are not yet fully supported, but, since these are not available in the C preprocessor either, enough of the Safer_C language has been implemented to allow the translation of all the ANSI C standard header files, such as <stdio.h>, <math.h>, and <stdlib.h>, into Safer_C translation-time functions. Since the dynamic loading of object modules at translation time is not yet supported, the source code for all translation-time function evaluations must be available at translation time.

13 Applicability of these Techniques

An attempt was made to judge the applicability of the techniques of this paper to real programs written by other programmers. For our analysis we chose code from three different projects:

1. Source code for the X11 library of the X Window System, release 5.
2. Source code for the kernel and SCSI device drivers of the LINUX operating system, version 1.1.59.
3. Source code for the Gnu C and C++ compilers (gcc and g++) version 2.5.8.

Because these freeware programs are designed to be portable across many operating systems and architectures, they make heavy use of preprocessor customization of source code. Since the sources were merely inspected for translatability to Safer_C, and not actually translated, some surprises may still arise. Nevertheless every attempt was made to do an accurate analysis.

By far the largest part of preprocessor usage in the code examined is plain and well behaved statements that can be easily and automatically translated into Safer_C: the simple definition of preprocessor constants with #define, the ordinary inclusion of header files with #include, and straightforward conditionally compiled source code using #if constructs.

Several instances of unusual code were found for which no direct translation would be advisable, since that would be duplicating the undesirable characteristic of preprocessors too. Recoding in a totally different style would be the best solution. In some cases, considerable thought had to be given as to how to use Safer_C constructs to provide the same effect as the preprocessor statements.

Usually the same problem recurs in the same form several times in the same source files, so once a translation scheme is found for one problem, it can be reapplied many times.

Ultimately, some of the translation problems encountered indicate that continued evolution of Safer_C is needed to provide for some of the uses of preprocessors. The two most important of these uses are:

1. Providing detailed control over declarations where control statements are currently not allowed in Safer_C, such as in formal parameter lists, and record structure declarations.
2. The stringizing of macro parameters, where the name of a formal parameter can be used as a string, has no equivalent in Safer_C, but is an especially useful feature for debugging and error reporting.

14   Sample Code

The following short Safer_C program is included to give the flavour of the language. Comments are delimited by an exclamation mark and the end of the line. In a style similar to CLU, semicolons are not required to end statements. Declarations and definitions are identified by a double colon. The name of a function is enclosed in French quotation marks (i.e. between $<<$ and $>>$) when it is being defined, but not when it is merely being declared. Most other constructs and operators that are not explained by comments follow C conventions.

```
!! Sample Safer_C/1 program.
!! ------------------------

!! Explicitly specify source language version.
Safer_C version 1.5

stdio_h()           !! Instead of "#include <stdio.h>".
math_h()            !! Instead of "#include <math.h>".

!! Pi is declared as a translation-time constant and
!! SIZE as a translation-time variable.
Pi :: tran const float := 3.141592654
SIZE :: tran int   !! Size of problem.

work :: extern func (x :: float) float


!! This translation-time function will be unfolded (in-lined).
<<map>> :: tran func (x :: float) int
body
      return (::int) (x/SIZE)   !! Cast Result to type int.
end
```

```
!! This run-time function will be specialized.
!! The type expression "-> T" means "pointer to type T".
<<swap>> :: run func (T :: type; a, b :: -> T) void
block
    temp :: T

    temp := a@    !! Dereference a and copy to temp.
    a@ := b@
    b@ := temp
end


!! Define the function "main".
<<main>> :: func () int
block
    !! Declare some translation-time symbols.
    IDX  :: tran int    !! Loop index.
    PHI  :: tran int

    !! Declare some run-time symbols.
    point, result :: float
    i :: int

    !! Translation-time I/O.
    fprintf (tranout, "Maximum size of problem? ")
    fscanf (tranin, "%d", &SIZE)

    !! Allocate enough zones for specified size.
    zones :: static [0..(2*SIZE)] float
    PHI := Pi/SIZE

    !! Translation-time initialization loop.
    #tran# for (IDX:=1; IDX < 2*SIZE; IDX++)
        zones[IDX] := sin(IDX*PHI)
    endfor

    !! A run-time, bottom-test loop.
    do
        printf ("Enter problem point: ")
        scanf ("%f", &point)
        result := work (point)
        printf ("    Result is: %g\en", result)
        i := map(point)
```

```
        swap (float, &result, zones+i)
        swap (float, &point, zones+i+1)
     while (result > 0.0)
     enddo
     return 0
end
```

References

1. Baier, R., Glück, R., Zöchling, R.: Partial evaluation of numerical programs in FORTRAN. *ACM SIGPLAN Workshop on Partial Evaluation and Semantics-Based Program Manipulation PEPM'94, Orlando, Florida, June 25, 1994. Technical Report 94/9*, Dept. of Comp. Sci., Univ. of Melbourne. (1994) 119–132
2. Consel, C., Danvy, O.: Tutorial notes on partial evaluation. *20-th Annual ACM SIGPLAN-SIGACT Symposium on Principles of Programming Languages POPL'93, Charleston, SC.* (1993) 493–501
3. Cormack, G. V.: Extensions to static scoping. *ACM SIGPLAN Notices* **18**, 6 (1983) 187–191
4. IBM: *OS and DOS PL/I Language Reference Manual.* Reference No. GC26-3977-1, File No. S370-29, IBM Corp., San Jose, CA (1984)
5. Jones, N. D., Gomard, C. K., Sestoft, Peter: *Partial evaluation and automatic program generation.* Prentice Hall Int'l., Hemel Hempstead, UK (1993)
6. Koenig, A.: *C Traps and Pitfalls.* Addison-Wesley, Reading, MA (1989)
7. Meyer, U.: Techniques for partial evaluation of imperative languages. *Symposium on Partial Evaluation and Semantics-Based Program Manipulation PEPM'91. Yale Univ., New Haven, CT, June 17-19, 1991. ACM SIGPLAN Notices* **26**, 9 (Sept. 1991) 94-105
8. Nirkhe, V., Pugh, W.: A partial evaluator for the Maruti hard real-time system. *Twelfth Real-Time Systems Symposium. IEEE Computer Society Press, Los Alamitos, CA, USA* (1991) 64-73
9. Salomon, D. J.: Four dimensions of programming-language independence. *SIGPLAN Notices* **27**, 3 (March 1992) 35-53
10. Salomon, D. J.: Safer_C: syntactically improving the C language for error resistance. *Tech. Rep. 95/07*, Dept. of Comp. Sci., Univ. of Manitoba (1995)
11. Stroustrup, B.: *The C++ Programming Language, 2-nd Ed.* Addison Wesley, Reading, MA. (1991)
12. Weise, D., Crew, R.: Programmable syntax macros. *ACM SIGPLAN Conference on Programming Language Design and Implementation PLDI'93. Albuquerque, NM, June 23-25, 1993. ACM SIGPLAN Notices* **28**, 6 (June 1993) 156-165

Incremental Computation of Static Single Assignment Form

Jong-Deok Choi[1] and Vivek Sarkar[2] and Edith Schonberg[3]

[1] IBM T.J. Watson Research Center, P. O. Box 704, Yorktown Heights, NY 10598
(jdchoi@watson.ibm.com)
[2] IBM Software Solutions Division, 555 Bailey Avenue, San Jose, CA 95141
(vivek_sarkar@vnet.ibm.com)
[3] IBM T.J. Watson Research Center, P. O. Box 704, Yorktown Heights, NY 10598
(schnbrg@watson.ibm.com)

Abstract. Static single assignment (SSA) form is an intermediate representation that is well suited for solving many data flow optimization problems. However, since the standard algorithm for building SSA form is exhaustive, maintaining correct SSA form throughout a multi-pass compilation process can be expensive. In this paper, we present incremental algorithms for restoring correct SSA form after program transformations. First, we specify incremental SSA algorithms for insertion and deletion of a use/definition of a variable, and for a large class of updates on intervals. We characterize several cases for which the cost of these algorithms will be proportional to the size of the transformed region and hence potentially much smaller than the cost of the exhaustive algorithm. Secondly, we specify customized SSA-update algorithms for a set of common loop transformations. These algorithms are highly efficient: the cost depends at worst on the size of the transformed code, and in many cases the cost is independent of the loop body size and depends only on the number of loops.

1   Introduction

Static single assignment (SSA) [8, 6] form is a compact intermediate program representation that is well suited to a large number of compiler optimization algorithms, including constant propagation [19], global value numbering [3], and program equivalence detection [21]. In SSA form, each variable appears as a target of an assignment at most once, so that each variable use is reached by a single definition. Special variable definitions called $\phi - functions$ are added to the program to represent multiple reaching definitions.

This paper addresses the problem of *rebuilding* SSA form after program transformation. The traditional algorithm for building minimal SSA form [8, 18] is efficient but exhaustive. Even when program changes are small, the cost of updating SSA with this algorithm is proportional to the size of the procedure. As a result, maintaining current and correct SSA form during a multi-pass compilation process is expensive.

As an alternative to exhaustive SSA reconstruction, we propose incremental SSA update techniques. We present general incremental algorithms for restoring correct SSA form:

- after an arbitrary insertion/deletion of a use/definition of a variable, and
- after an arbitrary update of a single interval.

We also characterize several cases for which the cost of these algorithms will be proportional to the size of the transformed region and hence potentially much smaller than the cost of the exhaustive algorithm.

Additionally, we present customized incremental SSA-update algorithms for a set of common loop transformations, which includes interchange of rectangular/trapezoidal loops, general iteration-reordering loop transformations, and loop fusion. These algorithms are highly efficient: the cost depends at worst on the size of the transformed code, and in many cases the cost is independent of the loop body size and depends only on the number of loops.

It is important to use more efficient customized SSA-update algorithms for common loop transformations because:

- Loop transformations are increasingly important in multi-pass compilers to facilitate instruction scheduling, increase parallelism, improve reference locality, and enable other optimizations [14].
- Loop transformations often constitute a small program change, relative to the size of the procedure.
- SSA form for loops has special properties which make incremental update on a single loop basis efficient and straightforward.

The rest of the paper is organized as follows. Section 2 describes comparison of our method with previous work. Section 3 presents definitions and background material on SSA form. Section 4 presents basic techniques for updating SSA form after changes to individual statements or to individual intervals. Section 5 gives more efficient update algorithms for specific loop transformations, and Section 6 presents our conclusions.

2   Related Work

We focus our discussion on incremental update of SSA form, since it is well-known how to perform incremental updates on other data structures such as the control flow graph and the intermediate language text for these loop transformations. Previous work on incremental data flow analysis focuses on obtaining an updated fixed-point solution after a small program change [5, 4, 13, 12]. These incremental data flow techniques apply to any monotone data flow problem expressed within the classic data flow framework. Our work differs from these exhaustive approaches in that we apply specialized update algorithms for particular changes in the program. Thereby, our methods incur costs proportional to the size of the changes in the program. Cytron and Gershbein [9] also present techniques for incrementally building SSA form to accommodate *may-aliases*.

Their techniques deal with only inserting special definitions, called *may-defs*, generated by may-aliases. They considered incrementality only in response to *specific* demands for data flow information over a program whose structure and contents remain constant. Ryder and Carroll [15] present techniques for incrementally updating the dominator tree of a directed graph.

In [11], Griswold and Notkin propose an incremental paradigm for updating the source abstract syntax tree (AST), control flow graph (CFG), and program dependence graph (PDG) representations of a program so as to properly reflect a program transformation supported by their tool. Each local/compensation transformation that is applied to the source AST by the tool has a corresponding subgraph substitution rule that is applied to the CFG/PDG. In contrast, we present substitution rules for updating the *SSA graph* for a variety of source transformations. Our technique could be used to extend the work reported in [11] so as to allow incremental update of the SSA graph representation in addition to incremental updates of the CFG and PDG. In fact, the SSA graph could be used as a more efficient representation of the data dependence edges in the PDG representation.

In [10], Giegerich et al study the problem of identifying conditions under which data flow information is unchanged after a program transformation is applied. They define the notion of invariance of an approximative semantics with respect to a given set of transformation rules. Their work could potentially be used as a basis for identifying transformations for which the SSA graph remains unchanged.

3 Background

In this section, we describe terminology and definitions used in the rest of the paper.

3.1 Program Representation

Definition 1. A *control flow graph* of a procedure P is a directed multigraph

$$CFG = < N_c, E_c, \textbf{Entry}, \textbf{Exit} >$$

A node $n_i \in N_c$ represents a statement w in P, and an edge $e_k = < n_i, n_j > \in E_c$ represents the transfer of control from the statement of n_i to the statement of n_j. We assume that each node is on a path from **Entry** to **Exit**. □

Definition 2. A node n *dominates* a node $\hat{n}$ in CFG if every directed path from **Entry** to $\hat{n}$ contains n. □

Definition 3. A *back edge* in CFG is an edge $< l, h >$ such that node h dominates node l. Node h is called a *header node*. A back edge defines a *strongly connected region* $STR(h, l)$, which consists of the nodes and edges belonging to all CFG simple paths from h to l, and also the back edge. □

Definition 4. Let $B(h) = \{< l, h > \in E_c \mid < l, h >$ is a back edge$\}$. Then, the *transitive interval with header* h, denoted by $I^*(h)$, is the union of all the $STR(h, l)$ defined by $B(h)$. The *interval with header* h, denoted by $Interval(h)$, is a directed graph $Interval(h) = < N_h, E_h, h >$ such that

- $N_h = \{n \in N_c \mid n \in (I^*(h) - \bigcup_{\hat{h} \in I^*(h), \hat{h} \neq h} I^*(\hat{h}))\}$, and
- $E_h = \{< n_i, n_j > \in E_c \mid n_i, n_j \in N_h\}$.

We denote the header node of interval I by $hdr(I)$. □

Informally, $Interval(h)$ is the union of all the nodes in $I^*(h)$ that do not "belong to" intervals nested in $I^*(h)$, and edges between these nodes.

3.2 Properties of SSA

Rendering a program into SSA form simplifies and increases the accuracy of solving a useful subset of data-flow optimization problems. These results are largely due to the statically functional nature of an SSA form program: each "variable" in the transformed program appears as the target of exactly one assignment statement. All uses are appropriately renamed so that the value flow from a variable's definition (*def*) to its use(s) is explicitly apparent in the program text.

To describe how to construct SSA form of a program, we introduce the following terminology.

Definition 5. Let n and m be nodes in CFG. If n dominates m and $n \neq m$, then n *strictly* dominates m. The *dominance frontier* $DF(n)$ of n is the set of all CFG nodes m such that n dominates a predecessor of m but does not strictly dominate m. □

Note that the dominator relation of a CFG forms a tree, called a *dominator tree*. Algorithmically, SSA form is constructed by identifying regions of a program dominated by a given def. Where control flow from different regions merge, the transformed program contains a ϕ-function that explicitly represents the merge of value defs. More specifically, the set of nodes containing ϕ-functions for variable v can be precomputed as the *iterated dominance frontier* of nodes containing defs of v [8, 18]. The SSA construction algorithm then traverses the dominator tree of the program's control flow graph, maintaining a stack of renamed defs for each variable.

Figure 1 shows an example program segment and its SSA form. Renaming in SSA form ensures that each variable in the transformed program appears as the target of exactly one assignment statement. A ϕ-function is introduced at statement $\hat{S}_4$ to explicitly represent the merge of value defs Y_1 and Y_2. Note that in this paper, we use x and y for the original variable names and use X_i and Y_j for the variable names renamed from x and y, respectively.

A statement in a program has a unique node in the corresponding CFG. Hence, in this paper, we will use statements and nodes (in CFG) interchangeably

$$
\begin{aligned}
&S_1: \quad x = \ldots; \\
&S_2: \quad \text{if } (x > 0) \qquad y = x + 10; \\
&S_3: \quad \text{else} \qquad\qquad y = x - 10; \\
&S_4: \\
&S_5: \quad x = x + y;
\end{aligned}
\qquad
\begin{aligned}
&\hat{S}_1: \quad X_1 = \ldots; \\
&\hat{S}_2: \quad \text{if } (X_1 > 0) \qquad Y_1 = X_1 + 10; \\
&\hat{S}_3: \quad \text{else} \qquad\qquad Y_2 = X_1 - 10; \\
&\hat{S}_4: \quad Y_3 = \phi(Y_1, Y_2); \\
&\hat{S}_5: \quad X_2 = X_1 + Y_3;
\end{aligned}
$$

Fig. 1. An Example program and Its SSA Form

when the meaning is clear. Our results are equally applicable to the case when a CFG node represents a basic block, which could contain multiple statements.

Property 1 Let n be a node in CFG with a def of X_i, and m be a node in CFG with a use of X_i that is a user statement, i.e. *not* a ϕ-function parameter. Then,

1. n dominates m; and
2. there is no node l with a def of x such that l dominates m and is in turn dominated by n.

Definition 6. Given a variable v and user statement S of a procedure in SSA form, *reaching_def*(S, v) is the def of v that reaches the statement S. For S_0, which is the entry of the procedure, *reaching_def*(S_0, v) is V_0, a def of v assumed to reach the entry of the procedure (interprocedurally).

Since S is a user program statement and not a ϕ-*function*, *reaching_def*(S, v) is unique and strictly dominates S. For X_i at a CFG node n to be *reaching_def*(m, x), node n and node m must satisfy Property 1.

Property 2 Let n be a node in CFG with a def of X_i, and m be a node in CFG with a use of X_i that *is* a ϕ-function parameter. Then,

1. m is a dominance frontier of n; and
2. $X_i = $ *reaching_def*(S, v), where S is a predecessor statement of m in CFG, if S does not have a def of x; or X_i is the def of x at S.

4 Incremental SSA Algorithms

This section explores general incremental properties of SSA. Given an insertion or deletion of a variable def or use, Section 4.1 presents algorithms for restoring correct SSA form. Section 4.2 generalizes these algorithms to work for updates of an interval.

4.1 Incremental SSA Techniques

When a variable def is deleted (inserted), $\phi-functions$ may have to be deleted (inserted) to restore minimal SSA form.[4] For example, in Figure 2, if the statement $S5$ is deleted in (a), $\phi-functions$ at statements $S4$, $S7$ and $S9$ must also be deleted, resulting in program (b). Similarly, inserting a def of x at location $\hat{S}5$ in (b) results in the inverse transformation. This insertion update procedure requires using the dominance frontier relation, and all four incremental algorithms presented below use the dominator tree. The variable def that reaches the change site plays a special role.

Theorem 7. Suppose a def of v is deleted (inserted) at statement S in an SSA-correct program P. Let $\hat{P}$ be the resulting SSA-correct program after the deletion (insertion), and $r = reaching\_def(S, v)$ in $\hat{P}$ (P). Then all modified statements in both P and $\hat{P}$ are dominated by r or are in the iterated dominance frontier of r. $\qquad\square$

Proof: It follows from Property 1 and Property 2. $\square$

In Figure 2, X_1 is $reaching\_def(S5, x)$ in (b), and dominates all modified statements. (Note that (b) corresponds to the transformed program $\hat{P}$ when S is deleted, and to the initial program P when S is inserted.)

$S1$: $X_1 = \ldots$	$\hat{S}1$: $X_1 = \ldots$
$S2$: if $\ldots$	$\hat{S}2$: if $\ldots$
$S3$: repeat	$\hat{S}3$: repeat
$S4$: $X_2 = \phi(X_1, X_3)$	$\hat{S}4$:
$S5$: $X_3 = \ldots$	$\hat{S}5$:
$S6$: until $\ldots$	$\hat{S}6$: until $\ldots$
$S7$: $X_4 = \phi(X_1, X_3)$	$\hat{S}7$:
$S8$: endif	$\hat{S}8$: endif
$S9$: $X_5 = \phi(X_1, X_4)$	$\hat{S}9$:
$S10$: $\ldots = X_5$	$\hat{S}10$: $\ldots = X_1$
(a)	(b)

Fig. 2. SSA form before and after deleting a def X_3.

A ϕ-function represents the merge of different value defs, which can become *redundant* if one or more of the defs get deleted. For example, the ϕ-functions at $S4$ and $S7$ in Figure 2 represent the merge of defs X_1 and X_3, and will become

---

[4] By minimal SSA form, we mean the SSA form that would be constructed by the exhaustive algorithm in [8].

redundant if X_3 gets deleted. A formal definition of a redundant ϕ-function is given as follows:

Definition 8. A ϕ-function F is *redundant* if all the parameters, except those identical to the target of the ϕ-function, are the same renamed variable.

Examples of redundant ϕ-functions are:

$$X_i = \phi(X_j, X_j, X_j), \qquad\qquad X_k = \phi(X_l, X_k, X_l).$$

In the incremental SSA update algorithms specified below, it is assumed that same-named variables are represented by def-use chains after variable renaming. Specifically, $Uses(d)$ is the set of uses reached by the def d. Using doubly-linked list representations for the $Uses$ sets, adding and deleting uses can be performed in constant time. Computing $r = reaching\_def(S, v)$ can be performed by searching ancestors in the dominator tree, so that the cost is proportional to the height of the tree.

Delete use u of variable v at statement S: Remove u from $Uses(r)$.

Insert use u of variable v at statement S: Add u to $Uses(r)$.

Delete def d of variable v at statement S: Like the original SSA algorithm in [8], the incremental update algorithm works in several steps:

1. *Update Uses sets:* All uses of d, including parameters of ϕ-functions, become uses of r, which is $reaching\_def(S, v)$.
2. *Delete redundant ϕ-functions:* If any ϕ-function F becomes redundant, F will be deleted and the whole process of (a) and (b) repeats, with the target of F as the new d.

   Example: To illustrate this algorithm, we delete $S5$ in Figure 2(a). X_3 in $S5$ is used in ϕ-functions at $S4$ and $S7$, and initially $reaching\_def(S5, x) = X_2$. Substituting X_2 for X_3, $S4$ becomes redundant and deleted. Step (a) is applied recursively with X_2 as the newly deleted d. The new $reaching\_def(S4, x)$ is X_1, which is propagated to the ϕ-function at $S7$, where X_2 appears as an input operand after the first iteration. Statement $S7$ is deleted as being redundant, and X_1, as the new $reaching\_def(S7, x)$, substitutes the use of X_4 at $S9$, resulting in a redundant ϕ-function at $S9$. With $X5$ at $S9$ deleted, the use of $X5$ at $S10$ becomes that of $X1$, resulting in Figure 2(b)

Insert def d of variable v at statement S:

1. *Insert new ϕ-functions:* For each node in the dominance frontier of S, if there is no $\phi-function$ for v create a new $\phi-function$, and perform this step recursively. (All the input operands of new $\phi-functions$ are initially assumed to be uses of r. Adjustments are made in step (c), when correct reaching defs are known.) For inserting defs at multiple nodes, a linear time algorithm for computing iterated dominance frontiers of these nodes can be used for placing $\phi-functions$ [18].
2. Update $Uses$ sets for all uses dominated by S, or all uses dominated by any of the new defs of the new $\phi-function$ assignments. This is done by walking down the dominator tree from each of these defs and identifying uses that, along with the def, satisfy Property 1.

3. Update each use that is a parameter of the newly created $\phi - functions$, according to Property 2.

Example: To illustrate this insertion algorithm, we insert '$x = ...$' at $\hat{S}5$ in Figure 2(b) and rename it X_3. $\hat{S}5$ has two dominance frontiers: $\hat{S}4$ and $\hat{S}7$, at which we insert new $\phi - functions$. We then rename the new def of x at $\hat{S}4$ as X_2, and the one at $\hat{S}7$ as X_4, which recursively creates a new def of x at its dominance frontier $\hat{S}9$ as X_5.

We now update $Uses$ sets for these new defs. None of X_2, X_3, or X_4 has uses dominated by them. However, X_5 has a use dominated by it at $\hat{S}10$, which used to be a use of X_1, that now becomes a use of X_5. The resulting SSA form is the same as that in Figure 2(a).

The cost of the insert and delete use algorithms is linear in the height of the dominator tree. The cost of the insert (delete) definition algorithm is linear in the size of the subgraph that is dominated by r ($\hat{r}$) or is in the iterated dominance frontier of r ($\hat{r}$). It is in the worst case as expensive as the exhaustive algorithm, but is often much more efficient.

Our incremental algorithm produces minimal SSA form when the CFG is reducible. For an irreducible CFG, restoring minimal SSA form, after a deletion of a def, requires an additional step of identifying and removing a set of ϕ-functions that have as their parameters only themselves plus a single, identical renamed variable. [7]

4.2 Incremental SSA for Updating an Interval

In this section, we generalize the above algorithms to handle arbitrary update of an interval. If interval I is transformed into interval $\hat{I}$, restoring correct SSA form involves: a) rebuilding SSA form of $\hat{I}$ and b) incrementally updating SSA as needed for intervals nested in $\hat{I}$ and intervals containing $\hat{I}$.

We use *augmented control flow graph* (CFG_{aug}) as the program representation. As compared to the original CFG, CFG_{aug} makes loop (interval) structure evident via *preheader* and *postexit* nodes [1, 16]. These extra nodes also provide convenient locations for summarizing data flow information for the loop. An interval I has a single preheader node, denoted by $prehdr(I)$, and there is an edge from the $prehdr(I)$ to $hdr(I)$, the header node. There is a postexit node for each distinct loop exit target. Also, for each interval node n which may exit the interval, there is an edge from n to the corresponding postexit node. Figure 3 shows an example code segment and the corresponding CFG_{aug}. More details on how to compute CFG_{aug} of a CFG are given in [1, 16].

Incrementally Updating Inner and Outer Intervals We first consider how to update the SSA form of inner untransformed intervals.

Definition 9. A use of variable A at node n is *upwards-exposed* at m if there is a CFG_{aug} path $P_{mn} : m \xrightarrow{*} n$ along which A is not defined. A use in I is *upwards-exposed in the interval* if it is upwards-exposed at $hdr(I)$.

Note that if interval I has no def of A, A_j, the unique def of A reaching $prehdr(I)$, will reach all the uses of A in I: all the uses of A in I will be converted into uses of A_j in the SSA form, which are all upwards-exposed at $hdr(I)$ as well as at $prehdr(I)$. If I has any def of A in it, there will be a def ϕ_{hdr}^A at $hdr(I)$. In this case, A_j is still upwards-exposed at $hdr(I)$ as a parameter of the ϕ_{hdr}^A. The following theorem follows from the above observations.

Theorem 10. If an inner interval I' is nested in a transformed interval, then restoring correct SSA form for I' involves updating upwards-exposed uses in I' only. □

Now we consider the effect of a transformation on the SSA form of outer intervals. If a variable A is defined in I but not in $\hat{I}$, $\phi-function$ ϕ_{px}^A at the postexit node of I becomes redundant and need be deleted. Correct SSA form for A in outer intervals can be restored by the procedure specified in Section 4.1 for deleting the def ϕ_{px}^A at the postexit node of I. Similarly, if A is defined in $\hat{I}$ but not in I, a def (ϕ_{px}^A) need inserted at the postexit node of I, so that the incremental insert-definition procedure in Section 4.1 can be applied.

Interval-based SSA Algorithm Correct SSA form for the new interval $\hat{I}$ is restored by performing the steps below. Following [8], S is a set of stacks of defs reaching the current CFG_{aug} node. For each variable A, $S(A)$ initially contains $reaching\_def(prehdr(I), A)$.

1. Rebuild CFG_{aug} dominator tree for $\hat{I}$.
2. Compute dominance frontier for $\hat{I}$.
3. Update $\phi-functions$ in $\hat{I}$.
4. Rename variables in $\hat{I}$, using an algorithm similar to [8], but without modifying the SSA structure of inner loops except for the upwards-exposed uses of variables in them.
5. Incrementally update SSA for outer intervals, using the algorithms in Section 4.1, for variables defined in $\hat{I}$ and not in I, and vice versa.

In many common cases, the set of variables defined in the interval does not change and hence the SSA form of outer intervals need not be updated. We call this the *conservative change property*. For example, this property is satisfied by the loop transformations discussed in Section 5. For such loop transformations, the cost of updating SSA form incrementally using this algorithm is on average linear in $N_I + UE(I)$, where N_I is the size of interval I, and $UE(I)$ is the number of upwards-exposed uses in intervals nested in I.

5 Efficient SSA Update for Common Loop Transformations

In this section, we discuss many popular loop-oriented program transformations, and present incremental update algorithms that can be even more efficient than the algorithms in Section 4 for these special-case loop transformations.

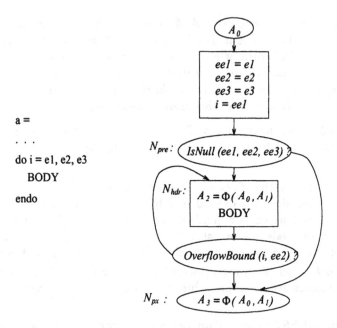

a =

. . .

do i = e1, e2, e3
    BODY

endo

Fig. 3. Schemata of Loop Construct, its CFG_{aug}, and its SSA numbering

5.1 Definition of Loop Construct

Before discussing the various loop transformations, we define the basic loop construct assumed as input to the loop transformations. This loop construct is essentially a well-structured loop with a single entry, single exit, and a single back edge. An example of such a loop construct is a Fortran do-loop with no premature exits. Figure 3 contains schemata of the loop construct, its augmented control flow graph (CFG_{aug}), and SSA numbering for all variables that have at least one def contained within the loop.

We assume that the scope of the index variable (i) is local to a loop construct thus making it unnecessary to perform SSA numbering for loop index variables (since each use of an index variable is associated with a unique loop construct). For convenience, we assume the existence of temporary variables, $ee1$, $ee2$, $ee3$ to capture the values of $e1$, $e2$, $e3$ on loop entry and thus keep those values invariant of the i loop.

We use the name A in Figure 3 to generically represent any variable (other than the index variable) that has at least one def contained within the loop. The four defs of variable A that are noteworthy are: def A_0 reaches the loop header from loop entry, def A_1 reaches the loop header from the back edge (A_0 and A_1 may be user defs or ϕ defs), def $A_2 = \phi(A_0, A_1)$ is the value of A used at the start of the loop body, and def $A_3 = \phi(A_0, A_1)$ is the value of A at loop exit. For all such variables A, there is a $\phi-function$ ϕ_{hdr}^A at the interval header, and a $\phi-function$ ϕ_{px}^A at the postexit node. In this example, A_2 is ϕ_{hdr}^A, and A_3 is ϕ_{px}^A.

5.2 Loop Interchange

The effect of loop interchange [20] is to interchange two perfectly nested loops as shown below in Fortran-like syntax:

```
do i = e1, e2, e3              do j = e7, e8, e9
  do j = e4, e5, e6              do i = e10, e11, e12
    BODY            --->            BODY
  enddo                          enddo
enddo                          enddo
```

The loop body is unchanged by the transformation.

If the loop nest is *rectangular* (i.e. if expressions e4, e5, e6 are independent of variable i), then the bounds expressions are not modified but only relocated (e7 = e4, e8 = e5, e9 = e6, e10 = e1, e11 = e2, e12 = e3). All SSA *Uses* sets remain unchanged after this transformation. The numbering for defs and uses of generic variable A is unchanged by the transformation even though the relative positions of loops i and j have been switched. Since we do not perform SSA numbering for loop index variables, there are no other SSA *Uses* sets that need to be changed. This incremental SSA result is also applicable to any general permutation of n rectangular loops.

In general, we have to consider cases when the loops are triangular or trapezoidal loops (i.e. cases in which e4, e5 are linear functions of i, and e3, e6 are compile-time constants). In such a case, it becomes necessary to generate new loop bound expressions that are different from the old loop bound expressions as in the following example from [20]:

```
do i = 1, n, 1                 do j = 1, n+n, 1
  do j = i, n+i, 1               do i = max(1,j-n), min(j,n), 1
    BODY            --->            BODY
  enddo                          enddo
enddo                          enddo
```

We observe that a def of a non-index-variable that is used in any of e7, e8, e9, e10, e11, e12 must also have been used in one of e1, e2, e3, e4, e5, e6 (since e7, e8, e9, e10, e11, e12 are derived from e1, e2, e3, e4, e5, e6). Therefore, the algorithm for updating *Uses* sets in trapezoidal loop interchange is equivalent to repeated application of the Insert-use and Delete-use algorithms in Section 4.1), such that uses of non-index-variables in e1, e2, e3, e4, e5, e6 are replaced by uses of the corresponding non-index-variables in e7, e8, e9, e10, e11, e12.

5.3 General Iteration-Reordering Loop Transformation

Any iteration-reordering loop transformation such as interchange, reversal, skewing, unimodular, blocking, coalescing or any combination thereof can be represented by the schema shown in Figure 4 for transforming a set of n perfectly nested loops into a set of n' perfectly nested loops with initialization

$$\text{do } x_1 = l_1, u_1, s_1$$
$$\vdots$$
$$\text{do } x_n = l_n, u_n, s_n$$
$$\text{BODY}$$

$\Longrightarrow$

$$\text{do } x'_1 = l'_1, u'_1, s'_1$$
$$\vdots$$
$$\text{do } x'_{n'} = l'_{n'}, u'_{n'}, s'_{n'}$$
$$x_1 = f_1(x'_1, \ldots, x'_{n'})$$
$$\vdots$$
$$x_n = f_n(x'_1, \ldots, x'_{n'})$$
$$\text{BODY}$$

Fig. 4. General structure of Iteration-reordering Loop Transformations

statements that map the new index variables $x'_1, \ldots, x'_{n'}$ to the old index variables $x_1, \ldots, x_n$ [17]. From our earlier assumption that an index variable is local in scope to its loop construct, we can assume that variables $x_1, \ldots, x_n$ are local in scope to the loop body of the transformed loop nest shown in Figure 4.

As in Section 5.2, we observe that a def of a non-index-variable that is used in the transformed loop nest must also have been used in the original loop nest. Therefore, the algorithm for updating $Uses$ sets in a general iteration-reordering transformation is as follows:

1. For each non-index variable A that has at least one def in BODY do
   (a) Let $A_0 =$ def of A that reaches entry to the original loop nest, and $A_1 =$ def of A that reaches end of BODY (as in Figure 3). Also let $A_m =$ def of A on exit from original loop nest. Defs A_0, A_1, A_m will be preserved by the SSA update.
   (b) For each loop $1 \le i \le n$ in the original loop nest, delete the ϕ-function associated with A at the entry of loop i (corresponding to ϕ-def A_2 in Figure 3).
   (c) For each loop $2 \le i \le n$ in the original loop nest, delete the ϕ-function associated with A at the exit of loop i (corresponding to ϕ-def A_3 in Figure 3). Note that the exit ϕ-function for the outermost loop (A_m) is not deleted.
   (d) For each loop $1 \le i' \le n'$ in the transformed loop nest, create a ϕ-function associated with A at the entry of the loop.
   (e) For each loop $2 \le i' \le n'$ in the transformed loop nest, create a ϕ-function associated with A at the exit of the loop. ϕ-def A_m will continue to be used as the exit ϕ-function for the outermost loop, $i' = 1$.
2. For each use u' of a non-index-variable in l'_i, u'_i, s'_i s.t. $1 \le i \le n'$ do
   (a) Let $u =$ corresponding use in one of l_i, u_i, s_i.
   (b) Insert u' in the $Uses$ set that u belongs to (this operation takes constant time with a doubly-linked list representation).
3. For each use u of a non-index-variable in l_i, u_i, s_i s.t. $1 \le i \le n$ do
   (a) Delete u from the $Uses$ set that it belongs to (this operation takes constant time with a doubly-linked list representation).

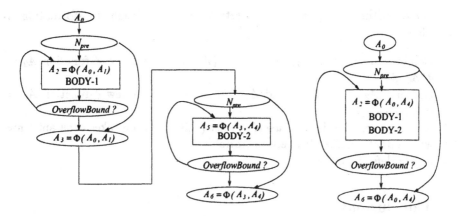

Fig. 5. SSA update for Loop Fusion

These updates will result in $Uses$ sets that are identical to the $Uses$ sets that would be obtained by exhaustively recomputing SSA form after the transformation. Even though the ϕ-functions associated with a generic variable A are changed, the defs A_0, A_1, A_m remain unchanged after the transformation. The above algorithm ensures that all uses in $l_i, u_i, s_i, l'_i, u'_i, s'_i$ are properly adjusted. Since we do not perform SSA numbering for loop index variables, there are no other SSA $Uses$ sets that need to be changed.

This SSA update has $O(n^2 + n'^2)$ execution-time complexity, which is independent of the size of the loop body.

5.4 Loop Fusion

The effect of loop fusion [2] is to fuse together the bodies of two adjacent conformable loops to obtain a single fused loop body:

```
a =
do i = e1, e2, e3              a =
  BODY-1                       do i = e1, e2, e3
enddo            --->            BODY-1
do i = e1, e2, e3               BODY-2
  BODY-2                      enddo
enddo
```

For simplicity, the above schema makes the following assumptions:

1. The two loops together form a single-entry, single-exit region.
2. The two loops use the same index variable and have identical loop bounds expressions.

Figure 5 outlines the low-level control flow and SSA numbering for the loop configurations before and after loop fusion.

The algorithm for updating $Uses$ sets after a loop fusion transformation is as follows:

1. Combine $A_2 = \phi(A_0, A_1)$ and $A_5 = \phi(A_3, A_4)$ into a new ϕ-function $A_2 = \phi(A_0, A_4)$
2. Combine $A_3 = \phi(A_0, A_1)$ and $A_6 = \phi(A_3, A_4)$ into a new ϕ-function $A_6 = \phi(A_0, A_4)$.
3. Append $uses(A_5)$ list into $uses(A_1)$ list (this operation takes constant time with a doubly-linked list representation).
4. Delete defs A_3 and A_5.

6 Conclusions

SSA form is a compact intermediate program representation that is well suited to a large number of compiler analysis and optimization algorithms. Though the current SSA construction algorithm has linear execution-time complexity, it is an exhaustive algorithm. For an intermediate form to be practical, it must be efficiently restorable after program transformations. We have therefore examined the question of incrementally maintaining correct SSA form after a number of common program transformations. We have concentrated on program statements and intervals as the basic units of incrementality. By treating intervals as collapsed statements, incremental SSA-updating for intervals can be seen as a generalization of incremental SSA-updating for statements. Finally, we have shown that it is possible to customize SSA-updating for common transformations of structured loops resulting in more efficient algorithms. In some cases (e.g. loop interchange, fusion), the cost is independent of the size of the loop body. In other cases, (e.g. loop distribution) the cost is proportional to the loop body sizes. These sample transformations illustrate that incremental SSA updating is a reasonable approach for a practical compiler: the advantages of SSA form can be repeatedly exploited without multiple costly reconstructions.

References

1. Frances Allen, Michael Burke, Philippe Charles, Ron Cytron, and Jeanne Ferrante. An overview of the ptran analysis system for multiprocessing. *Proceedings of the ACM 1987 International Conference on Supercomputing*, 1987. Also published in The Journal of Parallel and Distributed Computing, Oct., 1988, 5(5) pages 617-640.
2. Frances Allen and John Cocke. A catalogue of optimizing transformation. *Design and Optimization of Compilers*, pages 1–30, 1972.
3. Bowen Alpern, Mark N. Wegman, and F. Kenneth Zadeck. Detecting equality of variables in programs. *Fifteenth ACM Principles of Programming Languages Symposium*, pages 1–11, January 1988. San Diego, CA.
4. M.G. Burke and B.G. Ryder. A critical analysis of incremental iterative data flow analysis algorithms. *IEEE Transactions on Software Engineering*, 16(7):723–728, July 1990.

5. Michael Burke. An interval-based approach to exhaustive and incremental inter-procedural data-flow analysis. *ACM Transactions on Programming Languages and Systems*, 12(3):341–395, July 1990.

6. Jong-Deok Choi, Ron Cytron, and Jeanne Ferrante. Automatic construction of sparse data flow evaluation graphs. *Conference Record of the Eighteenth Annual ACM Symposium on Principles of Programming Languages*, January 1991.

7. Ron Cytron. private communication.

8. Ron Cytron, Jeanne Ferrante, Barry K. Rosen, Mark N. Wegman, and F. Kenneth Zadeck. Efficiently computing static single assignment form and the control dependence graph. *ACM Transactions on Programming Languages and Systems*, October 1991.

9. Ron Cytron and Reid Gershbein. Efficiently accommodating may-alias information in ssa form. *Proceedings of the ACM Conference on Programming Language Design and Implementation*, 1993.

10. Robert Giegerich, Ulrich Moencke, and Reinhard Wilhelm. Invariance of approximative semantics with respect to program transformation. *11th GI Annual Conference, Informatik-Fachberichte 50*, pages 1–10, October 1981.

11. William G. Griswold and David Notkin. Automated Assistance for Program Restructuring. *ACM Transactions on Software Engineering and Methodology*, 2(3):228–269, July 1993.

12. T. J. Marlowe and B. Ryder. An efficient hybrid algorithm for incremental data flow analysis. *ACM SIGPLAN Symp. on Principles of Programming Language*, pages 184–196, January 1990.

13. Thomas J. Marlowe. *Data Flow Analysis and Incremental Iteration*. PhD thesis, Rutgers University, October 1989.

14. David A. Padua and Michael J. Wolfe. Advanced compiler optimizations for supercomputers. *Communications of the ACM*, 29(12):1184–1201, December 1986.

15. Barbara G. Ryder and Martin D. Carroll. Incrementally updating the dominator tree of a rooted diagraph. Technical report, Rutgers U., December 1986. Center for Computer Aids for Industrial Productivity Technical Report CAIP-TR-029.

16. Vivek Sarkar. The ptran parallel programming system. *Parallel Functional Programming Languages and Compilers*, pages 309–391, 1991.

17. Vivek Sarkar and Radhika Thekkath. A general framework for iteration-reordering loop transformations. *Proceedings of the ACM SIGPLAN '92 Conference on Programming Language Design and Implementation*, pages 175–187, June 1992.

18. Vugranam C. Sreedhar and Guang R. Gao. A linear time algorithm for placing ϕ-nodes. In *22nd Annual ACM SIGACT-SIGPLAN Symposium on the Principles of Programming Languages*, pages 62–73, January 1995.

19. Mark Wegman and Ken Zadeck. Constant propagation with conditional branches. *ACM Transactions on Programming Languages and Systems*, pages 181–210, April 1991.

20. Michael J. Wolfe. *Optimizing Supercompilers for Supercomputers*. Pitman, London and The MIT Press, Cambridge, Massachusetts, 1989.

21. Wuu Yang, Susan Horwitz, and Thomas Reps. Detecting program components with equivalent behaviors. Technical report, University of Wisconsin, Madison, April 1989. Computer Sciences Technical Report Number 840.

Efficient Storage Reuse of Aggregates in Single Assignment Languages

Zhonghua Li and Chris C. Kirkham

Department of Computer Science, Manchester University, Manchester, M13 9PL, UK
{zhonghua,chris}@cs.man.ac.uk

Abstract. The storage reuse of aggregates is a key problem in implementing single assignment languages. In this paper, on the basis of a typical subset of the single assignment language SISAL, we analyze the inherent limits of storage reuse and define what the maximal storage reuse is. We propose an efficient method of achieving storage reuse, which is of polynomial complexity and linear in common cases. It achieves the maximal storage reuse for an extensive program class into which all common benchmark programs fall. We also show that no general method can guarantee the maximal storage reuse for programs outside the class. In this case, our method can choose the most likely operation to reuse the storage of an aggregate or a set of shared aggregates.

1 Introduction

The demand for higher speed from computational users continues to increase. Parallel processing has been considered as an important way to higher performance. Unfortunately, because of its extra complexity, software technology has yet to match architectural advances. For the development of parallel software, a brand-new methodology is needed. Language is an important aspect of the methodology. There are two possible choices, one is to take existent languages such as Fortran, and the other is to develop new languages. Although there has been a large production of software in existent languages and also programmers are familiar with them, these languages have been designed inherently for sequential machines, and are not suitable for parallel computations. The greatest hindrance to parallelization of conventional languages is that programs always overspecify, and impose too many unnecessary sequencing constraints. On the other hand, applicative languages, in particular, single assignment languages such as SISAL [6] have emerged as a promising approach to parallel programming. Because of referential transparency, only data dependencies define sequencing in applicative programs. Therefore, the identification of concurrency is trivial.

But, for applicative languages, aggregate structures such as arrays pose a problem for their efficient implementation. Because of their semantics, an update operation generally requires copying the entire array, and the update at appropriate indices is made in the new copy. The old copy needs to be kept intact because it may be referenced by other subcomputations in the program.

This simple implementation of the update operation leads to inefficient use of storage, and degrades the performance of an algorithm. In the context of scientific computing, where the manipulation of large aggregates is common-place, the copying can become intolerable. However, for most programs, the resulting copying operations are only inherent to language semantics and not the algorithms themselves. Storage reuse is essential to their efficient implementation, saving time by not copying values, and saving space by not re-allocating storage.

In this paper, we discuss the storage reuse of aggregates in a sequential implementation of first-order single assignment languages with nested aggregates. There are two reasons for us to restrict our attention to "sequential": (1) there has been no satisfactory solution to this problem and, (2) storage reuse in a sequential implementation is also an important part of parallel implementation since a partial sequentialization of programs is essential for an efficient parallel implementation. We analyze the inherent limits of storage reuse, define what a maximal storage reuse is, and give an efficient method of achieving storage reuse.

2 Background

2.1 The single assignment language

Single assignment languages are value-oriented. Their semantics deals with functions on values rather than destructive operations on data objects residing in memory. Even arrays are treated as values. In this paper, we consider the storage reuse for a subset of SISAL, called *SL*. We ignore the SISAL data types: *stream*, *union* and *record*. These simplifications make the resulting language *SL* a first-order strict functional language with nested aggregates, and enable us to focus on the storage reuse of arrays without need to consider unrelated aspects. In this section, we introduce the main features of interest.

An *SL* function computes one or more output values as a function of one or more input values. A function has no side effects and retains no state information from one invocation to another. Hence the values returned by any invocation of an *SL* function depend only on the arguments. Since *SL* is a side-effect free language, subexpressions may be evaluated in any order without affecting the results, provided all data dependencies are satisfied. Language constructs are provided for conditional and iterative expressions, which implicitly contain control dependencies. An iterative expression, called *while loop*, has a set of initial value definitions, a corresponding set of redefinitions used to define new values on every iteration, a loop control and a set of resulting values defined in terms of the values of the names during all the iterations or only in the last iteration. The keyword *old* is used to refer to the value of a name in the previous iteration. *SL* also offers a *for* construct for expressing parallel iterations with no cross iteration dependencies, called *forall loop*.

SL includes only one kind of data structure: *array*. An array has an integer index set and its components are of arbitrary but uniform type. Arrays can be nested to any depth. The operations on an array can be classified into three categories: initialization, reference, and modification. $array\_fill(l, h, v)$ creates an array with indices ranging from l to h and each element being equal to v. $A[j]$ selects the jth element of A. A typical array modification operation is $A[j : v]$, which produces a new value identical to A except that the element at the index j is substituted by v. A naive applicative implementation of the modification operation $A[j : v]$ requires construction of a new array almost identical to A. The time and storage requirements of this operation are linear to A's size. This is very expensive. A loop can greatly magnify the effect of an array modification in it. As [2] pointed out, the insertion sort program in a single assignment language may be several thousand times slower than the FORTRAN counterpart when sorting an array of 1000 floating point numbers.

2.2 The intermediate dataflow graph

Our discussions are based on the dataflow representation of a program which is similar to $IF1$[8]. A program can be described as a set of dataflow graphs with each representing a function and one of them being the main function graph where the computation starts. A **dataflow graph** is a quadruple (IP, OP, N, E) where IP, OP, N and E are a set of input ports, a set of output ports, a set of internal nodes and a set of arcs respectively. Nodes represent computations and arcs represent dependencies between them. For example, if there is an arc from node N_1 to N_2, then N_2 is dependent on N_1, i.e. N_1 must be finished before N_2 starts. We simply denote this as $N_1 \prec N_2$.

A node receives data from its input ports, fulfills a specific computation and puts the results to its output ports. There are mainly two kinds of nodes: atomic nodes and compound nodes. An atomic node represents an indivisible sequential computation. A compound node can embody a control structure to encapsulate a complex computation. It consists of a set of input ports, a set of output ports and a set of subgraphs. Typically, there are three kinds of compound nodes for representing an SL program, *conditional*, *product loop* and *non-product loop*, which correspond to a *conditional*, a *forall loop* and a *while loop* expression respectively. For example, a *conditional* node includes three subgraphs, the *condition*, *then* and *else* subgraphs corresponding to the predicate, *then* part and *else* part of a *conditional* expression respectively. There are control and data dependencies between subgraphs of a compound node. As shown in figure 1(a), we represent a node by a rectangle, an arc by an arrow and an aggregate port by a circle. Usually, we omit representations of other ports. We also omit representations of dependencies within a compound node unless we represent them by dashed arrows when necessary. For a *conditional* node, the upper subnode corresponds to the *predicate*, the left lower one to the *then* part and the right lower one to the *else* part as C1 and C2 in this figure.

2.3 Aggregates

An aggregate is a compound value consisting of simpler values, which are called components of the aggregate. In this paper, by an aggregate we mean an array. The aggregate operations fall into three categories, that is, *E-operations* which reference a whole aggregate returning the same aggregate as a result, *R-operations* which reference individual components of an aggregate, and *W-operations* [1] which change some components of an aggregate. We denote an *E-operation* on A by $E(A)$. We introduce a typical *R-operation* $read(A, i)$ and a typical *W-operation* $replace(A, i, a)$ to represent the *SL* expressions $A[i]$ and $A[i : v]$ respectively.

An aggregate, say A, may be a component of another bigger aggregate B. In this case, B is called a super-aggregate or nested aggregate and A is called a sub-aggregate of B. The *R-operation* $read(A, i)$ on a super-aggregate A can be taken as an *E-operation* on the sub-aggregate $A[i]$. The *W-operation* $replace(B, i, A)$ where A is an aggregate can be taken as an *E-operation* on A and $B[j]$ for $j \neq i$. A naive implementation of the *E-operation* $E(A)$ is to copy A into a new physical space to get a new value equal to A. Obviously, this is an inefficient way. In the following discussion, we assume the more efficient model: $E(A)$ represents the aggregate which is, not only logically but also physically, the same as A, that is, *E-operations* are implemented through sharing the same physical space. A related problem is the passing method of aggregate parameters of a function. Semantically, the call-by-value passing method is used for a strict functional language. This requires the copying of aggregate parameter values. Instead, we use the more efficient call-by-reference passing method for aggregate parameters in the implementation. In the following discussions, we use A, B, A', B', with or without subscripts to indicate aggregates.

3 Limits of Storage Reuse

3.1 Compilation granules

There can be more than one operation on an aggregate. A *W-operation* can reuse the storage of an aggregate only if it is the last operation on the aggregate. There are static and dynamic methods to achieve storage reuse. The former is to statically order the operations without violation of dependencies so that a *W-operation* can be done last on an aggregate to reuse its storage. The latter is to make decisions at run time, typically through reference counting. Because the static method involves less overheads, and the dynamic method can not achieve effective storage reuse without the static method, ordering the compilation granules is a basic part of any practical method of achieving storage reuse.

By a compilation granule, we mean a node whose execution is not interleaved with any node outside it, or a function call node. The size of a compilation granule (more exactly, the size and structure of a compilation granule, since a compilation granule can include compilation granules as its components) can

---

[1] There are two kinds of *W-operations* in SISAL, incremental construction and incremental modification. In this paper, we only introduce the latter. But our storage reuse method takes both of them into account, though an extra phase is needed for pre-allocating enough storage for in-place incremental construction operations.

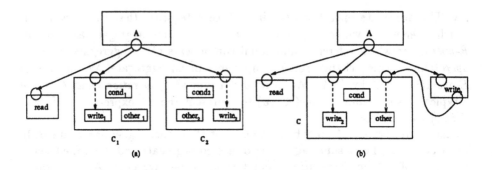

Fig. 1. Examples of conditional nodes

affect the degree to which the storage can be reused. In figure 1(a), C_1 and C_2 are two independent conditional nodes, and $write_1$ and $write_2$ are the *W-operations* on the aggregate A. $cond_1$ and $cond_2$ do not reference A and their values can vary with other input data. So, if a whole conditional node is a compilation granule, no method can guarantee that the storage of A can be reused reasonably efficiently. By "reasonably efficiently", we mean that the overheads from the reuse are less than the benefits from the reuse. On the other hand, if a conditional node can be decomposed into smaller compilation granules, e.g. the *condition* part, *then* part and *else* part, the storage of A can be reused through ordering these smaller compilation granules so that $cond_1$ and $cond_2$ are executed first and then making the further decision dynamically on the basis of their results as follows:

$cond_1$	$cond_2$	**the decision**
TRUE	TRUE	$write_1$ can reuse the storage
FALSE	FALSE	$write_2$ can reuse the storage
FALSE	TRUE	no *W-operation* is executed
TRUE	FALSE	both $write_1$ and $write_2$ will be executed
		the later one can reuse the storage

Generally, the smaller the compilation granules, the more opportunities for storage reuse through static ordering, but the compiler will be more complicated as the compilation granules become smaller. For simplicity of the compiler, the compound nodes, i.e. *conditional*, *product loop* and *non-product loop*, have been taken as compilation granules in some existing implementations[2]. In the rest of this paper, we make the same assumption. So, the control dependencies are encapsulated within compilation granules.

3.2 Aggregate operations and their degrees

We have described operations on an aggregate in §2.3. Generally, these operations are embedded in compilation granules. We are particularly interested in those outermost compilation granules including operations on an aggregate since effectively ordering them is an important part of achieving storage reuse. It will be convenient to also call them operations on this aggregate. By contrast, we call those operations in §2.3 atomic operations. So, an aggregate operation can be atomic or compound. In the latter case, it can operate on more than one aggregate and can include atomic *R-*, *W-* and/or *E-operations*. Some operations are certain to operate on an aggregate, while others are not. For example, $A[1:2]$ definitely operates on A, and, *if $x = 1$ then $A[1:2]$ else B end if* can operate on aggregate A only when x is equal to 1. Generally, an operation can be arbitrarily complicated. In different operations, probabilities that atomic *R-*, *E-* or *W-operations* are to be executed are different. We can statically assign W-Degree(op, A) to operation *op* to represent the probability that an atomic *W-operation* can be executed later than any atomic *R-* or *E-operation* on A. When a node is executed, one of the following cases can occur for an aggregate:

1. An atomic *W-operation* on it is certain to be executed later than any possible atomic *R-operation* or *E-operation* on it.
2. An atomic *R-operation* or *E-operation* on it is certain to be executed later than any possible atomic *W-operation* on it.
3. No atomic *W-operation* is executed on it.
4. An atomic *W-operation* may be executed on it, and if this occurs, it is later than any *R-operation* or *E-operation* on it.
5. An atomic *W-operation* may be executed on it, and whether or not the operation will be later than any possible *R-operation* or *E-operation* on it can not be predicted.

In the first case, the W-Degree assigned is one. In the second and third cases, the W-Degree assigned is zero. In the last two cases, the W-Degree is evaluated to a value between zero and one. Similarly, we can define R-Degree(op, A) for an operation *op* on an input aggregate A to represent the probability that an atomic *R-operation* on A can be executed in the operation; define E-Degree(op, A, B) for an operation *op* on an input aggregate A to represent the probability that A can be directly used as an output B of the operation; and E-Degree(op, A)=$\sum_B$E-Degree(op, A, B).

More generally, we call an operation *op* an *R-operation* on A if *R-Degree(op, A)>0 and W-Degree(op, A)=E-Degree(op, A)=0*; call it a *W-operation* on A if *W-Degree(op, A)>0*; and call it an *E-operation* on A if there is an output aggregate B, $E\text{-}Degree(op, A, B) > 0$. If there is indeed an atomic *W-operation* that is executed later than any atomic *R-operation* or *E-operation* on A in an execution of the *W-operation*, we say that it *acts as a physical W-operation on A in the execution*. If A is indeed directly used as an output in an execution of the E-operation, we say that it *acts as a physical E-operation* on A in the execution.

3.3 Dependencies

Without sharing After the compilation granules are fixed as §3.1, the inherent limits of storage reuse depend on the data dependencies. For a *W-operation wop* on A, if there is another operation op on A and $wop \prec op$, wop must be executed before op and can not reuse the storage of A. As illustrated in figure 1(b), $read$, $write_1$ and C are all the possible operations on aggregate A, and $write_1 \prec C$. $write_1$ can not reuse the storage of A, even if it is safe, e.g. when $cond$ is FALSE, and $write_1$ is the only W-$operation$ on A in the execution, since the safety of the reuse can not be justified in an execution generally. We call a W-$operation$ a *reuse candidate* on an aggregate if no operation on the same aggregate is dependent on it. Only a *reuse candidate* of an aggregate can reuse the storage.

The difficulties of reuse come from not only the dependencies between the operations on the same aggregate but also those on different aggregates. In the latter case, we call them interferences between these aggregates. In figure 2(a), due to the mutual interferences of A and B, the storage of only one of them can be reused. This is because, for a W-$operation$ on an aggregate to reuse the storage, we need to introduce extra *temporal dependencies* between it and all the R-$operations$ on the aggregate. We denote that op_1 *temporally precedes* op_2 by $op_1 \lhd op_2$ (represented as a dashed arrow in a diagram). These extra dependencies should not result in cycles. But, here, the dependency cycle, $w_A \prec r_B \lhd w_B \prec r_A \lhd w_A$, is formed.

Generally, suppose that $w_0, \ldots, w_{n-1}$ are reuse candidates on the aggregates $A_0, \ldots, A_{n-1}$ respectively. Let $k' = (k+1) mod\, n$. If there is a permutation $i_0, \ldots, i_{n-1}$ of $0, \ldots, n-1$ such that $\forall k\ (0 \le k < n)$ either w_{i_k} is also an R-$operation$ on $A_{i_{k'}}$ ($w_{i_k} \lhd w_{i_{k'}}$), or there is an R-$operation$ r on $A_{i_{k'}}$ and $w_{i_k} \prec r$ ($\lhd w_{i_{k'}}$), we say that they form an interference cycle. If all reuse candidates on these aggregates are in some cycle, then the storage of one of them can not be reused. We call such a cycle a *complete interference cycle*. An example is shown in figure 2(b) where op_1 is the W-$operation$ on A and the R-$operation$ on B and op_2 is the W-$operation$ on B and the R-$operation$ on A. Here, $op_1 op_2$ form a complete interference cycle. In the other cases, the interference cycle can be broken as follows without hindrance to storage reuse.

- There is a *reuse candidate* wop on A_{i_l} which is not in any interference cycle for some l, $0 \le l < n$. In this case, the cycle can be broken from w_{i_l} and we can schedule the above W-$operations$ in the following order: $w_{i_l} \ldots w_{i_{n-1}} w_{i_0} \ldots w_{i_{l-1}} wop$ so that the storage of $A_j (0 \le j < n \wedge j \ne i_l)$ can be reused by w_j and the storage of A_{i_l} can be reused by wop. For example, in figure 2(c), $w_A r_B w_B r_A$ is an interference cycle and $w1_A$ is not in any interference cycle. This cycle can be broken through scheduling nodes in the following order, $w_A r_B w_B r_A w1_A$.
- The cycle is adjacent to another interference cycle which can be broken. We say that two cycles are adjacent if there is a W-$operation$ w_1 in one cycle and a W-$operation$ w_2 in the other and w_1 and w_2 operate on the same aggregate. If one can be broken, the other can be broken, e.g. from w_2.

With sharing Semantically, an atomic E-$operation$ $E(A)$ on the aggregate A produces a new aggregate equal to A, say A', but A' is mapped into the same

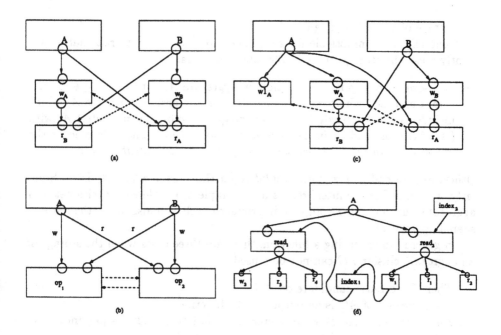

Fig. 2. Examples with dependencies

space as A instead of being allocated a new physical space. In this case, we call A and A' *inter-shared* or simply *shared*. Closely related to sharing is nesting of aggregates. We define the relation $\tilde{E}$ on $\mathcal{A}$, i.e. the set of all aggregates and sub-aggregates in a function, to describe the sharing among them. $\tilde{E}$ is the smallest equivalence relation satisfying the following condition:

For $A_1, A_2 \in \mathcal{A}$, if A_2 is generated through $E(A_1)$, $(A_1, A_2) \in \tilde{E}$.

$\tilde{E}$ is related to a specific execution of the program. For example, when E-$Degree(op, A, B) < 1$, whether $(A, B) \in \tilde{E}$ depends on whether op *acts as a physical E-operation* on A in the execution. Each equivalence class on $\tilde{E}$ represents a set of inter-shared aggregates or sub-aggregates which are mapped to the same physical space. We call such a class an *aggregate cluster* or simply a *cluster*. Each non-shared aggregate comprises a cluster of only one element.

The sharing and nesting of aggregates make storage reuse even more complicated. We need to consider a kind of specific dependency, index dependency. As illustrated in figure 2(d), A is a nested aggregate; $read_2$ and $read_1$ are two R-operations which reference A by the inputs from $index_2$ and $index_1$ respectively; w_1, r_1 and r_2 are operations on the sub-aggregate referenced by $read_2$; w_2, r_3 and r_4 are operations on the sub-aggregate referenced by $read_1$; $index_1$ is dependent on w_1. Due to this dependency, when w_1 is executed, it is impossible to reasonably efficiently decide whether the sub-aggregates referenced by $read_1$ and $read_2$ belong to the same cluster, and whether there are more operations on the cluster. Therefore, it is impossible for w_1 to reasonably efficiently reuse the storage of the sub-aggregate.

Generally, it is impossible for a *W-operation wop* on A_1 to reasonably efficiently reuse the storage of A_1 in the following cases:

- *wop* $\prec$ *op* where *op* is an operation on aggregate A_2 with $(A_1, A_2) \in \tilde{E}$; or
- *wop* $\prec$ *op.index* where *op* is an operation on the nested aggregate A_2 which includes a sub-aggregate (or a sub-aggregate of sub-aggregate, etc.) A'_2 with $(A_1, A'_2) \in \tilde{E}$, and *op.index* denotes the node whose output is used as the index of *op*. In this case, we say that *op* is *index-dependent* on *wop*.

Otherwise, we call *wop* a *reuse candidate* on the cluster which A_1 is in. Similarly, we can define the interferences and (complete) interference cycles between aggregate clusters, and a complete interference cycle can also affect the reuse of shared aggregates.

In general, in executing a function, there are three cases when the storage of an aggregate cluster AC can not be reused.

- There is no reuse candidate on AC.
- An aggregate of AC is an output of the function.
- An aggregate of AC is a parameter of the function, and this parameter can not be reused. (see §4.1)

We call the aggregate cluster AC non-reusable in these cases, otherwise reusable. Suppose for any function in a program, N_a is the total number of aggregate clusters, N_{nra} is the total number of non-reusable aggregate clusters and N_{cic} is the total number of complete interference cycles without any operation on non-reusable aggregate clusters. From the above analysis, we can conclude that, in executing the function, the *number* of aggregate clusters whose storage can be reasonably efficiently reused is not greater than $N_{mr} = N_a - N_{nra} - N_{cic}$. If the number of reused aggregate clusters is exactly equal to N_{mr}, we say that the maximal storage reuse is achieved.

4 The Method of Achieving Storage Reuse

In this section, we outline a storage reuse method. Statically, we order all nodes in each function so that the most likely *reuse candidate* is executed last on each aggregate. For shared aggregates, we can not, in general, statically determine whether such a *reuse candidate* is also the last one on the whole aggregate cluster. So, we introduce sharing counters for shared aggregates to dynamically capture the opportunities of storage reuse. In addition, we also need a dynamic mechanism to reuse the storage of an aggregate parameter of a function.

4.1 Dynamic mechanisms

1. A sharing counter is associated with the physical space of each aggregate cluster to reflect the number of aggregates mapped to it. An operation can

reuse the storage of the cluster only if (1) it is executed last on the current aggregate [2], and (2) the sharing count is 1.

2. The *E-operations* are implemented by incrementing the corresponding sharing-counter. After all the operations on an aggregate of this cluster are finished, the sharing counter is decremented.

3. In the static analysis, we assume that each aggregate parameter of a function is reusable. But, quite likely, there are multiple calls to the same function. Different calls have different environments, and so, for some calls, an aggregate parameter can be overwritten, while for the others, it can not be destructively written. Our strategy is: at compile time, an auxiliary parameter is generated for every aggregate parameter to indicate whether the storage for this aggregate can be reused in the current call.

4.2 Static methods

Definitions $\tilde{E}$ is related to a specific execution, and generally, it can not be calculated statically. In this section, we define the relation $\mathcal{R}$ to statically derive the possible sharing on all the aggregates and sub-aggregates in a function. We also introduce the concept of nesting degree.

1. $A \approx_{op} B$ denotes *E-Degree(op, A, B)*> 0.

2. $A \sqsubset_{op} B$ denotes that A may become a subaggregate of B through op; $A \sqsupset_{op} B$ denotes that B may be a subaggregate of A as a result of op, where A and B are input and output aggregates of op respectively.
   For example, for op: $B := A[i]$ where A is a nested aggregate, $A \sqsupset_{op} B$; for op: $B := C[i : A]$ where C and B are nested aggregates, $A \sqsubset_{op} B$; for op: $A := if\ cond\ then\ B[i]\ else\ C[i]\ end\ if$ where C and B are nested aggregates, $B \sqsupset_{op} A$ and $C \sqsupset_{op} A$.

3. Let $\mathcal{A}$ be the set of all the aggregates and sub-aggregates in a function, then $\mathcal{R}$ is the smallest equivalence relation on $\mathcal{A}$ satisfying the following condition: For $A, B \in \mathcal{A}$, if there is an op so that $A \approx_{op} B$ or $A \sqsubset_{op} B$ or $A \sqsupset_{op} B$ holds, then $(A, B) \in \mathcal{R}$. $\mathcal{R}(A)$ includes all possible aggregates which may share with A, or whose sub-aggregates (or sub-aggregates of sub-aggregates, ...) or whose super-aggregates (or super-aggregates of super-aggregates, ...) may.

4. the nesting degree of an aggregate A:

$$\text{N-Degree(A)} = \begin{cases} 1 & \text{if } A \text{ is a flat aggregate} \\ \text{N-Degree(sub(A))} + 1 & \text{otherwise} \end{cases}$$

where $sub(A)$ is any sub-aggregate of A.

---

[2] This is true if the aggregate is not a parameter of the current function. The more exact condition is reflected on the reusability tag. See §4.2

Priority rules The strategies of static ordering are embodied in the following priority rules. Suppose that op_1 and op_2 are two mutually independent operations and $(A, B) \in \mathcal{R}$.

1. **read-first**: If op_1 is an *R-operation* on A and op_2 is a *W-operation* on B, op_1 is executed before op_2.
2. **super-first**: If op_1 is a *W-operation* on A, op_2 is a *W-operation* on B, and $N\text{-}Degree(A) > N\text{-}Degree(B)$, op_1 is executed before op_2.
3. **highest-degree-last**: If op_1 is a *W-operation* on A, op_2 is a *W-operation* on B, and $W\text{-}Degree(op_1, A) < W\text{-}Degree(op_2, B)$, op_1 is executed before op_2.

The *read-first* and *highest-degree-last* rules are motivated for the most likely reuse candidate to be executed last on each aggregate cluster. The *super-first* rule is motivated for super-aggregates to be able to dereference their sub-aggregates as early as possible in order to increase the opportunity for operations on sub-aggregates to be done in place.

But the above rules can not always be completely implemented since there can be conflicting requirements for the storage reuse of different aggregates clusters. For example, a conflict occurs in enforcing the *highest-degree-last* rule if there are operations op_1 and op_2 on both A and B with $W\text{-}Degree(op_1, A) > W\text{-}Degree(op_2, A)$ and $W\text{-}Degree(op_1, B) < W\text{-}Degree(op_2, B)$. To get around this difficulty, we replace this rule by the following simpler one:

> 3′. *For two independent operations* op_1 *and* op_2, op_2 *is executed first if* $W\text{-}Degree(op_1) > W\text{-}Degree(op_2)$, *where* $W\text{-}Degree(op_i) = \sum_A W\text{-}Degree(op_i, A)$ $(i = 1, 2)$.

Similarly, there also can be conflicts in implementing the *read-first* and *super-first* rules. Figure 2(b) illustrates a conflict in implementing the read-first rule. Generally, these two rules can be completely implemented for a program only if the extra dependency arcs introduced to enforce them do not lead to dependency cycles. In these cases, we call this program *read-first-consistent* and *super-first-consistent* respectively.

Static steps
Phase 1: For each function,
1. Calculate the degrees of each aggregate operation;
2. Calculate the relation $\mathcal{R}$;
The process may be recursive due to recursive function calls, and the following analysis takes account of this. Suppose that n, m, k are the number of functions, the largest size of function (i.e. the maximal number of nodes and arcs within a function graph), and the maximal number of aggregate parameters to a function respectively. Because all the degrees of each aggregate are monotonically increasing in the calculation, by fixing the scale of degrees to a small constant s, the total time complexity of step 1 in the worst case is $O(s \cdot k \cdot n \cdot mn) = O(kmn^2)$, where skn is the maximal number of loops to calculate the fixed points, and mn represents the program size [5]. Similarly, the total time complexity of step

2 in the worst case is also $O(kmn^2)$. When k and n are quite small, they are basically linear to the program size. If there is no recursive function call, the time complexity of this phase is definitely linear.

Phase 2: For each function in the program, all nodes are ordered according to their dependencies and the above priority rules.

Input: a dataflow graph G;
Output: an ordered list of nodes L;
Algorithm **Order:**

1. Introduce a temporal dependency arc from op_1 to op_2 for each *R-operation* op_1 on A and each *W-operation op_2* on B where $(A, B) \in \mathcal{R}$ as long as no dependency cycles are formed;
2. Introduce a temporal dependency arc from op_1 to op_2 for each *W-operation* op_1 on A and each *W-operation op_2* on B where $(A, B) \in \mathcal{R}$ and *N-Degree(A)* $>$*N-Degree(B)* as long as no dependency cycles are formed;
3. Let T be an intermediate list. Initialize T to include the nodes which have no immediate predecessors and order them according to their *W-Degrees* so that node n_1 precedes node n_2 if *W-Degree(n_1)*$<$ *W-Degree(n_2)*;
4. If T is empty, output L and terminate; otherwise, $n = dequeue(T)$. If n is the last processed reuse candidate on A, then
   - if A is generated in the current graph, tag the corresponding input port of n "reusable"
   - otherwise (i.e. A is a parameter of the current function, or an input into the current compound node or subgraph node), copy the reusability tag of A into the corresponding input port of n (if any).
   If n is an atomic node, $L = L + n$; otherwise $L = L + Order_c(n)$. Delete n and all the arcs adjacent to it from G and insert the nodes whose sets of predecessors become empty into T according to their *W-Degrees*.
5. goto 4 ;

Here, $dequeue(T)$ deletes and outputs the first element of T; $L + m$ concatenates L and m where m is an element or a list. Step 1 and step 2 are to enforce the *read-first* and *super-first* priority rules respectively. Step 4 orders all nodes and identifies reusable input aggregates into each node. $Order_c$ orders all subgraphs in a compound node, identifies reusable input aggregates into a subgraph and recursively applies the algorithm $Order$ to each subgraph. $Order_c$ is similar to $Order$ and the only difference is that the former also uses the control dependencies encapsulated in the compound node. The worst case time complexity of this phase is polynomial since both step 1 and step 2 can be executed in $O(n^2 + e)$, and the worst-case complexity of steps 4 to 5 is also $O(n^2 + e)$ where n and e are the number of nodes and the number of arcs in the graph respectively. In common cases when the number of extra temporal dependency arcs is less than the size of the program, it is linear to the size of the program.

In sum, the static worst-case time complexity is polynomial to the size of the program. In common cases, it is linear.

4.3 Performance

Theorem 1. *The above method can achieve the maximal storage reuse under the following conditions for a* well-optimized *program* [3]:

1. *The program is read-first-consistent and super-first-consistent, and*
2. *For each operation op on an aggregate A, one of the following holds:*
   - *R-Degree(op, A)>0, W-Degree(op, A)=0, E-Degree(op, A)=0*
   - *W-Degree(op, A)+E-Degree(op, A)=1*

Proof: Due to the space limit, we only give an outline of the proof here. We consider a reusable aggregate cluster AC which includes nested aggregates (otherwise, the proof is simple). There must be reuse candidates on AC. Suppose that *wop* on $A \in AC$ is the latest executed one of them. Since the program is *read-first-consistent*, all the *R-operations* on AC must have been executed before *wop* by the *read-first* rule. Let us assume that *wop* fails in reusing the storage of AC. Then one of the following two cases must be true. **case 1**: *wop* does not *act as a physical W-operation* on A. By *condition 2*, it must *act as a physical E-operation* on A and output an aggregate $B \in AC$. But there is no operation on B since *wop* is the latest one on AC. So, B must be used as an output of the current function call (since the program is well-optimized). This contradicts the reusability of AC. **case 2**: The *sharing count* of AC is greater than 1. Since *wop* is the last operation on AC, there must be at least one super-aggregate which is still referencing an aggregate of AC. But this contradicts the premise that the program is *super-first-consistent*, by which the *super-first* rule can be completely implemented, and all the super-aggregates must have dereferenced aggregates of AC since no operation is *index-dependent* on *wop*. Thus, we conclude that the storage of any reusable aggregate cluster can be reused. □

We find that the program class described by Theorem 1 includes all the common benchmark programs: gaussian elimination, matrix transpose, matrix multiplication, LU-decomposition, quick-sort and insertion sort, where multiple-dimensional arrays are represented as nested one-dimensional arrays. The maximal storage reuse can be achieved for these programs. In fact, we can even loosen the read-first-consistency requirement to allow the existence of breakable cycles as in §3.3. In this case, we can modify the static ordering algorithm so that the nodes are ordered according to the reverse order of their dependencies to break all the cycles more easily. In other cases, static ordering is not sufficient for the maximal storage reuse and dynamically ordering operations can increase the opportunity of storage reuse. For the example illustrated in figure 3, $A_i \in \mathcal{R}(A)$ $(i = 1, 2)$ and $B_i \in \mathcal{R}(B)$ $(i = 1, 2)$, and according to the *read-first* rule, op_1 and op_3 must be executed next after *iop*. The other operations can be executed in the order $op_2 w_1 r_2 op_4 w_2 r_1$ for the maximal storage reuse if op_1 *acts as a physical W-operation* on A, since it has become clear that r_1 and op_2 do not operate on the same aggregate and r_1 need not precede op_2; otherwise,

---

[3] We call a program well-optimized if any value produced in a function call is always referenced later or used as an output of the function call.

in the order $op_4 w_2 r_1 op_2 w_1 r_2$ if op_3 *acts as a W-operation* on B. In the other cases when all the operations are in an interference cycle, no execution ordering, whether static or dynamic, can guarantee the maximal storage reuse. Whether the maximal storage reuse can be achieved can not be predicted, and on the basis of *degrees*, our method of static ordering tries to choose the most likely reuse candidate to operate last on each aggregate cluster to reuse its storage. But theoretical analysis of actual effects remains to be done.

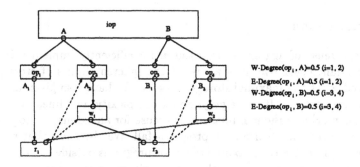

Fig. 3. A limiting case

5   Related Work

Storage optimization for applicative languages has been investigated by other researchers. But, almost all the results have been restricted to first-order functional languages without nested aggregates. Also, almost all the existing algorithms are potentially exponential except that in [7]. At Colorado, the SISAL group has developed a compiler for SISAL [2, 3]. They considered general iteration and function call boundaries with the assumption that there is no recursive function call. Although touching on nested aggregates, they did not propose a general solution and only attacked some special cases. Bloss considered update analysis to first-order lazy functional languages[1]. She defined path semantics to check whether an update can be performed destructively. But computing the path semantics of a program is at least exponentially complicated. So we do not consider it a practical method. In addition, in her work, the order of evaluation of arguments of primitive operations is statically fixed. This may decrease the opportunity of updates being done destructively. Gopinath proposed an approach to eliminating copies in divide and conquer problems through computing the target of an expression[4]. It also assumed a fixed pre-ordering of primitive operators. Also, his algorithm has very high time complexity, which makes it impractical. More recently, Sastry, Clinger and Ariola at University of Oregon claimed that their algorithm for strict functional languages with flat aggregates is the first practical one with a polynomial time complexity to solve the problem

[7]. But their algorithm is still quite conservative. For example, a function can be called from different sites with different environments. Parameters may be updated destructively under one environment but not under another one. However, according to their algorithm, if a parameter of the function can not be updated destructively in one site, then it is not allowed to be updated destructively in any environment. Obviously, this is over restrictive. None of this previous work has touched on the inherent limits of storage reuse and what the maximal storage reuse is.

6 Conclusions

The storage reuse of aggregates is essential for efficiently implementing single assignment languages. We have analyzed the inherent limits of storage reuse and defined what the maximal storage reuse is. We have also given an efficient storage reuse method. It is of polynomial complexity and linear in common cases and can achieve the maximal storage reuse for an extensive program class into which all common benchmark programs fall. We also show that no general method can guarantee the maximal reuse for programs outside the class, and in this case, our method can choose the most likely operation to reuse the storage of an aggregate or a set of shared aggregates.

Storage reuse and parallelization have conflicting requirements, e.g. although more pre-ordering can bring about more opportunities for reusing storage, it imposes more restrictions on exploitation of parallelism. Theoretical and experimental work has to be done to find their relationship.

References

1. A. Bloss. Update Analysis and Efficient Implementation of Function Aggregates. In *The 4th Int. Conf. on Functional Programming Language. and Computer Architecture*, pages 26–38, 1989.
2. D. C. Cann. *Compilation Techniques for High Performance Applicative Computation*. PhD thesis, Computer Science Department, Colorado State University, 1989.
3. D.C. Cann. Retire Fortran? A Debate Rekindled. *CACM*, 35(8):81–89, Aug 1992.
4. K. Gopinath. *Copy elimination in single assignment languages*. PhD thesis, Computer System Laboratory, Stanford University, 1989.
5. Z. Li and C. Kirkham. Efficient Implementation of Aggregates in United Functions and Objects. In *33rd ACM Southeast Conference*, pages 73–82, Mar. 95.
6. J. R. McGraw, S .K. Skedzielewski, S. J. Allan, R. R. Oldehoeft, J. Glauert, C. C. Kirkham, W. Noyce, and R. Thomas. *SISAL: Streams and Iteration in a Single Assignment Language*. Lawrence Livermore National Laboratory, reference manual 1.2, manual m-146, rev. first edition, 1985.
7. A. V. Sastry, W. Clinger, and Z. Ariola. Order-of-evaluation Analysis for Destructive Updates in Strict Functional Languages with Flat Aggregates. In *the 6th Int. Conf. on Functional Programming Languages and Computer Architectures*, 1993.
8. S. K. Skedzielewski and M. L. Welcome. Dataflow Graph Optimization in IF1. In J-P. Jouannaud, editor, *Functional Programming Languages and Computer Architecture*, pages 17–34. Springer-Verlag, NY, November 1985.

Effective Representation of Aliases and Indirect Memory Operations in SSA Form

Fred Chow, Sun Chan, Shin-Ming Liu, Raymond Lo, Mark Streich
Silicon Graphics Computer Systems
2011 N. Shoreline Blvd.
Mountain View, CA 94043

Contact: Fred Chow (E-mail: fchow@sgi.com, Phone: USA (415) 933-4270)

Abstract. This paper addresses the problems of representing aliases and indirect memory operations in SSA form. We propose a method that prevents explosion in the number of SSA variable versions in the presence of aliases. We also present a technique that allows indirect memory operations to be globally commonized. The result is a precise and compact SSA representation based on global value numbering, called HSSA, that uniformly handles both scalar variables and indirect memory operations. We discuss the capabilities of the HSSA representation and present measurements that show the effects of implementing our techniques in a production global optimizer.

Keywords. Aliasing, Factoring dependences, Hash tables, Indirect memory operations, Program representation, Static single assignment, Value numbering.

1 Introduction

The Static Single Assignment (SSA) form [CFR+91] is a popular and efficient representation for performing analyses and optimizations involving scalar variables. Effective algorithms based on SSA have been developed to perform constant propagation, redundant computation detection, dead code elimination, induction variable recognition, and others [AWZ88, RWZ88, WZ91, Wolfe92]. But until now, SSA has only been used mostly for distinct variable names in the program. When applied to indirect variable constructs, the representation is not straight-forward, and results in added complexities in the optimization algorithms that operate on the representation [CFR+91, CG93, CCF94]. This has prevented SSA from being widely used in production compilers.

In this paper, we devise a scheme that allows indirect memory operations to be represented together with ordinary scalar variables in SSA form. Since indirect memory accesses also affect scalar variables due to aliasing, we start by defining notations to model the effects of aliasing for scalars in SSA form. We also describe a technique to reduce the overhead in SSA representation in the presence of aliases. Next, we introduce the concept of *virtual variables*, which model indirect memory operations as if they are scalars. We then show how virtual variables can be used to derive identical or distinct versions for indirect memory operations, effectively putting them in SSA form together with the scalar variables. This SSA representation in turn reduces the cost of analyzing the scalar variables that have aliases by taking advantage of the versioning applied to the indirect memory operations aliased with the scalar variables. We then present a method that builds a uniform SSA representation of all the scalar and indirect memory operations of the program based on global value numbering, which we call the Hashed SSA representation (HSSA). The various optimizations for scalars can then automatically extend to indirect memory operations under this framework. Finally, we present measurements that show the effectiveness of our techniques in a production global optimizer that uses HSSA as its internal representation.

In this paper, indirect memory operations cover both the uses of arrays and accesses to memory locations through pointers. Our method is applicable to commonly used languages like C and FORTRAN.

2 SSA with Aliasing

In our discussion, the source program has been translated to an intermediate representation in which expressions are represented in tree form. The expression trees are associated with statements that use their computed results. In SSA form, each definition of a variable is given a unique version, and different versions of the same variable can be regarded as different program variables. Each use of a variable version can only refer to a single reaching definition. When several definitions of a variable, a_1, a_2, ..., a_m, reach a confluence node in the control flow graph of the program, a ϕ function assignment statement, $a_n = \phi(a_1, a_2, ..., a_m)$, is inserted to merge them into the definition of a new variable version a_n. Thus, the semantics of single reaching definitions is maintained. This introduction of a new variable version as the result of ϕ factors use-def edges over confluence nodes, reducing the total number of use-def edges required. As a result, the use-def chain of each variable can be provided in a compact form by trivially allowing each variable to point to its single definition. One important property in SSA form is that each definition must dominate all its uses in the control flow graph of the program. Another important property in SSA form is that identical versions of the same variable must have the same value.

Aliasing of a scalar variable occurs in one of four conditions: when its storage location partially overlaps another variable[1], when it is pointed to by a pointer used in indirect memory operations, when its address is passed in a procedure call, or when it is a non-local variable that can be accessed from another procedure in a call or return. Techniques have been developed to analyze pointers both intra-procedurally and inter-procedurally to provide more accurate information on what is affected by them so as to limit their ill effects on program optimizations [CWZ90, CBC93, Ruf95, WL95].

To characterize the effects of aliasing, we distinguish between two types of definitions of a variable: *MustDef* and *MayDef*.[2] Since a MustDef must redefine the variable, it blocks the references of previous definitions from that point on. A MayDef only potentially redefines the variable, and so does not prevent previous definitions of the

---

1. If they exactly overlap, our representation will handle them as a single variable.
2. In [CCF94], MustDefs and MayDefs are called Killing Defs and Preserving Defs respectively, while in [Steen95], they are called Strong Updates and Weak Updates.

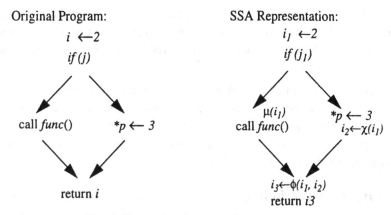

Fig. 1. Example of μ, χ **and** ϕ

same variable from being referenced later in the program. On the use side, in addition to real uses of the variable, there are places in the program where there are potential references to the variable that need to be taken into account in analyzing the program. We call these potential references *MayUse*.

To accommodate the MayDefs, we use the idea from [CCF94] in which SSA edges for the same variable are factored over its MayDefs. This is referred to as *location-factored SSA form* in [Steen95]. We model this effect by introducing the χ assignment operator in our SSA representation. χ links up the use-def edges through MayDefs. The operand of χ is the last version of the variable, and its result is the version after the potential definition. Thus, if variable i may be modified, we annotate the code with $i_2 = \chi(i_1)$, where i_1 is the current version of the variable.

To model MayUses, we introduce the μ operator in our SSA representation. μ takes as its operand the version of the variable that may be referenced, and produces no result. Thus, if variable i may be referenced, we annotate the code with $\mu(i_1)$, where i_1 is the current version of the variable.

In our internal representation, expressions cannot have side effects. Memory locations can only be modified by statements, which include direct and indirect store statements and calls. Thus, χ can only be associated with store and call statements. μ is associated with any dereferencing operation, like the unary operator * in C, which can happen within an expression. Thus, μ arises at both statements and expressions. We also mark return statements with μ for non-local variables to represent their liveness at function exits. Separating *MayDef* and *MayUse* allows us to model the effects of calls precisely. For example, a call that only references a variable will only cause a μ but no χ. For our modeling purpose, the μ takes effect just before the call, and the χ takes effect right after the call. Figure 1 gives an example of the use of μ, χ together with ϕ in our SSA representation. In the example, function *func* uses but does not modify variable i.

The inclusion of μ and χ in the SSA form does not impact the complexity of the algorithm that computes SSA form. A pre-pass inserts unnamed μ's and χ's for the aliased variables at the points of aliases in the program. In applying the SSA creation algorithm described in [CFR+91], the operands of the μ and χ are treated as uses and the χ's are treated as additional assignments. The variables in the μ and χ are renamed together with the rest of the program variables.

Transformations performed on SSA form have to take aliasing into account in order to preserve the safety of the optimization. In our SSA representation, it means taking into account the μ and χ annotations. For example, in performing dead code elimination using the algorithm presented in [CFR+91], a store can be deleted only if the store itself and all its associated χ's are not marked *live*.

3 SSA with Zero Versioning

In the previous section, we showed how to use μ and χ to model use-def information when aliases occur in a program. Even though use-def information is maintained, the number of versions multiplies because each χ introduces a new version and it may in turn cause new ϕ's to be inserted. Many of these versions have multiple possibly-defined values, and some of the defined values may also be unknown. As a result, it becomes relatively more expensive to represent programs in SSA form in the presence of aliases. In this section, we describe a technique to alleviate this problem.

We call occurrences of variables in the original program before conversion to SSA form *real* occurrences. In SSA form, variable occurrences in ϕ, μ and χ are thus not real occurrences. The variable versions that have no real occurrence do not directly affect the optimized output of the program once the program is converted back to ordinary form. But they do indirectly affect the optimizations that follow use-def chains that pass through ϕ, μ and χ. Once identified, these variable versions that have no real occurrence can be aggregately represented by a special version of the variable, thus reducing the number of versions of the variable that need to be represented, with only a slight impact on the quality of the optimized output. For the purpose of our discussion, we assign version 0 to this special version, and call it the *zero version*.

Definition 1. The *zero versions* are versions of variables that have no real occurrence and whose values come from at least one χ with zero or more intervening ϕ's.

Alternatively, we can define zero versions recursively as follows:

1. The left hand side of a χ is zero version if it has no real occurrence.
2. If an operand of a ϕ is zero version, the result of the ϕ is zero version if it has no real occurrence.

Zero versioning thus characterizes versions with no real occurrence whose values are affected by aliased stores. Since their values are not fixed, we do not assign unique versions to them and do not represent their use-def relationships.

We now give the algorithm to compute zero versions. We assume all variables have been renamed in the process of building the SSA form. Our algorithm assumes that def-use information, which is more expensive than use-def under SSA, is not maintained, and only use-def information is available.[1] The algorithm identifies the versions of variables that can be made zero-version and resets their versions to 0.

Algorithm 1. *Compute Zero Versions:*

1. Initialize flag *HasRealOcc* for each variable version created by SSA renaming to *false*.

2. Pass over the program. On visiting a real occurrence, set the *HasRealOcc* flag for the variable version to *true*.[2]

3. For each program variable, create *NonZeroPhiList* and initialize to empty.

4. Iterate through all variable versions:

   a. If *HasRealOcc* is *false* and it is defined by χ, set version to 0.

   b. If *HasRealOcc* is *false* and it is defined by ϕ:

      • If the version of one of the operands of the ϕ is 0, set version to 0.

      • Else if the *HasRealOcc* flag of all of the operands of the ϕ is *true*, set *HasRealOcc to* true.

      • Else add version to *NonZeroPhiList* for the variable.

5. For each program variable, iterate until its *NonZeroPhiList* no longer changes:

   a. For each version in *NonZeroPhiList*:

      • If the version of one of the operands of the ϕ is 0, set version to 0 and remove from *NonZeroPhiList*.

      • Else if the *HasRealOcc* flag of all the operands of the ϕ is *true*, set *HasRealOcc* to true and remove from *NonZeroPhiList*.

The first iteration through all the variable versions, represented by Step 4, completely processes all variable versions except those that are the results of ϕ whose operands have not yet been processed. These are collected into *NonZeroPhiList*. After the first iteration of Step 5, the versions still remaining in *NonZeroPhiList* all have at least one operand defined by ϕ. The upper bound on the number of iterations in Step 5 corresponds to the longest chain of contiguous ϕ assignments for the variable in the program. When no more zero versions can be propagated through each ϕ, the algorithm terminates.

Because zero versions can have multiple assignments statically, they do not have fixed or known values, so that two zero versions of the same variable cannot be assumed to be the same. The occurrence of a zero version breaks the use-def chain. Since the results of χ's have unknown values, zero versions do not affect the performance of optimizations that propagate known values, like constant propagation [WZ91], because they cannot be propagated across points of Maydefs to the variables. Optimizations that

---

1. If def-use information is present, a more efficient algorithm is possible.

2. The pass to set the *HasRealOcc* flag can coincide with another pass over the program that performs an unrelated optimization, e.g. dead store elimination.

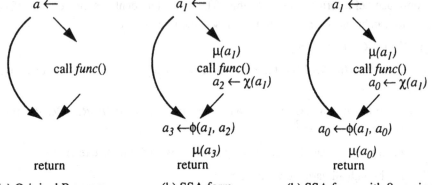

(a) Original Program   (b) SSA form   (b) SSA form with 0 versions

Fig. 2. Example of Using Zero Versions

operate on real occurrences, like equivalencing and redundancy detection [AWZ88, RWZ88], are also unaffected. In performing dead store elimination, zero versions have to be assumed live. Since zero versions can only have uses represented by μ's, the chance that stores associated with χ's to zero versions can be removed is small. However, it is possible that later optimizations delete the code that contains the μ's. Only in such situations would zero version prevent more dead store elimination.

Zero versions are created only when aliases occur. Our approach does not affect optimization when there is no aliasing. Zero versioning also does not prevent the SSA form from being used as a representation for various program transformations, because it is not applied to real occurrences. When aliases are prevalent in the program, zero versioning prevents the number of variable versions in the SSA form from exploding. In the example of Figure 2, since a is a global variable, it has a μ at the return statement. Our algorithm eliminates versions a_2 and a_3 by converting them to version 0.

4 SSA for Indirect Memory Operations

In an indirect memory operation, the memory location referenced depends on the values of the variables involved in the computation specified by the address expression. Figure 3 gives examples of indirect memory operations and their tree representation. Indirect memory operations are either indirect loads or indirect stores. We refer to them as loads and stores to *indirect* variables, as opposed to scalar variables. Indirect variables are identified by the form of their address expressions. We use the C dereferencing operator

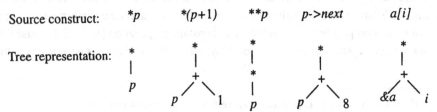

Fig. 3. Examples of Indirect Memory Operations

Original Program: SSA Representation:

$$.. *p ..$$

$$.. (*p_1)_1 ..$$

$$p \leftarrow p + 1$$

$$p_2 \leftarrow p_1 + 1$$

$$.. *p ..$$

$$.. (*p_2)_2 ..$$

Fig. 4. Renaming Indirect Variables

* to denote indirection. Given an address expression $<expr>$, $*<expr>$ represents a load of the indirect variable and $*<expr> \leftarrow$ represents a store to the indirect variable.

We can apply the same algorithm that computes SSA form for scalar variables to indirect variables, renaming them such that versions that statically have the same value get the same name. The difference is that each indirect variable needs to be treated as separate indirect variables if the variables involved in their address expressions are not of identical versions. This is illustrated in Figure 4, in which the two occurrences of $*p$ are renamed to different versions. Though $*p$ is not redefined between the two occurrences, p is redefined.

The obvious way to tackle the above problem is to apply the algorithm to compute SSA form multiple times to a program. The first application computes the versions for all scalar variables, the second application computes the versions for all indirect variables with one level of indirection, the third application computes the versions for all indirect variables with two levels of indirection, etc. Multiple invocation of the SSA computation algorithm would be prohibitively expensive and not practical. The only advantage with this approach is that, in between each application, it is possible to improve on the alias analysis by taking advantage of the version and thus use-def information just computed in the address expression.

We have formulated a scheme that allows us to compute the SSA form for all scalar and indirect variables in one pass. For this purpose, we introduce virtual variables to characterize indirect variables and include them in computing the SSA form.

Definition 2. The *virtual variable* of an indirect variable is an imaginary scalar variable that has identical alias characteristics as the indirect variable.

For all indirect variables that have similar alias behavior in the program, we assign a unique virtual variable. We use v superscripted with the indirect variable name to denote a virtual variable. Alias analysis is performed on the virtual variables together with the scalar variables. For virtual variables, alias analysis can additionally take into account the form of the address expression to determine when they are independent. For example, v^{*p} and $v^{*(p+1)}$ do not alias with each other. We then apply the algorithm to compute SSA form for all the scalar and indirect variables of the program. Since each virtual variable aliases with its indirect variable, the resulting SSA representation must have each occurrence of an indirect variable annotated with μ or χ of its virtual variable. The use-def relationship in the virtual variable now represents the use-def relationship of its

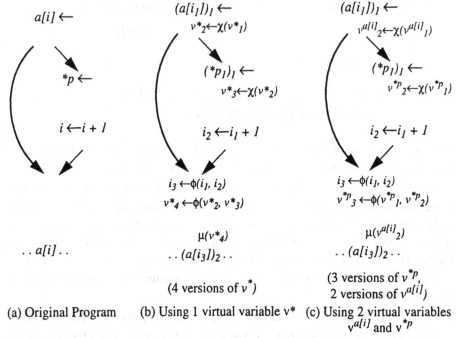

(a) Original Program   (b) Using 1 virtual variable v*   (c) Using 2 virtual variables $v^{a[i]}$ and v^{*p}

Indirect variables $a[i]$ and $*p$ do not alias with each other

Fig. 5. SSA for indirects using different numbers of virtual variables

indirect variable. Each occurrence of a indirect variable can then be given the version number of the virtual variable that annotates it in the μ or χ, except that new versions need to be generated when the address expression contains different versions of variables. We can easily handle this by regarding indirect variables whose address expressions have been renamed differently to be different indirect variables, even though they share the same virtual variable due to similar alias behavior. In Figure 4, after p has been renamed, $*p_1$ and $*p_2$ are regarded as different indirect variables. This causes different version numbers to be assigned to the $*p$'s, $(*p_1)_1$ and $(*p_2)_2$, even though the version of the virtual variable v^{*p} has not changed.

It is possible to cut down the number of virtual variables by making each virtual variable represent more indirect variables. This is referred to as *assignment factoring* in [Steen95]. It has the effect of replacing multiple use-def chains belonging to different virtual variables with one use-def chain that has more nodes and thus versions of the virtual variable, at the expense of higher analysis cost while going up the use-def chain. In the extreme case, one virtual variable can be used to represent all indirect variables in the program. Figure 5 gives examples of using different numbers of virtual variables in n a program. In that example, $a[i_1]$ and $a[i_2]$ are determined to be different versions because of the different versions of i used in them, and we assign versions 1 and 2 (shown as subscripts after the parentheses that enclose them) respectively. In part (b) of Figure 5, when we use a single virtual variable v^* for both $a[i]$ and p, even though they do not alias with each other, the single use-def chain has to pass through the appearances of both of them, and is thus less accurate.

In practice, we do not use assignment factoring among variables that do not alias among themselves, so that we do not have to incur the additional cost of analyzing the alias relationship between different variables while traversing the use-def chains. For example, we assign distinct virtual variables to $a[i]$ and $b[i]$ where arrays a and b do not overlap with each other. While traversing the use-def chains, we look for the presence of non-aliasing in indirects by analyzing their address expressions. For example, $a[i_j]$ does not alias with $a[i_j+1]$ even though they share the same virtual variable.

Zero versions can also be applied to virtual variables, in which virtual variables appearing in the μ and χ next to their corresponding indirect variables are regarded as real occurrences. This also helps to reduce the number of versions for virtual variables.

5 Global Value Numbering for Indirect Memory Operations

In this section, we apply the various ideas presented in this paper to build a concise SSA representation of the entire program based on global value numbering (GVN). We call our representation *Hashed SSA* (HSSA) because of the use of hashing in value numbering. HSSA serves as the internal program representation of our optimizer, on which most optimizations are performed.

Value numbering [CS70] is a technique to recognize expressions that compute the same value. It uses a hash table to store all program expressions. Each entry in the hash table is either an operand (leaf) or an operator (internal) node. The hash table index of each entry corresponds to its unique value number. The value number of an internal node is a function of the operator and the value numbers of all its immediate operands. Any two nodes with the same value number must compute the same value. Value numbering yields a directed acyclic graph (DAG) representation of the expressions in the program.

Without SSA form, value numbering can only be performed at the basic block level, as in [Chow83]. SSA enables value numbering to be performed globally. The representation is more compact, because each variable version maps to a unique value number and occupies only one entry in the hash table, no matter how many times it occurs in the program[1]. Expressions made up of variables with identical versions are represented just once in the hash table, regardless of where they are located in the control flow graph.

In value numbering, when two indirect memory operations yield the same hash value, they may not be assigned the same value number because the memory locations may contain different values. In straight-line code, any potential modification to the memory location can be detected by monitoring operations that affect memory while

---

1. The identification of each variable version is its unique node in the hash table, and the version number can be discarded.

traversing the code. But with GVN, this method cannot be used because GVN is flow-insensitive. One possibility is to give up commonizing the indirect operators by always creating a new value number for each indirect operator. This approach is undesirable, since it decreases the optimality and effectiveness of the GVN. To solve this problem, we apply the method described in the previous section of renaming indirect operations. During GVN, we map a value number to each unique version of indirect operations that our method has determined.

Our GVN has some similarity to that described in [Click95], in that expressions are hashed into the hash table bottom-up. However, our representation is in the form of expression trees, instead of triplets. Since we do not use triplets, variables are distinct from operators. Statements are not value-numbered. Instead, they are linked together on a per-block basis to represent the execution flow of each basic block. The DAG structure allows us to provide use-def information cheaply and succinctly, via a single link from each variable node to its defining statement. The HSSA representation by default does not provide def-use chains.

Our HSSA representation has five types of nodes. Three of them are leaf nodes: *const* for constants, *addr* for addresses and *var* for variables. Type *op* represents general expression operators. Indirect variables are represented by nodes of type *ivar*. Type *ivar* is a hybrid between type *var* and type *op*. It is like type *op* because it has an expression associated with it. It is like type *var* because it represents memory locations. The *ivar* node corresponds to the C dereferencing operator *. Both *var* and *ivar* nodes have links to their defining statements.

We now outline the steps to build the HSSA representation of the program:

Algorithm 2. *Build HSSA*:

1. Assign virtual variables to indirect variables in the program.

2. Perform alias analysis and insert μ and χ for all scalar and virtual variables.

3. Insert ϕ using the algorithm described in [CFR+91], including the χ as assignments.

4. Rename all scalar and virtual variables using the algorithm described in [CFR+91].

5. Perform the following simultaneously:

    a. Perform dead code elimination to eliminate dead assignments, including ϕ and χ, using the algorithm described in [CFR+91].

    b. Perform Steps 1 and 2 of the Compute Zero Version algorithm described in Section 3 to set the *HasRealOcc* flag for all variable versions.

6. Perform Steps 3, 4 and 5 of the Compute Zero Version algorithm to set variable versions to 0.

7. Hash a unique value number and create the corresponding hash table *var* node for each scalar and virtual variable version that are determined to be live in Step 5a. Only one node needs to be created for the zero versions of each variable.

8. Conduct a pre-order traversal of the dominator tree of the control flow graph of the program and apply global value numbering to the code in each basic block:

   a. Hash expression trees bottom up into the hash table, searching for any existing matching entry before creating each new value number and entry. At a *var* node, use the node created in Step 7 for that variable version.

   b. For two ivar nodes to match, two conditions must be satisfied: (1) their address expressions have the same value number, and (2) the versions of their virtual variables are either the same, or are separated by definitions that do not alias with the ivar.

   c. For each assignment statement, including ϕ and χ, represent its left hand side by making the statement point to the *var* or *ivar* node for direct and indirect assignments respectively. Also make the *var* or *ivar* node point back to its defining statement.

   d. Update all ϕ, μ and χ operands and results to make them refer to entries in the hash table.

The second condition of Step 8b requires us to go up the use-def chain of the virtual variable starting from the current version to look for occurrences of the same *ivar* node that are unaffected by stores associated with the same virtual variable. For example, a store to $a[i_1+1]$ after a use of $a[i_1]$ does not invalidate $a[i_1]$. Because we have to go up the use-def chain, processing the program in a pre-order traversal of the dominator tree of the control flow graph guarantees that we have always processed the earlier definitions.

Once the entire program has been represented in HSSA form, the original input program can be deleted. Figure 6 gives a conceptual HSSA representation for the example of Figure 4. In our actual implementation, each entry of the hash table uses a linked list

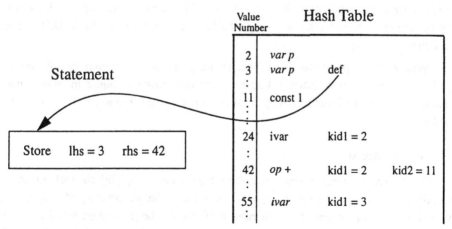

Fig. 6. HSSA representation for the example in Figure 5

for all the entries whose hash numbers collide, and the value number is represented by the pair *<index, depth>*.

6 Using HSSA

The HSSA form is more memory efficient than ordinary representations because of structure sharing resulting from DAGs. Compared to ordinary SSA form, HSSA also uses less memory because it does not provide def-use information, while use-def information is much less expensive because multiple uses are represented by a common node. Many optimizations can run faster on HSSA because they only need to be applied just once on the shared nodes. The various optimizations can also take advantage of the fact that it is trivial to check if two expressions compute the same value in HSSA.

An indirect memory operation is a hybrid between expression and variable, because it is not a leaf node but operates on memory. Our HSSA representation captures this property, so that it can benefit from optimizations applied to either expressions or variables.

Optimizations developed for scalar variables in SSA form can now be applied to indirect memory operations. With the use-def information for indirect variables, we can substitute indirect loads with their known values, performing constant propagation or forward substitution. We can recognize and exploit equivalences among expressions that include indirect memory operations. We can also remove useless direct and indirect stores at the same time while performing dead code elimination.

The most effective way to optimize indirect memory operations is to promote them to scalars when possible. We call this optimization *indirection removal*, which refers to the conversion of an indirect store and its subsequent indirect loads to direct store and loads. This promotion to scalar form enables it to be allocated to register, thus eliminating accesses to memory. An indirect variable can be promoted to a scalar whenever it is free of aliases. This can be verified by checking for the presence of its virtual variables in μ's and χ's. Promotion of an *ivar* node can be effected by overwriting it with the contents of the new *var* node, thus avoiding rehashing its ancestor nodes in the DAG representation.

Optimization opportunites in indirect memory operations depends heavily on the quality or extent of alias analysis. Implementing the above techniques in an optimizer enables programs to benefit directly from any improvement in the results of the alias analyzer.

7 Measurements

We now present measurements that show the effects of applying the techniques we described in this paper. The measurements are made in the production global optimizer WOPT, a main component of the compiler suite that will be shipped on MIPS R10000-based systems in May of 1996. In addition to the optimizations described in Section 6,

Routine	Language	Description
tomcatv	FORTRAN	101.tomcatv, SPECfp95
loops	FORTRAN	subroutine loops from 103.su2cor, SPECfp95
kernel	FORTRAN	routine containing the 24 Lawrence Livermore Kernels
twldrv	FORTRAN	subroutine twldrv from 145.fpppp, SPECfp95
Data_path	C	function Data_path from 124.m88ksim, SPECint95
compress	C	function compress from 129.compress, SPECint95
Query_Ass	C	function Query_AssertOnObject from 147.vortex, SPECint95
eval	C	function eval from 134.perl, SPECint95

Table 1. Description of routines used in measurements

WOPT also performs bit-vector-based partial redundancy elimination and strength reduction. From the input program, it builds HSSA and uses it as its only internal program representation until it finishes performing all its optimizations. We focus on the effects that zero versioning and the commonizing of indirect variables have on the HSSA representation in the optimizer. We have picked a set of 8 routines, 7 of which are from the SPEC95 benchmark suites. Table 1 describes these routines. We have picked progressively larger routines to show the effects of our techniques as the size of the routines increases. The numbers shown do not include the effects of inter-procedural alias analysis.

We characterize the HSSA representation by the number of nodes in the hash table needed to represent the program. The different types of nodes are described earlier in Section 5. Without zero versioning, Table 2 shows that *var* nodes can account for up to 94% of all the nodes in the hash table. Applying zero versioning decreases the number of *var* nodes by 41% to 90%. The numbers of nodes needed to represent the programs are reduced from 30% to 85%. Note that the counts for non-*var* nodes remain constant, since only variables without real occurrences are converted to zero versions. Having to deal with less nodes, the time spent in performing global optimization is reduced from 2% to 45%. The effect of zero versioning depends on the amount of aliasing in the program. Zero versioning also has bigger effects on large programs, since there are more variables affected by each alias. We have found no noticeable difference in the running time of the benchmarks due to zero versioning.

With zero versioning being applied, Table 3 shows the effects of commonizing indirect variables on the HSSA representation. *Ivar* nodes account for from 6% to 21% of the total number of nodes in our sample programs. Commonizing *ivar* nodes reduces the *ivar* nodes by 3% to 58%. In each case, the total number of nodes decreases more than the number of *ivar* nodes, showing that commonizing the *ivar* nodes in turn enables other operators that operate on them to be commonized. Though the change in the total number of hash table nodes is not significant, the main effect of this technique is in preventing missed optimizations, like global common subexpressions, among indirect memory operations.

routines	number of nodes				percentage reduction		compilation speedup
	zero version off		zero version on				
	all	vars	all	vars	all	vars	
tomcatv	1803	1399	844	440	53%	69%	4%
loops	7694	6552	2493	1351	68%	79%	9%
kernel	9303	8077	2974	1748	68%	78%	6%
twldrv	33683	31285	6297	3899	81%	88%	11%
Data_path	489	365	340	216	30%	41%	2%
compress	759	647	367	255	52%	61%	4%
Query_Ass	5109	4653	1229	773	76%	83%	12%
eval	62966	59164	9689	5887	85%	90%	45%

Table 2. Effects of zero versioning

routines	number of nodes				percentage reduction	
	ivar commoning off		ivar commoning on			
	all nodes	ivar nodes	all nodes	ivar nodes	all nodes	ivar nodes
tomcatv	844	124	828	111	2%	10%
loops	2493	453	2421	381	3%	16%
kernel	2974	398	2854	306	4%	23%
twldrv	6297	506	6117	333	3%	34%
Data_path	340	44	320	30	6%	32%
compress	367	21	365	19	0.5%	10%
Query_Ass	1229	183	1218	173	1%	5%
eval	9689	1994	9114	1504	6%	25%

Table 3. Effects of the global commonizing of ivar nodes

8 Conclusion

We have presented practical methods that efficiently model aliases and indirect memory operations in SSA form. Zero versioning prevents large variations in the representation overhead due to the amount of aliasing in the program, with minimal impact on the quality of the optimizations. The HSSA form captures the benefits of SSA while efficiently representing program constructs using global value numbering. Under HSSA, the integration of alias handling, SSA and global value numbering enables indirect memory operations to be globally commonized. Generalizing SSA to indirect memory operations in turn allows them to benefit from optimizations developed for scalar variables. We believe that these are all necessary ingredients for SSA to be used in a production-quality global optimizer.

Acknowledgement

The authors would like to thank Peter Dahl, Earl Killian and Peng Tu for their helpful comments in improving the quality of this paper. Peter Dahl also contributed to the work in this paper.

References

[AWZ88] Alpern, B., Wegman, M. and Zadeck, K. Detecting Equality Of Variables in Programs. Conference Record of the 15th ACM Symposium on the Principles of Programming Languages, Jan. 1988.

[CWZ90] Chase, D., Wegman, M. and Zadeck, K. Analysis of Pointers and Structures. Proceedings of the SIGPLAN '90 Conference on Programming Language Design and Implementation, June 1990.

[Chow83] Chow, F. "A Portable Machine-independent Global Optimizer — Design and Measurements," Ph.D. Thesis and Technical Report 83-254, Computer System Lab, Stanford University, Dec. 1983.

[Click95] Click, C., Global Code Motion Global Value Numbering, Proceedings of the SIGPLAN '95 Conference on Programming Language Design and Implementation, June 1995.

[CBC93] Choi, J., Burke, M. and Carini, P. Efficient Flow-Sensitive Interprocedural Computation of Pointer-Induced Aliases and Side Effects. Conference Record of the 20th ACM Symposium on the Principles of Programming Languages, Jan. 1993.

[CCF94] Choi, J., Cytron, R. and Ferrante, J. On the Efficient Engineering of Ambitious Program Analysis. *IEEE Transactions on Software Engineering*, February 1994, pp. 105-113.

[CS70] Cocke, J. and Schwartz, J. *Programming Languages and Their Compilers.* Courant Institute of Mathematical Sciences, New York University, April 1970.

[CFR+91] Cytron, R., Ferrante, J., Rosen B., Wegman, M. and Zadeck, K., Efficiently Computing Static Single Assignment Form and the Control Dependence Graph. *ACM Transactions on Programming Languages and Systems,* October 1991, pp. 451-490.

[CG93] Cytron, R. and Gershbein, R., Efficient Accomodation of May-alias Information in SSA Form, Proceedings of the SIGPLAN '93 Conference on Programming Language Design and Implementation, June 1993.

[RWZ88] Rosen, B., Wegman, M. and Zadeck K. Global Value Numbers and Redundant Computation. Conference Record of the 15th ACM Symposium on the Principles of Programming Languages, Jan. 1988.

[Ruf95] Ruf, E. Context-Insensitive Alias Analysis Reconsidered. Proceedings of the SIGPLAN '95 Conference on Programming Language Design and Implementation, June 1995.

[Steen95] Steensgaard, B. Sparse Functional Stores for Imperative Programs. Proceedings of the SIGPLAN '95 Workshop on Intermediate Representations, Jan. 1995.

[WL95] Wilson, B. and Lam, M. Efficient Context Sensitive Pointer Analysis for C Programs. Proceedings of the SIGPLAN '95 Conference on Programming Language Design and Implementation, June 1995.

[WZ91] Wegman, M. and Zadeck, K. Constant Propagation with Conditional Branches. *ACM Transactions on Programming Languages and Systems,* April 1991, pp. 181-210.

[Wolfe92] Wolfe, M. Beyond induction variables. Proceedings of the SIGPLAN '92 Conference on Programming Language Design and Implementation, June 1992.

Maptool – Supporting Modular Syntax Development

Basim M. Kadhim and William M. Waite

{Basim.Kadhim,William.Waite}@Colorado.EDU
University of Colorado, Boulder, CO 80309-0425, USA

Abstract. In building textual translators, implementors often distinguish between a concrete syntax and an abstract syntax. The concrete syntax describes the phrase structure of the input language and the abstract syntax describes a tree structure that can be used as the basis for performing semantic computations. Having two grammars imposes the requirement that there exist a mapping from the concrete syntax to the abstract syntax. The research presented in this paper led to a tool, called Maptool, that is designed to simplify the development of the two grammars. Maptool supports a modular approach to syntax development that mirrors the modularity found in semantic computations. This is done by allowing users to specify each of the syntaxes only partially as long as the sum of the fragments allows deduction of the complete syntaxes.

Keywords: Abstract syntax, concrete syntax, modularity, parsing grammar, syntax development, syntax mapping, tree construction

1 Introduction

The meaning of a construct in a programming language is often described in terms of the meanings of the components of that construct. A tree embodies the relationship between constructs and their components, and therefore much of the analysis that a compiler performs on a source program is conveniently expressed in the form of computations over a tree. Although the structure of this tree is related to the phrase structure of the source program text, the two are generally not identical.

Both the phrase structure and the tree structure can be defined by context-free grammars. The grammar describing the phrase structure is called the *concrete syntax*, while the grammar describing the tree structure is called the *abstract syntax*. Together, the two grammars provide the foundation for verifying the syntactic and semantic correctness of a program in the language. The desirability of distinguishing between a concrete and abstract syntax is discussed in [3, 4].

A concrete syntax can be input to a parser generator, which will then produce a parser for the language. In order for the concrete syntax to be usable by a parser generator, it must be unambiguous and typically must have either the LL(1) or LALR(1) property (depending on the parser generator being used) [12].

An abstract syntax describes the structure of trees over which computations are to be performed. While symbols and rules are included in a concrete syntax to handle things like operator precedence and associativity, these distinctions are unimportant in describing semantic computations. It is inconvenient to force the abstract syntax to have such symbols and rules only so that it is also usable by a parser generator. Including such rules in the abstract syntax also unnecessarily increases the size of the tree. Consequently, it is desirable to allow for differences between the syntaxes by supporting a set of mappings.

Semantic computations can most often be divided into several different modules [7]. Name analysis, type analysis, and output generation are examples of common semantic computations that can be thought of as individual modules and can in many cases be implemented in isolation from one another. Each of these modules typically only specifies computations for some of the nodes in the tree. If the concrete syntax is completely specified, it should not be necessary to specify abstract tree fragments other than those involved in the current computation being considered. It is also desirable to be able to test each of these modules in isolation from one another.

For existing languages, it is very often the case that the implementor of a language would begin with a complete concrete syntax as assumed in the last paragraph. With a new language, an implementor might not be concerned with the syntactic structure of the language and might begin by describing the semantics of the language based on an abstract syntax tree. In this case, it should not be necessary to completely specify the concrete syntax, but rather only describe those fragments that resolve ambiguities present in the abstract syntax and those that add desired syntactic sugar.

With these strategies in mind, the research presented in this paper (and implemented in a tool called Maptool) addresses the following points:

1. It should not be required that both the concrete and abstract syntaxes provided in the input be complete as long as the two together specify a complete grammar.
2. There must be a statically verifiable mapping between the concrete and the abstract syntax.
3. Mappings between rules in the concrete and the abstract syntax must exist such that the abstract syntax can be designed to simplify the development of semantic computations.

Static verifiability of the mapping ensures that the syntaxes can be modified independently of one another, and that a module can be generated to construct an abstract syntax tree automatically from the syntax descriptions and a mapping specification.

The remainder of the paper begins with a discussion of related work in Sect. 2. Section 3 discusses the rules for mapping between the two syntaxes and notations for describing mappings that cannot be determined implicitly. Section 4 shows how the concrete and abstract syntaxes are made complete. The paper concludes with some notes about the implementation of Maptool and its use in the Eli Compiler Construction System [6].

2 Related Work

Rosenkrantz and Hunt [11] use the notion of symbolic equivalence to join several abstract symbols into a single concrete symbol in order to find a concrete grammar that falls into a parsable class (such as LL(1) or LR(1)). This work is consistent with other research in the area of grammatical covers [9]. It is our experience, however, that the notion of symbolic equivalence is more useful in the opposite direction: several concrete symbols form an equivalence class that is represented by a single symbol in the abstract syntax. This technique was first implemented in the Eli system by a tool called CAGT [2]. The research in this paper will also discuss a technique for dealing with cases in which the abstract syntax needs to distinguish, based on context, between constructs that have identical phrase structure.

Some of the mappings described in this paper bear strong resemblance to *Transduction Grammars* [5], however Transduction Grammars require that the same nonterminals be used in the original and the transformed versions of rules. This does not allow the grouping of symbols into symbolic equivalence classes. The work of Ballance et. al. [3] on grammatical abstraction is also closely related to the work presented here. Grammatical abstraction, however, does not allow the abstract syntax to distinguish between constructs with identical phrase structure.

We are unaware of any efforts directed towards the merging of syntax fragments in support of modular development.

3 Mapping

Through the remainder of the paper, we will assume that the user has provided a set of productions, P and P', representing fragments of the concrete and abstract syntaxes, respectively. Productions in P are all of the form $N \to x_1 \ldots x_n$, while productions in P' have either the form $N' \to x'_1 \ldots x'_n$ or $N' \hookrightarrow x'_1 \mid \ldots \mid x'_n$. The latter form represents a variadic node in the abstract syntax tree. Variadic nodes are used to represent lists of structures, where the number of those structures is determined at run-time and the syntactic glue (literal symbols) between those structures is not relevant to the semantics of the input. A symbol that precedes a $\hookrightarrow$ may not appear on the left hand side of any other production in P'.

The same symbol may appear in both P and P'. Symbols that appear on the left hand side of any production in P or P' are classified as nonterminals, while symbols that only occur on the right hand side of productions in P and P' are classified as terminal symbols. (These initial classifications are based only on the fragments provided in P and P' - they may be altered during the mapping.)

In addition to P and P', the user may provide a mapping specification that can contain two kinds of mappings: symbol mappings and rule mappings. These are the subject of the next two subsections. The last subsection discusses several mappings not implemented in Maptool and the reasons for their omission.

3.1 Symbol Mappings

Symbol mappings, or *symbolic equivalence classes*, are the means for specifying a group of symbols from P that are represented by a single symbol in P'. As an example, consider the concrete syntax fragment of Fig. 1, which describes a typical arithmetic expression language. The symbols *Expr*, *Term*, *Factor*, and *Primary* are used to indicate precedence levels of operators. Once the input is parsed and the abstract syntax tree is constructed, the structure of the tree embodies the precedence levels of the operators in the input. For most processors, the symbolic distinction between *Expr*, *Term*, *Factor*, and *Primary* becomes superfluous and even cumbersome. To solve this problem, Maptool allows users

$$Expr \rightarrow Expr \text{ '+' } Term \qquad (1)$$
$$| \ Expr \text{ '-' } Term \qquad (2)$$
$$| \ Term \qquad (3)$$
$$Term \rightarrow Term \text{ '*' } Factor \qquad (4)$$
$$| \ Term \text{ '/' } Factor \qquad (5)$$
$$| \ Factor \qquad (6)$$
$$Factor \rightarrow \text{ '-' } Factor \qquad (7)$$
$$| \ Primary \qquad (8)$$
$$Primary \rightarrow Integer \qquad (9)$$
$$| \ Identifier \qquad (10)$$
$$| \ \text{'(' } Expr \text{ ')'} \qquad (11)$$

Fig. 1. Concrete Expression Syntax Fragment

to specify a group of symbols from P that are represented by a single symbol in P'. The notation $Expr \Leftrightarrow Term\ Factor\ Primary$ indicates that $Expr$ is the *symbolic equivalent* in P' for *Expr*, *Term*, *Factor*, and *Primary* of P. More formally, $V' \Leftrightarrow x_1 \ldots x_n$ specifies that V' is the symbolic equivalent for $x_1, \ldots, x_n$ subject to the following restrictions:

1. $x_1, \ldots, x_n$ are symbols that only occur in productions of P.
2. $x_1, \ldots, x_n$ may not appear in more than one symbolic equivalence class.
3. $x_1, \ldots, x_n$ must all be classified as nonterminal symbols or all be classified as terminal symbols.
4. The classification of V' must "agree" with the classification of $x_1, \ldots, x_n$:
   (a) If V' appears in P, then its classification must be the same as that of $x_1, \ldots, x_n$.
   (b) If V' appears as a nonterminal in P', then $x_1, \ldots, x_n$ must also be classified as nonterminals.

(c) If V' appears as a terminal in P' or does not appear in either P or P', then V' assumes the classifications of $x_1, \ldots, x_n$. (The reason for this will be clarified by an example in Sect. 4.)

Every symbol in productions of P has a symbolic equivalent in the productions of P'. Symbols which do not appear in a symbol mapping specification are their own symbolic equivalents. Symbolic equivalents that do not appear in productions of P' will be added to the abstract syntax when the syntaxes are completed as described in Sect. 4. This ensures that any phrase derived from a symbol in the concrete syntax is represented by a tree that is rooted by its symbolic equivalent. As will be seen in the next section, many of the mappings between rules are inferred as a result of the symbolic equivalence class specifications defined in this section.

Applying a symbolic equivalence class to concrete rules means replacing each occurrence of a symbol in the production with its symbolic equivalent. In our example in Fig. 1, applying the symbolic equivalence class $Expr \Leftrightarrow Term\ Factor\ Primary$ causes rules 3, 6, and 8 to have the form $Expr \rightarrow Expr$. These are called *trivial chain productions*. They serve no purpose in the abstract syntax and do not require tree nodes to represent them. Eliminating them can result in significant reduction in the size of the abstract syntax tree.

3.2 Rule Mapping

Rule mapping provides the basis for the completion of the syntaxes described in the next section. It is also the determining factor in how the module to automatically construct the abstract syntax tree is generated. While it is possible to specify rule mappings explicitly, the rule mappings can be determined implicitly in most cases.

For each mapping, we will briefly discuss how the abstract syntax tree fragment is constructed. The tree construction is based on a scheme in which constructed subtrees are placed on a stack and used when concrete syntax rules are reduced to construct new subtrees to place on the stack. This is very much like the scheme used for tree transduction grammars [5].

Variadic Nodes Languages are replete with lists of things, such as lists of declarations or lists of statements. While parsing grammars require the introduction of recursive rules to describe such lists, it is convenient to view such a list as a single flat context when describing the semantics. This can result in a reduction in the size of the abstract syntax tree, because numerous nonterminals used in the concrete syntax to adequately disambiguate the phrase structure need not be represented in the abstract syntax tree.

As an example, consider the concrete syntax fragment in Fig. 2 representing a list of *Decl*'s followed by a list of *Stmt*'s. All of the rules in the figure can map to a variadic production in the abstract syntax of the form $Program \hookrightarrow Decl \mid Stmt$. The concrete syntax fragment includes the syntactic sugar (brackets, commas, and semicolons) and rules that enforce the requirement that *Decl* nodes precede

Stmt nodes. Neither the syntactic sugar nor the ordering need be specified in the abstract syntax. Omitting them prevents over-specification and allows one to describe semantic computations that are less specific to the exact phrase structure of the input language. In this example, the size of the abstract syntax tree is also reduced because *StmtList* and *DeclList* nodes are not represented in the tree.

$$Program \rightarrow \text{'['} \: DeclList \: \text{']'} \: StmtList$$
$$DeclList \rightarrow DeclList \: \text{','} \: Decl$$
$$\mid Decl$$
$$StmtList \rightarrow StmtList \: \text{';'} \: Stmt$$
$$\mid Stmt$$

Fig. 2. Concrete Representation of a Variadic Node

Variadic productions in the abstract syntax fragment P' are the first to be mapped. The process begins by examining the left hand side symbol, N', of the production. We add N' and any symbols that have N' as their symbolic equivalent to a set of symbols, R, that represents the root of the variadic context. Assume that S represents the set of symbols that appear on the right hand side of the variadic production and all symbols that have a member of S as their symbolic equivalent. Each rule in P that appears along a derivation path from a member of R to a member of S is marked as being mapped to the variadic production. More formally, the set of rules mapped to the variadic production can be described as follows:

$$\{N \rightarrow x_1 \ldots x_n \mid \exists (r \in R, s \in S) \text{ such that } r \overset{*}{\Rightarrow} N \overset{+}{\Rightarrow} s\}$$

(In the above notation, $\overset{*}{\Rightarrow}$ and $\overset{+}{\Rightarrow}$ denote the application of zero or more and one or more productions from P, respectively.)

Each non-literal symbol that appears on a derivation path from a member of R to a member of S is called an *intermediate nonterminal*. An error has occurred if any intermediate nonterminal appears in any productions of P that are not mapped to the variadic production. In other words, there can be no symbols in P from which a derivation exists to any of the intermediate nonterminals without passing through a member of R.

An error must also be signalled if a non-literal terminal symbol that is not a member of S is found on the right hand side of any production encountered on any derivation path from members of R to members of S. This would imply that an element of the input other than those specified by the variadic production was found on a derivation sequence from the root of the variadic context.

Based on this mapping, we must establish how to build the abstract syntax tree fragment representing the variadic node given the set of mapped concrete syntax rules. For each production mapped to the variadic context, the right hand side symbols that are members of S have subtree fragments on the tree construction stack. The reduction of a mapped rule must append these fragments to a running list. Every concrete production that has a member of R on its right hand side and is not mapped to the variadic production must finalize the list to create the variadic node. The reason for doing the finalization in the parent context is that it is possible for a member of R to be recursively defined. In such a case, trying to finalize the variadic node in a context that defines a member of R might execute the finalization prematurely.

Implicit Rule Mapping We say that variadic productions are mapped *implicitly* to a set of rules in the concrete syntax fragment, because the user provides no additional information to Maptool to deduce the mapping. The more general form of implicit rule mapping simply maps rules that have identical signatures. Only mapping rules with identical signatures, however, does not allow users to semantically distinguish between constructs that are syntactically the same. Fig. 3 shows two concrete rules that represent different contexts for the terminal symbol *Identifier*. Semantically, one represents the definition of an identifier and the other represents the use of an identifier.

$$Decl \rightarrow Type\ Identifier$$
$$AssignStmt \rightarrow Identifier\ ' =' \ Expression$$

Fig. 3. Concrete Syntax for Identifier Definitions and Uses

Symbolically distinguishing between these two different uses of *Identifier* may simplify semantic computations. Systems (like Eli [6]) where computations can be provided for occurrences of symbols in the abstract syntax tree benefit by not having to distinguish between occurrences of the same symbol in different contexts. This technique is used heavily in developing modular and reusable attribute grammars as demonstrated in [7].

The abstract syntax fragment that distinguishes between identifier uses and definitions is shown in Fig. 4. The figure shows that two new symbols, *IdDef* and *IdUse*, are introduced to represent definitions and uses, respectively. To retain a mapping with the concrete syntax, *chain productions* are added between the new nonterminal and *Identifier*. To facilitate such mappings, Maptool not only maps rules that have identical signatures, but also rules that differ only in the names of their right hand side non-literal symbols. In cases where these symbols differ, there must be a series of chain productions connecting the two symbols.

$$Decl \rightarrow Type \ IdDef$$
$$AssignStmt \rightarrow IdUse \ '=' \ Expression$$
$$IdDef \rightarrow Identifier$$
$$IdUse \rightarrow Identifier$$

Fig. 4. Abstract Syntax for Identifier Definitions and Uses

More formally, Maptool takes rules from the concrete syntax (from P) that were not mapped to a variadic context and tries to map them to rules in P'. A rule from P is mapped to a rule in P' if the following conditions hold:

1. The rules differ only in the names of their nonterminals.
2. The left hand side nonterminal symbols of the two productions belong to the same symbolic equivalence class.
3. For each pair of right hand side symbols that differ in the two productions, they either both belong to the same equivalence class or the symbol from the production in P is *coercible* to the symbol from the production in P'.

For a symbol X to be coercible to another symbol Y, there must be a series of chain productions in P' such that one can derive X from Y using those chain productions. Chain productions are productions that have only a single nonterminal symbol on the right hand side. If more than one rule in P' satisfies the above criteria, then the mapping that requires the use of the fewest chain productions is chosen. If the map is still ambiguous, an error must be signalled to the user.

The reason that coercions are possible is that, when reducing a concrete syntax rule, we can check to see what symbols are at the roots of the tree fragments on the tree construction stack. If the symbol does not match what is expected for the particular tree construction function invoked, then the tree constructor can coerce the found symbol to the expected symbol by inserting the chain productions representing the coercion sequence between the two symbols.

Explicit Rule Mapping There are times when symbolic equivalence classes and implicit rule mapping do not provide enough flexibility. For example, DeRemer recognized the desire for *standardization* of certain language constructs [4]. The example he gives involves "let expressions" and "where expressions." "Let expressions" have the form $LetExpr \rightarrow$ 'let' $Definitions$ 'in' $Expr$, while "where expressions" have the form $WhereExpr \rightarrow Expr$ 'where' $Definitions$. The syntax is different, but the semantics of the two kinds of expressions are identical.

If we have a language that allows both, we would like to have a single abstract syntax tree structure to represent both syntactic constructs. For example, our abstract syntax might have the form $BoundExpr \rightarrow Definitions \ Expr$.

To implement this kind of transformation, we allow users to provide a mapping specification that rewrites the right hand side of certain concrete syntax rules before implicit rule mapping is performed. In this case, we would have the following specification:

$$LetExpr \rightarrow \text{'let'} \; Definitions \; \text{'in'} \; Expr \; < \$1 \; \$2 >$$

$$WhereExpr \rightarrow Expr \; \text{'where'} \; Definitions \; < \$2 \; \$1 >$$

The symbols between angle brackets specify how the rule is to be rewritten. Literal symbols may be included in the rewrite and the non-literal symbols in the rule are represented by the $ symbol followed by a number, i, that represents the i-th non-literal symbol on the right hand side of the rule. Here we have stripped the literal symbols from the rules and reordered the non-literals in the case of the where expression.

3.3 Mappings Not Implemented

Maptool has been in use for over a year and implements those syntax mappings that we have found most useful. Three other possible mappings have been suggested to us. In two cases, the mappings do not agree with our goal for modular syntax development and we have not yet found compelling reasons to implement the third.

Deducing Symbolic Equivalence Classes The first suggestion was to deduce symbolic equivalence classes. Currently, Maptool requires that an explicit specification for equivalence classes be supplied by a user.

In the example in Fig. 1, the symbols $Expr$, $Term$, $Factor$, and $Primary$ are all connected by chain productions. If $Expr$ is the only symbol specified in an abstract syntax fragment supplied by the user, one could deduce that all of the symbols connected to $Expr$ by chain productions should belong to the same equivalence class.

The problem with this deduction arises when developing syntaxes piece by piece in a modular fashion. (It is important to note that Maptool results derived from syntax fragments under development have been very heavily used, particularly with large grammars.) Consider the concrete syntax fragment in Fig. 5 in conjunction with the expression language from Fig. 1. Together they specify the complete concrete syntax for an expression language with bound variables. In developing the abstract syntax, we might first use Maptool to deduce a complete version of the abstract syntax without supplying any abstract syntax fragment.

If we allowed Maptool to deduce symbolic equivalence classes, it would deduce an equivalence among $Computation$, $Expr$, $LetExpr$, $WhereExpr$, $Term$, $Factor$, and $Primary$, because they are all connected by chain productions. For some semantic computations, however, $Computation$ should not be considered part of the equivalence class. Consequently, $Computation$ would either not appear in the resulting abstract syntax or would appear in unexpected contexts

$$Computation \rightarrow Expr$$
$$| \ LetExpr$$
$$| \ WhereExpr$$
$$LetExpr \rightarrow \text{'let'} \ Definitions \ \text{'in'} \ Expr$$
$$WhereExpr \rightarrow Expr \ \text{'where'} \ Definitions$$
$$Definitions \rightarrow Definitions \ \text{','} \ Definition$$
$$| \ Definition$$
$$Definition \rightarrow Identifier \ \text{'='} \ Expr$$

Fig. 5. Concrete Syntax Fragment

(depending on which of the symbols is chosen by the tool to be the symbolic equivalent).

Given the size of the example just given, such a misleading result from a mapping tool would be simple to correct by adding rules to the abstract syntax fragment. Unfortunately, the larger the syntax the more difficult it becomes to detect and correct such inconsistencies. As a result, we find it preferable to force the user to specify symbolic equivalence classes explicitly.

Adding Chain Rules Another possibility that has been suggested is to deduce similarities in the signatures of rules in the concrete and the abstract syntax, and to introduce chain rules between the differing symbols in cases where it would facilitate a match. As an example, consider the concrete and the abstract syntax fragments from Figs. 3 and 4. Given the concrete syntax fragment from Fig. 3, the suggested mapping would relieve the user from having to supply the last two rules of Fig. 4. The similarity of the first two rules of the abstract syntax fragment with the two rules in the concrete syntax fragment would be deduced by the tool and the appropriate chain rules would be automatically introduced.

The problem with this approach is that it may deduce a similarity between rules that are clearly not meant to be matched. Figure 6 shows two similar concrete syntax rules that might appear in the same grammar. Maptool aims to support a style of development in which users can develop semantic computations for *Declarations* and *Statements* separately and test those computations in isolation from one another. In such a case, suppose that the user provides computations for *Declarations* (i.e. the first rule of Fig. 6 also appears in the abstract syntax fragment). If the second rule does not also appear in the abstract syntax fragment, then the suggested mapping would introduce a chain rule between *Statements* and *Declarations*. Since we want to develop separate computations for *Statements* and *Declarations*, this is clearly not the desired effect and is likely to be misleading.

$$Section \rightarrow \text{'begin'} \; Declarations \; \text{'end'}$$
$$Section \rightarrow \text{'begin'} \; Statements \; \text{'end'}$$

Fig. 6. Two Similar Concrete Syntax Rules

Multi-Level Matching Given the concrete syntax rule $A \rightarrow B \; C \; D$, it has been suggested that one might want to construct two contexts in the abstract syntax. These might be of the form $A \rightarrow X \; D$ and $X \rightarrow C \; D$. Conversely, one might consider mapping two concrete syntax rules of the form $A \rightarrow X \; D$ and $X \rightarrow C \; D$ to a single abstract syntax rule of the form $A \rightarrow B \; C \; D$.

Maptool does not currently support these kinds of mappings. We have not yet found compelling examples to warrant the effort required to add them. The implementation for the first of the two mappings would be fairly straightforward. The second mapping, however, would require techniques described by Ballance et al.[3] for either grammar modification or the computation of yield states in the parser.

4 Completing the Syntaxes

After the mappings are complete, Maptool must try to generate reduced context free grammars from the fragments provided. The basic technique is that rules in P are added to the abstract syntax if they do not map to any rules in P' and rules in P' are added to the concrete syntax if there aren't any rules in P that map to them. This basic technique is subject to the following restrictions:

1. All symbolic equivalence classes are applied to rules from P before they are added to the abstract syntax.
2. As indicated in Sect. 3.1, trivial chain productions are not added to the abstract syntax.
3. *Literal chain productions* are also not added to the abstract syntax. Literal chain productions are rules that have the form, $N' \rightarrow x \; N' \; y$, where x and y are sequences of literals and x or y is non-empty. The rationale here is that such a context is only needed in the abstract syntax tree if there is actually some computation associated with it, in which case it should be included in P'.
4. A chain production $X' \rightarrow Y'$ of P' is only added to the concrete syntax if X' is a symbol that already exists in productions of the concrete syntax. If X' does not already exist in the concrete syntax, then introducing the rule would result in X' being unreachable. Such productions are often present in the abstract syntax to define coercions as described in Sect. 3.2. Note that adding the chain production may result in the addition of Y' to the concrete syntax. This means that all abstract chain productions must be checked for inclusion each time a new rule is added.

5. If no rules in P are found to map to a variadic production in P', then a canonical left-recursive version of the rule is added to the concrete syntax.

Once the basic technique has been applied, Maptool must verify that the grammars are, in fact, reduced by checking that neither has more than one potential root symbol.

In Sect. 3.1 it was indicated that symbols that appear as terminals in P' assume the nonterminal classification if they are symbolic equivalents for nonterminals in P. This is because rules defining the nonterminals from P will be added to the abstract syntax making the symbolic equivalent in P' a nonterminal.

Maptool does not attempt to "undo" symbolic equivalence classes for rules in P' that are added to the concrete syntax. The reason for this can be seen in the example in Fig. 1. Again assume that we define the symbolic equivalence class, $Expr \Leftrightarrow Term\ Factor\ Primary$. Now consider the case in which we have a rule from P' that needs to be included in P and that has $Expr$ on its right hand side. we would have to generate four instances of this rule in the concrete syntax, one for each member of the symbolic equivalence class. Doing so would make the grammar ambiguous.

5 Implementation

Maptool is described by a set of specifications. Eli uses these specifications to produce a C program, which can be compiled and executed independent of Eli. The generated program takes as input a BNF grammar specifying the concrete syntax fragment, an attribute grammar specifying the abstract syntax fragment, and a mapping specification written in a language designed for Maptool.

Given these inputs, Maptool yields a complete concrete syntax annotated with reduction actions that build the appropriate abstract syntax tree using the tree construction module exported by the LIGA attribute grammar evaluator [8]. It also produces a complete abstract syntax in notation usable as input to LIGA.

An interesting part of the Maptool implementation is its use of OIL, an operator identification library available in the Eli system. Operator identification is a well understood process, first discussed by Aho and Johnson in 1976 [1, 10]. The signatures of abstract productions can quite easily be cast as operators, chain rules are represented by coercions, and the signature of the concrete syntax rules are analogous to expressions whose operators must be determined. A cost value of 1 is associated with each coercion so that the mapping requiring the fewest chain productions is chosen.

Maptool has been a component of the Eli system for over a year and has been successful in supporting the development of modular specifications in concert with the support for modularity afforded by the LIGA evaluator [7].

6 Acknowledgments

We would like to thank the members of the Eli team, with special thanks to Dr. Uwe Kastens, for their numerous contributions to this research.

This work was partially supported by the US Army Research Office under grant DAAL03-92-G-0158.

References

1. Alfred V. Aho and Stephen C. Johnson. Optimal code generation for expression trees. *Journal of the ACM*, 23(3):488–501, July 1976.

2. Ali Bahrami. CAGT – an automated approach to abstract and parsing grammars. Master's thesis, Department of Electrical and Computer Engineering, University of Colorado, Boulder, CO, 1986.

3. Robert A. Ballance, Jacob Butcher, and Susan L. Graham. Grammatical abstraction and incremental syntax analysis in a language-based editor. In *Proceedings of the SIGPLAN '88 Conference on Programming Language Design and Implementation*, pages 185–198. SIGPLAN, ACM, June 1988.

4. Franklin L. DeRemer. *Compiler Construction; An Advanced Course*, chapter 2.E., pages 121–145. Springer-Verlag, New York, Heidelberg, Berlin, second edition, 1976.

5. Franklin L. DeRemer. *Compiler Construction; An Advanced Course*, chapter 2.A., pages 37–56. Springer-Verlag, New York, Heidelberg, Berlin, second edition, 1976.

6. Robert W. Gray, Vincent P. Heuring, Steve P. Levi, Anthony M. Sloane, and William M. Waite. Eli: A complete, flexible compiler construction system. *Communications of the ACM*, 35(2):121–131, February 1992.

7. U. Kastens and W. M. Waite. Modularity and reusability in attribute grammars. *Acta Informatica*, 31:601–627, 1994.

8. Uwe Kastens. LIGA: A language independent generator for attribute evaluators. Technical Report Reihe Informatik 63, Universität-GH Paderborn, Fachbereich Mathematik-Informatik, 1989.

9. Anton Nijholt. *Context-Free Grammars: Covers, Normal Forms, and Parsing*, volume 93 of *Lecture Notes in Computer Science*. Springer-Verlag, Berlin, Heidelberg, New York, 1980.

10. Guido Persch, Georg Winterstein, Manfred Dausmann, and Sophia Drossopoulou. Overloading in preliminary Ada. *SIGPLAN Notices*, 15(11):47–56, November 1980.

11. D. J. Rosenkrantz and H. B. Hunt. Efficient algorithms for automatic construction and compactification of parsing grammars. *Transactions on Programming Languages and Systems*, 9(4):543–566, October 1987.

12. William M. Waite and Gerhard Goos. *Compiler Construction*. Texts and Monographs in Computer Science. Springer-Verlag, New York, Berlin, Heidelberg, Tokyo, 1984.

A Faster Earley Parser

Philippe McLean & R. Nigel Horspool

Dept. of Computer Science, University of Victoria
Victoria, BC, Canada V8W 3P6
E-mail: pmclean@csc.uvic.ca, nigelh@csc.uvic.ca

Abstract. We present a parsing technique which is a hybrid of Earley's method and the LR(k) methods. The new method retains the ability of Earley's method to parse using arbitrary context-free grammars. However, by using precomputed LR(k) sets of items, we obtain much faster recognition speeds while also reducing memory requirements.

1 Introduction

The parsing method invented by Earley [2,4] is a highly practical parsing technique for general context-free grammars (CFGs). If n is the length of the input to be recognized, the parser requires time proportional to n^3 to recognize arbitrary context-free languages, n^2 for unambiguous languages, and n for a large class of languages.

The amount of processing performed while recognizing an input string is large compared to table-driven techniques such as the LR parser family, which includes the LR(0), SLR(1), LALR(1) and LR(1) methods. These LR methods, however, cannot accept arbitrary CFGs. They are limited to subsets of unambiguous grammars. In general, the LR parsing table constructed for an arbitrary CFG will contain conflicts. That is, one or more states will provide a choice of actions to perform for some inputs.

A parsing method due to Tomita [6,4] overcomes the limitations of the LR methods. It uses LR tables that may contain conflicts. Whenever the parser encounters a choice of parsing actions, it in effect clones new copies of itself to track each of the conflicting actions simultaneously. Some copies of the parser may subsequently reach a state where parsing cannot proceed (i.e. the input symbol is invalid for that state) and these copies of the parsers simply terminate execution. In practice, the Tomita parser simulates parallel execution of multiple copies of a LR parser, and it uses a DAG data structure to reduce the storage needed by all the parse stacks. A Tomita parser is particularly efficient when few conflicts are encountered in the LR states.

If all we need to do is recognize the input, a Tomita parser would likely be the method of choice. However, we will usually wish to execute semantic actions while precisely *one* of the parses is being performed. This is not so easy for a Tomita parser because many parses are being performed in parallel. One possible solution is for each copy of the LR parser to construct a parse tree. At the end of the input, we can traverse one of these parse trees to perform the desired semantic actions. We consider that the computational work of building the parse trees negates the advantage of Tomita's method.

The Earley parser builds a data structure, a threaded sequence of states, which represents all possible parses of the input. After the input has been processed, it is straightforward to traverse the sequence of states to build a parse tree for one possible parse of the input, or to execute semantic actions for just the one parse.

We have developed a variation on Earley's method which, like Tomita's method, uses LR parse tables for efficiency, while retaining the advantage of permitting semantic actions to be easily associated with the grammar. The LR tables, in effect, capture precomputations of all the run-time actions performed by an Earley parser. Our parsing method, which we call LRE(k), uses information from the LR tables and therefore avoids recomputing this information at run-time. The name LRE(k) reflects the fact that our method can be viewed as a combination of LR(k) parsing with Earley parsing.

2 Terminology and Notation

2.1 Context-Free Grammars

A context free grammar G is a four-tuple $\langle V_T, V_N, P, Start \rangle$ where V_T is a set of terminal symbols, V_N is a set of nonterminal symbols, $V_N \cap V_T = \varnothing$, P is a set of productions, and $Start \in V_N$ is the start symbol or goal symbol of the grammar. The vocabulary $V = V_N \cup V_T$.

An augmented grammar G' is formed from G by adding a special goal rule

$$G' = \langle V_T \cup \{ \dashv \}, V_N \cup \{ S' \}, P \cup \{ Start' \rightarrow \vdash Start \dashv \}, Start' \rangle.$$

where the tokens $\vdash$ and $\dashv$ are delimiters that represent the beginning and end of input.

Lower-case letters near the front of the alphabet (i.e. a, b, c ...) represent elements of V_T, upper-case letters near the front of the alphabet (i.e. A, B, C ...) represent elements of V_N, and upper-case letters near the end of the alphabet (i.e. X, Y, Z) represent elements of V. A superscript represents repetitions of a symbol, so that, for example, a^3 represents the string aaa. Greek letters α, β, ... represent sequences of zero or more vocabulary symbols.

2.2 LR(k) Recognizers

An *item* is a production which contains a marker, written as a dot, to indicate how much of the right-hand side (RHS) has been recognized. Associated with each item is a string of k symbols ($k \geq 0$). The string represents lookahead or right context for the production. For example, if k is 2, a possible item is [A $\rightarrow$ a b • B c, dd]. This item indicates that we have matched the first two symbols on the right-hand side of the rule A $\rightarrow$ a b B c. If the complete RHS is successfully matched, then the next two symbols in the input should be dd for this production to be valid in a parse of the input at this point.

We use S to denote the set of LR(k) sets of items for the augmented grammar G'. Each element of S corresponds to a state in the LR(k) recognizer for G'. The recognizer has an initial state

$$I_{initial} = \{ \, [\, Start' \rightarrow \bullet \vdash Start \dashv, \dashv^k \,] \, \} \in S,$$

and it has an accept state

$$I_{accept} = \{ \, [\, Start' \rightarrow \vdash Start \dashv \bullet, \dashv^k \,] \, \} \in S.$$

The transition function between the recognizer's states is

goto : $S \times V \rightarrow S \cup \{\varnothing\}$

The function $goto(I, x)$ is defined as the set of all items $[\, A \rightarrow \alpha \, x \bullet \beta, t_1 \ldots t_k \,]$ such that $[\, A \rightarrow \alpha \bullet x \, \beta, t_1 \ldots t_k \,] \in I$. If the set $goto(I,x)$ is an empty set, the transition is illegal. (I.e., the string $x \, t_1 \ldots t_k$ cannot follow the symbols that have been accepted so far in a syntactically valid input.)

The closure of an itemset I is defined as the least set J such that $I \subseteq J$, and $[\, A \rightarrow \alpha \bullet B \, \beta, t_1 \ldots t_k \,] \in J$ implies that $\forall \eta \, (\eta \in first_k(\beta, t_1 \ldots t_k))$: $\{ \, [\, B \rightarrow \bullet \, \gamma, \eta] \, | \, B \rightarrow \gamma \in P \, \} \subseteq J$.

The function $first_k(\beta, \gamma) \equiv_{def} \{ \, prefix_k(\sigma) \, | \, \beta\gamma \Rightarrow^* \sigma, \, \sigma \in V_T^* \, \}$, where $prefix_k(\sigma)$ is the k-symbol prefix of σ.

The set of items for each state may be partitioned into kernel items and non-kernel items. The former are those items which are not added to a state by closure, while the latter (also called completion items) are those which are added to a state by closure.

3   Conventional Earley Recognizers

A conventional Earley recognizer has two inputs: a context-free grammar G and a token string $x_1 \, x_2 \ldots x_n$, and determines if the string may be derived by G. For simplicity, lookahead will not be considered in this discussion $(k = 0)$.

The recognizer constructs a sequence $E_1, E_2 \ldots, E_{n+1}$, of sets of tuples. Each tuple has the form $<i, p>$ where i is an item $[\, A \rightarrow \alpha \bullet \beta \,]$ and p is an integer referring to the parent Earley set E_p where the tuple containing the item with the marker at the beginning of the RHS was introduced. The k-th set is formed as a result of recognizing the first k-1 input tokens.

Tuples in a state may be partitioned into active and predicted tuples. Active tuples may be introduced in two ways: by a *SCANNER* operation, and by a *COMPLETER* operation. The SCANNER operation introduces tuples from the previous state where the marker appears before the current input token; the marker is advanced past that token in the new item. This is the process of matching terminal tokens in a production's RHS, and corresponds to a shift operation in an LR parser. The COMPLETER operation identifies each tuple where an item's marker is at the end of a RHS, and moves the marker past the LHS in items in the tuple's parent state. This operation identifies the derivation of a non-terminal, in the recognition of some RHS; an LR parser would perform a reduction in exactly this case.

The COMPLETER operation introduces new tuples for every item where the marker appears before a non-terminal. This operation begins the recognition of possible derivations for a non-terminal; it is the closure of a set of items. Closure is performed at parse time in a conventional Earley parser. However these closure items are implicit in the LR(k) recognizer.

Earley's doctoral dissertation [3] contains a proof of correctness for a conventional Earley recognizer, and an analysis of its algorithmic complexity. Parse trees may be enumerated for all derivations of the input string by examining the sets E_i, $1 \leq i \leq n+1$.

The conventional recognizer affords a simple implementation. However, observation of the parser's actions reveals that the parser spends much of its time introducing new items during the completion operation. Many prediction items may not be used during the parse. The computation of item-set closures, a grammar-dependent operation, is performed at parse time. It is natural to wonder whether the Earley items can be grouped in a manner that exploits pre-computed properties of the grammar. Our solution is to group items into sets in exactly the same way as in the states of a deterministic (and possibly inadequate) LR(k) finite-state automaton.

4   LRE – A Faster Earley Recognizer

The new parsing method is named LRE(k); this represents the hybrid nature of the algorithm as a composition of the LR(k) and Earley parsing methods.

In the following description, we use $x_1 \, x_2 \, ... \, x_n$ to represent the input to the recognizer. So that lookahead sets are properly defined, we assume that the input is terminated by k end-of-file delimiters. I.e., $x_{n+i} = \dashv$, for $1 \leq i \leq k$.

Our algorithm is based on a conventional Earley parser and its correct operation may be established by comparing its actions to an Earley parser's actions. A conventional Earley parser uses items of the form $[A \rightarrow \alpha \bullet \beta, t_1 \, ... \, t_k, p]$, where $A \rightarrow \alpha \bullet \beta$ is a marked production, $t_1 \, ... \, t_k$ is the lookahead for the item, and p is a reference back to the state where recognition of the rule $A \rightarrow \alpha \beta$ commenced. Our algorithm takes advantage of the fact that the first two components of the Earley item represent an item in one or more states of the LR(k) recognizer. We therefore implement states in our LRE parser in terms of states in the LR(k) recognizer. The advantages of our representation are (1) we can use the LR(k) recognizer's tables to determine actions for the Earley parser, (2) the lookahead strings are not computed dynamically, and (3) the new representation can be implemented in a manner which uses much less storage.

A state in our LRE recognizer will be called an *Earley state*, and will be written as E_m. State E_m is reached after recognizing the token string $x_1 \, x_2 \, ... \, x_{m-1}$. The state E_m is represented by a set of tuples $\{ \, \langle I_1, B_1 \rangle, \langle I_2, B_2 \rangle, \, ... \, \}$ where each $I_i \in S$ is the number of some state in the LR(k) recognizer and B_i is an organized collection of back-pointers to Earley states. In programming terms, each B_i could be implemented as an array of lists of LRE state numbers, where elements in the array are in one-to-one correspondence with items in LR(k) state I_i. In more formal terms, we can represent B_i as a list of list of integers $[\, [b_{i\,1\,1}, b_{i\,1\,2}, b_{i\,1\,3} \,...], [b_{i\,2\,1}, b_{i\,2\,2}, ...], \, ... \, [b_{i\,n\,1}, b_{i\,n\,2}, ...] \,]$ where each $b_{i\,x\,y}$ is an integer in the range 0 to k inclusive, and LR(k) state I has n items.

As an example, suppose that LRE state E_3 has the following representation:
$$\{ \, \langle 17, [\, [1,2], [3], [3] \,] \, \rangle, \langle 23, [\, [2] \,] \rangle \, \}$$
This would mean that state E_3 represents a mixture of the same items as found in the LR(k) states numbered 17 and 23. State 17 must have three items (the length of the list that completes the tuple with state number 17) – let us suppose that these items are:

$$A \to A \cdot B C \qquad \alpha_1$$
$$X \to a A \cdot D \qquad \alpha_2$$
$$A \to \cdot b \qquad \alpha_3$$

where we have written the lookahead strings as α_1, α_2 and α_3 respectively. Similarly, LR(k) state 23 must have just one item and let us suppose that this item is

$$C \to a b \cdot b \qquad \beta_1$$

Now, our LRE state represents an Earley state which contains exactly these items:

$$\{ \langle A \to A \cdot B C, \alpha_1, 1 \rangle, \langle A \to A \cdot B C, \alpha_1, 2 \rangle, \langle X \to a A \cdot D, \alpha_2, 3 \rangle,$$
$$\langle A \to \cdot b, \alpha_3, 3 \rangle, \langle C \to a b \cdot b, \beta_1, 2 \rangle \}$$

The first tuple in E_3 represents two copies of the first item of LR state 17, where one copy is associated with a pointer back to state 1 and the other with a pointer back to state 2. And similarly for the other items in LR states 17 and 23.

Our parsing algorithm is based on Earley's, but it has been modified to work with the different state representation. It has two main functions named SCAN and RECOGNIZER.

Given a LRE state E_s, the function SCAN(E_s, X, t) constructs a new LRE state which represents Earley items where the marker has been past the token X in all applicable Earley items represented in set E_s.

The procedure RECOGNIZER(x_1, ..., x_n, ..., x_{n+k}) determines whether the token string $x_1 \ldots x_n$ is in the language generated by G. Note that each of the symbols x_{n+1}, $x_{n+2} \ldots x_{n+k}$ is the symbol ⊣. These extra k symbols are needed to provide right context for the final reductions in the parse. RECOGNIZER constructs a sequence of Earley states, from which a set of valid parse trees may be enumerated. Code for the SCAN function is shown in Figure 1, while code for the RECOGNIZER is given in Figure 2.

The code uses the data structures and tables explained below. The tables may be created during the LR(k) parser construction algorithm.

- Each LRE state is represented by a set whose elements are structures with two fields. One field is named `State` and holds a state number for the LR(k) recognizer. The other field is named `BackPtrs` and is an array of lists of integers. An element `BackPtrs[i]` holds the state numbers that should be associated with the i-th item of LR(k) state with number `State`.
- The array `NumberOfItems[i]` gives the number of items in LR(k) state i.
- The array `SHIFT[s,x]` holds the shift actions for the LR(k) recognizer. If the current LR(k) state is numbered s, then `SHIFT[s,x]` gives the number of the destination state to shift on symbol x. If a valid shift action is not defined for symbol x, `SHIFT[s,x]` holds -1.
- The array `DestItemPosition[m,i]` gives the correspondence between items in one LR(k) state and those in another LR(k) state. In particular, if item i in the LR(k) state numbered m is $A \to \alpha \cdot X \beta$, then a shift on the symbol X will lead to a unique destination LR(k) state that contains the item $A \to \alpha X \cdot \beta$. The number held in `DestItemPosition[m,i]` is the number of this item in the destination state. If item i in state m does not have the specified form (i.e. the marker is at the end of the right-hand side), we assume that `DestItemPosition[m,i]` holds the value -1.

```
function SCAN(Eₛ, X, t)
begin
    result := ∅;
    for origin := each tuple in Eₛ do
    begin
        dest := Shift[origin.State,X];
        if dest ≥ 0 then
        begin
            newTuple := < dest, emptyBackPtrArray >;
            (* process kernel items of new state *)
            for i := 1 to NumberOfItems[origin] do
            begin
                j := DestItemPosition[origin,i];
                if j ≥ 0 then
                    newTuple.BackPtrs[j]:= origin.BackPtrs[i]
            end;
            (* process non-kernel items of new state *)
            for j := 1 to NumberOfItems[dest] do
            begin
                if newTuple.BackPtrs[j] = empty then
                    newTuple.BackPtrs[j] := [t]
            end;
            result := MERGE1(result, newTuple)
        end
    end;
    return result
end SCAN;


(* MERGE1 is an auxiliary function called by SCAN *)
function MERGE1( L, T )
begin
    for elem := each element of L do
        if elem.State = T.State then
        begin
            for i := each index of elem.BackPtrs do
                elem.BackPtrs[i] := elem.BackPtrs[i] ∪
                                        T.BackPtrs[i];
            return L;
        end;
    return L ∪ { T };
end MERGE1;
```

Fig. 1. The SCAN Function

```
function RECOGNIZER( x₁ ... xₙ₊ₖ )
begin
    E₀ := { < I_initial, [[0]] > };
    E₁ := SCAN(E₀, ⊢, 1);
    for i = 1 to n do
    begin
        E_{i+1} := SCAN(E_i, x_i, i+1);
        repeat
            for LS := each element in E_{i+1} do
            begin
                (* process reduce items *)
                rs := ReduceItemList(LS.State, x_{i+1}x_{i+2}...x_{i+k});
                for i := each element in rs do
                begin
                    lhs := LeftHandSymbol[LS.State,i];
                    for j := each element in
                                    LS.BackPtrs[i] do
                        E_{i+1} := MERGE(E_{i+1}, SCAN(E_j,lhs,i+1));
                end
            end
        until E_{i+1} does not change;
        if E_{i+1} = ∅ then return failure;
    end
    if E_{n+1} = { < I_accept, [[0]] > } then
        return success
    else
        return failure
end RECOGNIZER;


(* MERGE is an auxiliary function used above *)
function MERGE( E1, E2 )
begin
    result := E1;
    for elem := each element in E2 do
        result := MERGE1(result, elem);
    return result;
end MERGE;
```

Fig. 2. The RECOGNIZER Function

- The array `ReduceItemList[m, α]` is a list of the positions of all items in LR(k) state m where the marker is at the end of the right-hand side and where the lookahead string for these items is $α$.
- The array `LeftHandSymbol[m, i]` gives the symbol which appears on the left-hand side of the i-th item in LR(k) state m.

5 An Example of Operation

To illustrate the operation of the LRE(k) parsing method, we use the ambiguous grammar:

1. E → E + E
2. E → n

This grammar is augmented by the extra rule

0. S → ⊢ E ⊣

For simplicity, we choose $k = 0$. From this grammar, we can derive the LR(0) recognizer which has the states and actions shown below in Table 1. Each shift action is preceded by the symbol which selects that shift action. Because a LR(0) parser does not use lookahead, a reduce action is performed no matter what the next symbol is. The word *any* represents the fact that any symbol selects the specified reduce action. The table contains conflicts, in particular note that state 7 implicitly contains two different actions for the case when the lookahead symbol is +.

Table 1: LR(0) Recognizer for the Example Grammar

State	Item No.	Item	Parse Actions	
1	1	[S → • ⊢ E ⊣]	⊢	Shift 2
2	1	[S → ⊢ • E ⊣]	E	Shift 3
	2	[E → • E + E]	n	Shift 4
	3	[E → • n]		
3	1	[S → ⊢ E • ⊣]	+	Shift 6
	2	[E → E • + E]	⊣	Shift 5
4	1	[E → n •]	*any*	Reduce 2
5	1	[S → ⊢ E ⊣ •]	*any*	Reduce 0
6	1	[E → E + • E]	E	Shift 7
	2	[E → • E + E]	n	Shift 4
	3	[E → • n]		
7	1	[E → E + E •]	+	Shift 6
	2	[E → E • + E]	*any*	Reduce 1

From that LR(0) table we derive the tables shown below in Figure 3. Only the significant entries in the two rectangular arrays, DestItemPosition and LeftHandSymbol are shown (the missing elements in these arrays should never be accessed). Similarly, only the significant entries in the Shift array are shown; if any other element is accessed the result should be -1.

Fig. 3. Tables Used In Parser Example

State	Item No.	DestItem Position	LeftHand Symbol
1	1	1	S
2	1	1	S
2	2	2	E
2	3	1	E
3	1	1	S
3	2	1	E
4	1	-1	E
5	1	-1	S
6	1	1	E
6	2	2	E
6	3	1	E
7	1	-1	E
7	2	1	E

State	Number Of Items	Reduce-ItemList
1	1	[]
2	3	[]
3	2	[]
4	1	[1]
5	1	[1]
6	3	[]
7	2	[1]

State	Symbol	Shift
1	⊢	2
2	E	3
2	n	4
3	+	6
3	⊣	5
6	E	7
6	n	4
7	+	6

We now trace the states of the LRE(0) parser on the input string n+n+n. The RECOGNIZER function begins by initializing the set E_0 with the initial LRE state $\{\langle 1,[0] \rangle\}$. It represents item 1 of state 1 in the LR(0) recognizer – indicating that the RHS of the rule S→ ⊢ E ⊣ is to be recognized.

Each numbered step in our trace corresponds to the processing of one input symbol, and begins by showing the LRE state that is computed after seeing that input symbol. An explanation of the state's derivation is provided for the first few steps only.

=== The start of input symbol ⊢ is processed ===

1. $E_1 = \{ \langle 2,[[0], [1], [1]] \rangle \}$. RECOGNIZER called SCAN(E_0, ⊢, 1), which looked

up the action for LR(0) state 1 when the input is ⊢. Thus it created the LRE item $\langle 2, [\ [], [], []] \rangle$ and then it filled in the back pointers. The list [0] was copied from the origin item, while the two lists containing [1] correspond to completion items.

=== The first input symbol n is now processed ===

2. $E_2 = \{\ \langle 4, [\ [1]] \rangle, \langle 3, [\ [0], [1]] \rangle\ \}$. RECOGNIZER called SCAN(E_1, n, 2). The $\langle 4, [\ [1]] \rangle$ element is created because of the LR(0) action for state 2 when the lookahead symbol is n. The other items are created by RECOGNIZER because item 1 in LR(0) state 4 is a reduce item, and the reduce action is triggered by the next input symbol which is +. The LHS symbol for that item is E, and RECOG-NIZER called SCAN(E_1, E, 1) to create the two extra items.

=== The second input symbol + is processed ===

3. $E_3 = \{\ \langle 6, [\ [1], [3], [3]] \rangle\ \}$.

=== The input symbol n is processed ===

4. $E_4 = \{\ \langle 4, [\ [3]] \rangle, \langle 7, [\ [1], [3]] \rangle, \langle 3, [\ [0], [1]] \rangle\ \}$.

=== The input symbol + is processed ===

5. $E_5 = \{\ \langle 6, [\ [1,3], [5], [5]] \rangle\ \}$.

=== The input symbol n is processed ===

6. $E_6 = \{\ \langle 4, [\ [5]] \rangle, \langle 7, [\ [1,3], [3,5]] \rangle, \langle 3, [\ [0], [1]] \rangle\ \}$.

=== The end-of-input symbol ⊣ is processed ===

7. $E_7 = \{\ \langle 5, [0] \rangle\ \}$.

6   An Additional Enhancement

The algorithm presented above can be further improved. The implementation used in our experiments does not immediately record non-kernel items in a LRE state (except when handling productions with an empty RHS). Their processing is deferred until scanning to the next state occurs. By recording the number of kernel items in each LR(k) state, and by consulting the DestItemPosition table, it can be determined whether or not a particular item in a destination state came from a kernel item in the source state. If it did, the BackPtr list is copied from the previous state. If it did not, the list [t-1] is supplied, where t is the number of the current LRE state.

The additional improvement achieves significant space and time savings, because many predictions items in an Earley parser are fruitless

7   Experimental Results

Lookahead significantly affects the speed of an Earley parser. In general, it is used to eliminate items from the sets of items maintained by the parser. Fewer items imply that fewer fruitless parsing possibilities are explored. On the other hand, a conventional

Earley parser computes the lookahead contexts for items at run-time, and choosing a large value for the lookahead k will waste execution time. In Figure 4, we compare the speed of a conventional Earley parser and our LRE parsing method for $k=0$ and $k=1$.

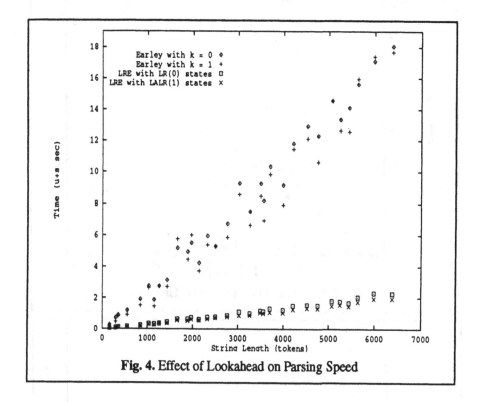

Fig. 4. Effect of Lookahead on Parsing Speed

Figure 4 already demonstrates that LRE(k) is a much faster parsing method than the conventional Earley parsing method. In Figure 5, we show an additional comparison against a parser generated by the freely distributed parser generator *bison* [1]. (Other measurements, not displayed here, reveal that a parser generated by *yacc* [5] yields very similar results.) Our grammar for these experiments was Roskind's ANSI C grammar. The grammar contains one ambiguity, namely the dangling *else* problem. This ambiguity is automatically eliminated from the generated parser when *yacc* and *bison* are used; it is retained by the Earley parsers.

For an unambiguous grammar (or when the ambiguities have been eliminated, such as with the *bison*'s interpretation of the Roskind C grammar), recognition time is proportional to the length of the input. For an ambiguous grammar, the recognition time may increase as the cube of the length of the input. Figure 6 shows timing measurements when parsing with the ambiguous grammar:

$$S \rightarrow S\ S\ |\ a,$$

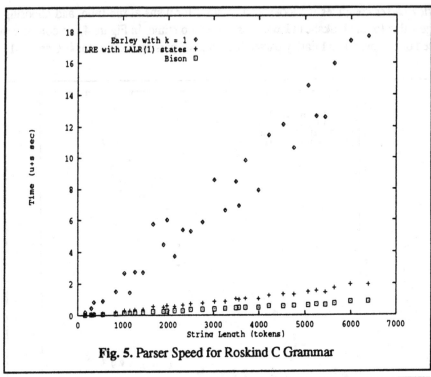

Fig. 5. Parser Speed for Roskind C Grammar

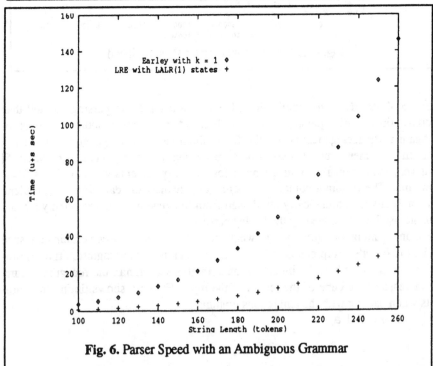

Fig. 6. Parser Speed with an Ambiguous Grammar

8 Conclusions

We have modified Earley's parsing method so that it can take advantage of precomputed LR(k) sets of items. The result is a hybrid parsing method, LRE(k), which can still handle general context-free grammars but which is comparable in speed to a *yacc*-generated or *bison*-generated parser. However, *yacc* and *bison* can, of course, only recognize unambiguous languages that are based on LALR(1) grammars with conflict elimination in the generated parser. The LRE(k) parsing method is 10 to 15 times faster than a conventional Earley parser, while requiring less than half the storage.

Acknowledgements

Funding for this research was provided by the Natural Sciences and Engineering Research Council of Canada in the form of a summer fellowship for the first author and a research grant for the second author. The initial motivation for working on this problem is due to Gordon Cormack.

References

1. Donnelly, C., and Stallman, R. *BISON: Reference Manual*. Free Software Foundation, Cambridge, MA, 1992 .
2. Earley, J. *An Efficient Context-Free Parsing Algorithm*. Comm. ACM **13**, **2** (Feb. 1970), 94-102.
3. Earley, J. *An Efficient Context-Free Parsing Algorithm*. Ph.D. Thesis, Carnegie-Mellon University, 1968.
4. Grune, D., and Jacob, C.J.H. *Parsing Techniques: a practical guide*. Ellis Horwood, Chichester, 1990.
5. Johnson, S.C. *YACC: Yet Another Compiler-Compiler*. UNIX Programmer's Supplementary Documents, vol 1, 1986.
6. Tomita, M. *Efficient Parsing for Natural Language*. Kluwer Academic Publishers, Boston, 1986.

One-Pass, Optimal Tree Parsing — With Or Without Trees

Todd A. Proebsting   Benjamin R. Whaley

Department of Computer Science
University of Arizona
Tucson, AZ 85721 USA
{todd,bwhaley}@cs.arizona.edu

Abstract

This paper describes the theory behind and implementation of wburg, a code-generator generator that accepts tree grammars as input and produces a code generator that emits an optimal parse of an IR tree in just a single bottom-up pass. Furthermore, wburg eliminates the need for an explicit IR tree altogether. The grammars that wburg-generated parsers can parse are a proper subset of those that two-pass systems can handle. However, analysis indicates that wburg can optimally handle grammars for most instruction sets (e.g., SPARC, MIPS R3000, and x86).

1 Introduction

Compilers often use intermediate representation (IR) trees to represent expressions. A compiler's front end generates an IR tree, and the back end walks the tree, emitting appropriate assembly language instructions and operands.

Several automatically generated code generators perform pattern matching on IR trees to emit optimal code. The code-generator generator consumes a cost-augmented tree grammar with associated semantic actions. The resulting code generator requires two passes over the IR tree to determine a least-cost parse and to execute the associated semantic actions. Code-generator generators based on this model include BEG [ESL89], twig [AGT89], burg [FHP92b, Pro92], iburg [FHP92a], and lburg [FH95].

This paper describes the theory behind and implementation of wburg, a code-generator generator that accepts tree grammars as input and produces a code generator that emits an optimal parse of an IR tree in just a single bottom-up pass. Furthermore, wburg eliminates the need for an explicit IR tree altogether. The generated parser emits optimal code, and can do so without retaining an entire IR tree during its single pass. The grammars that wburg-generated parsers can parse are a proper subset of those that the two-pass systems can handle. However, analysis indicates that wburg can optimally handle grammars for most major instruction sets, including the SPARC, the MIPS R3000, and the x86.

Our system has the advantage of not requiring a dynamically allocated IR tree, but sometimes suffers from its small amount of additional bookkeeping. Preliminary experiments indicate that wburg's one-pass parsers run over 30% faster than two-pass burg-generated parsers that use malloc and free. Even when the overhead of dynamic allocation is completely factored out, the one-pass parsers ranged from over 50% *faster* to 3% slower than burg's parsers.

2 Related Work

Many code-generator generators use cost-augmented instruction patterns to produce code generators that optimally parse IR trees. The resulting code generator uses tree pattern matching and dynamic programming to find least-cost instruction sequences for realizing the given IR tree's computations. The various code-generator generators differ in the pattern-matching technology they use, and in when they perform dynamic programming. Pattern-matching techniques vary widely in theoretical efficiency [HO82]. Previous code generators have employed many of these pattern-matching technologies, ranging from the slowest, naive [ESL89, FHP92a, FH95], to top-down [AGT89], to the fastest, bottom-up [FHP92b, Pro92, BDB90, PLG88]. Most systems perform dynamic programming at compile-time [ESL89, AGT89, FHP92a, FH95]; those based on bottom-up rewrite system (BURS) technology do all dynamic programming at compile-compile time [FHP92b, Pro92, BDB90, PLG88].

Previous tree-pattern matching systems required two passes over the IR tree: one for labeling the tree with dynamic programming information, and another for selecting the least-cost parse based on that information. To enable two tree walks, this design requires allocating and building an explicit IR tree. In contrast, wburg's parsers can find an optimal parse in a single pass. Surprisingly, an explicit IR tree is not needed at all. The procedure invocations necessary to build a tree in a bottom-up fashion form a trace of the tree's structure — much like a recursive-descent parser traces out a parse tree — which is all that is necessary for our system to produce optimal code.

The Oberon compiler's code generator works in a single pass without the benefit of an explicit IR tree [WG92]. In order to generate complex addressing modes, the code generator retains a constant amount of information to guide subsequent instruction selection decisions. wburg's parsers must also retain a constant amount of information for subsequent decisions. Oberon's code generator, however, does not generate optimal code for all expressions, and is not automatically generated.

3 burg Automata

burg is a code-generator generator that accepts a cost-augmented tree grammar as input and automatically produces a tree-parser that gives an optimal parse of an IR tree using a two-pass algorithm [FHP92b]. burg does all dynamic programming at compile-compile time and creates a state machine for guiding

```
stmt: ASGN(addr, reg)    = 1 (1);
addr: ADD(reg, con)      = 2 (0);
addr: reg                = 3 (0);
reg:  ADD(reg, con)      = 4 (1);
reg:  con                = 5 (1);
con:  CONST              = 6 (0);
```

Figure 1: A burg-Style Grammar, G

all subsequent pattern matching and instruction selection decisions. Rules in a burg grammar have the form

nonterminal : *rule* = *rule_number* (*cost*);

Consider the burg grammar, G, in Figure 1. The fourth rule specifies that the result of adding an immediate value to a value held in a register can be placed in a register at the cost of one. The second rule in Figure 1 corresponds to the "register-offset" addressing mode supported by many architectures, which is free. A burg grammar describes the operations and addressing modes of a particular architecture. Rules in a burg grammar have one of two forms. A *chain rule* has only a single nonterminal on its right-hand side, while a *base rule* always has a terminal (operator) on its right-hand side. In Figure 1, rules 3 and 5 are the only chain rules.

We restrict our analysis to grammars in *normal form* [BDB90]. A grammar is in normal form if all patterns are either chain rules, or base rules of the form $n_0 \rightarrow \theta(n_1, \ldots, n_k)$ where n_i are all nonterminals, θ is an operator, and k is the arity of θ. Normal-form grammars are no less expressive than other tree grammars, and this restriction greatly simplifies our discussion. We also restrict our discussion to binary, unary, and leaf operators.

Parsers produced by burg use a two-pass algorithm to give an optimal (least-cost) parse of a tree. The first, bottom-up pass over the tree *labels* each node with a state. A state encodes, for each nonterminal in the grammar, the rule to apply at the current node to derive that nonterminal at least cost. (The burg states and transition function implicitly encode the cost of each rule, and therefore explicit cost comparisons are avoided completely at compile-time — this is one of burg's major advantages.) The second, top-down pass finds the least-cost parse based on those states. This second pass *reduces* the tree by applying the appropriate rules at nodes in the tree.

Figure 2 shows the set of burg-generated states for grammar G (Figure 1). State 1 encodes the fact that an ADD node labeled with state 1 is reduced to an addr nonterminal using rule 2 and to a reg using rule 4. State 3 represents the label for all CONST nodes. CONST nodes are reduced directly to a con nonterminal via rule 6, but require the application of chain rules for addr and reg nonterminal reductions. Note that reducing a CONST node to an addr would require two

State 1	*Nonterminal*	*Rule*	*#*
(op = ADD)	stmt	(none)	
	addr	addr : ADD(reg, con)	= 2
	reg	reg : ADD(reg, con)	= 4
	con	(none)	

State 2	*Nonterminal*	*Rule*	*#*
(op = ASGN)	stmt	stmt: ASGN(addr, reg)	= 1
	addr	(none)	
	reg	(none)	
	con	(none)	

State 3	*Nonterminal*	*Rule*	*#*
(op = CONST)	stmt	(none)	
	addr	addr: reg	= 3
	reg	reg: con	= 5
	con	con: CONST	= 6

Figure 2: The burg States for G

chain rule applications (rules 3 and 5) followed by the base rule 6. Also note that there is not necessarily a 1 : 1 correspondence between between states and operators; more than one state corresponding to a particular operator may exist. All reductions at a state follow this pattern of zero or more chain rules followed by exactly one base rule. (Bottom-up reductions would reverse that order.) The application of a base rule at a node with children will cause those children to be reduced to the nonterminals on the right-hand side of the base rule.

4 One-Pass Tree Parsers

A two-pass system defers all reduction decisions until labeling is complete. Because every node in the tree contains a label, an unbounded amount of information must be retained prior to starting the reduction process. If reductions could be done during the bottom-up labeling pass, any subtree that is reduced could be discarded since reduction is the last phase of pattern matching. The labeler would only retain unreduced subtrees until they could be reduced.

(Note: Reducers normally apply rules in a top-down order, but the semantic actions associated with those rules typically are applied in bottom-up order — the order in which code is emitted. From this point forward, we will assume that reducers reduce trees bottom-up.)

For some states, optimal reductions can be made during the bottom-up labeling pass. Because rule 1 is the only rule in state 2, it must be used to reduce any node labeled with state 2. Therefore, the labeling pass can *immediately* apply rule 1 to any node it labels with state 2. wburg creates an array, *reduce_now[ ]*, that is indexed by state numbers. Whenever a state contains only one base rule,

state	1	2	3
nonterminal	$\perp$	stmt	con

Figure 3: Array *reduce_now* for Grammar G

wburg places the appropriate nonterminal (the nonterminal appearing on the left-hand side of that base rule) into the table.

Reducing a node via a base rule will cause all descendents of that node to be reduced, and thus no longer needed. Although not true for state 2, applying a base rule does *not* always completely reduce the given node. Subsequent reductions of ancestor nodes may require the application of chain rules at this node in order to derive a nonterminal other than the left-hand side of the base rule. Therefore, the node itself must be retained for the possible chain-rule applications later.

Now consider state 1, which contains two base rules, 2 and 4. The labeler cannot immediately determine the appropriate reduction when it reaches such a node. Therefore, wburg must mark state 2's entry in *reduce_now[ ]* as unknown ($\perp$). Figure 3 gives *reduce_now[ ]* for grammar G. Formally,

$reduce\_now[A] \equiv N$ iff state A contains only one base rule, $N \rightarrow \theta(\ldots)$.

Although state 1 contains two base rules, and a decision about which to apply depends on reductions at ancestor nodes, the state does contain enough information to guide the reductions of its children. Both base rules have the same vector of nonterminals — (reg, con) — on the right-hand side. Therefore, any node labeled with state 1 can immediately reduce its left child to reg and its right child to con. This fully reduces its children. The labeler must defer reductions of the state 1 node, however.

wburg could generate vectors like *reduce_now[ ]* to map states to the nonterminals to which their children should be reduced. Instead, we generalize this notion and create tables that guide child reductions based on the states of both the child and the parent. Two two-dimensional arrays, *left_nt[ ][ ]* and *right_nt[ ][ ]*, hold the nonterminals to which a node's children should be reduced. *left_nt[B][A]* holds the nonterminal to which a node labeled with B should be reduced if it is the left child of a node labeled with A.

An entry is put in *left_nt[B][A]* if every left-most nonterminal on the right-hand side of every base rule in A derives from the same base rule in B via zero or more chain rules. Under these conditions, the nonterminal on the left-hand side of B's base rule, N, is put in the table. This condition ensures that wburg knows which base rule in B ultimately will be applied when B is the left child of A. *right_nt* is similar. Formally,

$left\_nt[B][A] \equiv N$ iff $X \rightarrow \theta(Y, -) \in A$ implies $N \rightarrow \phi(\ldots) \in B$ and $Y \overset{*}{\Rightarrow} N$ in B.
$right\_nt[B][A] \equiv N$ iff $X \rightarrow \theta(-, Y) \in A$ implies $N \rightarrow \phi(\ldots) \in B$ and $Y \overset{*}{\Rightarrow} N$ in B.

Figure 4 gives the tables for G. A "$\perp$" indicates that no immediate reduction is possible.

$left\_nt$		Parent's State		
		1	2	3
Left	1	reg	addr	$\perp$
Child's	2	$\perp$	$\perp$	$\perp$
State	3	con	con	$\perp$

$right\_nt$		Parent's State		
		1	2	3
Right	1	$\perp$	reg	$\perp$
Child's	2	$\perp$	$\perp$	$\perp$
State	3	con	con	$\perp$

Figure 4: Arrays $left\_nt$ and $right\_nt$ for Grammar G

4.1 Characteristic burg Graph

For each cost-augmented tree grammar, burg generates at compile-compile time a function state that, when invoked at compile-time, computes the state of a particular node given its operator and the states of its children.

$$\text{state} : operator \times state_{left} \times state_{right} \rightarrow state$$

Using state, we can generate a *characteristic* directed graph to represent states and state transitions. Nodes represent states, and edges represent possible state transitions. Edges are annotated with either *left* or *right*, depending on whether the target node represents the left or right child of the source node. Formally,

$$A \xrightarrow{left} B \quad \text{iff } \exists \theta, X \text{ such that } \text{state}(\theta, B, X) \equiv A$$
$$A \xrightarrow{right} B \quad \text{iff } \exists \theta, X \text{ such that } \text{state}(\theta, X, B) \equiv A$$

Figure 5 shows the characteristic graph for G. A characteristic graph depicts which states can be derived from combinations of operators and certain child states. For instance, the given graph indicates that a node in state 1 must have a state 3 right child, but can have a state 1 or 3 left child. We can use the characteristic graph to generate "trees" of states by starting out at a root node (state 2 in this example), and doing a traversal of the graph, following one *left*- and one *right*-labeled edge each time we encounter a node. (Different edges may be chosen each time a given node is encountered in a traversal.) The nodes visited and the edges followed represent a tree of states. In general, the characteristic graph can generate a superset of the trees that a grammar describes because not all combinations of *left* and *right*-labeled arcs leaving a particular state can actually be combined to generate that state. Only cyclic graphs generate trees of unbounded size.

A bound on the sizes of the trees generated by an acyclic graph is simply the size of the largest tree in the graph. Therefore, this bound is the maximum amount of information that must be retained between passes of a two-pass parser.

4.2 Arc Pruning

Analysis of the characteristic graph leads to a method of doing one-pass parsing that retains only a constant amount of information about the reduction of any

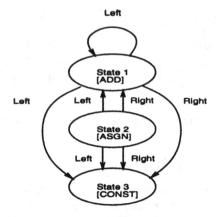

Figure 5: Transition Graph for **burg** States of Grammar G

labeled node and the subtree it roots. **wburg** will prune an arc from the graph if the arc corresponds to a state transition for which a correct base-rule reduction of the child node is known. The remaining arcs represent the reductions that the analysis cannot immediately determine and therefore must postpone until the parser can safely reduce an ancestor. If the pruned graph is acyclic, then only a bounded number of nodes must ever be retained for subsequent reduction. Because the original graph (Figure 5) is cyclic, one-pass parsing with grammar G is not possible without arc pruning.

Arcs leaving state 2 may be pruned because the parser can immediately reduce the left and right children of a state 2 node. After the parser reduces the children of a state 2 node, the parser would retain those nodes, but not their children (the node's grandchildren). The children may require subsequent chain-rule reductions, but the grandchildren will be completely reduced at this point. (The condition for pruning arcs only guarantees that one of the child's base rules can be applied immediately — application of the child's chain rules may be deferred, and so it is necessary to record the last nonterminal to which the child was reduced.)

The entries in *left_nt* and *right_nt* correspond directly to the pruned arcs. An arc $A \overset{left}{\to} B$ may be pruned if $left\_nt[B][A] \neq \perp$ because the labeler can immediately reduce B to the given nonterminal, which forces the reduction by its base rule.

If, after applying the arc pruning rule, the resulting graph contains no cycles, then the grammar can be parsed optimally during the single, bottom-up labeling pass while retaining only a constant number of unreduced nodes at any given point. A conservative upper bound on the number of unreduced nodes is the size of the largest tree generated by the pruned graph *plus* information about deferred chain rule reductions of the nodes just off the leaves of that tree.

If the pruning rule removes all directed edges from the graph (as it will for grammar G), then the largest subtree whose reduction may have to be deferred consists of a tree node and its children. Its children will lack, at most, chain-rule applications.

5 A Code-Generator Generator

5.1 One-Pass, Optimal Parsing of IR Trees

If the application of the pruning rule creates an arc-free graph, then labeling and reducing the tree can be done in a single-pass while deferring at most three nodes worth of reductions at the most recently labeled node: the reductions at that node, and possible chain rule reductions at its children. All descendents further down the tree must be completely reduced.

wburg is a system for generating optimal, single-pass tree-parsers for grammars for which the characteristic graph can be completely pruned of arcs. Note that this is the same class of grammars for which wburg can fill all entries in *left_nt* and *right_nt* that correspond to valid state transitions.

Because the reductions induced by wburg's *reduce_now*, *left_nt*, and *right_nt* tables are identical to the reductions that burg's parser would apply, both systems find identical least-cost parses.

Consider the procedure *Compose* in Figure 6, which creates a new node from an operator and two child nodes. *Compose* labels a node and attaches that node to its children. Then, it initializes the node's nonterminal field to zero, indicating that the current node has not yet been reduced. The procedure checks the array *reduce_now* to see whether the node itself can be reduced immediately. If so, *Compose* will immediately reduce the entire subtree rooted at this node (except, of course, previously reduced nodes).

If *reduce_now* cannot help, the parser consults *left_nt* and *right_nt* to obtain the appropriate nonterminals to which the children should be reduced and performs those reductions. In this case, *Compose* does no reductions at *node* itself, but it does invoke reductions of its children. The node's reductions and the children's chain rule reductions must wait until this node's parent is labeled and causes subsequent reductions.

Figure 7 gives the code for *reduce*, which performs reductions. Nodes previously reduced to the desired nonterminal will terminate the reduction. *arity(rule_number)* gives the number of nonterminals on the right-hand side of *rule_number*, which represents the number of subsequent reductions this rule must invoke. For chain rules, *kids[ ]* simply holds *node*; for base rules, it is a vector of the node's children. *nts[ ][ ]* is a table of the nonterminals to which the *kids[ ]* should be reduced based on the rule number.

5.2 One-Pass, Optimal Parsing *Without* Trees

Because burg and other tree-parsing algorithms require two-passes over the IR tree, the IR tree must be retained until the second pass is complete. Because a tree may be of arbitrary size, the tree nodes must be dynamically allocated and deallocated. wburg's parsers parse an IR tree in a single bottom-up pass, but

```
procedure Compose(out node_ptr node,
                    in int op, in node_ptr left_child, in node_ptr right_child)
    node.left = left_child                                    // Assemble tree.
    node.right = right_child
    node.state = state(op, left_child.state, right_child.state) // Label tree.
    node.nt = 0                                               // Node is not reduced.
    if (reduce_now[node.state] ≠ ⊥) then
        reduce(node, reduce_now[node.state])                 // Reduce immediately.
    else
        left_nt = left_nt[left_child.state][node.state]
        right_nt = right_nt[right_child.state][node.state]
        reduce(left_child, left_nt)                          // Reduce children's
        reduce(right_child, right_nt)                        //      base rules.
    end if
end procedure
```

Figure 6: Procedure *Compose*

```
procedure reduce(in/out node_ptr node, in int nt)
    if nt = node.nt then return                              // Previously reduced.
    rule_number = rule(node.state, nt)                       // Find rule to apply.
    for i ← 1 to arity(rule_number) do                      // Invoke subsequent
        reduce(node.kids[i], nts[rule_number][i])           //      reductions.
    end for
    // Invoke semantic action for rule here.
    node.nt = nt                                             // Record reduction.
end procedure
```

Figure 7: Procedure *reduce*

reductions at a given node may require reducing child nodes further. This seems to indicate that the subtrees descending from each node must be retained until the entire tree is reduced, but that is not the case.

Retaining entire subtrees is overly conservative. The analysis described in Section 4 guarantees that when *Compose* processes a node, the only deferred reductions possible for the subtree rooted at that node are chain rule reductions at its children, and reductions at itself. No deferred reductions can exist below its children. Therefore, all deferred reductions at a given node can be summarized by the *state* and *nt* fields of that node and its children. Of course, this information can be kept (via copying) in the node itself, thus eliminating any need to retain child nodes at all after creating a new node. A node exists only until its parent is created. Thus, it is possible for the parser to eliminate the creation of the explicit IR tree. Furthermore, the parser can use the run-time stack to store nodes, eliminating the need for any dynamic heap allocation or deallocation.

Consider the modified *Compose* procedure, *Compose'*, in Figure 8. *Compose'*

```
procedure Compose'(out node_ptr node,
                in int op, in node_ptr left_child, in node_ptr right_child)
    node.self.state = state(op, left_child.self.state, right_child.self.state)
    node.self.nt = 0
    if (reduce_now[node.self.state] ≠ ⊥) then
        node.self.left = left_child.self              // Create (tiny) tree for
        node.self.right = right_child.self            //     immediate reduction of
        reduce(node.self, reduce_now[node.self.state]) //    node (and its children).
    else
        left_nt = left_nt[left_child.self.state][node.self.state]
        right_nt = right_nt[right_child.self.state][node.self.state]
        reduce(left_child.self, left_nt)              // Reduce children.
        reduce(right_child.self, right_nt)
        node.retain_left = left_child.self            // Retain children for later
        node.retain_right = right_child.self          //     chain rule applications.
        node.self.left = addressof node.retain_left   // node represents 3-node tree.
        node.self.right = addressof node.retain_right
    end if
end procedure
```

Figure 8: Procedure *Compose'*

invokes *reduce* whenever possible. Nodes retain all necessary information for the deferred reductions of their children. The node retains the summary of its state (*node.self*) and the retained state of its children (*node.retain_left* and *node.retain_right*) — the pruning analysis guarantees that this is sufficient for one-pass parsing. Each node maintains pointers (*left* and *right*) to its children to give the reducer the illusion of an actual tree. *Compose'* must maintain these pointers, invoke the reducer when possible, and copy the states of the children into the root node when necessary. (Note that the *left* and *right* children of *node.retain_left/right* are never accessed because the only rules they may defer are chain rules.)

If the array *reduce_now* indicates that an immediate reduction of the current node can be made, then pointers to the two children are copied into the node, and the entire subtree rooted at the current node is reduced. If the reduction of the current node must be deferred, the left and right children are reduced, and their root nodes are copied into *node.retain_left* and *node.retain_right* for later chain-rule reductions. The node's *left* and *right* pointers are set to point to those fields.

Compose' constructs nodes and invokes parsing reductions. Each node retains all the information necessary for any deferred reductions at, or below, itself. Therefore, the nodes from which it was built are no longer needed. Bottom-up tree building may require maintaining multiple nodes that each represent the unreduced portion of an entire subtree. Fortunately, such nodes can often be kept on the run-time stack.

Platform	Grammar	System			
		burg w/ alloc	burg w/o alloc	wburg w/ trees	wburg w/o trees
Alpha	SPARC	19.1	13.5	13.6	13.9
	x86	22.3	17.7	16.6	17.1
SPARC	SPARC	258.6	192.5	125.8	124.9
	x86	321.5	249.9	151.3	159.7

Table 1: Speeds of Parsers (in sec.).

Appendix A contains a complete one-pass parsing example.

6   Implementation

wburg is an extension of burg. wburg and burg, therefore, have identical specification languages. wburg uses the output of burg to build and prune the characteristic graph. For suitable grammars, it creates *reduce_now*, *left_nt*, and *right_nt* tables.

6.1   Experimental Results

While the set of grammars that can be parsed optimally using wburg's parsers is a proper subset of the grammars that can be parsed optimally using burg's, analysis indicates that most useful grammars, including those describing the SPARC, the MIPS R3000, and the x86 architectures, fall within this subset.

We compared the speed of wburg's one-pass parsers with burg's two-pass parsers. To the best of our knowledge, burg produces faster two-pass parsers than any other parser-generator system. We present speeds for burg's parsers both with and without dynamic memory allocation. For dynamic allocation, we use malloc and free. We also present wburg's parsers both with explicit trees (using *Compose*) and without trees (using *Compose'*). wburg's parsers with trees do not do dynamic memory allocation. Tests utilized modified versions of lcc grammars for the SPARC and the x86 [FH95].

The tests consisted of labeling and reducing the 1,234 unique trees lcc generates when it compiles itself. Each test parsed a set of 1,234 trees (a total of 11,587 nodes) 500 times. The tests were performed on lightly loaded DEC Alpha and Sun SPARCstation workstations. The times in Table 1 were measured using the system clock.

Clearly, wburg's parsers without trees are faster than burg's when burg's trees are allocated via malloc and free.

When both burg and wburg parsers operate on trees and do no dynamic memory allocation, wburg's parsers must do bookkeeping to avoid redundant reductions that burg's do not need to do. wburg's parsers avoid a second tree walk, but occasionally must visit a node a second time to do deferred chain-rule reductions. When measured with pixie on the Alpha, the number of cycles executed for wburg's parsers was only 1–2% greater than those for burg's. The difference in actual running time ranged between +3% and −7%, and we believe this is due to cache-effects, which are not measured by pixie.

On the SPARC, wburg's parsers were over 50% faster than burg's even though they were saddled with additional bookkeeping to avoid redundant reductions. While very pleased by these results, we cannot currently explain them other than to speculate. Possible explanations include reduced register-window spilling from only one recursive tree walk and beneficial cache-effects.

The relative speeds of burg's parsers and wburg's parsers appear to be independent of grammar, which is what we expected. Because of the overhead of copying child states into parent nodes, wburg's parsers without trees are slower than those with trees.

6.2 lcc Grammars

The lcc grammars are written for the lburg code-generator generator, and we modified them for burg. lcc grammars allow rule costs to be determined at runtime, which burg cannot handle, so we had to alter the grammar to use constant costs. We also put lcc grammars into normal form. After the changes, all three grammars met the sufficient restrictions for one-pass optimal code generation without further modification. lcc puts all trees in a canonical form (e.g., all constant operands appear as the right child of commutative operators), and this greatly simplifies the code generation grammars. Tests demonstrate, however, that wburg can handle non-canonical grammars for all possible permutations of complex addressing modes.

7 Conclusion

We have developed the theoretical basis for optimal, one-pass tree pattern matching. Using this theory, we have developed wburg, a code-generation system based on optimal tree-pattern matching that has two important advantages over previous systems: the code generator does labeling and reducing in a single parsing pass, and the code generator does not need to build an explicit IR tree. Both advances result in time and space advantages.

References

[AGT89]   Alfred V. Aho, Mahedevan Ganapathi, and Steven W. K. Tjiang. Code generation using tree matching and dynamic programming. *ACM Transactions on Programming Languages and Systems*, 11(4):491–516, October 1989.

[BDB90]   A. Balachandran, D. M. Dhamdhere, and S. Biswas. Efficient retargetable code generation using bottom-up tree pattern matching. *Computer Languages*, 15(3):127–140, 1990.

[ESL89]   Helmut Emmelmann, Friedrich-Wilhelm Schröer, and Rudolf Landwehr. BEG—a generator for efficient back ends. In *Proceedings of the SIGPLAN '89 Conference on Programming Language Design and Implementation*, pages 227–237, New York, 1989. ACM.

[FH95]   Christopher W. Fraser and David R. Hanson. *A Retargetable C Compiler: Design and Implementation*. Benjamin/Cummings, Redwood City, California, 1995.

[FHP92a]   Christopher W. Fraser, David R. Hanson, and Todd A. Proebsting. Engineering a simple, efficient code-generator generator. *ACM Letters on Programming Languages and Systems*, 1(3):213–226, September 1992.

[FHP92b]   Christopher W. Fraser, Robert R. Henry, and Todd A. Proebsting. BURG — fast optimal instruction selection and tree parsing. *SIGPLAN Notices*, 27(4):68–76, April 1992.

[HO82]   Christoph M. Hoffmann and Michael J. O'Donnell. Pattern matching in trees. *Journal of the ACM*, 29(1):68–95, January 1982.

[PLG88]   Eduardo Pelegri-Llopart and Susan L. Graham. Optimal code generation for expression trees: An application of BURS theory. In *Proceedings of the 15th Annual Symposium on Principles of Programming Languages*, pages 294–308, New York, 1988. ACM.

[Pro92]   Todd A. Proebsting. Simple and efficient BURS table generation. In *Proceedings of the SIGPLAN '92 Conference on Programming Language Design and Implementation*, pages 331–340, New York, June 1992. ACM.

[WG92]   N. Wirth and J. Gutknecht. *Project Oberon, the Design of an Operating System and Computer*. Addison Wesley, 1992.

A   Example One-Pass Parsing

We will outline the one-pass construction and reduction of the seven-node tree given in Figure 9. This example utilizes the grammar and tables described throughout this paper. burg states appear underneath the operators in the tree. burg's left-to-right, bottom-up reduction of the example tree appears in Figure 10. Each rule in the reduction is annotated with the node at which the rule was applied.

Figure 11 gives the necessary calls for building and reducing the example tree using a wburg-derived one-pass parser. A–G are the tree nodes being composed, which correspond to the labels in Figure 9. The final call to *reduce* guarantees that the root node is fully reduced to the goal nonterminal, stmt.

Figure 12 gives the (nearly identical) calls for reducing the same tree, only *without* actually constructing the tree. Note that the nodes X–Z are reused after they serve as children in a prior composition — this is a benefit of one-pass parsing without trees.

Figure 13 outlines the actions that a one-pass parser takes during the eight function calls given in Figure 11. (The reductions induced by the calls in Figure 12 are identical.) The *Nonterminal* column indicates which of the one-pass parsing tables (*reduce_now*, *left_nt*, or *right_nt*) is determining the reductions.

The reductions at node A demonstrate the subtleties of one-pass parsing. Note that visits to A for possible reductions occur as a consequence of actions at nodes A, C, and E. When visiting A for the first time, *reduce_now* causes a reduction to **con**, which results in the application of rule "**con: CONST**." Then, A's parent node, C, uses *left_nt* to determine that A should be reduced to **con**. Since A was previously reduced to **con**, this visit by *reduce* does not cause another reduction. At this point, the parser has not applied a base rule at C. Finally, E uses *left_nt* to determine that C must be reduced to **reg**, which causes an application of rule "**reg: ADD(reg, con)**" at C. Before making that reduction, A must be revisited, and reduced via chain rule "**reg: con**" because the base rule at C requires A be reduced to a **reg**.

wburg-derived parsers do not produce a simple left-to-right reduction order because of the way reductions are deferred. The reductions do, however, maintain a bottom-up ordering.

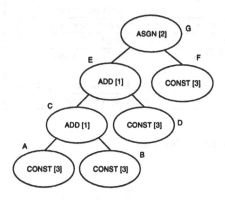

Reductions		Node
con:	CONST	A
reg:	con	A
con:	CONST	B
reg:	ADD(reg, con)	C
con:	CONST	D
addr:	ADD(reg, con)	E
con:	CONST	F
reg:	con	F
stmt:	ASGN(addr, reg)	G

Figure 9: Example IR Tree With State Labels

Figure 10: burg's left-to-right, bottom-up reduction.

Compose(A, CONST, —, —)	*Compose'(X, CONST, —, —)*
Compose(B, CONST, —, —)	*Compose'(Y, CONST, —, —)*
Compose(C, ADD, A, B)	*Compose'(Z, ADD, X, Y)*
Compose(D, CONST, —, —)	*Compose'(X, CONST, —, —)*
Compose(E, ADD, C, D)	*Compose'(Y, ADD, Z, X)*
Compose(F, CONST, —, —)	*Compose'(X, CONST, —, —)*
Compose(G, ASGN, E, F)	*Compose'(Z, ASGN, Y, X)*
reduce(G, stmt)	*reduce(Z, stmt)*

Figure 11: One-Pass Parsing With a Tree.

Figure 12: One-Pass Parsing *Without* a Tree.

Statement	Nonterminal	Reductions		Node
Compose(A, CONST, -, -)	*reduce_now[3]* ≡ con	⇒ con:	CONST	A
Compose(B, CONST, -, -)	*reduce_now[3]* ≡ con	⇒ con:	CONST	B
Compose(C, ADD, A, B)	*left_nt[3][1]* ≡ con	⇒ (Previously reduced)		A
	right_nt[3][1] ≡ con	⇒ (Previously reduced)		B
Compose(D, CONST, -, -)	*reduce_now[3]* ≡ con	⇒ con:	CONST	D
Compose(E, ADD, C, D)	*left_nt[1][1]* ≡ reg	⇒ reg:	con	A
		reg:	ADD(reg, con)	C
	right_nt[3][1] ≡ con	⇒ (Previously reduced)		D
Compose(F, CONST, -, -)	*reduce_now[3]* ≡ con	⇒ con:	CONST	F
Compose(G, ASGN, E, F)	*reduce_now[2]* ≡ stmt	⇒ addr:	ADD(reg, con)	E
		reg:	con	F
		stmt:	ASGN(addr, reg)	G
reduce(G, stmt)		(Previously reduced)		G

Figure 13: One-Pass Reductions

Compact Dispatch Tables for Dynamically Typed Object Oriented Languages

Jan Vitek

Object Systems Group, CUI,
Univ. of Geneva, 24 rue General-Dufour,
1211 Geneva 4, Switzerland
jvitek@cui.unige.ch

R. Nigel Horspool

Dept. of Computer Science,
Univ. of Victoria, P.O. Box 3055,
Victoria BC, Canada V8W 3P6.
nigelh@csr.uvic.ca

Abstract. Dynamically typed object-oriented languages must perform dynamic binding for most message sends. Typically this is slow. A number of papers have reported on attempts to adapt C++-style selector table indexing to dynamically typed languages, but it is difficul to generate space-efficient tables. Our algorithm generates considerably smaller dispatch tables for languages with single inheritance than its predecessors at the cost of a small dispatch time penalty.

1 Introduction

Message passing is the heart of object-oriented programming. Messages are ubiquitous, often appearing in the most basic operations such as assignment or integer addition. It is therefore not surprising that fast message dispatch is a major issue for implementations of object-oriented languages. The difficulty lies in finding an implementation technique which is fast but does not sacrifice space efficiency.

Message passing refers to the process of binding a message to an implementation. This binding depends on the value of the message receiver, or rather, on the class of the receiver. If known at compile-time, the message send reduces to a procedure call. Otherwise, the binding is resolved at run-time. This is called *dynamic binding* or late binding. In object-oriented programming, dynamic binding is an expensive and frequent operation. It is therefore worthwhile to try to minimize its overhead. There are two complementary ways to do that, either by binding at compile-time, or by speeding up dynamic binding. The first approach is motivated by the observation that the majority of call sites have a constant receiver class. In other words, they are always bound to the same method. Static binding of those call sites would not affect the program's semantics. But the difficulty lies in deciding which call sites can safely be bound statically. In the best case, only a portion of the calls will be bound statically [10], [12], [14]. The second solution is to reduce the cost of dynamic binding. Efficient implementations of dynamic binding have been the focus of much research, yet it is customary to see modern dynamically typed object-oriented languages spend more than 20% of their time handling messages. This paper takes the second approach.

A generic dynamic binding algorithm can be defined as follows:

1. Determine the message receiver's class;
2. if the class implements a message with this selector, execute it;
3. otherwise, recursively check parent classes;
4. if no implementation is found, signal an error.

The algorithm either succeeds and executes a method, or it fails and signals a type error. The difference between dynamically typed languages and statically typed ones is that former *detect* type errors at run-time while the latter prevent them at compile time. The most straightforward implementation of dynamic binding is called *dispatch table search* (DTS). With DTS, look-up proceeds exactly as outlined above. Although conceptually simple, DTS it is too slow to be practical. Its overhead must be reduced. A number of techniques have been proposed to this end. They can be classified in two categories: static techniques and dynamic techniques. *Static techniques* use information obtained by analysis of the program source to pre-compute part of the look-up. These techniques guarantee that message dispatch incurs a small and constant[1] overhead. *Dynamic techniques* adapt to the program run-time behaviour by caching the result of previous look-ups. Their speed is a function of the cost of probing the cache and of the cost, as well as frequency, of cache misses. On current hardware, static techniques are faster and more predictable. Their drawback is that they require static type information without which space requirements become unrealistic. For instance, applying a static technique to the OBJECTWORKS SMALLTALK library would generate 16MB of tables.

This paper presents a fast and intuitive technique for generating compact selector-indexed dispatch tables for dynamically typed languages with single inheritance. The criteria used to evaluate such algorithms are (1) dispatch table size, (2) generation time, (3) cost per call site of a message send, (4) message send speed and (5) number of machine registers required by the message send operation. Our algorithm has the following characteristics. For the OBJECTWORKS class library (776 classes and 5,325 selectors) the algorithm generates 221 KB of dispatch tables in 1.5 seconds. The cost of message passing is two memory references, one indirect function call, a comparison and a branch, that is 4 instructions at the call site and 3 instruction in the prologue of each method. It takes 11 cycles on a SPARC and requires 3 registers. This represents a marked improvement over previous algorithms.

2 Canonical Implementations of Dynamic Binding

We present two extremes in the spectrum of dynamic binding algorithms: *dispatch table search* (DTS) and *selector indexed dispatch tables* (STI), and discuss their relative merits. The algorithms presented here have been implemented in hand optimized assembly language [16]. To get a meaningful comparison of dispatch speed, we chose a concrete target architecture: the SUN SPARC processor. For space comparisons we use data extracted from OBJECTWORKS SMALLTALK; a real-life class library. We use the hierarchy of Figure 1 to illustrate the algorithms. (Class names are in upper case and methods in lower case. Table 1 gives the addresses of the methods.)

2.1 Dispatch Table Search (DTS)

The obvious way to implement dynamic binding is to follow the letter of the definition of method look-up. This means, search classes one by one, in the order specified by the inheritance rules, until a method is found or the list of classes is exhausted.

---

1. Actually message passing is performed by executing a constant *number of instructions*, instruction cache misses can account for considerable differences in time.

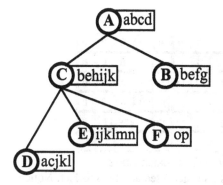

method	ref	method	ref	method	ref	method	ref
A::a	1	C::b	9	D::j	17	E::n	25
A::b	2	C::e	10	D::k	18	F::o	26
A::c	3	C::h	11	D::l	19	F::p	27
A::d	4	C::i	12	E::i	20	msg	0
B::b	5	C::j	13	E::j	21	Not	
B::e	6	C::k	14	E::k	22	Under-	
B::f	7	D::a	15	E::l	23	stood	
B::g	8	D::c	16	E::m	24		

Figure 1 Sample class hierarchy.   **Table 1** Method addresses.

The speed of DTS depends on two factors: the cost of searching a dispatch table and the number of tables to search. Hash tables offer a good compromise between access speed and memory requirements and are, thus, used for implementing dispatch tables. Each class has its own hash table of <selector, method address> pairs. The look-up procedure hashes the method selector to obtain an index into the table. If the selector in the table matches, control is transferred. Otherwise, a collision has occurred and the table must be probed until the method is found or an empty entry is encountered. In the latter case, search continues in the table of the superclass. The cost of DTS is a function of the cost of probing the hash table, of the average number of probes per table, and of the average number of tables visited per message send [5]. For SMALLTALK-80, a message requires, on average, 8.48 hash table probes [2]. The cost of DTS is estimated as 250 cycles [13], [10]. Although very slow, DTS is space efficient. For this reason, it is used as a backup strategy in SMALLTALK-80 [3], LISP [11] and SELF [10]. Driesen [6] estimates the memory requirements of DTS to be $2MH$, where M is the number of methods in the system and H is the hash table overhead (133%). OBJECTWORKS has 8,780 methods, and thus 93 KB of hash tables.

A call site requires two instructions: a call and a load of the selector number (if small enough to be loaded in one instruction). The code size for the 50,696 send sites of the reference library is thus 405 KB, which brings the total space consumption to 498 KB.

2.2   Selector Indexed Dispatch Tables (STI)

Indexing is an extreme form of hashing which favours access time over space. *Selector table indexing* (STI) is an attractive candidate for implementing dynamic binding because it delivers fast constant time look-up, and is conceptually simple. For a system of C classes and S selectors, the idea is to construct a two-dimensional array of C by S entries. Classes and selectors are given consecutive numbers on each axis. The array is filled by pre-computing the look-up for each class and selector. Array entries contain a reference to the method implementing the message, or to messageNotUnderstood. The look-up procedure is reduced to an indexing operation on this array. Figure 2 gives the STI tables for the hierarchy of Figure 1.

The look-up code is short and can be inlined, thus avoiding one control transfer. A concrete STI procedure is shown below. The variable self holds a pointer to the receiver.

	a	b	c	d	e	f	g	h	i	j	k	l	m	n	o	p
A	01	02	03	04	0	0	0	0	0	0	0	0	0	0	0	0
B	01	05	03	04	06	07	08	0	0	0	0	0	0	0	0	0
C	01	09	03	04	10	0	0	11	12	13	14	0	0	0	0	0
D	15	09	26	04	10	0	0	11	12	17	18	19	0	0	0	0
E	01	09	03	04	10	0	0	11	20	21	22	23	24	25	0	0
F	01	09	03	04	10	0	0	11	12	13	14	0	0	0	26	27

Figure 2 Class hierarchy and STI dispatch tables.

The '#' symbol is prefixed to constants. The class is accessed at a fixed offset. Notice that all offsets are hard-wired in the code.

```
load [self + #class_offset], class
load [class + #selector_offset], method
call method
nop
```

Taking into account a one cycle load latency, a look-up requires $T_{STI} = 6$ cycles. The delay slot after the call is filled with a no-op, so the code size is 4 instructions per call site. The data size is an array of $S*C$ addresses. The space for dispatch tables for the reference library is 16.5MB and the space required for call sites is 811KB.

Note that STI is inherently global and static. Tables are computed for a complete system, and are very sensitive to changes in the class hierarchy. Such changes may affect the entire system, forcing regeneration of tables and changing offsets in the code.

3   Practical Implementations of Message Passing

3.1   Static Techniques

Static techniques follow the principle of STI but with smaller tables (with STI, tables are typically more than 90% msgNotUnderstood). The schemes described in this section assume that objects are represented by records with one field referring to a shared dispatch table, Figure 3, which is an array of method references.

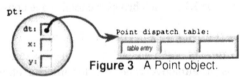

Figure 3 A Point object.

3.1.1   Virtual Function Tables (VTBL)

In the context of statically typed programming languages such as C++ [9], virtual function tables (VTBL) are dispatch tables with no empty entries. VTBL dispatching takes two memory references and one indirect function call before method specific code is reached. For each class, the dispatch table is constructed by assigning consecutive indices to all the selectors it understands and storing the corresponding method addresses in the table. These offsets are scoped by their defining type. This allows any selector to have a different offset in independent classes (this also makes separate compilation easier). Inheritance adds one additional constraint: subclass conformance—a subclass must be compatible with its superclass. If the same compiled code is going to manipulate instances of the class as well as instances of subclasses, subclasses should share their parent's memory layout. The dispatch tables for the sample hierarchy are shown in Figure 4. This technique assumes the availability of static type information.

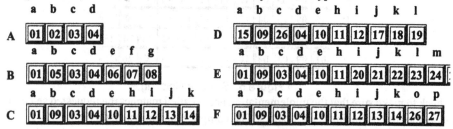

Figure 4 Virtual Function Tables.

For large systems, the memory requirements of VTBLs can be high. The reason is that classes inherit considerably more methods than they define. There are few differences in the VTBLs of subclasses and most of their content is redundant. A C++ implementation of the OBJECTWORKS hierarchy (with all methods virtual) would require 868KB of dispatch tables, and roughly the same amount for the code.

3.1.2 Dispatch Table Compression Techniques

Virtual function tables can not be used for dynamically typed languages as we lack the type information. Instead we will try to compress the STI tables. Previous work on dispatch table compression techniques falls in two categories: *graph coloring schemes* and *row displacement schemes*. Graph coloring schemes attempt to minimize the length of each table by a judicious choice of indices. Row displacement schemes compress dispatch tables by merging all tables into one master array in a way that takes advantage of their sparse nature.

3.1.3 Selector Colouring (SC)

Selector colouring merges rows which do not have differing significant values in any column position. The goal is to find a partition of all rows into groups, or colours, such that rows of the same colour do not collide. A partition with the minimal number of groups represents an optimal compression of table rows. If the table is still sparse, columns can be compressed in a similar way. This problem is equivalent to finding the minimal coloring of a graph. Since the problem is NP-complete, heuristics are used to find approximate solutions [6], [4], [1]. For the purpose of compressing dispatch table, msgNotUnderstood entries are considered "empty". Two selectors can share the same offset, if they are understood by two disjoint sets of classes. Although much smaller than STI, the compressed table still contains a non negligible proportion of empty entries, which may be as high as 43%. Selector colouring for the sample hierarchy of Figure 1 is shown in Figure 5.

As with any compression technique, gains in space are paid for by additional effort to access elements. Offsets assigned to more than one selector are called aliased offsets. The dispatching procedure is identical to STI, except that aliased offsets require an extra

	a	b	c	d	e	f (h, i)	g	j	k	l	m (o)	n (p)
A	01	02	03	04	0	0	0	0	0	0	0	0
B	01	05	03	04	06	07	08	0	0	0	0	0
C	01	09	03	04	10	11	12	13	14	0	0	0
D	15	09	26	04	10	11	12	17	18	19	0	0
E	01	09	03	04	10	11	20	21	22	23	24	25
F	01	09	03	04	10	11	12	13	14	0	26	27

Figure 5 Selector Coloring.

check to make sure that the implementation being called matches the requested selector. Consider the following send: object f. The compiler may translate this into:

```
table = object->dt;
method = table[5];      — the offset of f in Figure 5 is 5.
method(object);
```

Whether this is correct or not depends on the class of the object. If the object is an instance of B the message send is valid. On the other hand, if it is an instance of class C, the message will quietly execute the code of h. So, when accessing aliased offsets, it is necessary to check that the selector at the call site matches the implementation. The dispatching code is as follows:

call site:
```
1. table = object->dt;
2. method = table[ #color_offset ];
3. method(object, #selector_code, ...);
```

method prologue:
```
4. if (s != #The_selector_number)
5.    messageNotUnderstood();
```

Figure 6 Dynamic binding with Selector Colouring.

The calling code is 4 instructions long and 3 instructions in the prologue. It executes in 9 cycles. Data size is $O_{SC} = 1.15MB$ and code size is 916 KB.

3.1.4   Row Displacement (RD)

Row displacement [5] is another way of compressing STI dispatch tables. It slices the two-dimensional STI table into rows corresponding to classes and fits the rows into a one-dimensional array so that non-empty entries overlap only with empty ones (Figure 7). The algorithm minimizes the size of the resulting master array by minimizing the number of empty entries, 33% in [6] and if the table is sliced according to columns the table can be filled to 99.5% [7]. When the row displacement scheme is applied to the sample hierarchy, Figure 7, the result is a single array with overlapping tables.

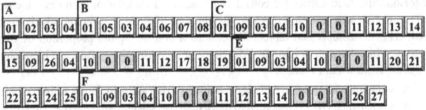

Figure 7 Row Displacement.

Like selector colouring, row displacement requires extra work to access table elements. At run-time, depending on the class of the receiver, a different starting offset in the master array will be used. From that starting index, adding the selector offset will yield the address of a method. The code for a look-up is the same as that of SC. Table space is $O_{RD} = O_{VTBL} * 101\% = 819KB$ and code space is 916KB.

3.2 Dynamic Techniques

Dynamic techniques speed up message passing by caching results of previous look-ups. Caching relies on temporal locality: a cache is profitable when its contents are used numerous times before being evicted. Programs exhibit good locality when the same message is sent repeatedly to same class. Empirical data suggests that pure object-oriented languages have better locality than hybrid languages [10]. But the very nature of caching techniques means that performance can vary between the time of a successful probe, and the time required for handling a miss and updating the cache.

There are two major approaches to caching: one is to have one global look-up cache, and the other is to have small inline caches at each call site.

3.2.1 Global Look-up Caches (LC)

This technique uses a global cache of frequently invoked methods to accelerate look-up [2], [3], [13]. The cache is a table of triples (selector, class identifier, method address). Hashing a class and a selector returns a slot in the cache. If the class and selector stored in the cache match, control is transferred to the method. Otherwise, a backup dispatching technique is used, usually DTS, and the cache is updated with the new triple before transferring control to the method.

The cache hit rate depends heavily on program behaviour (85%–95% hit ratios have been reported [3], [10]). The run-time memory required is small: usually a fixed amount for the cache plus the overhead of the backup technique. Hash functions and cache insertion routines are discussed in [2]. To get a lower bound for the speed of hashing, we used a simple hash function that takes an exclusive OR of the class and the selector [7]. Even with this simple function, look-up is unacceptably slow. A hit executes 19 instructions before method specific code is reached. The cost of a cache miss is the cost of DTS, plus hashing, and a few extra cycles to update the cache.

3.2.2 Inline Caches (IC)

Inline caching stores the result of the previous look-up in the code itself taking advantage of the type locality at call sites. In SMALLTALK, 95% of sites have constant receiver classes [3], [13]. IC changes the call instruction itself. It overwrites it with a direct invocation of the method found by the default system look-up procedure. Thus, a hit is only a little more expensive than a procedure call. The secondary look-up is performed by a global look-up cache and, finally, by dispatch table search. The cost of a miss is therefore the cost of LC plus the overhead of overwriting the calling instruction.

A cache hit takes 7 cycles, a miss takes an average of 113 cycles [7] with a 95% average hit rate [13]. The speed of inline caching is 12.3 cycles, giving a marked improvement over DTS and LC. Inline caching has reasonable space requirements: 4 instructions per call site and 3 instructions per method prologue. The space required by

IC is $O_{IC} = 94$KB. The code size is $4c+3M = 916$KB. The speed is computed by $T_{IC} = hitTime_{IC}*hitRate + (1-hitRate)*(82+T_{LC})$.

A recent study conducted by Driesen, Hölzle and the first author [7] suggests that inline caching and its cousin, polymorphic inline caching, can outperform VTBL-style dispatching on modern architectures. This is because an indirect function call causes a break in the pipeline, while a hit with inline caching does not stall the processor. Thus even statically typed programming languages may find it profitable to combine IC or PIC (described below) with VTBL.

3.2.3 Polymorphic Inline Caches (PIC)

Polymorphic inline caches (PIC) represent a straightforward extension of inline caches [10]. Studies have shown that ICs behave badly for polymorphic call sites; measurements of the SELF-90 system showed that it spent up to 25% of its time handling cache misses [10]. PICs alleviate that problem by caching more than one type at each polymorphic call site. For each site, a small stub routine is created. This stub grows as more receiver classes are encountered. The performance of PICs drops for call sites with a great number of receiver classes. In these cases it may be better to adopt a fall-back strategy like IC.

4 Compact Dispatch Tables, a first look: CT-94

How do we compress the dispatch tables while, at the same time, retaining most of the speed-up obtained by the dispatch table technique? In an earlier paper [14], we proposed the *compact dispatch table* (CT-94) techniques. We give a short description of CT-94 as it is the basis for the work described in this paper. A detailed account can be found in [14] and [16]. The technique applies four different optimizations to the full STI tables, and a pre-processing and a post-processing step.

4.1 Factoring Out Conflict Selectors

The first step of our algorithm performs pre-processing, separating the STI tables of Figure 2 into two. One contains normal selectors and the other contains *conflict selectors*. A conflict selector is a selector that is implemented by two classes unrelated by inheritance. A second set of dispatch tables, Figure 8, called conflict tables, is created and conflict selectors are assigned offsets in these tables. The compiler must generate code to access either a normal or a conflict dispatch table depending on the selector.

	a	b	c	d	f	g	h	i	j	k	m	n	o	p		e	l	
A	01	02	03	04	0	0	0	0	0	0	0	0	0	0		0	0	A
B	01	05	03	04	07	08	0	0	0	0	0	0	0	0		06	0	B
C	01	09	03	04	0	0	11	12	13	14	0	0	0	0		10	0	C
D	15	09	26	04	0	0	11	12	17	18	0	0	0	0		10	19	D
E	01	09	03	04	0	0	11	20	21	22	24	25	0	0		10	23	E
F	01	09	03	04	0	0	11	12	13	14	0	0	26	27		10	0	F

Figure 8 Factoring conflict selectors.

4.2 Dispatch Table Trimming

Dispatch table trimming removes trailing empty entries from dispatch tables. After trimming, the dispatch tables can differ in size; therefore the compiler should generate code to prevent indexing errors. Figure 9 shows the trimmed tables.

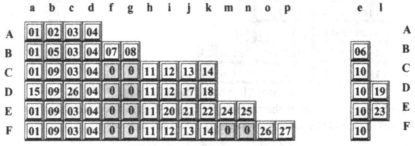

Figure 9 Trimming the tables.

4.3 Selector Aliasing

After trimming, dispatch tables still mostly consist of empty entries. Selector aliasing packs tables by assigning the same offset to different selectors with the constraint that each selector has a disjoint set of classes. For dynamically typed languages, aliasing introduces additional run-time type checks. These checks are detailed below. Aliasing is applied to the dispatch tables to yield the tables shown in Figure 10.

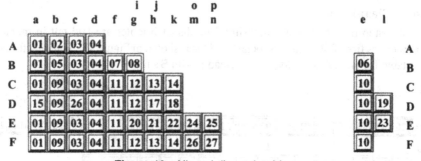

Figure 10 Aliased dispatch tables.

4.4 Dispatch Table Sharing

Identical dispatch or conflict tables can be shared. Usually, many conflict tables can be shared but only a small portion of dispatch tables. The potential for sharing is fully realized only in conjunction with table entry overloading (below). In our running example, only one of the conflict tables can be shared, as demonstrated by Figure 11. This optimization entails no additional run-time cost.

4.5 Table Entry Overloading

Table sharing merges identical tables. But the majority of dispatch tables differ, if only in a small way, from their parents' tables. The idea is to merge sufficiently "similar" tables by overloading entries with multiple implementations. This is done by walking the inheritance tree and trying to merge each child table with its parent's. The degree of

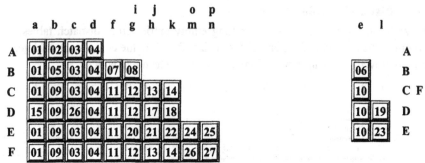

Figure 11 Shared dispatch tables.

similarity is a parameter of the algorithm. Figure 12 shows one possible overloading: Table A and B, and C and F are overloaded.

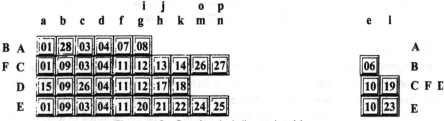

Figure 12 Overloaded dispatch tables.

4.6 Cleaning up

The last step performs post-processing. The dispatch tables are laid out in memory, superclasses first, followed by subclasses. This is shown in Figure 13. Note that the conflict table for class A is empty, we overload it with B's table.

Figure 13 Complete dispatch table layout.

5 Run Time Issues

The space gained by overloading has to be balanced against the additional run-time cost of retrieving entries. Overloaded entries point to a small dispatch routine which must select one of the overloaded classes. When there are many different classes overloading the same entry, the speed of dispatching deteriorates. The code sequence for a non overloaded entry is 8 instructions long and executes in 11 cycles. For an overloaded entry the code sequence is 8 instructions long plus 4 per subclass test. A call to overloaded entry executes in 13 cycles plus 4 per subclass test. Each call site requires 5 instructions. The speed is thus $T_{CT-94} = (1 - overload) * 11 + overload * (13 + 4\ avgTests) = 11.9$ cycles. Table size is $O_{CT-94} = 158\text{KB}$.

5.1 What's wrong with CT-94?

At first sight CT-94 seems pretty good. The overhead of STI has been brought down to 158 KB. The dispatch speed is much faster than DTS. But, there are several hidden problems. Firstly, the formula for speed assumes that each table *entry* is used with the same relative frequency. But, recall that some entries are aliased to multiple selectors and/or overloaded with multiple methods. If we assume, instead that every *method* is equiprobable, then overloaded entries are used more frequently and speed drops 12.8 cycles. Secondly, when we consider space usage, we should not overlook that if over-loading decreases table sizes, it increases code size because stub and prologue code has to be generated. A better measure of data size includes prologue and stubs with the tables, as shown in Figure 14. As overloading increases, gains become small. Finally, perhaps the worst news is that the per-call site overhead of CT-95 is 5 instructions. This means that for the OBJECTWORKS system slightly more than 1 MB of send code is required. Table 3 gives the true cost of CT-94: it is slower than SC and RD, and the gains in size are small. The only marked improvement is the running time of the algo-rithm as the table can be computed about 100 times faster than with RD. The average number of tests, avgTests, is 2.28 and the frequency of overloaded calls is 16%.

speed	$T_{CT-94} = (1 - overload) * 11 + overload * (13 + 4\ avgTests)$	12.8 cycles
data size	O_{CT-94}	378 KB
code size	$5c$	1 MB

Table 2 Compact Dispatch Tables (CT-94).

6 Compact Dispatch Tables revisited: CT-95

The design goals of the new dispatch table algorithm were to reduce code size, obtain constant time message dispatch speed, improve the algorithm running time and retain good table compression rates. This section presents an algorithm which meets these goals. These improvements have been made possible by the addition of a new tech-

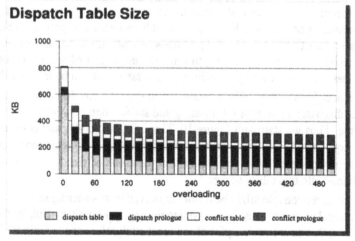

Figure 14 CT-94 tables for OBJECTWORKS SMALLTALK.

nique, which we call *partitioning*, to our toolbox of optimizations. It turns out that partitioning makes overloading and trimming redundant; without overloading message passing becomes a constant time operation. Space requirement are about the same as we lose a little table compression but gain on code size.

6.1 Partitioning

The idea of partitioning is to improve sharing of dispatch tables by allowing the sharing of portions of tables. Consider a subclass which inherits one hundred methods from its superclass and only redefines five of them. Would it not be simpler to have one table with the ninety-five common entries, and two separate tables with the five methods that actually differ?

The principle of partitioning is to cut dispatch and conflict tables into partitions. The table allocation procedure tries to share (or overload) partitions instead of entire tables. Actually, we were already doing that in CT-94, but with only two partitions: the dispatch table and the conflict table. Increasing the number of partitions does not really change dispatching. The compiler must only know, for each selector, to which partition it belongs and its offset in that partition. The data structure for a class consists of an array of pointers to partitions. Each partition is a table of methods addresses. This organization is illustrated in Figure 15. This figure shows a class composed of 6 partitions. The first partition is an array of 4 method addresses.

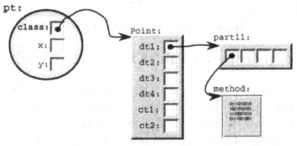

Figure 15 Objects, classes, partitions and methods.

The structure of classes and partitions has to be regular. Each class must have the same number of partitions, otherwise it would be necessary to perform a bound check before accessing partitions. Also, all partitions accessed from the same offset must have the same size. In the example above, this means that the size of the first partition is four for all classes in the hierarchy. This implies that tables can not be trimmed (4.2).

CT-95 proceeds as follows. The new algorithm starts by creating dispatch and conflict tables as discussed in section 4.1, aliasing and sharing optimizations are applied at the same time. Thus we start with Figure 10. Then, dispatch tables and conflict tables are cut into equal sized partitions. Partitions which have equal contents can be shared. Figure 16 shows dispatch tables divided in four partitions of size 3. Conflict tables have been divided into two tables of size 1.

The compression rate might be further improved by re-ordering selectors and choosing individual partition sizes that maximize sharing opportunities. But, in order to keep table generation time low, we picked the most straightforward technique. The size of

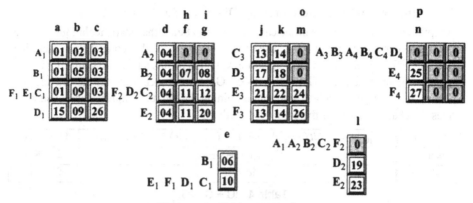

Figure 16 Table partitioning.

the table is such a small factor in the overall space requirements (compared to the per call site overhead) that the additional effort would not be worth it.

Choosing a fixed partition size means that there will be some trailing empty entries and thus some amount of wasted space. See, for instance, partitions E_4 and F_4 above. Again, in practice, wasted space amounts to a negligible portion of the overall system.

For a practical algorithm we need to know what partition sizes give best results, whether it is possible to retain the same partition size for different hierarchies, and whether to allow overloading of similar partitions or just sharing of equals.

What is the best partition size? Smaller partitions improve the chance that two partitions will be similar. Thus, the best partition size for reducing sheer table size is 1. Then, the dispatch tables have as many entries as there are method definitions. The problem is that every class needs a data structure with one pointer per partition. Reducing partition size increases the number of partitions and thus the size of class objects. We tested the algorithm with various table sizes, partition of 14 entries seem to give good results [16].

6.2   Results

Doing away with overloading and trimming allows more regular code to be generated for message passing. To send a message it is necessary to load a partition, access it at the right offset to retrieve a method address, load a selector code, and transfer control to the method. At the call site we simply check that the selector code matches that of the implementation and then execute the method body. This is exactly the same code sequence as that of the non-overloaded entries of CT-94. It consists of 5 instructions at the call site 3 in the method prologue, and it executes in 11 cycles, see the appendix. For OBJECTWORKS, we have 221 KB of data in 23 partitions in total (18 dispatch and 5 conflict). The prologue code size is 62 KB and the call site overhead is still at 1 MB. Table 3 summarizes those results.

speed	T_{CT-95}	11 cycles
data size	O_{CT-95}	221 KB
code size	$5c$	1 MB

Table 3 Compact Dispatch Tables (CT-95).

6.3   Inline Caching and Compact Dispatch Tables (IC+CT-95)

Adaptive techniques such as inline caching perform better than static techniques on certain computer architecture [7] because of their more predictable control flow. But, they rely on DTS as their backup look-up strategy, which means a high miss time. Could we improve IC by replacing DTS with CT-95? On current architectures, the branch miss penalty is not large enough to warrant combining the two techniques. Table 4 summarizes the characteristics of the combined method.

speed	$T_{IC+CT-95} = hitTime_{IC} * hitRate + (1-hitRate) * (82 + T_{CT-95})$	11.3 cycles
data size	$O_{IC+CT-95} = O_{CT-95}$	221 KB
code size	$4c + 3M$	916 KB

Table 4   IC + CT-95.

7   Space, Time and Efficiency Measurements

Space. The compression rates for the five static table-based algorithms discussed in this paper are compared in Figure 17 for OBJECTWORKS SMALLTALK-80. Both compact dispatch table algorithms (CT-94 and CT-95) produce good compression. Notice that even for a medium sized system like this one, C++-style selector indexed tables (VTBL) require in excess of 800KB of tables. It is also interesting to note that Driesen's row displacement technique (RD) provides almost as good compression as VTBL with no type information. Selector colouring (SC) requires considerably more space.

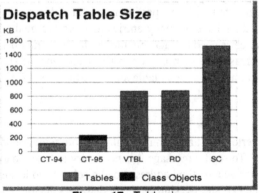

Figure 17   Table sizes.

The data size is only one contributor to the space cost of these algorithms. Code size has to be accounted for to give a meaningful comparison. We have computed the total number of call sites for the OBJECTWORKS system (50,696 call sites) and used that figure to compute the size of the dispatching code. This is shown in Figure 19. Note that these figures represent an upper bound as many call sites can be resolved statically by an optimizing compiler. It is interesting to note that CT-95 performs better than CT-94 because the latter had to include a large number of code stubs to resolve overloading. It is also interesting to note how code size dominates space costs. The data sizes of other libraries are shown in Figure 19. It is interesting to note that for Visualworks 2.0 and Digitalk 3.0 both VTBL and RD require in excess of 2.5MB.

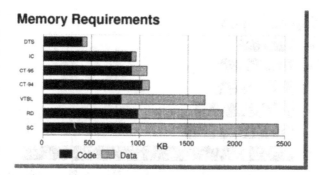

Figure 18 Memory requirements of dispatching algorithms

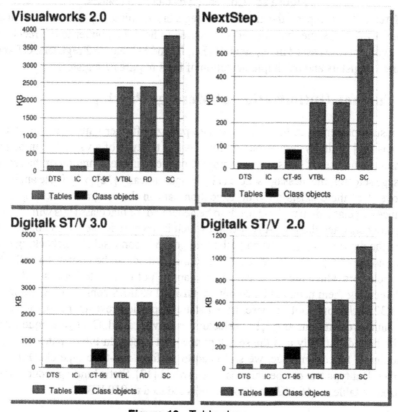

Figure 19 Table sizes.

Time. We implemented our algorithm in approximately 1,500 lines of C. The algorithm completes dispatch table allocation between 1.5 seconds (NextStep) and 4.8 seconds (Visualworks 2.0). The time is the sum of user and system time on a SPARCstation-5. **Speed.** We compare the speed of the different dispatching techniques based on the hand coded assembly code of Appendix A and [7]. VTBLs (on the target architecture) have the best performance. SC and RD are followed by CT and IC. As expected, DTS is far more expensive. This data is given in Figure 20.

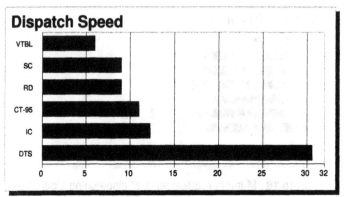

Figure 20 Comparing dispatching speeds.

Registers. We compare the number of registers required by the various dispatch sequences. We assume that one register is used to hold the pointer to the receiver and that arguments are passed in registers. VTBL, IC and SC require 2 registers. CT and RD require 3 registers and our implementation of DTS requires 7 registers.

8   Further Optimization of Message Passing

The results presented in this paper can be optimized further with some modest static analysis [14] of the system. First and foremost, if the type of a variable can be pinned down to a small set of classes which provide only one implementation of the requested message selector, the message send can be bound statically [12] [14]. If the analysis can discover that there exists no valid execution path in the program which creates any instance of a class, then nothing needs to be generated for that class (this will be the case for purely abstract classes). Any method which is never redefined does not need to be put in the dispatch tables. The compiler will generate some subclass checking code in the prologue to type-check the receiver and the method can be bound statically. Similarly, selectors which are never called need not be put in dispatch tables and methods implementing them need not be compiled. OBJECTWORKS consists of 8,780 methods and 5,325 selectors. Out of these, trivial static inspection reveals that 4,154 selectors have unique definitions and 1,197 selectors are never called. Calls to unique selectors can be bound statically and the selectors need not appear in the dispatch tables. In a dynamically typed language, we still need to perform run-time type checking of the receiver. But type test can be very fast as shown in [17]. Static binding reduces the size of dispatch tables to 160 KB and code size is reduced to 910 KB.

9   Conclusion

There is a gap in performance between statically typed programming languages such as C++ and dynamically typed ones such as OBJECTIVE-C. This paper improves on previously published techniques for implementing message passing in dynamically typed object-oriented programming languages with single inheritance. Our algorithm generates dispatch tables which are consistently smaller than C++-style VTBLs. It provides constant-time fast dispatching for dynamically typed languages. Thus further reducing the gap between statically typed and dynamically typed languages.

References

[1] André, P., Royer, J.-C.: Optimizing Method Search with Lookup Caches and Incremental Coloring. In *OOPSLA '92*, 1992.

[2] Conroy, T., Pelegri-Llopart, E.: An Assessment of Method-Lookup Caches for Smalltalk-80 Implementations. In *Smalltalk-80: The Language and its Implementation*, Addison-Wesley, 1985.

[3] Deutsch, L.P., Schiffman, A.: Efficient Implementation of the Smalltalk-80 System. In Proc. 11th POPL, Salt Lake City, UT, 1984.

[4] Dixon, R., McKee, T., Schweitzer, P., Vaughan, M.: A Fast Method Dispatcher for Compiled Languages with Multiple Inheritance. Proc. OOPSLA'89, New Orleans, LA, Oct. 1989.

[5] Driesen, K.: Selector Table Indexing & Sparse Arrays. Proc. OOPSLA'93, Washington, DC, 1993.

[6] Driesen, K.: Method Lookup Strategies in Dynamically Typed Object-Oriented Programming Languages. M.Sc., Vrije Univ. Brussel, 1993.

[7] Driesen, K., Hölzle, U., Vitek, J.: Message Dispatch on Pipelined Processors. In ECOOP 95.

[8] Karel Driesen, Urs Hölzle, "Minimizing Row Displacement Dispatch Tables". In OOPSLA'95.

[9] Ellis, M.A., Stroustrup, B.: *The Annotated C++ Reference Manual*. Addison-Wesley, 1990.

[10] Hölzle, U., Chambers, C., Ungar, D.: Optimizing Dynamically-Typed Object-Oriented Languages With Polymorphic Inline Caches. Proc. ECOOP'93, Springer-Verlag, 1993.

[11] Kiczales, G., Rodriguez, L.: Efficient Method Dispatch in PCL. In *LFP '90*, 1990.

[12] Plevyak, J., Chien, A.A.: Precise Concrete Type Inference for Object-Oriented Languages, Proc. OOPSLA'94, Portland, Oregon, October 1994.

[13] Ungar, D.: The Design and Evaluation of a High Performance Smalltalk System. PhD Thesis, The MIT Press, 1987.

[14] Vitek, J, Horspool, R.N., Uhl, J.: Compile-time analysis of object-oriented programs, Proc. CC'92, Paderborn, Germany, 1992, *LNCS 641*.

[15] Vitek, J, Horspool, R.N: Taming Message Passing: Efficient method lookup for dynamically typed object-oriented languages. In *ECOOP '94*, *LNCS 821*, Springer-Verlag, 1994.

[16] Vitek, J: Compact Dispatch Tables for Dynamically Typed Programming Language. M.Sc. Thesis, University of Victoria, 1995.

[17] Vitek, J., Horspool, R.N.: Fast Constant Time Type Inclusion Testing. Submitted, Sept. 1995.

Appendix A: CT-95 dispatch sequence

The code sequence for dynamic binding with CT-95 is listed below. The constants #table_offset, #selector_offset and #selector_color can be determined at compile-time.

call site:

```
1.  load   [object + #class_offset], class
2.  load   [class + #table_offset], table
3.  load   [table + #selector_offset], method
4.  call   method
5.  setlo  #selector_color, color
```

method prologue:

```
5.  cmp    #expected_color, color
6.  bne    #message_not_understood
7.  nop
8.  <first instruction of target method>
```

Delegating Compiler Objects
An Object-Oriented Approach to Crafting Compilers

Jan Bosch*

Department of Computer Science and Business Administration,
University of Karlskrona/Ronneby,
S-372 25, Ronneby, Sweden.

E-mail: Jan.Bosch@ide.hk-r.se,
URL: http://www.pt.hk-r.se/~bosch

Abstract. Conventional compilers often are large entities that are highly complex, difficult to maintain and hard to reuse. In this article it is argued that this is due to the inherently *functional* approach to compiler construction. An alternative approach to compiler construction is proposed, based on object-oriented principles, which solves (or at least lessens) the problems of compiler construction. The approach is based on *delegating compiler objects* (DCOs) that provide a structural decomposition of compilers in addition to the conventional functional decomposition. The DCO approach makes use of the *parser delegation* and *lexer delegation* techniques, that provide reuse and modularisation of syntactical, respectively, lexical specifications.

1 Introduction

Traditionally, compiler constructors have taken a functional approach to the process of compiling program text. In its simplest form, the process consists of a lexical analyser, converting program text into a token stream, a parser, converting the token stream into a parse tree and a code generator, converting the parse tree into output code. Both the lexical analyser and the parser are monolithic entities in that only a single instance of each exists in an application.

The monolithic approach to compiler construction is becoming increasingly problematic due to changing requirements on compiler construction techniques. Whereas previously applications were built using one of the few general purpose languages, nowaday often a specialised, application domain languages is used. Examples can be found in the fourth generation development environments, e.g. Paradox[2], and formal specification environments, e.g. SDL. Another example is the use of compilation techniques to obtain structured input from the user as in, e.g. modern phones. In a modern phone exchange, the user can request services by dialing the digits associated with a service. Example services are *follow-me*

---

* This work has been supported by the Blekinge Forskningsstiftelse.
[2] Paradox is a trademark of Borland International, Inc.

and *tele-conference*. The digits are parsed by a parser and the requested service is activated for the user. The available services in most systems, however, are subject to regular change. A third example are the *extensible* language models. An extensible language can be extended with new constructs and the semantics of existing language constructs can be changed. In this article, an extensible object-oriented language, LAYOM, is used as an example.

The changing requirements described above call for modularisation and reuse of compiler specifications. These new requirements would benefit from means to modularise and reuse compiler specifications as it would reduce the required effort in the construction of compilers.

In this article *delegating compiler objects* (DCOs) are proposed as an approach to compiler construction that supports modularisation and reuse of compiler specifications. The DCO approach to compiler development allows one to recursively decompose a compiler into *structural components*, i.e. nested compilers. The DCO concept provides a structural decomposition of a compiler in addition to the traditional functional compiler decomposition. When using DCOs, an input program text is not compiled by a single compiler, but by a set of cooperating compiler objects. A compiler object can delegate parts of the compilation process to other compiler objects. The advantage of this approach is that reusability and maintainability are increased considerably due to the modular approach.

To evaluate the mechanism, a tool, PHEST, has been implemented that implements the DCO concept. Using this tool, compilers have been constructed that convert LAYOM code into C++ and C code.

The remainder of this article is organised as follows. In the next section, the problems of traditional compiler construction techniques that we identified are described. Section 3 describes the layered object model that will be used as the running example throughout the paper. Section 4 describes the DCO approach to compiler construction, whereas sections 4.2, 4.3 and 4.4 respectively describe the *parser delegation*, *lexer delegation* and *parse graph node object* techniques employed by the DCO approach. Section 5 describes the PHEST tool supporting the techniques discussed in this paper. Section 6 describes related work and the paper is concluded in section 7.

2 The Problems of Conventional Compilers

Traditionally, the compilation process is decomposed towards the different *functions* that convert program code into a description in another language, e.g. lexing, parsing and code generation. We have identified three problems of this approach to compiler construction:

- *Complexity*: A traditional, monolithic compiler tries to deal with the complexity of a compiler application through decomposing the compilation process into a number of subsequent phases. Although this indeed decreases the complexity, this approach is not *scaleable* because a large problem cannot *recursively* be decomposed into smaller components. In order to deal with large, complex or often changing compilers, the one level decomposition into lexing, parsing, semantic analysis and code generation phases we have experienced to be insufficient.

- *Maintainability*: Although the compilation process is decomposed into multiple phases, each phase itself can be a large and complex entity with many interdependencies. Maintaining the parser, for example, can be a difficult task when the syntax description is large and has many interdependencies between the production rules. In the traditional approaches, the syntax description of the language cannot be decomposed into smaller, independent components.

- *Reuseability*: Although the domain of compilers has a rich theoretical base, building a compiler often means starting from scratch, even when similar applications are available. The notion of reusability has no supporting mechanism in compiler construction. Nevertheless, crafting a compiler generally is a large and expensive undertaking and reuse, when available, would be highly beneficial.

Summarising, the conventional approach to compiler construction results in large, complex modules that result in the aforementioned problems. This is due to the one-level functional decomposition. We consider an object-oriented approach to compiler construction that supports reuse and modularisation of compiler specifications provides a solution the aforementioned problems.

3 Example: Layered Object Model

The layered object model (IAYOM) [6] is an *extensible* object model that extends the conventional object model to improve expressiveness. An object in IAYOM (see figure 1) consists of five major components, i.e. *variables* (nested objects), *methods*, *states*, *categories* and *layers*. The IAYOM object model can be further extended by adding new types of layers or new object model components.

The variables and methods of a IAYOM object are defined as in most object-oriented languages. A state, as defined in IAYOM, is a dimension of the abstract object state [5]. The notion of *abstract object state* provides an a systematic and structured approach to make the *conceptual* state of the object accessible at the interface. A category is used to define a client category, i.e. a distinguishing characteristic of a group of clients that are to be treated similar.

The *layers* encapsulate the object such that messages sent to the object or sent by the object itself have to pass all layers. Each layer can change, delay, redirect or respond to a message or just let is pass. Layers are, among others, used for representing and implementing inter-object relations [4] and design patterns [7].

4 Delegating Compiler Objects

The delegating compiler object (DCO) approach aims at modular, extensible and maintainable implementations of compilers. In section 2 it was concluded that

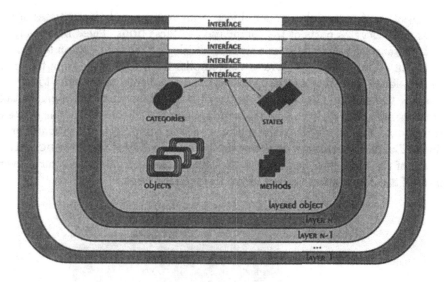

Fig. 1. IAYOM object

traditional approaches to compiler compilation had difficulty providing required features due to the lack of modularisation and reuse. The underlying rationale of DCOs is that next to the functional decomposition into a lexer, parser and code generator, we offer another structural decomposition dimension that can be used to decompose a compiler into a set of subcompilers. Rather than having a single compiler consisting of a lexer, parser and code generator, an input text can be compiled by a group of compiler objects that cooperate to achieve their task. Each compiler object consists of one or more lexers, one or more parsers and a parse graph. A compiler object, when detecting that a particular part of the syntax is to be compiled, can instantiate a new compiler object and delegate the compilation of that particular part to the new compiler object.

The delegating compiler object concept makes use of *parser delegation* and *lexer delegation* for achieving the structural decomposition of grammar, respectively, lexer specification. These techniques will be described in section 4.2 and 4.3. Section 4.4 discusses the parse graph node objects

4.1 Delegating Compiler Objects

A delegating compiler object (DCO) is a generalisation of a conventional compiler in that the conventional compiler is used as a component in the DCO approach. In this approach, a compiler object consists of one or more lexers, one or more parsers and a parse graph.

A consequence of decomposing a compiler into subcompilers is that the syntax of the compiled language should be decomposed into the main constructs of the language. Each construct is then compiled by a DCO. Each DCO can instantiate and interact with other DCOs. The compilation process starts with the instantiation of an initial compiler object. This DCO generally instantiates other DCOs and delegates parts of the compilation to these DCOs. These DCOs can, in turn, instantiate other compiler objects and delegate the compilation to them.

As an example, the structure of the compiler for LAYOM is shown in figure 2. As mentioned, LAYOM is an extensible language, requiring its compiler to be extensible. In addition, the layer types part of LAYOM have their individual syntax and semantics, but with considerable overlap. The LAYOM compiler is constructed using DCOs since modularisation and reuse of the compiler specification is provided. The initial compiler object of the LAYOM compiler is the *class* DCO. The parser of the class DCO instantiates the other DCOs and delegates control over parts of the compilation process to the instantiated DCOs.

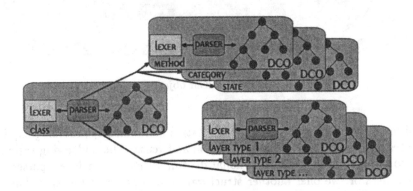

Fig. 2. DCO-based LAYOM compiler

A DCO-based compiler consists, as described, of a set of DCOs that cooperate to compile an input text. Each DCO consists of one or more lexers, one or more parsers and a parse graph, consisting of node objects. When a DCO has multiple parsers or lexers this can be to modularise the parser or lexer specification for the DCO or to reuse existing parser or lexer specifications. The interaction between different parsers or lexers is achieved through *parser delegation* and *lexer delegation*, respectively. In figure 3, an overview of a DCO-based compiler is shown. Each DCO has a parse graph G consisting of node objects. The classes of the node objects are in the *node space* and the DCO specifies which node classes it requires.

The concept of delegating compiler objects makes use of *parser delegation* [3], *lexer delegation* and *parse graph node objects* [6]. These techniques will be discussed in the following sections.

4.2 Parser Delegation

Parser delegation is a mechanism that allows one to modularise and to reuse grammar specifications. In case of modularisation, a parser can instantiate other

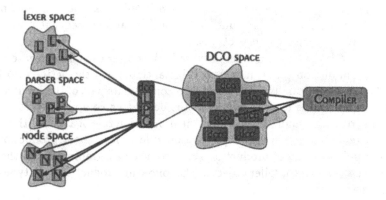

Fig. 3. Overview of a DCO-based Compiler

parsers and redirect the input token stream to the instantiated parser. The instantiated parser will parse the input token stream until it reaches the end of its syntax specification. It will subsequently return to the instantiating parser, which will continue to parse from the point where the subparser stopped. In case of reuse, the designer can specify for a new grammar specification the names of one or more existing grammar specifications. The new grammar is extended with the production rules and the semantic actions of the reused grammar(s), but has the possibility to override and extend reused production rules and actions.

We define a monolithic grammar as $G = (\ I,\ N,\ T,\ P)$, where I is the name of the grammar, N is the set of nonterminals, T is the set of terminals and P is the set of production rules. The set $V = N \cup T$ is the vocabulary of the grammar. Each production rule $p \in P$ is defined as $p = (q, A)$, where q is defined as $q : x \rightarrow \alpha$ where $x \in N$ and $\alpha \in V^*$ and A is the set of semantic actions associated with the production rule q. Different from most YACC-like grammar specifications (e.g. [1, 19]), a grammar in this definition has a name, and the start symbol is simply denoted by the production called *start*.

Parser delegation extends the monolithic grammar specification in several ways to achieve reuse and modularisation. First, one can specify in a grammar that other grammars are reused. In situations where a designer has to define a grammar and a related grammar specification exists, one would like to reuse the existing grammar and extend and redefine parts of it. If a grammar is reused, all the production rules and semantic actions become available to the reusing grammar specification. In our approach, reuse of an existing grammar is achieved by creating an instance of a parser for the *reused* grammar upon instantiation of the parser for the *reusing* grammar. The reusing parser uses the reused parser by *delegating* parts of the parsing process to the reused parser.

When modularising a grammar specification, the grammar specification is divided into a collection of grammar module classes. When a parser object decides to delegate parsing, it creates a new parser object. The active parser object delegates parsing to the new parser object, which will gain control over the input token stream. The new parser object, now referred to as the *delegated* parser, parses the input token stream until it is finished and subsequently it returns control to the delegating parser object.

Instead of delegating to a different parser, the parser can also delegate control to a new compiler object. A new DCO is instantiated and the active DCO leaves control to the new DCO. The delegated DCO compiles its part of the input syntax. When it is finished it returns control to the delegating compiler object.

To describe the required behaviour, the production rule of a monolithic parser has been replaced with a set of production rule types. These production rule types control the reuse of production rules from reused grammars and the delegation to parser and compiler objects. The following production rule types have been defined:

- $n : v_1\ v_2\ ...\ v_m$, where $n \in N$ and $v_i \in V$
  All productions $n \rightarrow V^*$ from G_{reused} are excluded from the grammar specification and only the productions n from $G_{reusing}$ are included. This is the *overriding* production rule type since it overrides all productions n from the reused grammars.
- $n +: v_1\ v_2\ ...\ v_m$, where $n \in N$ and $v_i \in V$
  The production rule $n \rightarrow v_1\ v_2\ ...\ v_m$, if existing in G_{reused} is replaced by the specified production rule n. The *extending* production rule type facilitates the definition of new alternative right hand sides for a production n.
- $n\ [id]: v_1\ v_2\ ...\ v_m$, where $n \in N$ and $v_i \in V$
  The element *id* must contain the name of a parser class which will be instantiated and parsing will be delegated to this new parser. When the delegated parser is finished parsing, it returns control to the delegating parser. The results of the delegated parser are stored in the parse graph. When i is used as an identifier, v_i must have a valid parser class name as its value. The *delegating* production rule type initiates delegation to another parser object.
- $n\ [[id]]: v_1\ v_2\ ...\ v_n$, where $n \in N$, the set of all non terminals and $v_i \in V$, the vocabulary of the grammar.
  The element *id* must contain the name of a delegating compiler object type which will be instantiated and the process of compilation will be delegated to this new compiler object. When the delegated compiler object is finished compiling its part of the program, it returns the control over the compilation process to the originating compiler object. The originating compiler object receives, as a result, a reference to the delegated compiler object which contains the resulting parse graph. The delegating parser stores the reference to the delegated DCO in the parse graph using a DCO-node. Next to using an explicit name for the *id*, one can also use i as an identifier, in which case v_i must have a valid compiler object class name as its value. The DCO production rule type causes the delegation of the compilation process to another DCO.

In figure 4 the process of parser delegation for modularising purposes is illustrated. In (1) a delegating production rule is executed. This results (2) in the

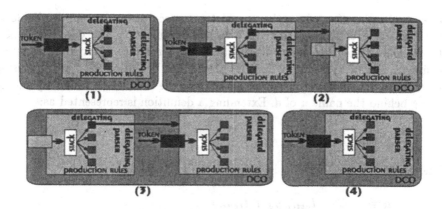

Fig. 4. Parser Delegation for Grammar Modularisation

instantiation of a new, dedicated parser object. In (3) the control over the input token stream has been delegated to the new parser, which parses its section of the token stream. In (4) the new parser has finished parsing and it has returned the control to the originating parser. This parser stores a reference to the dedicated parser as it contains the parsing results. Note that the lexer and parse graph are not shown for space reasons.

We refer to [3, 6] for more detailed discussion of parser delegation.

4.3 Lexer Delegation

The *lexer delegation* concept provides support for *modularisation* and *reuse* of lexical analysis specifications. Especially in domains where applications change regularly and new applications are often defined modularisation and reuse are very important features. Lexer delegation can be seen as an *object-oriented* approach to lexical analysis.

A monolithic lexer can be defined as $L = (I, D, R, S)$, where I is the identifier of the lexer specification, D is the set of definitions, R is the set of rules and S is the set of programmer subroutines. Each definition $d \in D$ is defined as $d = (n, t)$, where n is a name, $n \in N$, the set of all identifiers, and t is a translation, $t \in T$, the set of all translations. Each rule $r \in R$ is defined as $r = (p, a)$, where p is a regular expression, $p \in P$, the set of all regular expressions, and a is an action, $a \in A$, the set of all actions. Each subroutine $s \in S$ is a routine in the output language which will be incorporated in the lexer generated by the lexer generator. Different from most lexical analysis specifications languages, a lexer specification in our definition has a *identifier* which will be used in later sections to refer to different lexical specifications.

Lexer delegation, analogous to parser delegation, extends the monolithic lexer specification to achieve modularisation and reuse. The designer, when defining a new lexer specification, can specify the lexer specifications that should be reused by the new lexer. When a lexer specification is reused, all definitions, rules and subroutines from the reused lexer specification become available at the reusing lexer specification. In a lexical specification, the designer is able to exclude or override *definitions*, *rules* and *subroutines*. Overriding a reused definition $d = (n, t)$ is simply done by providing a definition for d in the reusing lexer definition. One can, however, also *extend* the translation t for d by adding a $=+$ behind the name n of d. Extending a definition is represented as:

$$\text{n} =+ \qquad t_{extended}$$

The result of extending this definition is the following:

$$\text{n} = \qquad t_{extended} \; ? \; t_{reused}$$

A reused rule $r = (p, a)$ can also be overridden by defining a rule $r' = (p, a')$, i.e. a rule with the same regular expression p. One can interpret extending a rule in two ways. The first way is to interpret it as extending the action associated with the rule. The second way is to extend the regular expression associated with an action. Both types of rule extensions are supported by *lexer delegation*. Extending the regular expression p is represented as follows:

$$p' \qquad |+ \; p$$

When a lexer specification is modularised, it is decomposed into smaller modules that contain parts of the lexer specification. One of the modules is the *initial lexer* which is instantiated at the start of the lexing process. The extensions for lexer modularisation consist of two new actions that can be used in the action part of rules in the lexer specifications. Lexer delegation occurs in the action part of the lexing rules. The semantics of these actions are the following:

- **Delegate(<lexer-class>)**: This action is part of the action part of a lexing rule and is generally followed by a *return(<token>)* statement. The delegate action instantiates a new lexer object of class *<lexer-class>* and installs the lexer object such that any following token requests are delegated to the new lexer object. The delegate action is now finished and the next action in the action block is executed.
- **Undelegate**: The undelegate action is also contained in the action part of a lexing rule. The undelegate action, as the name implies, does the opposite of the delegate action. It changes the delegating lexer object such that the next token request is handled by the delegating lexer object and delegation is terminated. The lexer object does not contain any state that needs to be stored for future reference, so the object is simply removed after finishing the action block.

For a more detailed discussion of lexer delegation we refer to [6].

4.4 Parse Graph Node Objects

In the delegating compiler object approach, an object-oriented, rather than a functional approach, is taken to parse tree and code generation. Instead of using passive data structures as the nodes in the parse tree as was done in the conventional approach, the DCO approach uses *objects* as nodes. A node object is instantiated by a production rule of the parser. Upon instantiation, the node object also receives a number of arguments which it uses to initialise itself. Another difference from traditional approaches is that, rather than having an separate code generation function using the parse tree as data, the node objects themselves contains knowledge for generating the output code associated with their semantics.

A parse graph node object, or simply node object, contains three parts of functionality. The first is the *constructor* method, which instantiates and initialises a new instance of the node object class. The constructor method is used by the production rules of the parser to create new nodes in the parse graph. The second part is the *code generation* method, which is invoked during the generation of output code. The third part consists of a set of methods that are used to access the state of the node object, e.g. the name of an identifier or a reference to another node object.

The grammar has facilities for parse graph node instantiation. An example production rule could be the following:

```
method   :   name '(' arguments ')' 'begin' temps statements 'end'
             [ MethodNode($1, $3, $6, $7) ]
         ;
```

The parse graph, generally, consists of a large number of node objects. There is a root object that represents the point of access to the parse graph. When the compiler decides to generate code from the parse graph, it sends a **generateCode** message to the root node object. The root node object will generate some code and subsequently invoke its children parse nodes with a **generateCode** message. The children parse nodes will generate their code and invoke all their children.

5 DCO Tool Set

In order to be able to experiment with the concepts described in this paper, an integrated tool, PHEST, has been developed. The PHEST tool provides the functionality of DCO approach. It incorporates two previously developed tools, i.e. D-YACC and D-LEX, that implement parser delegation and lexer delegation. Another tool part of PHEST supports the definition of parse graph node classes. The PHEST tool itself facilitates the definition of a compiler by composing a cooperating set of DCOs that, when combined, provide the required functionality. A second aspect of the PHEST tool is the composition of compiler objects based on the available lexers, parsers and parse graph node classes.

In figure 5, the user interface of the PHEST tool is shown. A designer using the tool can have several projects, representing different compilers. One project

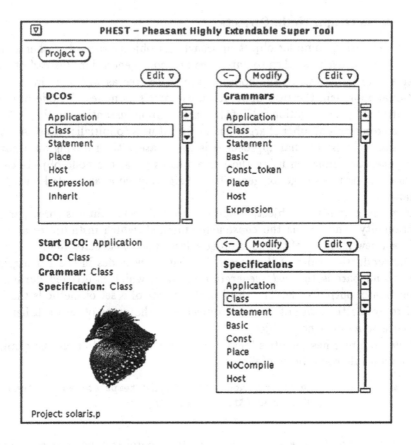

Fig. 5. DCO tool

can be open and worked on using the tool. In the left subwindow, the list of DCOs contained in the current project (or compiler) is shown. The **class** DCO is selected and below the aforementioned window, information on the name of the grammar and lexer used in by the **class** DCO. In this case, the grammar and the lexer also have the name **class**. In the upper right window, the list of grammars contained in the project is shown. Note that the number of grammars is larger than the number of DCOs. The reason for that is that some grammars, e.g. **basic**, are used to as 'abstract classes', i.e. only used for reuse, but never 'instantiated' in a DCO. The lower right window shows the lexers defined within the project.

When satisfied with the configuration, the designer can request the PHEST tool to generate an executable compiler. For pragmatic reasons, PHEST makes use of YACC for the actual parser generation. This is done by first converting a grammar expressed in D-YACC, the extended grammar definition syntax for parser delegation, to an equivalent YACC specification. This specification is converted to C++ by YACC. The resulting C++ code is preprocessed and subsequently added to the c++ code for the executable compiler. The lexer specifications are treated in an analogous fashion. For the implementation details of *phest* tool, we refer to [6, 18].

The PHEST tool has been used to construct two compilers for the IAYOM object model discussed in section 3. One compiler generates c++ output code for the Sun Solaris environment. The second compiler generates *Neuron c* output code for the Lonworks environment. The students that built the compilers noted that the modularisation and reusability provided by the DCO approach indeed simplified compiler development.

6 Related work

In [10, 11] a different approach to language engineering, TaLE, is presented. Rather than using a meta-language like LEX or YACC for specifying a language, the user edits the classes that make up the implementation using a specialised editor. TaLE not immediately intended for the implementation of traditional programming languages, but primarily for the implementation of languages that have more dynamic characteristics, like application-oriented languages. *Reuse* is one of the key requirements in TaLE and it is supported in three ways: first, language structures are implemented by independent classes, leading to a distributed implementation model; second, general language concepts can be specialised for particular languages; third, the system supports a library of standard language components.

The TaLE approach is different from the delegating compiler object (DCO) approach in, at least, two aspects. First, TaLE does not make use of metalanguages like LEX and YACC, whereas the DCO approach took these metalanguages as a basis and extended on them. This property makes it more difficult to compare the two approaches. Second, the classes in TaLE used for language implementation seem only to be used for language parts at the level of individual production rules, whereas DCOs are particularly intended for, possibly small, groups of production rules representing a major concept in the language.

In [2] a mechanism for reuse of grammar specifications, *grammar inheritance* is described. It allows a grammar to inherit production rules from one or more predefined grammars. Inherited production rules can be overridden in the inheriting grammar, but exclusion of rules is not supported. Although inheritance offers a mechanism to reuse existing grammar specifications, no support for modularising a grammar specification is offered. Therefore, for purposes of modularising a large grammar specification, we are convinced that delegation is a better mechanism than inheritance. The rational for this is that delegation allows one to separate a grammar specification at the object level, whereas inheritance would still require the definition of a monolithic parser, although being composed of inherited grammar specifications. Also, delegation offers a *uniform* mechanism for both reuse *and* modularisation of grammar specifications.

In [8], a persistent system for compiler construction is proposed. The approach is to define a compiler as a collection of modules with various functionalities that can be combined in several ways to form a compiler family. The modules have a type description which is used to determine whether components can be combined.

The approach proposed in [8] is different from the DCO approach in the following aspects. First, although the approach enhances the traditional compiler modularisation, modularisation and reuse of individual modules, e.g. the grammar specification, is not supported. Secondly, judging from the paper, it does not seem feasible to have multiple compilers cooperating on a single input specification, as in the DCO approach.

The Mjølner Orm system [13, 14, 15] is an approach to object-oriented compiler development that is purely grammar-driven. Different from the traditional grammar-driven systems that generate a language compiler from the grammar, Orm uses *grammar interpretation*. The advantage of the interpretive approach is that changes to the grammar immediately are incorporated in the language. A grammar in Orm is represented as an object and consists of four parts: an *abstract grammar* defining the structure of the language; a *concrete grammar* that defines the textual presentation of the language constructs; a *semantic grammar* that defines the static semantics and a *code-generation grammar* that translates the language into an intermediate language. Orm may be used to implement an existing language or for language prototyping, e.g. for application-domain specific languages.

Although the researchers behind the Orm system do recognise the importance of grammar and code reuse, see e.g. [16], this is deferred to future work. The Orm system addresses the complexity of language implementation through, among others, the decomposition of a grammar specification into an *abstract* and *concrete* grammar. Extensibility and reusability are not addressed. Thus, there are several differences between the Orm approach and the DCO approach. First, Orm takes the grammar-interpretive approach, whereas DCOs extend the conventional generative approach. Second, a language implementation can be decomposed into multiple DCOs, whereas an equivalent Orm implementation would consist of a single abstract, concrete, etc. grammar, even when the size of the language implementation would justify a structural decomposition. Furthermore, the goals of the Orm system and the DCO approach are quite different. The Orm system aims at an interactive, incrementally compiling environment, whereas DCOs aim at improving the modularity and reusability of the traditional compiler construction techniques. It is thus difficult to compare these approaches.

7   Conclusion

The requirements on compiler construction techniques are changing due to certain trends that one can recognise, e.g. application domain languages, fourth generation languages and extensible language models. Due to this, the traditional, functional approach to compiler construction has been proven insufficient and leads to *complexity, maintainability* and *reusability* problems.

To address these problems, a way to structurally decompose a compiler into subcompilers, in addition to the traditional functional decomposition into a lexer, parser and code generator, is required. In this article, the notion of *delegating compiler objects* (DCO) is proposed as a solution. The major difference with a traditional compiler is that an input text, in the DCO approach, is compiled by a cooperating group of compiler objects rather than be a single, monolithic compiler. The result is a compiler that is much more modular, flexible and extensible than the conventional, monolithic compiler. The DCO approach is based on the ability of compiler objects to instantiate new compiler objects and delegate the compilation of pieces of the input syntax to these specialised compiler objects.

The delegating compiler object approach builds on the *parser delegation* and *lexer delegation* techniques. Traditional parsing approaches suffer from problems related to *complexity, extensibility* and *reusability*. Parser delegation offers an object-oriented approach to parsing which does not suffer from these problems. The parser specification syntax has been extended to support reuse and modularisation. Each grammar has a name and possibly a list of grammars it reuses. The production rules syntax has been extended to support extension and overriding of reused production rules.

Traditional lexing approaches, analogous to conventional parsing approaches, suffer from problems related to *complexity, flexibility, extensibility* and *reusability*. Lexer delegation is proposed as an object-oriented solution to these problems that facilitates modularisation and reuse of lexical analysis specifications. The syntax for lexical analysis specifications has been extended with elements for the specification of modularisation and reuse and for the extension and overriding of reused specifications.

The contribution of *delegating compiler objects, parser delegation* and *lexer delegation* is that these techniques comprise a novel approach to compiler construction which supports structural decomposition and reuse of existing specifications. The complexity, maintainability, extensibility and reusability of the resulting compiler is significantly better than the conventional approaches to compiler development.

Acknowledgements

Many thanks to the students that were involved in the construction of the PHEST, D-YACC and D-LEX tools.

References

1. A.V. Aho, R. Sethi, J.D. Ullman, "Compilers Principles, Techniques, and Tools," Addison Wesley Publishing Company, March 1986.
2. M. Aksit, R. Mostert, B. Haverkort, "Compiler Generation Based on Grammar Inheritance," *Technical Report 90-07*, Department of Computer Science, University of Twente, February 1990.
3. J. Bosch, "Parser Delegation – An Object-Oriented Approach to Parsing," in Proceedings of *TOOLS Europe '95*, 1995.

4. J. Bosch, "Relations as First-Class Entities in IA¥OM," accepted for publication in *Journal of Programming Languages*, 1995.
5. J. Bosch, "Abstracting Object State," submitted to *Object-Oriented Systems*, December 1994.
6. J. Bosch, "Layered Object Model – Investigating Paradigm Extensibility," *Ph.D Thesis* (in preparation), Department of Computer Science, Lund University, October 1995.
7. J. Bosch, "Language Support for Design Patterns," to be published in proceedings of *TOOLS Europe '96*, 1996.
8. A. Dearle, "Constructing Compilers in a Persistent Environment," Technical Report, Computational Science Department, University of St. Andrews, 1988.
9. B. Fischer, C. Hammer, W. Struckmann, "ALADIN: A Scanner Generator for Incremental Programming Environments," *Software – Practice & Experience*, Vol. 22, No. 11, pp. 1011-1026, November 1992.
10. E. Järnvall, K. Koskimies, "Language Implementation Model in TaLE," *Report A-1993-1*, Department of Computer Science, University of Tampere, 1993.
11. E. Järnvall, K. Koskimies, M. Niittymäki, "Object-Oriented Language Engineering with TaLE," to appear in *Object-Oriented Systems*, 1995.
12. M.E. Lesk, "Lex – A Lexical Analyzer Generator," *Science Technical Report 39*, At&T Bell Laboratories, Murray Hill, 1975.
13. B. Magnusson, M. Bengtsson, L.O. Dahlin, G. Fries, A, Gustavsson, G. Hedin, S. Minör, D. Oscarsson, M. Taube, "An Overview of the Mjølner/Orm Environment: Incremental Language and Software Development," *Report LU-CS-TR:90:57*, Department of Computer Science, Lund University, 1990.
14. B. Magnusson, "The Mjølner Orm system," in: *Object-Oriented Environments - The Mjølner Approach*, J. Lindskov Knudsen, M. Löfgren, O. Lehrmann Madsen, B. Magnusson (eds.), Prentice Hall, 1994.
15. B. Magnusson, "The Mjølner Orm architecture," in: *Object-Oriented Environments - The Mjølner Approach*, J. Lindskov Knudsen, M. Löfgren, O. Lehrmann Madsen, B. Magnusson (eds.), Prentice Hall, 1994.
16. S. Minör, B. Magnusson, "Using Mjølner Orm as a Structure-Based Meta Environment," To be published in *Structure-Oriented Editors and Environments*, L. Neal and G. Swillus (eds), 1994.
17. V. Paxson, "Flex – Manual Pages," *Public Domain Software*, 1988.
18. Pheasant student project, *Pheasant project documentation*, University of Karlskrona/Ronneby, 1995.
19. Sun Microsystems Inc., "Yet Another Compiler Compiler," *Programming Utilities and Libraries*, Solaris 1.1 SMCC Release A Answerbook, June 1992.

A Parallel Debugger with Support for Distributed Arrays, Multiple Executables and Dynamic Processes

Peter Fritzson, Roland Wismüller[1],Olav Hansen[2],
Jonas Sala[3], Peter Skov
PELAB, Dept. of Computer and Information Science
Linköping University, S-581 83 Linköping, Sweden
Email: petfr@ida.liu.se;
Phone: +46-13-281000; Fax: +46-13-282666

Abstract. In this paper we present the parallel debugger DETOP with special emphasis on new support for debugging of programs with distributed data structures such as arrays that have been partitioned over a number of processors. The new array visualizer within DETOP supports transparent browsing and visualization of distributed arrays which occur in languages such as High Performance Fortran. Visualization of sparse arrays is supported through an array mapper facility, as well as transparent visualization of arrays which have been partitioned by hand for applications in C or Fortran77. Color coding makes the visualization more expressive and easier to read.

DETOP provides a graphical user interface that is simple to use even for inexperienced users and supports not only static data parallel programs, but also dynamic programs and parallel applications based on functional decomposition. The combination of support for applications that include dynamic process creation, multiple executables, processes and threads, and distributed data structures, makes DETOP rather unique among parallel debuggers. DETOP has been implemented for Parsytec PowerPC based multicomputers with Sparcstation frontends. Ongoing efforts include portable versions of DETOP for PVM and MPI run-time environments.

1 Introduction

The state of the art in programming large scale parallel applications are programs with explicit parallelism. The parallelism is either defined in a programming model with explicit message passing or by giving data distributions like those in High Performance Fortran. To achieve more effective development of correct and efficient parallel programs, support must be provided for all phases of the program design and implementation. In this paper, however, we focus on the support of the debugging process of programs that have been implemented and are being executed on parallel hardware platforms. Existing tools in this area have deficiencies that limit their usability to a subclass of typical applications. Easy-to-use debugging tools have so far been limited to single threaded programs or to programs that have a static process structure. Programs that dynamically create new processes and consist

---

1. Department of Computer Science, University of Technology, Munich, D-802 90 München, Germany. Email: wismuell@informatik.tu-muenchen.de

2. Affiliation during this work: PELAB; Current affiliation: Parsytec Gmbh, Jülicher Strasse 338, D-52070 Aachen, Germany. Email: olav@parsytec.de

3. Parallel Systems, Dalvägen 8, S-171 23, Solna, Sweden

of multiple executables are not supported by most other debugging tools.

We present the parallel debugger DETOP which is available for Parsytec PowerPC based parallel computing systems (PowerXplorer, GC/ PowerPlus, CC) running the PARIX operating system. DETOP supports debugging of applications containing both functional and data parallelism. Applications may consist of multiple threads and multiple program modules. Visualization of distributed arrays partitioned over multiple processes is supported. Prototypes of DETOP [BeWi94] were developed at LRR, the Technical University of Munich. The new support for visualization of distributed arrays was developed at PELAB, Linköping University, Sweden. The run-time debugging support (similar to the Unix Ptrace mechanism) within PARIX was implemented by Parsytec. The DETOP effort is thus an excellent example of both European cooperation between universities, and successful cooperation between universities and industry.

In the next section we give a brief overview on existing debugging tools including their limitations. In section 3 we present the primary design goals that should be satisfied. Section 4 introduces the user interface and command set of DETOP, while the next section gives some details on the implementation. A short conclusion and future plans are presented in section 6.

2 Related Work

To support the process of detecting and locating bugs in a program, a debugger must provide functionality to watch the internal execution of that program. There are two different methods how to gather, analyze and present run time information: the off-line and the on-line approaches.

Most parallel computing platforms provide tools that allow recording and viewing event traces, e.g. ParaGraph [Heath93]. Though mostly aimed towards performance analysis, these tools can, to some extent, also be used for correctness debugging. However, the way in which event traces are visualized is not suitable for massively parallel or dynamic systems.

Ariadne [CFH+93] uses event abstractions to deal with the difficulty of presenting large amounts of events to the user. Instead of visualizing the raw event streams, Ariadne allows the user to define abstract events and to ask if and where these abstract events occur. DARTS [TGL93] even goes further and transforms event streams into Prolog fact bases. In this way, the trace can be automatically related to the program's source code. Furthermore, Prolog can be used as a very powerful query language. Although these tools avoid the problem of displaying large event traces, they still need a global event trace that cannot be gathered in a scalable way. Furthermore, they only allow monitoring of a very restricted set of events, usually only communication events. Thus the obtained information is often too coarse grained to track down the cause of a bug in the source code.

On-line debuggers allow a more detailed view on program execution. They provide functions to stop threads at given locations in the source code, to view or modify data structures, to determine the source code position where threads are stopped and to execute threads in a controlled fashion, e. g. in single steps. Usually, the user is allowed to specify a group of processor nodes, processes or threads. A command is then executed independently for each element in that group.

Some of these tools, like ndb or ipd [BCS93] are based on pure textual interfaces that are difficult to use for non-computer scientists. However, debuggers using graphical interfaces, e. g. Prism [Sist92] are becoming more common. There are also a number of graphical interfaces built on top of text-based debuggers, e.g. xipd [Ries93] or Panorama [MaBe93]. These tools usually provide visualization of arrays and thread states to simplify debugging of complex applications.

However, such advanced features are only usable for data parallel or SIMD-style programs. Current debuggers don't support applications that create or delete threads dynamically or are composed of multiple executables due to dynamically loaded codes. Most debuggers even require a one-to-one mapping between threads and processing nodes, i. e. they support only one thread per node, due to the way breakpoints are implemented and since the visualization of thread states is often based on a fixed hardware topology.

The array visualization functionality of DETOP described in Section 4.1 has both similarities and differences compared to the numeric visualizers of the Prism [Sist92] programming environment for the Connection Machine. DETOP provides a general mapping (also suitable for sparse arrays) of array partitions distributed on processors of MIMD machines/workstation clusters into a single logical array, whereas Prism lacks such a general mapping and is oriented towards SIMD computers. The DETOP visualizer integrates color coding into the numeric visualizer, whereas Prism provides several separate types of graphic visualizers. Both systems show multidimensional data through selected two-dimensional projections, and provide panning up/down and left/right.

3 Primary Design Goals

The design goals for DETOP are to create an easy-to-use and comprehensive tool that can handle most aspects of explicitly parallel application programs, including more difficult aspects such as dynamic process creation, multiple executables and large volumes of data. Here we briefly review some important goals.

- *Ease of use*. Graphical interfaces and guided user interaction can help inexperienced users. A systematically designed user interface is another important aspect. The system should support a systematic bug localization strategy, e.g. top-down by first localizing bugs in coarse-grained context (processes, procedures) and later conveniently observing single statements, messages or variables.

- *Global system-oriented overview*. The debugger should provide information on the system as a whole and on the interaction between system components. This implies a need for global event detection, global breakpoints and monitoring of communication and synchronization.

- *Detailed analysis*. The debugger should provide detailed information that is needed to locate bugs. For example, to inspect single threads or messages; or single statements, procedures or source lines.

- *Data overview*. The system should allow convenient inspection and browsing of large application data structures that often occur in parallel applications.

- *Low intrusion*. The monitor part of the debugger should have minimal intrusion on the application program. This can be partly achieved by only monitoring those events that are of current interest for the user, which is practical using an on-line mode of operation.

- *Dynamic applications*. The system should be able to handle applications consisting of multiple executables and also support debugging for applications with dynamic process and thread creation, and dynamic loading of code.

- *Multiple parallel programming models.* Debugging of parallel programs using different forms of parallelism should be supported, e.g. processes, threads, message-passing style, data-parallel style.
- *Scalable data handling.* Handling and presentation of data collected during monitoring should be scalable, i.e. some data-reduction might be performed during on-line operation. Data representations and presentation methods useful for hundreds or thousands of processors should be selected.

4 The Parallel Debugger DETOP

DETOP provides a graphical user interface whose main component is a debugger window as shown in Figure 1. For data parallel applications, a single window is often sufficient and offers the most convenient and comprehensive way to debug all threads of a program. For data viewing of large objects, separate windows such as the array visualizer (see Figure 3), are created. However, in order to also support other paradigms of parallel programming, especially functional decomposition, DETOP has been designed to allow multiple debugger windows.

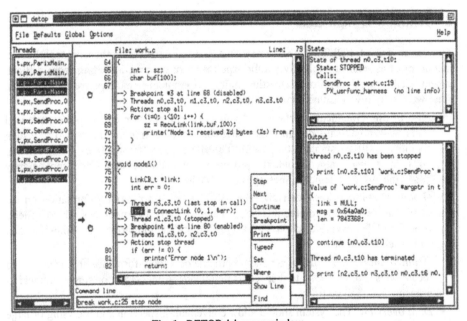

Fig. 1. DETOP debugger window

Each of these multiple debugger windows may be associated with an arbitrary set of threads. Thus, for data parallel programs a single window can be used for all threads, while separate windows can be used for different parts of applications according to their functional decomposition. Multiple windows also makes it possible to let one window show a coarse grained overview of the whole application, while another is used for detailed inspection of one selected thread.

The center of each window shows a listing of the threads' source code. The currently active locations of the threads associated with this window and the breakpoints that have been set for these threads are indicated in the listing by small icons and additional descriptions inserted into the source code (see Figure 1). The listing subwindow is also used for quick and intuitive command input.

We use an input scheme that is object oriented in some sense: the user may select an object in the listing, e.g. a line, a variable name or a breakpoint marker. Based on the type of this object, he or she will then get a popup menu containing commands appropriate for the selected object. Thus, if a line or variable is selected, the menu will allow setting of a breakpoint or printing the type or contents of the variable. If a breakpoint marker has been selected, the menu will show items for deleting or modifying this breakpoint.

In contrast to other debuggers providing graphical input, commands use both the selected piece of text and the position of this text in the source code. Thus, if a variable i is selected in a procedure foo, the print command will print the value of i in this procedure, even if it is not on top of the call stack. This is what users expect intuitively, which substantially simplifies usage. In addition to menu input there is also a command line for more experienced users and complex commands. Command line syntax supports both C and Fortran 77.

The left side of the debugger window displays the list of threads currently associated with that window. The list may be changed at any time using a separate window (see Figure 2) that allows selection of a new thread from the list of currently existing threads. In this list a subset of threads may also be selected. All commands entered in the debugger window will then be applied to all selected threads. In addition, there are global commands that always affect the whole application, e.g. a global stop.

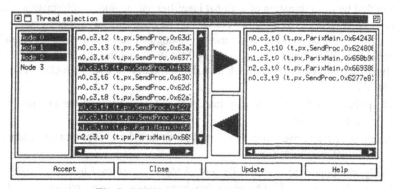

Fig. 2. DETOP thread selection window

DETOP provides two different forms of command output. Output may either be appended to a log file or updated in-place. The first mode is used for all unconditional commands, but may also be used to generate traces of events or other data. The second mode is, for example, used to display the state and the procedure call back-trace of threads. Each time a thread is stopped, the state display (in the upper right of Figure 1) is updated and shows the current stopping point.

The debugging commands offered by DETOP fall into six major groups:

1. *Execution control:* It is possible to start, stop and single step any thread at any time. In addition, there is also a global start and stop.

2. *Inspection of program state:* These commands retrieve information about the program's current state, e.g. the list of all existing threads, the point of execution and procedure traceback of threads and the types and values of variables or expressions, including visualization of arrays.

3. *Modification of program state:* Currently only modification of variables is supported.

4. *Events and actions (breakpoints):* Breakpoints may be set on source code lines or procedure entries for an arbitrary set of threads. A breakpoint consists of an execution event and an associated stop action. The event is raised whenever one of the selected threads reaches a given position in the source code. The stop action can either stop the thread that raised the event, the thread's processing node or the whole application. The latter modes are essential in order to obtain consistent views of shared variables or the program's global state.

   Additionally, there are several types of events that are always monitored by DETOP, e.g. exceptions or termination of a thread. It is also possible to define a special breakpoint that will stop dynamically created threads immediately before they start executing.

5. *Miscellaneous:* There are also commands to display a source file, to set defaults, e.g. a default action for breakpoints, and to configure the user graphical interface.

6. *Help:* DETOP also provides full context sensitive on-line help.

Since support for dynamic applications has been a major design goal, there are also special features that simplify debugging of programs that dynamically create new threads. Threads are identified by a combination of a global identifier and additional information related to the source code. The global identifier consists of the node number, a context number and a thread number. The context number is used to distinguish between threads having different executable files. The thread number starts at 0 for the initial thread and is incremented for each dynamically created thread. Additional information is used to make identification easier for the user:

- For applications that dynamically load new code, the name of the executable file is given for each thread.
- The name of the thread's root function is given in order to support applications based on functional decomposition.
- Finally, the pointer to the thread's control block, as returned by the `CreateThread` library call is shown. If the pointer has been stored in some program variable, the corresponding thread can be identified in this way.

Threads are always selected from lists displaying global identifiers and additional information (see Figure 2). Once a thread has been selected for debugging, its symbol table is automatically loaded into the debugger, if it is not already available. Thus, only the symbol tables needed for the current debugging session are loaded; there is no need for the user to explicitly specify the symbol tables to be used.

DETOP also supports two additional event types that are essential for debugging

347

dynamic applications. Termination of debugged threads is always monitored. When a thread terminates, a message is printed and the thread is removed from all thread lists. A special option requests the debugger to also monitor creation of new threads. When a new thread is created, a message containing the thread's identifier is printed, and the thread is stopped immediately before it starts executing. It is then possible to select this thread for debugging, to set breakpoints in this thread and to start it. Thus, even a dynamically created thread can be debugged from the very beginning of its execution.

4.1 Visualization of Distributed Arrays

For parallel programs on MIMD computers with distributed memory, large arrays with massive amounts of data are typically partitioned and distributed over several processors. DETOP allows a separate window, called a visualizer, to be created for each array to be visualized. Visualizers give the user an efficient way to navigate through and interpret large amounts of data typically found in parallel programs.

Visualizers are designed to view multi-dimensional arrays of data, but due to the two-dimensional nature of computer screens, two dimensions at a time are selected for visualization. Data is fetched using the DETOP monitoring mechanism, which means that programs do not have to be modified to display a visualizer. The user simply runs a program to a breakpoint and specifies the array to be visualized. The visualizer displays a two-dimensional slice of the data, and the user may pan around in this slice using simple mouse commands to the scroll bars.

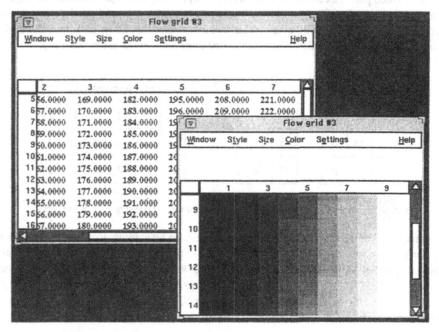

Fig. 3. Two array visualizer windows, one numeric and one graphic.
Combined numeric-graphic is also possible.

Figure 3 shows two typical array visualizers. The data is shown in numeric format. Color coding can be applied to the displayed values, which allows faster the user easier overview of many numbers, and quick visual detection of any numbers with strange values. Threshold or range conditions may also be specified, which causes the visualizer to only display those values that fulfill the conditions. Future extensions may include purely graphic visualizers, e.g. displaying fields of 2-D or 3-D vectors as arrays of small graphical arrows. Other extensions are animations, i.e. visualizing a sequence of snapshots of the same array, and observing modifications over time. A variation of the animation theme is to only display the array elements that change value between different iterations of some application algorithm.

The array visualization functionality of DETOP described here has both similarities and differences compared to the numeric visualizers of the Prism [Sist92] programming environment for the Connection Machine. DETOP provides a general mapping (also suitable for sparse arrays) of array partitions distributed on processors of MIMD machines/ workstation clusters into a single logical array, whereas Prism lacks such a general mapping and is oriented towards SIMD computers. The DETOP visualizer integrates color coding into the numeric visualizer, whereas Prism provides several separate types of graphic visualizers. Both systems show multidimensional data through selected two-dimensional projections, and provide panning up/down and left/right.

4.2 Mapping for Array Visualization

The array mapping facility of the array visualizer allows the user to specify a mapping from the distributed parts that comprise the array, to a single array that is presented as one logical entity to the user. The example below shows how every other column from the array part in process1 is combined with every other column from the array part in column 2, corresponding to a cyclic distribution in the first dimension of the combined array.

Array in process 1   Array in process 2   Logically combined array

11	12	13
14	15	16
17	18	19

21	22	23
24	25	26
27	28	29

11	21	12	22	13	23
14	24	15	25	16	26
17	27	18	28	19	29

Fig. 4. Example of two distributed array pieces presented transparently as one array.

The mapping can be specified in a general way, column by column, by filling in a number of *Entry Definitions* as shown in Figure 5 applied to the above example. The mapping can also be specified in the High Performance Fortran way, by filling in (CYCLIC,*) in the *Dimension field*, thus avoiding the need for a general specification of the mapping. Mappings need to be specified when debugging C or Fortran77 code with explicitly programmed data distributions.

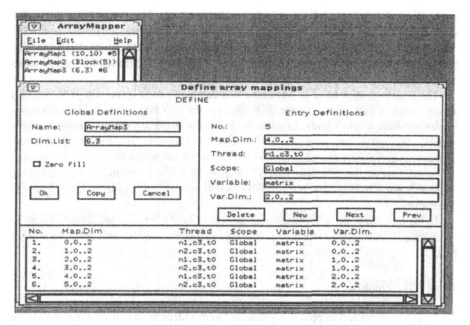

Fig. 5. The arraymapper window, when specifying a general mapping.
In this case the cyclic distribution shown in Figure 4 is specified.

For High Performance Fortran, mapping information could automatically be obtained from the compiler generated symbol table. There are plans to integrate DETOP with the PREPARE High Performance Fortran compiler [BCSK95]. The general way of specifying a mapping is however still needed for non-standard data distributions, e.g. sparse arrays, for which the *Zero fill* button of the array mapper window can be checked, which means that all array elements which are not explicitly mapped are assumed to be zero.

We explain the array mapping example in Figure 5 in somewhat more detail. Process 1 is specified as thread: (n1,c3,t0), i.e. processor node 1, context 3 (process address space), thread 0; Process 2 as thread: (n2,c3,to) on processor node 2. There are 6 mapping entry definitions specified; the fields of the entry currently selected for editing are visible in the upper right part of the form. The *Var.Dim* field describes which elements from the local array should be mapped into corresponding elements in the combined array, as specified by the *Map.Dim* field. For example, in entry No 3 for process 1, Var.Dim = 1,0..2 and Map.Dim = 2,0..2, which means the elements indexed 0..2 in column 1 of the local array (column 1 = the second column, for which in this case the first array index = 1) are mapped into column 2, elements 0..2 of the combined array.

5 Implementation

The debugger has been designed in an hierarchical way in order to simplify portability and maintenance. The debugger's basis is a distributed monitoring system that consists of one monitor on each of the parallel computer's nodes. DETOP itself can be executed on any workstation allowing network access to the parallel computer. The host part is again divided into two layers: the graphical user interface and an underlying transformation layer. The main tasks of this layer are transformation between source language level and machine level, i e. symbol table management, distribution of commands to the appropriate monitors and management of events and actions.

The transformation layer is connected to a communication server via TCP/ IP. This server, which is part of the monitor on Node 0 for the GC/ PowerPlus and PowerXplorer implementation, acts as a bridge between the TCP/ IP network and the monitoring system's internal communication network. Communication between the monitor system and debugger is completely asynchronous, so in contrast to sequential and most other parallel debuggers neither the debugger interface is blocked while a monitor is busy on some command, nor it is necessary to interrupt the whole application in order to issue debugger commands.

In the following, we will discuss four aspects of DETOP's implementation: the array visualizer, the monitoring system, symbol table management and the user interface in more detail.

5.1 Array Visualizer

The array visualizer and mapper is implemented as an independent Unix process, see Figure 6, that communicates with the main debugger process via ToolTalk. It is also possible to connect the array visualizer directly to an application, if that should be desired. The user interface parts of the visualizer are implemented in Tk/Tcl with a number of call-back routines in C, which keep track of what parts of the array data that have been transferred to the visualizer process. Data is transferred either on demand, depending on the scrolling and panning actions of the user, or all data at once for a whole array if a snapshot is desired. The main debugger process can initiate some actions, for example refreshing of the array data in the visualizer process.

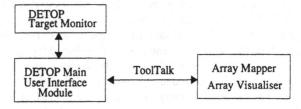

Fig. 6. Communication structure between parts of DETOP.

5.2 Monitoring System

The task of the monitoring system is to provide the tools with adequate information. Since monitoring is also needed for other tasks beside debugging, a universal and flexible monitoring system is used. All other members of the TOPSYS tool family [BeBo91], such as the performance analyzer PATOP [Hans94] and the visualizing tool VISTOP [BeBr93] are based on this monitoring system.

The structure of the monitoring system for one node is depicted in Figure 7. In order to perform data reduction, monitor processes are present on each node of the multicomputer system. The monitor process collects information, condenses this information, and combines it with information from adjacent nodes, e.g. to form average values. For example, in the Parsytec/PARIX implementation information is sent to Node 0, and reduced, before being communicated to the host. The monitor itself is programmable, in order to be flexible to the needs of different debugging and performance analysis tasks. Small pieces of programs in a simple language are downloaded to the monitor. Another important function performed by the monitor is to recognize events and to initiate the corresponding event handling.

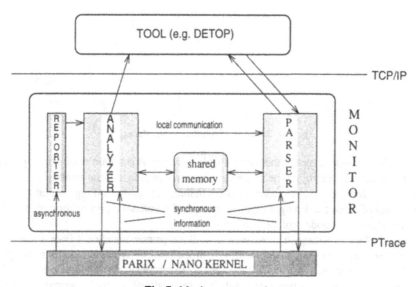

Fig. 7. Monitor on one node

5.3 Symbol table management

When a program is compiled for debugging, compilers emit a symbol table that is stored in the program's executable file. The symbol table is used to link machine addresses to source code items, e.g. variables, procedures or lines in a source file. Though this information is mainly needed for correctness debugging, it is also important for performance analysis, if performance values have to be related to the source code, e.g. by restricting a measurement to a some procedure.

There are a couple of different symbol table formats and also a variety of extensions for different source languages. In order to keep our tools portable, we have developed a symbol table management library that can read various formats and offers a uniform interface for accessing symbol table information that is independent of format and source language. Since the library is able to manage several symbol tables at the same time, it allows us to support both applications where code is loaded dynamically, i.e. applications consisting of more than one executable, as well as programs on heterogeneous systems, where there are different executables for the different types of node processors. Mixed language programs, e.g. written in C and Fortran, are also supported.

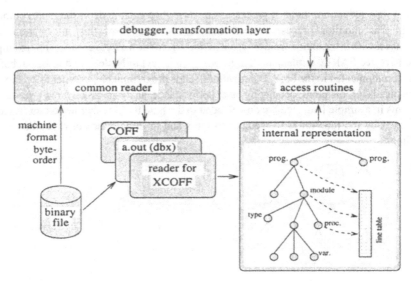

Fig. 8. Structure of Symbol Table Manager

Figure 8 shows the structure of this symbol table manager. A common reader first opens the executable file and determines the target machine, its byte order and the symbol table format used. Next, a format-specific reader is called, building up an internal representation that is independent of format and programming language. The internal representation is a tree-like structure where each node represents a symbol.

The interface to access this structure acts like a pattern matcher. Given a start node representing a context, e.g. a source file or procedure, all symbols matching the given specification are returned. A specification consists of symbol name or address, symbol class (e.g. procedure, variable, type) and subclass (e.g. global symbol, parameter), where wildcards are possible for each component. Several search types are available, e.g. to search for all descendent symbols, for local symbols only, or for symbols within scope of the program structure represented by the start node. Thus, the interface provides a uniform support for both searching specific symbols and retrieving the set of all symbols with a given class, e.g. a list of all procedures in an application.

5.4 User interface

The main user interface window has been built on top of X Windows using the Motif widget set. We have used C++ and the Widget Creation Library (Wcl) for rapid prototyping of the main debugger window. The array visualizer was implemented more recently, using Tk/Tcl (versions 4.0/7.4) and ToolTalk for communication between the array browser and the main debugger process. The Motif look and feel is used by all window types to provide a consistent user interface.

6 Conclusion and Future Work

We have presented the parallel debugger DETOP with special emphasis on new functionality for debugging of programs with distributed array data structures, combined with support not only for static data parallel programs but also for applications with dynamic process creation and programs based on functional partitioning. Thus, DETOP provides a rather unique combination of debugging facilities covering most aspects of explicitly parallel programming.

An earlier version of the debugger [ObWi95] is distributed by Parsytec for their GC/ Powerplus and PowerXplorer systems since Dec. 1994. It is complemented by the performance analysis tool PATOP [Hans94], developed by the group in Munich. The smooth cooperation between the PELAB group at Linköping University and the group at the Technical University of Munich is another nice aspect of this effort.

The performance of the monitoring system that is used by both DETOP and PATOP appears to be reasonable. For example, when using PATOP do online drawing of a few curves of properties of threads or processes, the overhead is usually around 10-15% for the application. The overhead of using DETOP is much less, except, of course, when hitting a breakpoint.

Future work on DETOP includes more graphic support in the array visualizers, e.g. showing arrays of small arrows; options for snapshots of whole arrays and animation of array contents over time, etc. Other possible future extensions involve integrating distributed dynamic slicing [KKF96] into the debugger. Slicing can trace data dependencies through messages between processes and through statements and procedure calls, which gives the debugger capabilities to answer queries about which parts of the parallel program influences the computation of a certain (faulty) data item. There are also future plans to integrate DETOP with the PREPARE High Performance Fortran compiler so that data distribution information for distributed arrays in that language can be automatically obtained from the symbol table instead of being specified in the array mapper.

Other future plans include extending the capabilities of DETOP for debugging communication between threads, e.g. by allowing breakpoints to be set on links. A thread sending to or receiving from the link will then be stopped before it completes communication. Thus, it is possible to watch communication on a link. This type of breakpoint also allows to stop the receiver of a message, so processing of that message can be debugged. It is also planned to port both DETOP and PATOP to the PVM and MPI parallel programming models, both for execution on networks of workstations and for a version running on top of PARIX for Parsytec parallel computers.

7 Acknowledgements

The main debugger functionality (except for the distributed array visualization and mapping reported here) has been designed and implemented by the group at the Lehrstuhl für Rechnertechnik und Rechnerorganisation, Technical University of Munich (TUM), including Roland Wismüller, Michael Oberhuber (until Dec 1994, the TUM group also included Olav Hansen, who was at PELAB during the work reported here, but since Nov 95 is affiliated with Parsytec), and some more people. The nanokernel Ptrace-like debugging support mechanism used by the monitor has been implemented by Parsytec. Support for the

354

visualizer work has been obtained from the European Commission through the Esprit-3 PREPARE project, from NUTEK – the Swedish Board for Technical Development, and for the main debugger work from the German Science Foundation special research grant SFB 342.

References

[BeWi94] T. Bemmerl and R. Wismüller. On-line Distributed Debugging on Scalable Multiprocessor Architectures. In W. Gentzsch and U. Harms, editors, *High-Performance Computing and Networking, Volume II: Networking and Tools*, volume 797 of *Lecture Notes in Computer Science*, pages 394–400, München, April 1994. Springer-Verlag.

[BCS91] D. Breazeal, K. Callaghan, and W. D. Smith. IPD: A Debugger for Parallel Heterogeneous Systems. In *Proceedings of ACM/ONR Workshop on Parallel and Distributed Debugging*, pages 216–218, Santa Cruz, CA, May 1991.

[BeBo91] T.Bemmerl and A. Bode. An integrated tool environment for programming distributed memory multiprocessors. *Distributed Memory Computing*, 487 of LNCS:130 – 142, 1991.

[BeBr93] T. Bemmerl and P. Braun. Visualization of Message Passing Parallel Programs with the TOPSYS Parallel Programming Environment. *Journal of Parallel and Distributed Computing (Special Issue on Tools and Methods for Visualization of Parallel Systems and Computations*, 18(2):118 – 128, June 1993.

[BCSK95] Peter Brezany, Olivier Chéron, Kamran Sanjari, Erik van Konijnenburg. Efficient Translation of Irregular Code by the PREPARE HPF Compiler. In Proc. of *Fifth Workshop on Compilers for Parallel Computers,* Tech. report UMA-DAC_95/09, Dept. of Computer Science, University of Malaga, Malaga, June 23-30, 1995.

[CFH+93] J. Cuny, G. Forman, A. Hough, J. Kundu, C. Lin, L. Snyder, and D. Stemple. The Ariadne Debugger: Scalabe Application of Event-Based Abstraction. In *Proceedings of the ACM/ONR Workshop on Parallel and Distributed Debugging*, pages 85–95, San Diego, California, May 1993. ACM.

[Hans94] Olav Hansen. A tool for optimizing programs on massively parallel computer architectures. In W. Gentzsch and U. Harms, editors, *High-Performance Computing and Networking, Volume II: Networking and Tools*, volume 797 of *Lecture Notes in Computer Science*, pages 350 – 356, Munich, April 1994. Springer-Verlag.

[Heath93] Michael T. Heath. Recent Developments and Case Studies in Performance Visualization using ParaGraph. In G. Kotsis and G. Haring, editors, *Proc. of Workshop on Monitoring and Visualization of Parallel Processing Systems*, pages 175 – 200, Moravany and Váhom, CSFR, October 1992. Elsevier, Amsterdam, 1993.

[KKF95] Mariam Kamkar, Patrik Krajina, Peter Fritzson. Distributed Dynamic Slicing. In Proc of EuroMicro'96, Braga, Portugal, 1996.

[MaBe93] J. May and F. Berman. Panorama: A Portable, Extensible Parallel Debugger. In *Proceedings of the ACM/ONR Workshop on Parallel and Distributed Debugging*, pages 96–106, San Diego, California, May 1993. ACM.

[ObWi95] Michael Oberhuber, Roland Wismüller. DETOP - An Interactive Debugger for PowerPC Based Multicomputers. In (P. Fritzson, L. Finmo, Eds.) Proc. of *ZEUS'95 – Workshop on Parallel Programming and Applications,* Linköping, May 17-18, 1995. IOS Press, Amsterdam, 1995.

[Ries93] B. Ries, R. Anderson, W. Auld, D. Breazeal, K. Callaghan, E. Richards, and W. Smith. The Paragon performance monitoring environment. In *Proc. of Supercomputing '93,* pages 850–859, Portland, Or., November 1993. IEEE.

[Sist92]   Steve Sistare, Don Allen, Rich Bowker, Karen Jourdenais, Josh Simons, Rish Title. Data Visualization and Performance Analysis in the Prism Programming Environment. In N. Topham, R. Ibbett and T. Bemmerl (Eds), *IFIP Working Conference on Programming Environments for Parallel Computing*, Edinburgh, Elsevier Science Publishers B.V. (North-Holland), April 1992.

[TGL93]   M. Timmerman, F. Gielen, and P. Lambrix. High Level Tools for the Debugging of Real Time Multiprocessor Systems. In *Proceedings of the ACM/ONR Workshop on Parallel and Distributed Debugging*, pages 151–157, San Diego, California, May 1993. ACM.

[TT94]   Thomas Treml. *Monitoring Paralleler Programme*. PhD thesis, Munich University of Technology, 1994.

Lecture Notes in Computer Science

For information about Vols. 1–987

please contact your bookseller or Springer-Verlag